DURHAM PUBLIC

P9-CEV-186

THE
SOLEMN SENTENCE
OF DEATH

✳

DURHAM PUBLIC LIBRARY

THE
SOLEMN SENTENCE
OF DEATH

✳

Capital Punishment
in Connecticut

✳

Lawrence B. Goodheart

University of Massachusetts Press

AMHERST AND BOSTON

Copyright © 2011 by University of Massachusetts Press
All rights reserved
Printed in the United States of America

LC 2010051761
ISBN 978-1-55849-847-1 (paper); 846-4 (library cloth)

Designed by Dennis Anderson
Set in Dante with Goudy Oldstyle display by
Westchester Book, Inc.
Printed and bound by Thomson-Shore, Inc.

Library of Congress Cataloging-in-Publication Data

Goodheart, Lawrence B., 1944–
The solemn sentence of death : capital punishment in Connecticut /
Lawrence B. Goodheart.
p.   cm.
Includes bibliographical references and index.
ISBN 978-1-55849-847-1 (pbk. : alk. paper)—
ISBN 978-1-55849-846-4 (library cloth : alk. paper)
1. Capital punishment—Connecticut—History.
2. Criminal justice, Administration of—Connecticut—History.   I. Title.
HV8699.U6C848 2011
364.6609746—dc22
                                                            2010051761

British Library Cataloguing in Publication data are available.

To Ellen and Anna

CONTENTS

TABLES

ACKNOWLEDGMENTS

THIS DETAILED study of capital punishment since colonial times in one jurisdiction was feasible only because of extensive archival holdings and other
primary sources at the Connecticut State Library in Hartford. Without such
repositories and their capable staffs, projects like this one would not be possible. It is essential to the vitality of democracy that such institutions be
supported by generous public funding and free access to materials. Without
informed knowledge of the collective past, current discussion of critical social
issues is impoverished and restricts our ability to do the right thing.

This book is the result of the contributions of a number of people, and I
thank them very much. Over the years, Mark H. Jones, state archivist, has been
a friend and guide to important sources at the Connecticut State Library.
Bruce Stark, assistant state archivist, and Carolyn Picciano, Kevin Johnson,
Richard Roberts, Jeannie Sherman, and Mel Smith of the History and Genealogy Department as well as law librarian Hilary Frye and serial specialists
provided valuable help on numerous occasions.

In addition, I relied extensively on the services of the University of Connecticut Libraries, particularly the reference department. Lana Babij at inter-
library loan secured much-needed microfilm of judicial proceedings and
pamphlet literature. The ever-growing access to documents and newspapers
online that the library supports proved a boon.

I also benefited from a variety of human rights activities that have occurred
over the years at the University of Connecticut. During early stages of
research, I was the recipient of awards from the Human Rights Institute and
the Research Foundation. Cindy Carvalho, a graduate assistant, provided
valuable help at this time. I also thank Sharon M. Harris, director of the
Humanities Institute, David W. Williams, director of the Greater Hartford
Campus, and Shirley Roe, head of the Department of History, for kindly
providing subvention funds for publication. I also benefited from presentations I gave at the Association for the Study of Connecticut History, the
National Association of African American Studies, the Social Science History

Association, and University of Connecticut venues at West Hartford and Waterbury. In addition, it was a pleasure to participate in Karyl Evans's documentary film, *The Rise and Fall of Newgate Prison*.

It was a pleasure to work again with the University of Massachusetts Press, particularly Senior Editor Clark Dougan and Managing Editor Carol Betsch. Kathleen Lafferty was a conscientious copy editor. Most of all, I thank my wife, Ellen Embardo, and daughter, Anna, to whom this book is dedicated.

THE
SOLEMN SENTENCE
OF DEATH

*

INTRODUCTION
The Paradox of Capital Punishment

It seems strange to me that in these days when capital punishment has been
abolished in many states, that Connecticut, one of the leading and most liberal
states in the United States, still uses capital punishment.

Rabbi Dr. David S. Hachen to Governor John Dempsey, April 14, 1967

ON NOVEMBER 13, 1817, more than 15,000 people—men, women, and children—
converged on Danbury, Connecticut. It was an unusually large gathering
for the time. Some had traveled from as far away as twenty-five miles and
arrived the previous night. They came to see the public execution that day
of Amos Adams, a twenty-eight-year-old African American who had been
convicted of raping Lelea Thorp, a married white woman and mother. Adams was to be the last person in Connecticut executed for a capital crime
other than homicide.[1]

In contrast, Michael Ross in 2005 died by lethal injection in a supermaximum prison during the early morning hours. An admitted sexual sadist, he
had manually strangled eight girls and young women after raping most of
them. Only a few witnesses were permitted at the execution, and protesters
against the death penalty were kept well away. Despite a judicial process
that would have continued to stay his already much-delayed execution, Ross
voluntarily waived his legal rights and opted to die. His was the only legal
execution in New England since 1960, when Connecticut electrocuted Joseph
Taborsky, another serial killer who relinquished further appeals. At a time of
declining execution rates in the United States and the abolition of capital
punishment in much of the western world, Connecticut is the only state in
New England to have executed anyone during the last half century. As of
2010, it had ten inmates on death row, by far the most in New England.[2]

The opening quotation by Rabbi Hachen asks why, and *The Solemn Sentence of Death: Capital Punishment in Connecticut* responds to that question.[3]

1

This book examines what happened in one jurisdiction over nearly four hundred years. Criminologist David Garland observed that "the social meaning of punishment is badly understood." He added, "To say—correctly—that punishment is a form of power immediately raises the question: 'what kind of power?' Is it authorized? Does it command popular support? What values does it convey? Which objectives does it seek? How is it shaped by sensibilities and in what kind of culture and morality is it grounded?"[4]

The death penalty, the most extreme and irreversible form of retribution, is intrinsically a social and legal artifact. The focus is the criminal justice system, but the larger context is the ethical values of New England culture. In Connecticut over the centuries, 158 people have been judicially executed in civilian courts. In sheer numbers, that is slightly more than the number of people executed—154—during the five years that George W. Bush was governor of Texas from 1995 to 2000. The contrast is striking and points to significant regional variation in the United States. No southern or far western state, areas with indelible traditions of racial suppression and vigilantism, has abolished the death penalty. In New England and the Northeast (excluding Pennsylvania), only New Hampshire and Connecticut retain a capital code, yet no systematic historical analysis of capital punishment exists for Connecticut. In addition, only recently has a comprehensive study appeared for another state (Massachusetts, which executed 237 people from 1630 to its last in 1947).[5] This book, then, explores new ground.[6]

The major conclusion of this work is that after nearly four centuries, capital punishment in Connecticut presents a paradox. The current restrictive statute and the lengthy appeals process have in recent decades blocked executions unless, ironically, the convict stipulates for death, as Taborsky and Ross did. State policy seeks to have it both ways: a commitment to the death penalty, but one that is not carried out. There is an uneasy tension between supporters and opponents that has resulted in halfway measures. Public opinion, the General Assembly (except in 2009), most governors, and the courts (state and federal) sustain the death penalty, at least for particularly cruel and heinous murders. A substantial majority of citizens believed that Taborsky and Ross got what they deserved. At the same time, however, there has been a judicial mandate to limit the scope of the law to the extent that it is virtually ineffective. The result is that the death penalty in Connecticut is contradictory in principle and unworkable in practice.

Ambiguity, ambivalence, and alteration have characterized the death penalty since the colonial era. A number of religious proscriptions adopted by the first colonists were never implemented, and others, such as execution for witchcraft, were blocked after 1663 even though they remained on the books for decades. The 1750 Connecticut Code of Laws dropped all biblical citations. There was a steady diminution in the types of crimes considered capital offenses. Concern with proportionate punishment during the Enlightenment led to imprisonment in place of corporal punishment or shaming for eventually all capital crimes except first-degree murder. A long tradition of the rule of law and adherence to a fair trial obstructed mob lynching so characteristic of the Wild West and Jim Crow South. A two-eyewitness standard of evidence, jury proceedings, and representation by attorneys have been standard in capital cases since the colonial era. The capital codes excluded the mentally disordered and eventually youths under eighteen years old. An unofficial gender convention has barred the execution of females since 1786. Connecticut established the first office of public defender during the early twentieth century. By the late 1950s, court decisions expanded defendants' rights and impeded implementation of the death penalty. With few exceptions, the underclass constituted those judicially executed. There is no way to determine how many people with more privilege escaped such punishment. What is clear is that those on the social margins were most vulnerable.

Before 1833, executions were public. The gallows provided a ritual of death emblematic of divine wrath and civic retribution for all to see. The funeral sermon held forth hope of repentance and salvation for all sinners, including the prisoner. By 1833, the morbid event was seen as too crass, brutalizing, and degrading for citizens of a democratic republic, and the gallows were banished to the confines of county jails. Sheriffs continued to admit dozens of spectators, however, until in 1893 hangings were sequestered in the state prison and only a select few were admitted. Executions were secretive and isolated, out of sight and out of mind, as it were. The latest technology—the automatic gallows, electric chair, and lethal injection—rendered a gruesome event more expeditious, more modern, and less offensive, it was hoped.

Abolitionist efforts reached their zenith during the late antebellum period, during the 1950s, and in 2009 when a gubernatorial veto blocked such legislation. Ethically based opposition contended that state-sanctioned killing was wrong, whereas proponents supported the righteousness of retribution. Despite a petition campaign and gubernatorial support, opponents during an era of reform in the 1840s and 1850s failed to sway the legislature, a time during which Michigan in 1846 was the first state to abolish the death penalty. The bloody Civil War forestalled further efforts. After the horrors of World

War II, Governor Abraham Ribicoff and the *Hartford Courant* supported broad-based efforts to end capital punishment, but the General Assembly voted down abolition and the shocking murder spree of Taborsky undermined the cause. Taborsky's multiple murders left a lasting legacy of support for capital punishment, albeit with many restrictions that have resulted in an unofficial moratorium, interrupted by the self-willed execution of Michael Ross in 2005. Then, in 2009, for the first time the General Assembly, with Democratic majorities in both houses, voted to abolish the death penalty, but Republican Governor M. Jodi Rell vetoed the bill.[7] The present law is riddled with contradictions.

This book is organized on a thematic and chronological format. Each chapter examines the capital code, the criminal justice system, a profile of the executed person, and the broader cultural context. Table 1 breaks down the number of persons judicially executed in Connecticut by the same groupings as the chapters in this book.

In 1976, the United States Supreme Court in *Gregg v. Georgia* lifted the ban on capital punishment that it had imposed four years earlier in *Furman v. Georgia*. Since then, more than one thousand people have been executed in the United States. Starting in the late 1990s, however, the number of convicts executed and the number of people sentenced to death have declined significantly nationwide. The growing reliability of DNA evidence has contributed to the exoneration and freedom of dozens of wrongly convicted prisoners, including those on death row. The documentation of bias in the criminal justice system is clear; for example, low-income black men convicted

TABLE 1

Number of Persons Judicially Executed in Connecticut, by Chapter

Chapter in This Volume	Number of Persons Executed
1. Biblical Retribution, 1636–1699	31
2. Emergence of Yankee Justice, 1700–1772	17
3. Era of Newgate Prison, 1773–1827	16
4. Debate over Capital Punishment, 1828–1879	12
5. Menace of the Criminal Class, 1880–1929	60
6. Waning of Executions, 1930–1960	21
7. Unofficial Moratorium, 1961–2004	0
8. Execution of Michael Ross, 2005	1
Total	158

of murdering whites are particularly vulnerable to capital punishment.[8] Moratoria on the death penalty exist in a dozen states, including Illinois, where Governor George Ryan called the system broken. The U.S. Supreme Court has recently excluded juveniles and the mentally retarded from capital punishment on the basis of mental competency. In 2008, it also ruled that the death penalty for rape is unconstitutional because it is not a graduated response according to the Eighth Amendment's injunction against cruel and unusual punishment. The Court upheld the death penalty, but only in crimes against individuals when a life is taken. In the majority decision, Justice Anthony Kennedy cautioned, "When the law punishes by death, it risks its own sudden descent into brutality, transgressing the constitutional commitment to decency and restraint."[9]

Indeed, the death penalty is an emotionally charged and polarizing topic. Opponents such as Sister Helen Prejean ultimately base their opposition not on the injustice of the criminal system, but on the premise that judicial execution is an evil per se, a cruel and unusual punishment banned by the Eighth Amendment. Defenders such as state's attorney John Connolly reply that Connecticut's capital punishment is limited to the worst of the worst, for which execution is a just and appropriate retribution. Like abortion, evolution, flag burning, gay marriage, gun control, and school prayer, capital punishment is an integral part of the cultural politics that have significantly reshaped the electoral landscape since Ronald Reagan's presidency of the 1980s. After nearly four centuries of capital punishment, Connecticut is exceptional in its region in still carrying out the statute. It appears that a substantial majority of the state's citizens wish to preserve the death penalty, at least for multiple murderers such as Taborsky and Ross.

This book concludes that there were—and are—inherent tensions in the capital code and application of the death penalty. The effort to resolve these contradictions led to revisions and the unsuccessful effort to abolish capital punishment. A profound ambivalence has further complicated the issue. Moral repugnance at state-sanctioned killing contends with a still popular emotion that certain crimes demand death if for no other reason than communal revenge for the victim. The concern with due process and the fear of executing an innocent person act as restraints; however, the animus against arbitrary government rests uncomfortably with the belief that capital punishment is an essential function of state power. Over the course of four centuries, legislation, more recently prompted by federal court decisions, has greatly restricted but not eliminated capital punishment. The death penalty remains on the books because enough citizens believe that it is a necessary and just retribution. In rural eastern Connecticut, where most of Ross's young victims had lived, one of several large plywood signs posted along a highway in 2005 celebrated, "EXECUTE ROSS! TIME FOR A PARTY!"[10] The sentiment was widespread.

1

BIBLICAL RETRIBUTION
1636–1699

The Saints maintain God in his ordinances, the want of which is under the
penalty of death and condemnation.

Thomas Hooker, 1641

We have endeavored not only to ground our capital laws upon the word of
God, but also all our other Laws upon the justice and equity held forth in that
word which is a most perfect rule.

Connecticut Code of Laws, 1672

CAPITAL PUNISHMENT was not a casual or arbitrary matter for the Puritans
of New England. Scrupulous attention was paid to law and procedure, which
were influenced by English tradition and scriptural interpretation. The saints,
God's elect, held the individual responsible for his or her actions, which were
measured against the law, and the law's ultimate basis was believed to be sa-
cred.[1] In the Connecticut and New Haven Colonies (two separate plantations
until the latter merged with the former in 1665), thirty-one people were judicially executed in nonmilitary situations over the course of the seventeenth
century. Puritan statutes did not explicitly impose differential standards
based on a person's identity or standing in the community. The ideal, as the
1672 Connecticut Code of Laws stated, was to ensure "justice and equity," an
earthly reflection of the "most perfect rule" of heaven. Based largely on biblical retribution, certain crimes were capital, but who was executed, and why?

The Religious Mandate for the Death Penalty

New England was a Puritan redoubt in the contentious religious wars that
continued a century after the origins of the Reformation. Among those seeking refuge from Anglican persecution of nonconformist ministers were the

influential John Cotton, Thomas Hooker, and Samuel Stone, all graduates of Cambridge University in England, who arrived at Boston aboard the ship *Griffin* in 1634. Hooker and his assistant Stone joined their followers in New Towne (Cambridge), Massachusetts, where they were ordained. The New Towne residents were eager for farmland and looked westward toward the fertile valley of the Connecticut River. Already in 1633 the Dutch from New Netherlands had established a trading post with the Indians in Hartford on the Connecticut. Pilgrims from Plymouth Colony in the same year established a base to the north at Windsor, which received additional arrivals in 1635 from a congregation in Dorchester, Massachusetts. In 1634, another Connecticut River town was formed south of Hartford at Wethersfield, principally by emigrants from Watertown, Massachusetts, and people from other locations, including directly from England. With permission from the Massachusetts General Court, Hooker and Stone in 1636 moved their congregation 100 miles overland to the Dutch settlement at Hartford. On January 14, 1639, the residents of Windsor, Wethersfield, and Hartford "in Combination and Confederation together" adopted the Fundamental Orders of Connecticut "to maintain the purity of the gospel of Lord Jesus."[2]

With his appointment in 1633 as archbishop of Canterbury, William Laud escalated harassment of dissidents, demanding complete uniformity to Anglican doctrine. John Davenport, a principled nonconformist, fled his London church for exile in Holland. Hooker and Cotton had earlier failed to convince Davenport to emigrate with them, but now under the threat of arrest he was convinced that relocation to New England was imperative. Returning to England in disguise, he organized his congregation for an expedition to Massachusetts Bay Colony. These expatriates were staunch Puritans and included prominent merchants, among them Davenport's confidant Theophilus Eaton, who were eager to establish a "Bible State."[3] Governor John Winthrop welcomed their arrival in Boston in the early summer of 1637. The attraction of Quinnipiac (New Haven) with a good harbor on Long Island Sound, suitable for mercantile endeavors, spurred the original company and new arrivals to found New Haven Colony in the spring of 1638. They subsequently acquired extensive landholdings, ceded by compliant Indians, along the coast and well into the interior. In organizing their church and civil government in 1639, the colonists adopted a code of laws, "a Model of Moses his judicials compiled in an exact method," a blueprint that Cotton had drawn up in 1636. New Haven Colony had no royal charter, it was distant from Massachusetts Bay to the east, and it was independent of Connecticut to the north. Cotton's model fit their needs nicely and in its religious rigor gave distinct rendering to the criminal justice system. The General Court for New Haven Colony in 1644 officially mandated "the judicial laws of God, as they were delivered by Moses," throughout its jurisdiction.[4]

The rationale for the death penalty was deeply embedded in the religious foundation of New England. It was the logical, albeit extreme, extension of presuppositions about human nature and civil society. "The Puritans," Perry Miller observed, "were gifted—or cursed—with an overwhelming realization of an inexorable power at work not only in nature but in themselves, which they called God."[5] These dissenters believed that humans were almost irrevocably flawed by original sin, an innate human propensity to disobey divine will. The Puritans, however, had modified the relentless predestination of John Calvin in which a hidden, unknowable God had eternally damned the many and elected the few. Although mindful of divine absolutism, the theology of Thomas Hooker stressed human volition, especially the hope that the righteous might gain gradual assurance of regeneration.[6] "God of an unwilling will, doth make a willing will," Hooker preached.[7] "We must sin," he acknowledged, but Hooker demanded that we "look sin in the face, and discern it to the full." And, he said, with the gift of divine grace, we would *cure these inordinate and raging lusts* and thence wil follow a stil and quiet composure of mind."[8] Sin was a choice; people were accountable, particularly for criminal conduct. Puritanism demanded a rigorous regime of inner discipline, self-regulation, spiritual examination, and dedicated work ethic.[9]

Furthermore, the Bible commonwealth was an external check on individual tendencies toward wrongdoing. It was expected that the populace accept the social covenant, as they had the spiritual compact, and defer to the most worthy saints. The rule by male elders, as Stone famously said, was "a speaking aristocracy in the face of a silent democracy."[10] The magistrates and ministers were predictably the colony's elite: the college educated, the major landowners, and the well connected. Government was hierarchical and mirrored a stratified social order with medieval vestiges that banned usury, set fixed prices, and observed sumptuary laws. Mindful of Stuart abuses and their own sinful proclivities, New Englanders feared that liberty might degenerate into license and authority into absolutism. Cotton warned, "There is a straine in a mans heart that will sometime or other runne out to excesse, unless the Lord restraine it, but is not good to venture it."[11] Original sin would produce obstinacy from some, for whom correction was necessary. And if the fault was a grievous one, death was divinely mandated, but subject to human implementation.

The Legal Culture of Capital Punishment

In creating a body of law, the Puritans selected applicable scriptural mandates that identified capital crimes. English statutes also made frequent biblical references, but the Puritans, given their religiosity, made even more. The scriptural emphasis in Connecticut and New Haven Colonies allowed for flexibility and innovation in the traditional law code. The stamp of divine approval meant that the colonists might revise English statutes and make more explicit what was often vague in common law. Until the establishment of the Dominion of New England by King James II in 1686, English law did not apply if not mentioned in colonial law. The Puritans kept parts of the old system while incorporating what was pertinent to their New England experience, part of the Americanization experience. England and New England concurred that witches be executed. In vivo evisceration, burning alive, and being racked and broken on the wheel were practiced in Europe, but were never sanctioned in New England. The 1672 Connecticut Code of Laws stated in regard to punishment that "none shall be inflicted that are Inhumane, Barbarous or Cruel."[12] Adultery was not a capital crime in England, but the Puritans, concerned with confining sexual relations to marriage, made it a violation punishable by death. Ecclesiastical courts in England oversaw morals; in New England, civil courts were the censors. What an omnipotent divinity had made incumbent upon the Jews with the covenant of Abraham currently applied to the Puritans. The Mosaic code, however, was subject to interpretation. The Hebraic stoning of adulterous women was a remnant of tribal patriarchy beyond the pale for seventeenth-century Europeans.[13]

Rather than an escape from orthodoxy in Massachusetts, Connecticut and New Haven were its western extension. Connecticut's capital crimes

TABLE 2
Connecticut Colony's Capital Laws, 1642

1. Idolatry	5. Killing through guile	9. Rape
2. Witchcraft	6. Bestiality	10. Man-stealing
3. Blasphemy	7. Sodomy (male)	11. Perjury (to take a life)
4. Murder (killing with malice)	8. Adultery	12. Rebellion

Sources: J. Hammond Trumbull, *The Public Records of the Colony of Connecticut, Prior to the Union with New Haven Colony, May, 1665,* (Hartford: Brown and Parsons, 1850), 1:77–78; and Edgar J. McManus, *Law and Liberty in New England* (Amherst: University of Massachusetts Press, 1993), 189. I have used McManus's classification.

TABLE 3

Connecticut Colony's Capital Laws, 1650

1–12. Same as 1642, although the sequence changed	15. Defiance by a rebellious son
13. Cursing a natural parent	16. Burglary (third offense)
14. Smiting a natural parent	17. Robbery (third offense)

Sources: J. Hammond Trumbull, *The Public Records of the Colony of Connecticut, from 1665–1678* (Hartford, Conn.: F. A. Brown, 1852), 1:515; and Edgar J. McManus, *Law and Liberty in New England* (Amherst: University of Massachusetts Press, 1993), 190. I have used McManus's classification.

enacted in 1642 (table 2) closely copied Massachusetts's list of a year earlier. Only the crime of rebellion did not have a clear biblical imprimatur. Now that the Puritans were establishing their own fledgling regimes, however, sedition and treason were seen as crimes that must be severely punished. Accommodation to worldly necessity made a breech in the spiritual fortress, one that would widen by the end of the seventeenth century. Indeed, the Puritan dilemma, as Edmund Morgan pointed out in the case of Winthrop, was "the paradox that required a man to live in the world without being of it."[14] Seventeenth-century law made further compromises with scripture. Willful intent to defame religion or deny God was necessary to demonstrate blasphemy. False witness in a capital trial applied only if the perjurer deliberately lied to convict the accused. And conviction for adultery required direct evidence of the sexual act, not merely the presence of a man in the bed or boudoir of a married or betrothed woman who was not his wife or fiancée.

After Massachusetts revised its law in 1648, Roger Ludlow, Connecticut's only formally trained lawyer, followed its lead and devised a new law code that added five new capital crimes to the original dozen (table 3). The founding generation revealed a disturbing diminution in filiopiety at midcentury. In keeping with their own traditions, not the Bible, the Puritans made age sixteen the demarcation point so that sons younger than that age were not subject to the death penalty. The authorities instructed parents to encourage literacy so that, in part, children could read the "Capitall Lawes" and appreciate the dire consequence of not honoring their parents.[15] Because "many persons," it was thought, were engaged in robbery and burglary in homes and on highways, those common-law crimes were also added to the list. These property crimes were graduated, however. The first and second offenses provided for branding the letter *B* on the forehead and a severe whipping, and if the offense occurred on the Sabbath, the ears were cropped. For the third conviction, the incorrigible could be hanged.[16] Unlike the 1642

TABLE 4

New Haven Colony's Capital Laws, 1656

1. Idolatry	12. Adultery
2. Witchcraft	13. Man-stealing
3. Blasphemy	14. Perjury (to take a life)
4. Murder	15. Rebellion
5. Manslaughter (involving anger or cruelty)	16. Cursing a natural parent
	17. Smiting a natural parent
6. Killing through guile	18. Defiance by a rebellious son
7. Bestiality	19. Rape (death penalty not mandatory)
8. Sodomy (male)	20. Incest
9. Sodomy (heterosexual)	21. Burglary (third offense)
10. Fornication with very young ("unripe") female	22. Robbery (third offense)
	23. Profaning the Sabbath (provocatively)
11. Masturbation (male)	

Sources: John D. Cushing, *The Earliest Laws of the New Haven and Connecticut Colonies, 1639–1673* (Wilmington, Del.: Michael Glazier, 1977), 18; and Edgar J. McManus, *Law and Liberty in New England* (Amherst: University of Massachusetts Press, 1993), 190. I have used McManus's classification.

code, manslaughter was now distinguished from murder as justifiable homicide committed in self-defense. Trained at Oxford and the Inner Temple, Ludlow made clear the commitment to individual rights and the rule of law: "No mans life shall be taken away . . . no mans person shall be arrested, restrained banished, dismembered nor any way punnished . . . vnless it bee by the virtue or equity of some express Law of the Country warranteing the same, established by a Generall Courte, and sufficiently published, or in case of the defect of a Law in any particular case, by the word of God."[17]

New Haven Colony in 1639 had adopted Cotton's *Judicial,* the most rigorous biblical codicil in New England, which conveniently met the colonists' high expectations. Its strict Puritanism influenced the formal law code adopted in 1656 (table 4). Scripture underscored capital cases. Unlike its sister colonies, New Haven made provocative profanation of the Sabbath a hanging offense. A recidivist convicted of burglary for a second time on the Sabbath not only was branded and whipped, but had to stand in the pillory and "wear a halter in the day time constantly and visibly about his neck, as a mark of infamy."[18] Sexual infractions set New Haven apart the most. It was the only colony to adopt literally the Hebraic ban on incest, to punish heterosexual sodomy, and to outlaw male masturbation with the death penalty. The Mosaic code, which allowed a rapist to marry his victim and pay restoration to her family, did not fit Puritan sensibilities. New Haven made rape of an unmarried woman and statutory rape of a girl under age ten hanging offenses. The latter was included broadly under the concept of sodomy, an unnatural sexual act. The rape of married and betrothed women fell under the category of adultery, which in this case condemned the male assailant. No provision of marital rape existed in a patriarchal system. The 1656 code echoed New Haven's affirmation of the rule of law and due process in death penalty cases.

The restoration of the Stuart monarchy under King Charles II in 1660 and the end of the Puritan interregnum confronted Connecticut and New Haven with a crisis. Neither colony had a royal charter. Connecticut's Governor John Winthrop Jr., the capable, eldest son of Massachusetts's founder, agreed to represent both colonies in England. He gained one, not two, charters from the king in 1662 that allowed for a remarkable amount of self-government but only for Connecticut. New Haven was reluctant to accept its extinction. With only 2,500 settlers, however, it was in an untenable position. Eaton died in 1658 at a time when his dynamic leadership was wanted. The colony's ultra-Puritanism might well have caused problems in gaining legal sanction from London. To the west, it was bounded by Anglican New York and to the North blocked by Connecticut. As the uncertain situation threatened the political integrity of New England, New Haven Colony reluctantly merged with Connecticut in 1665.[19]

In the revision of statutes in 1672 (table 5), Connecticut significantly avoided the provisions in the capital crimes that had made New Haven distinctive. Adultery was dropped as a capital crime, the first time in the

TABLE 5
Connecticut's Capital Laws, 1672

1. Idolatry	10. Man-stealing
2. Blasphemy	11. Perjury (to take a life)
3. Witchcraft	12. Rebellion
4. Murder (killing with malice or cruelty)	13. Arson
5. Killing through guile	14. Cursing a natural parent
6. Bestiality	15. Smiting a natural parent
7. Sodomy (male)	16. Defiance by a rebellious son
8. Incest	17. Burglary (third offense)
9. Rape	18. Robbery (third offense)

Sources: John D. Cushing, *The Earliest Laws of the New Haven and Connecticut Colonies, 1639–1673* (Wilmington, Del.: Michael Glazier, 1977), 9–10; and Edgar J. McManus, *Law and Liberty in New England* (Amherst: University of Massachusetts Press, 1993), 190. I have used McManus's classification.

colony that such a deletion had occurred. The substitution for the death penalty was whipping, branding on the forehead with the letter *A,* and wearing a halter around the neck while in the colony.[20] Connecticut added incest, but limited the definition to parents and children, not the biblical literalism of New Haven. Both parties were to be executed, unless "the Woman was forced or under *fourteen years* of age," the time of discretion.[21] A case of father–daughter incest the year before in Norwich had forced the subject on the books. Arson was a serious concern in an era of wood-frame structures and uncertain fire protection. The colony distinguished, however, between conflagrations that were set that threatened property and those that endangered human life.

The statutes are deceptive as to what occurred in practice. The laws represented a religious ideal, a public declaration, as the 1672 code put it, of what was "suitable for the people of Israel."[22] The judicial system was much more lenient. The courts aspired to be scrupulous and fair. There was concern to balance individual protection with the greater good. Drawing on centuries of English tradition, the Puritans upheld civil rights, including no unreasonable search or seizure, no double jeopardy, no compulsory self-incrimination, no torture, no cruel or barbarous punishments, right to bail (except in capital cases), grand and petite juries in capital cases, speedy trial, presumption of innocence, and the right to confront accusers in open court. New Haven did not have a jury system because there was no scriptural basis for it.[23] Attorneys did not usually function in either colony; the wise and impartial rule of the magistrates was deemed sufficient. The plaintiff managed the prosecution, called witnesses, and presented evidence. The defendant responded and called witnesses. The judges interrogated deponents and commented on the evidence; their function was to clarify the matter for the jury.

The royal charter of 1662 provided for different levels of courts. Oversight rested with the General Court. The Court of Assistants (composed of the governor, deputy governor, and magistrates or assistants) was the immediate venue for all crimes punishable by banishment, dismemberment, or death. There was a reluctance to execute unless there was a confession of the accused or two eyewitnesses of "competent age, of sound understanding, and good reputation."[24] This amended biblical stipulation based on Deuteronomy 17:16 is an outstanding example of how scriptural compunction acted to limit executions. Another check on the rush to judgment was that a two-thirds majority was needed for a jury indictment; otherwise, a jury might declare itself *ignoramus* and not arrive at a verdict. The magistrates could twice return a verdict to the jury, which usually meant reconsideration of a sentence of death.[25] Most capital crimes in Connecticut and New Haven during the seventeenth century—including blasphemy, burglary, fornication with a young female, heterosexual sodomy, killing through guile, man-stealing, perjury, profanation of the Sabbath, rape, robbery, and various forms of filial disrespect—did not end on the gallows. Instead, there was a graduation of punishment available that fell short of execution. For noncapital crimes such as drunkenness, fornication, lascivious behavior, and theft, among others, fines were most common. A variant was the requirement to post a bond for good behavior or, if appropriate, provide a financial restoration.

Low-status people were more likely to appear in criminal proceedings and less likely to be able to pay pecuniary penalties than were better-off people.[26] The courts could also employ other possibilities that fell disproportionately on the nonelite. Shaming techniques were common in these face-to-face communities. Public humiliation included being set in the stocks (three hours maximum in Connecticut and four in New Haven), standing in the pillory, and ascending the ladder on the gallows with a rope around the neck, a symbolic form of hanging. In 1672, a conviction of adultery required wearing a halter around the neck. Among corporal punishments, public whipping (limited to thirty stripes in Connecticut and forty in New Haven) of both sexes was routine, with the directive to be severely whipped on the naked body while tied to a post. For the incorrigible, branding with a hot iron left a permanent mark of disrepute. Seared into the forehead or hand were the insignia *A* for adultery, *B* for burglary, or *H* for heretic. Connecticut cropped the ears of hardened thieves, and New Haven permitted boring through the tongue with a hot iron for Quakers for a fourth offense of irreligion, an indignity never carried out. The judicial repertory included banishment (even to Barbados) and instruction of fornicators to wed. Incarceration in Hartford's house of correction was a temporary measure, reserved for defendants awaiting trial and others awaiting their punishment, including death row. With a population of less than 13,000 in 1680, long-term jailing was not practical or economic.[27]

Some capital cases are notable because the court imposed alternatives to death. A Quillipiock Indian, Panquash, in New Haven blasphemed Jesus, for which he was whipped. The court in 1646 warned him that a repetition "would hazard his life."[28] In 1666, the Court of Assistants overturned a jury's verdict of death for Hannah Hackleton for "notorious criminal acts" of sexual misconduct and blasphemy. Instead, she was held in jail, "corrected by severe whipping on ye naked body" of thirty lashes, and then ascended the ladder

to the gallows with a rope around her neck for one hour.[29] In 1655, an insolent youth named Samuel Ford injured a young boy, disobeyed his father,
sassed his mother, and defied Sabbath observance. When an elder sought to
correct him, "he turned up his breech and bid him kiss it." The New Haven
magistrates did not enact the full force of biblical retribution. Instead, they
whipped Ford and warned, "Take heed."[30] Mercy Brown of Wallingford
confessed to the homicide of her son with an ax. The court found in 1691
that she had "generally been in a crazed or distracted condition as well long
before she committed the [act]." According to long-standing English tradition, the court withheld a sentence of death because Brown was not morally
responsible.[31] Abraham, an African American slave, with one name defining
his racial bondage, confessed to "breaking open" several houses on the Sabbath and other robberies as well as escaping jail in Fairfield. Rather than
execution, this recidivist in 1698 was "severely whipt" and branded with a *B*
on his forehead.[32]

Judicial Executions

Thirty-one people in criminal proceedings did not, however, escape execution during the seventeenth century in the colonies of Connecticut and New
Haven. The original sources of the period are often incomplete and, when
they do exist, fail to provide a full description. The executed nevertheless
fall into three broad categories: homicide (nine cases), sexual violations
(eleven cases), and witchcraft (eleven cases). Witchcraft was confined to the
period, as were some of the sexual violations. Here, the cases are restricted
to civilian trials; excluded are combat and courts martial during the Pequot
War (1637) and King Philip's War (1675–1676) in which thousands of Native
Americans and European Americans died, civilians and combatants alike.
These bloody conflicts in which killing and retribution took many forms
warrant separate study.[33] To learn what was distinctive about the thirty-one
executions, each of the three categories will be examined in turn.

Homicide

The interchange between colonists and Indians became one-sided with the
willingness of the English to use their growing numbers and technological
superiority to establish hegemony. During the initial period of contact, both
sides found it mutually advantageous to accommodate to the other's concept of
justice. "When mutual recognition of reciprocity failed," historian Katherine

TABLE 6
Executions for Homicide, 1636–1699

	Year of Execution	Name	Race	Gender	Location of Crime or Execution
1	1639	Nepaupuck	Indian	Male	New Haven
2	1644	Busheage	Indian	Male	New Haven
3	1667	Peter Abbott	White	Male	Fairfield
4	1668	Ruth Briggs	White	Female	New Haven*
5	1675	Cloyes Negro	Black	Male	Stamford
6	1677	Benjamin Tuttle	White	Male	Stamford
7	1678	John Stoddard	White	Male	New London
8	1682	Allumchoyse	Indian	Male	Wethersfield
9	1685	Squampam	Indian	Male	Wethersfield
10	1699	Amy Mun	White	Female	Farmington

* Convicted of adultery and infanticide; see table 7.

Hermes writes, "the Anglo-European legal system and the power it represented began the ascent to dominance."[34] Antagonism, including violence and atrocities, came quickly. An unprovoked Pequot raid on Wethersfield on April 23, 1637, in which a dozen residents were killed or kidnapped escalated existing tensions. In retaliation, on May 1 the General Court at Hartford authorized an offensive war on the Pequot. On May 26, with Narragansett and Mohegan allies, Captain John Mason commanded a massacre on a redoubt at Mystic that killed by his estimate some 600 to 700 men, women, and children. Captain John Underhill responded to stiff resistance by burning the village, blocking the exits, and shooting escapees. The victors enslaved the survivors, a number of whom were transported to the West Indies. Other Pequot, not at the fort, were later hunted down. Indian allies delivered severed heads, including that of Sassacus the Pequot sachem, to the colonists at Hartford and Wethersfield as tokens of friendship.[35] Extensive killing, particularly of noncombatants, was characteristic of European religious wars, such as the concurrent Thirty Years War in Germany, and presaged Oliver Cromwell's ruthless occupation of Ireland. What the Puritans heralded as the Lord's judgment on the heathen reverberated in the bloodthirsty words of Ezekiel 9:5–6: "Go yet after him through the city and smite: let not your eye spare, neither have ye pity: slaughter old and young, both maids and little children." The English slaughtered the Pequot and took their land.

As shown in table 6, the first colonial execution on October 30, 1639, was a sequel to the Pequot War. The magistrate and deputies in New Haven had learned through examination of the Quillipiock sagamore that a member of their tribe, Nepaupuck, had boasted of killing colonists, cutting off their hands, and presenting them to Sassacus. Nepaupuck first denied the charge. Further interrogation led to a confession that he had murdered Abraham Finch and others at Wethersfield, kidnapped a child of Samuel Swaine, and killed three white men on a boat on the Connecticut River. The cooperation of tribal leaders was essential to the criminal proceedings. The General Court found "such pregnant proof" that the accused was decapitated and his head "pitched upon a pole in the marketplace." The standard biblical justification was God's commandment to Noah, "He that shed man's blood, by man shall his blood be shed" (Genesis 9:6).[36]

A homicide occurred as part of Kieft's War in New Netherlands, with Indians seeking Dutch victims but straying into English border towns. One Busheage was convicted in May 1644 of a murder in Stamford. He entered a house, struck a mother with infant on the head three times with a lathing hammer, and stole clothes. She survived long enough to identify the assailant, and a Potatuck Indian delivered the suspect to the New Haven authorities. He confessed, produced the stolen clothes, and was sentenced to death. Governor Winthrop of Massachusetts, who was consulted on the case, described the punishment: "The executioner would strike off his head with a falchion [a sword with a curved blade], but he had eight blows at it before he could effect it, and the Indian sat upright and stirred not all the time."[37] New Haven authorities racially set apart Nepaupuck and Busheage with beheading, but the cruel execution ended decapitation in New Haven.

With the subjugation of Indians during King Philip's War, the colonial homicide statutes held sway. An Indian, Allumchoyse, pleaded guilty to the murder of Elizabeth Randall, a Wethersfield woman, whom he stabbed in the back with a knife. He had a translator, but did not contest his execution on June 28, 1682.[38] In another case, a jury on October 1, 1685, found Squampam of Wethersfield guilty of murdering an Indian man and woman with a broad ax in Samuel Wright's home. He was hanged on a Friday at 1 p.m.[39] No motive was offered in either case. Overwhelming English victory in devastating wars made it less necessary for the capital code to accommodate to an Indian sense of justice.

Other homicide cases were also procedurally straightforward. "Cloyes Negro," an African American slave in Stamford, was convicted on May 25, 1675, of the ax murder of his wife. The failure of the court records to identify the husband, except as his master's possession, and not to name his wife, as also occurred with Squampam's Indian victims, documents a pervasive white supremacy and patriarchy. During the seventeenth century, Connecticut and New Haven enslaved more Indians than Africans, although the number of slaves was low, particularly in proportion to a population of 12,500 whites after midcentury. The practice of bondage was rich in scriptural justification (see Leviticus 25:45, 46), but racially limited in New England to non-European people.[40] "Cloyes Negro" confessed and was the first person of African ancestry hanged in Connecticut.[41]

Nor was there much question of Benjamin Tuttle's guilt in the ax murder of his sister, Sarah Slasson, in Stamford in 1676, for which he was hanged on June 13, 1677. Several witnesses, including Slasson's husband and two children, testified that Tuttle had admitted the crime. The siblings were quarrelsome and had "a falling out." Tuttle was afraid that his sister "would have done to him as he did to her." Enraged, he split her skull with several blows.[42]

Scrupulous detective work prevented the execution of two innocent Indians, Resuekquinek and Sucquanch, for multiple murders in New London. What seemed like persuasive evidence led authorities to arrest these men for the hatchet murder of Zipporah Bolles and two young children at her home on June 6, 1678. Then, on July 25, sixteen-year-old John Stoddard alerted officials that Indians had assaulted his infant stepbrother with a hatchet blow to the head. He had been tending the baby while his mother and stepfather were away. Under persistent questioning by the magistrates, Stoddard, who had been questioned in the Bolles's murders, admitted the crimes. Zipporah Bolles had angered the youth, who may have had sexual motives, when she refused to let him stay the night at her house during her husband's absence. Stoddard claimed that she thrust him out of the house and struck him. He admitted that his one-year-old stepbrother had annoyed him with his crying. Rage and revenge were the overt motives.

As historian Nancy Steenburg points out, the Court of Assistants did not take mitigating factors into account. The age of discretion in Connecticut law was fourteen, so Stoddard's youthful age did not bar execution. At this time, it was not customary to appoint a defense attorney or other advocate to oversee due process of the law, even for a juvenile offender. Furthermore, the youth had a history of delinquency, his father had died two years ago, and he did not get along with his quarrelsome stepfather. Indeed, Stoddard told the court that he had no love for his stepfather or stepbrother. According to the standards of the day, Stoddard was hanged on October 9, 1678, and was the youngest person executed in the state for more than a hundred years. Only two years after the racial violence of King Philip's War, Native Americans, whom Stoddard sought to scapegoat, did not die for his crimes. Justice in this sense did prevail.[43]

Evidence of insanity did not stop the October 16, 1667, execution of Peter Abbott of Fairfield. He confessed to having slit the throat of his wife, Elizabeth, and child as they slept. Elizabeth died; the child survived. The documents are scant, but record that he had been "taken . . . with a lunacy." In English jurisprudence, mental disorder might well void the prerequisite of mens rea, of criminal intent in committing the act. Neither the jury nor the Court of Assistants, however, blocked the hanging.[44] In contrast, Mercy Brown was spared execution for the homicide of her son in 1691. Gershom Buckeley, a minister and physician, put the matter directly: "If she were not compos mentis at the time of the fact it is no felony and consequently no willful or malicious murder; and if she be known to be a lunatic, though she have her lucid intervals, there need be very good and satisfactory proof that she was compos mentis for the law favors life."[45] Family and neighbors added that "we do believe in our consciences that she was a distracted woman when she committed this horrid act."[46]

For most of the seventeenth century, no special statute covered infanticide. It was common-law murder. The two-eyewitness rule made conviction difficult unless a confession was forthcoming. The desperate effort of Amy Mun in 1699 to conceal a birth led to a draconian change in the law. Mun, an unmarried servant in the Farmington household of Samuel Wadsworth, claimed to have hidden a stillbirth and admitted she was only guilty of fornication. The prosecution charged a series of offenses: she had intended an abortion, injured the baby during birth, neglected the infant, and ultimately cut its throat to the bone. Her employers corroborated the last point. The indictment continued, "To add to her wickedness," she lied about willful murder and sought to perjure witnesses.[47] The jury found her guilty of murder. As a result, the General Assembly passed shortly thereafter a specific law modeled on a severe English statute of 1624 that Massachusetts had adopted in 1696 stating that the concealment of an illegitimate child's death was presumptive evidence of murder, unless one witness could rebut that there was a stillbirth.[48] Mun's egregious situation heightened concerns of sexual immorality and social disorder at the end the seventeenth century that punitive legislation sought to correct. She was likely hanged under the old homicide law. The new statute expedited execution and made unmarried mothers particularly vulnerable.[49]

The circumstances surrounding these nine people executed for homicide reveal the following profile. Eight men were executed, compared with one woman, who died for the gender-specific crime of infanticide as a result of an illegitimate birth. Male violence was often directed at women, of whom six were murdered. Excluding infanticide, intrafamily violence included two husbands who murdered their wives and one brother who killed his sister. In six of eight known cases, perpetrators were known to victims. All perpetrators were hanged, except for two Indians who were beheaded in the first decade of settlement, the only murderers executed in New Haven Colony. In interracial homicide, three Indians were executed for killing whites, but no whites were convicted for killing Indians. A black man killed his African American wife and was hanged. Alcohol is indicated in one murder, an Indian assault on a white woman. No firearms were involved; blunt and sharp instruments (knife, hatchet, hammer, and ax), common to households of the day, predominated as the instruments of murder. A miscarriage of justice may well have occurred in the execution of Peter Abbott, whose sanity was in question. Four young children and infants died, including three at the hand of John Stoddard, himself just sixteen years old, who was hanged as a culpable adult. Beyond the scope of this study, there looms the bloody multitude that died violently in two racial wars.

Sexual Crimes

Contrary to a persistent stereotype, the Puritans were not particularly prudish for their day. The lesson of original sin for the Puritans was that humans were flawed and had difficulty obeying divine precepts, including carnal restraint. Puritans sought to contain sexuality within marriage, couple it with reproduction, and ensure the survival of the saints. The errand into the wilderness gave special urgency to the divine injunction to go forth and multiply. They sought to regulate, not renounce. Outside of marriage, sexual intercourse was banned. New Haven's sweeping prohibition that prescribed death for "carnal knowledge of another sexual vessel than God in nature appointed to become one flesh" included heterosexual sodomy, which was not mentioned in the Bible.[50] The courts generally dealt with most sexual violations, especially noncapital offenses, with moderation and graduated punishment.[51] In keeping with its strictures, New Haven with seven of eleven executions for sexual crimes outpaced Connecticut (table 7). These specific cases—involving bestiality, male sodomy, adultery, incest, and rape—had distinct circumstances that led to the gallows, however. These executions represented extremes that affirmed sexual taboos at the intersection of law, religion, and community standards.

TABLE 7
Executions for Sexual Infractions, 1636–1699

	Year of Execution	Name	Crime	Race	Gender	Location of Crime	Location of Execution
1	1642	George Spencer	Bestiality	White	Male	New Haven	New Haven
2	1646	William Plaine	Sodomy	White	Male	Guilford	New Haven
3	1647	John Newberry	Bestiality	White	Male	Windsor	Hartford?
4	1650	Unknown	Adultery	White	Unknown	New Haven	New Haven
5	1650	Unknown	Sodomy	White	Male	New Haven	New Haven
6	1654	Walter Robinson	Bestiality	White	Male	Milford	New Haven
7	1655	John Knight	Sodomy	White	Male	New Haven	New Haven
8	1662	William Potter	Bestiality	White	Male	New Haven	New Haven
9	1668	Ruth Briggs	Adultery and infanticide	White	Female	New Haven	New Haven
10	1672	Thomas Rood	Incest	White	Male	Norwich	Hartford
11	1694	Daniel Matthews	Rape	White	Male	Fairfield and Wethersfield	Hartford

Bestiality was a capital offense throughout New England. The statute adopted from Leviticus included men and women and directed that "the beast shall be slaine, buried, and not eaten."[52] Only men were ever accused. The act was typically a private and secretive affair that, in legal terms, required more than hearsay or a salacious reputation to convict. The standard requirement of two eyewitnesses or confessions was necessary to establish guilt. A total of six white males were hanged for the crime in New England, including John Newberry (1647) in Connecticut and George Spencer (1642), Walter Robinson (1654), and William Potter (1662) in New Haven.[53]

The example of Aaron Stark, a servant in Windsor, occurred before the statute against bestiality appeared in the Connecticut Code of Laws of 1642. In the late 1630s, he was sentenced to stand in the pillory and then be whipped for "unclean practices" with Mary Holt. He paid Holt's parents a fine, compensation for the violation of their daughter, and the letter R (for wrong?) was burned on his cheek. The crime was probably premarital sexual intercourse.[54] With a tarnished background, Stark was later accused in the summer of 1642 of bestiality with a heifer. Confined in jail by lock and chain, at hard labor, and under a coarse diet, he eventually confessed. He maintained that he had twice mounted the animal's flanks, but the young cow was "too narrow." Without the capital statute on the books and no proof that the act was consummated, he escaped the gallows.[55]

George Spencer, the first white man executed in what is now Connecticut, was convicted of bestiality in 1642.[56] Issues of folk culture, class, and badgering of the accused were determinative in the litigation. John Wakeman, a planter and church member, reported to the magistrates that his sow had given stillbirth to a "prodigious monster." He reported, "The most straing, itt had butt one eye in the middle of the face, and that large and open, like some blemished eye of a man; over the eye, in the bottome of the foreheade which was like a childs, a thng of flesh grew forth and hung down, itt was hollow, and like a mans instrument of genration." Officials examined the innards and found them aberrant. Spencer had been the servant of Henry Browning, who had sold the pregnant sow to Wakeman. Unfortunately for the lowly Spencer, he too had one eye and the other "whitish and deformed," a simulacrum of the fetal monster. In addition, he was "notorious in the plantation for a prophane, lying, scoffing, and lewd spirit." Given the assumptions of the day, Goodwife Wakeman and others concluded that Spencer "had beene actor in unnatureall and abominable filthyness with the sow."[57]

Officials jailed Spencer on suspicion of bestiality. Magistrates, ministers, and marshal "wished to give glory to God, in a free confession of his sin."

Coerced and intimidated, Spencer confessed, a fatal admission, on February 25 that "the sow came into the stable, and then the temptation and his corruption did worke, and he drove the sow into the stye, and then committed that filthyness." The next day, the Reverend John Davenport and other prominent citizens further queried him about irreligion and carnal temptation. Spencer acknowledged "that Satan had hardened his hart." The General Court in New Haven on March 2 charged him with bestiality. For the court, it was self-evident that "the monster shewed, upon which God from heaven seamed both to stamp out the sin, and as wth his finger to single out the actor." Spencer, however, "impudently" repudiated "all that he had formerly confessed." A variety of people recounted that Spencer had told them he was guilty, including how he had copulated with the sow for a half hour. Despite his recantation, the court found him guilty because "he was acted by a lying speritt in his denyalls."[58]

At sentencing on April 6, Spencer again repudiated his confession. He was confronted by testimony that he had admitted the act. Given a last chance in court to acknowledge "his sinful and abominable filthyness," the defendant responded that "he would leave it to God, adding that he had condemned himself by his former confession." Indeed, he had. The confession stood; the court rejected his renunciation.[59]

On April 8, a cart brought Spencer to the outskirts of a field near the seaside. Upon seeing the gallows, he "seemed to be much amazed and trembled." He mounted the scaffold. Prodded by officials to play his scripted role, Spencer spoke perfunctorily, after a noticeable pause, to servants gathered before him to not neglect "the means of grace." Urged to confess, he admitted sins but not bestiality. The halter was fastened to the gallows and fitted around his neck. The ministers prompted him that this was an ill time to provoke God with "his impudency and atheisme." At the last moment, he admitted bestiality and called his sentence just, so the record says. He called a fellow servant, Will Harding, forward, blaming him for "the murder of his soul." He charged Harding with telling him to deny the charge so that he would not be convicted. Harding's counsel had denied him repentance and redemption during the several weeks purposely set aside between the verdict and execution. Harding denied the accusation. The ministers now pressed Spencer to talk about his apprehensions and anticipation of the mercy of Jesus Christ. He said not a word. As he watched, the sow was slain, run through with a sword. The high-pitched squeal and gushing blood were demonic, a premonition of the tortures of hell. Then Spencer was launched into eternity. The epitaph bore Davenport's imprimatur: "He ended his course here, God opening his mouth before his death, to give him the glory of his righteousness, to the full satisfaction of all then present, but in other respects leaving him a terrible example of divine justice and wrath."[60] The rationale for biblical retribution has not been put more directly.

Not surprisingly, the situation left an indelible mark on death penalty jurisprudence, no more so than four years later in New Haven when the unhappily named servant Thomas Hogg was suspected of bestiality with a sow that produced "two monsters." For his mistress, Mrs. Lamberton, it was divine déjà vu. "One of them had a faire and white skinne, and head, as Thomas Hoggs is," she told authorities. "Another wth a head lik a childs and one eye lik him, the biger on the right side, as if God would describe the party, with the description of the instrument of bestyalie." The uncanny resemblance was proof positive. Like Spencer, Hogg was disreputable. Women of various ranks noted that his penis and scrotum, "his filthy nakedness," showed through his breeches. He did not avail himself of the needle and thread that Goody Camp gave him. And Lucretia, a "neagar" woman of the governor, had seen him "act filthynesse with his hands by the fireside." In this case, a slave woman testified against a lowly white man. Hogg explained that "his belly was broake, and his breeches were straight, and he wore a steele trusse, and soe it might happen his members might be seene." The attention to the genitals was, at least in part, the awkward arrangements of a workman suffering from a painful inguinal hernia. He also denied that he snitched dumplings out of the pot or pilfered cheese from the buttery.[61]

Governor Theophilus Eaton and his deputy brought Hogg to the pigsty for a New World application of Baconian empiricism. At their direction, Hogg scratched the sow in question under the ear, which immediately aroused "a working of lust . . . that she poured out seede before them." A second sow similarly scratched was not stimulated. To the frustration of the officials' clever experiment, Hogg denied that he committed bestiality. Without a confession, the colony could not hang the "impudent lyar." Instead, they "severely whipped" the lewd pig herder and, while he was jailed, kept him on "a mean diet and hard labor, that his lusts not be fed."[62]

Two guilt-ridden adolescent boys confessed to bestiality and were hanged. Seventeen-year-old John Newberry of Windsor admitted to several attempts, once to penetration but without "effution of seed."[63] That was enough for him to be hanged in Hartford in 1647. Walter Robinson of Milford, a fifteen-year-old shepherd, was seen by a fisherman copulating with a "bitch" while he tended his flock. Before he was hanged in New Haven in 1654, he watched his sheep dog killed, run through with a sword. They were buried together.[64] Both boys were of the age when pious youths ought to have owned the covenant, not embraced lubricity. Powerful pressure by their superiors worked on these malleable lads, whereas it failed for the older, obstinate Thomas Hogg who saved his neck. Writing from Boston, based on local reports, John Winthrop posthumously praised the young Newberry, who "upon his own confession out of horror of Conscience etc: to glorify God, his Repentance and godly end very observable."[65] These are the very words that a defiant George Spencer refused to mouth even at the point of death.

The last execution for bestiality in what is now Connecticut occurred in New Haven in 1662. William Potter was convicted of the "sin of bestiality with sundry creatures" that included cows, dogs, horses, pigs, and sheep. His wife and son testified against him. His son had caught his father copulating with a sow. At first Potter denied the charge, but under relentless interrogation he confessed; "God hath brought it out of his own mouth."[66] His sexual initiation with animals had begun at age eleven in England. He struggled to control his urges, even hanging a bitch that tempted him. The threat of death, however, had not deterred his barnyard exploits, which spanned a half century. Otherwise, he had confined sexual intercourse exclusively to his wife. Cotton Mather recorded that Davenport declared a "Solemn Day of Humiliation on this Occasion" to excommunicate this "Unclean Devil" from the church. As Potter approached the gallows, Mather approvingly noted that the repentant sinner "was Awakened unto a most Unutterable and Intolerable Anguish of Soul, and made most Lamentably Desperate Out cries." Before he was hanged, he watched a cow, two heifers, three sheep, and two sows slaughtered before his eyes. He was a literate farmer of some social standing, but sexual excess was his fatal flaw.[67]

For the Puritans, sodomy was a catchall term for homosexual practices, particularly anal intercourse. Unlike other New England colonies, New Haven extended scriptural prohibitions to include sex between women; anal penetration of women and children, male and female; vaginal penetration of prepubescent girls; and public masturbation or encouraging others in the act. ("Self-pollution" itself might warrant whipping, but not hanging.) In effect, "carnal knowledge of another vessel than God in nature hath appointed to become one flesh" defined "Sodomiticall filthinesse." Unlike vaginal intercourse between married partners, sodomy tended "to the destruction of the race of mankind." Those engaged in sodomy who were coerced "against his or her will" or those under fourteen years of age were exempt from the death penalty.[68] The only three executions for sodomy in New England occurred in New Haven Colony.[69]

The first, William Plaine, was a married servant in New Guilford whose practice of sodomy had begun in London before he immigrated in 1639. John Winthrop in Massachusetts, who was consulted by Governor Eaton, recorded that Plaine "corrupted a great parte of the youth of New Guilford by masturbation, which he had committed, and provoked others to the like, aboue 100: tymes." The miscreant added to the outrage by sowing "the seeds of Atheism, questioning whither there were a God" when officials interrogated him about pederasty. Although two eyewitnesses could not be produced to verify a specific act, officials hanged him at New Haven in 1646.[70]

The second, an unknown person, undoubtedly a white male, was likely executed for sodomy in New Haven sometime between May 28 and June 11, 1650. During that time, Governor Eaton spoke of "another under ye sentence of death for unnaturall filthynes." The latter term was similar to wording in the 1656 New Haven Code of Laws that referred to "Sodomiticall filthiness."[71]

With similar words, several witnesses corroborated that John Knight had engaged in "filthyness in a sodomatical way." His two partners were a fourteen-year-old Peter Vinson and Mary Clark, a maidservant whom he had buggered. Vinson and Clark were whipped for concealing evidence and complicity, respectively. The court ruled that an unrepentant Knight was not "fitt to live among men," and he was hanged at New Haven in 1655, the third and final execution for sodomy in New England.[72]

Unlike Plaine and Knight, Nicholas Sension, a prosperous resident of Windsor, escaped execution despite a long history of active homoeroticism in the community. He had been charged with sodomy as early as the 1640s and again a decade later, but no punishment had been meted out. Unlike Plaine and Knight, Sension's social status allowed him more leeway than those near the bottom of the ladder. Apparently, there was a certain amount of toleration for a married man of means to pursue his inclinations as long as they were discrete assignations.

By 1677, however, a tipping point was reached. A dozen men told of being accosted by Sension, who offered to pay for sex. Sension's liaisons had become flagrant in the Puritan village. His servant and frequent, if reluctant, partner, Nathaniel Pond, died in 1675. Two witnesses testified that they had seen the master sodomize his servant. One recalled that a creaking bed that the two shared was but one indication that "Sension was very familiar with Nathaniel Pond." Sension was also observed hugging and fondling Pond. Pond had pleaded with his fellow workers not to report their relationship. He was fearful because his subaltern status made him vulnerable, whereas Sension's prominence emboldened him. Without Pond available, had Sension become reckless in his solicitations? Two servants, for example, offered explicit accounts of attempted male rape. In tight quarters, men often shared beds for the night. Daniel Saxton awoke face down, his underclothes off, and an aroused Sension mounting him; he physically repulsed the assailant. Another servant, Thomas Barber, elbowed Sension in the belly when he awakened to find that his bedmate "with his yard [sought] to enter my body."[73] Barber told his master that he would never again sleep with him. A capital jury found that the defendant "hast most wickedly committed or at least attempted that Horible sin of sodomy." Sension was disfranchised, shamed in a symbolic hanging, severely whipped, and forced to post a £100 bond for good behavior.[74] The punishment was extreme for a gentleman, but he was not executed.

The capital statute on adultery in early New England defined the felony as one committed with a married or espoused woman. The marital status of the man was not a factor. Sexual relations between a married man and a single woman were not deemed adultery, but fornication. The Puritans adopted the Hebraic proscription that protected the husband's bloodline by punishing the straying wife. The full weight of the law, however, was narrowed procedurally by the need to produce actual proof of illicit relations. There were only three documented executions exclusively for adultery in New England. Mary Latham and Thomas Britton were tried and executed together at Boston in 1644. The third is an unnamed person whom Governor Eaton described as "one executed for Adultery" sometime between May 28 and June 11, 1650, presumably in New Haven. Apparently only "one" partner of the couple, not both as in Boston, was hanged. The gender, social status, and other information are unknown.[75]

There was a reluctance to enforce the death penalty for adultery. Of all the capital crimes in New England for which people were actually hanged, adultery accounted for the fewest (three) and the earliest date (1650), after which no one went to the gallows. Adultery was the first death penalty offense in New England to be removed from the capital list when Connecticut deleted it in 1672. Population growth and demographic shifts after midcentury helped undermine the law. A severe whipping, branding by a hot iron with the letter *A* on the forehead, and the wearing of a halter in public were substituted for execution. The General Court granted more divorces in cases of adultery and desertion. The resort to divorce became an expedient to deal with marital impasses short of a capital charge, an alternative with increasing appeal.[76] In a case with scant documentation, the Court of Assistants convicted Ruth Briggs for adultery and infanticide of an illegitimate child. A woman on the margins of respectability in New Haven, she was hanged in 1668. It is difficult to know how the dual capital charges were weighed. Nonetheless, it seems fair to conclude that conviction of infanticide coupled with adultery provided the momentum for execution.[77]

Incest was initially a capital crime only in zealous New Haven. The other New England colonies were deterred from a formal statute by the involved proscriptions in Leviticus that would have criminalized a number of marriages in a small Puritan village where extensive exogamy was not practical.[78] Instead, magistrates were left to deal with the issue in an ad hoc manner. When the behavior of the paterfamilias was flagrantly lascivious, however, serious punishment followed. Such was the case in Connecticut when in 1672 Thomas Rood of Norwich was tried before the Court of Assistants in Hartford for incest with his daughter Sarah, who at twenty-three years old was half her father's age. Without a positive law on the books, Governor Winthrop in June prudently asked the counsel of four ministers, including the judicious Gershom Buckeley. They concluded that the religious and secular prescriptions mandated the death penalty. The father, who had impregnated his daughter, was tried on October 8 and hanged eight days later, the only such execution in New Haven and Connecticut at any time. One day before the hanging, on October 17, 1672, the General Court added father–daughter and mother–son incest to the capital code.[79] This law was more instrumental than dependent on biblical literalism.

Such pragmatism applied to Sarah Rood's situation. Although she pleaded guilty, the magistrates were reluctant to execute her. The trial was postponed until May 1673 to allow time for reflection on the sentence. The court found her "a person so ignorant and weake in minde" that she was less culpable than her overbearing father who had taken advantage of her.[80] The description suggests, but does not prove, that she was mentally retarded or, at least, deficient. Although there were mitigating factors, she had submitted more than once and was found complicit. She was severely whipped in public, once in Hartford and again in Norwich, so that "others may heare and feare."[81]

Similar to its handling of incest, Hebraic law did not provide a clear model for a statute on rape.[82] Roger Williams in Rhode Island drew on English tradition and made carnal copulation by force and without consent, which included consensual relations with a girl under the age of ten, a capital crime. Connecticut and New Haven generally accepted this understanding. Connecticut in 1642 made rape a hanging offense but only against betrothed or married women. The 1672 law extended protection to "any Maid or Woman," but there was no mention of underage girls. The rape law of the 1656 New Haven code extended to unmarried women, but the death pen-alty was discretionary, depending on the circumstances. The abuse of the "unripe vessel of a Girl," however, specified the death penalty. In addition, the sexual assault of married women presumably made the perpetrator liable under the capital statute of adultery.[83]

A double standard existed for women in the prosecution of witchcraft and for a range of moral lapses in New England. Historian Cornelia Hughes Dayton points out that, in contrast to extreme male dominance in England, women's legal standing before the court was nonetheless encouraged in important ways. "The Puritans' emphasis on each individual's obedience to God's strictures," she writes, "led them to insist on punishing men's abuse of authority and sinful behavior. In the cases of sexual assault, wife-abuse, and premarital sex, seventeenth-century magistrates gave credence to women's charges and meted out swift, severe sentences to men."[84] In sexual assault cases, punishment was meted out to men and to anyone who concealed evi-dence. Women's accounts were respected because the perpetrator would likely lie, and the victim's voice was crucial in an adversarial proceeding. In a dozen indictments of sexual assault spanning the seventeenth century, the vast majority of indicted men were convicted.

There were some important constraints. In the spirit of the femme co-vert, the father or husband was expected to take the initiative in prosecu-tion. If sexual assaults were not reported or legally pursued, justice was de-nied. The contention of whether an encounter was consensual or coercive was also crucial. Women on the margins of respectability also had an uphill battle. A New Haven court in 1653 in an alleged rape convicted the defen-dant of the lesser charge of lascivious carriage because the plaintiff was a woman of doubtful character.[85] In addition, the concept of bed-and-board marriage allowed the husband free access to his wife's body.

Moreover, of the dozen cases of successful prosecution of sexual assault, only two men were found guilty of rape; the others were mostly convicted of attempted rape and were severely whipped. The two rapists, Arthur Teague and Daniel Matthews, were outsiders to the community, used aliases, and were not acquaintances of their victims. They were the proverbial "other" for whom harsher punishment was reserved. Teague, who claimed as a dubious mitigating factor that his wife was barren, was found guilty in New Haven in 1667 of raping an unmarried servant, yet despite the capital statute, he es-caped with a severe whipping and fine of £10.[86]

Daniel Matthews was the only person to be executed for rape during this period in what is now Connecticut. Matthews was an itinerant tailor who crossed into the colony from New York. The Court of Assistants found him guilty of the "forcible ravishment" of two girls: Elizabeth Colley, age ten, in Fairfield on April 15, 1693, and Mary Goodrich, age twelve, in Wethersfield on June 20. After the first incident, Matthews was indicted. Two men testified that blood was found on his shirt, and two women added that Elizabeth Colley was "abused" and "bruised." Imprisoned at Fairfield, Matthews broke out of jail. Two months later, the fugitive claimed another young victim. Rebecca Goodrich provided a graphic account of what her daughter, Mary, told her had happened. Matthews had enticed Mary with money to an out-of-the-way place. She resisted his advances and screamed, but he knocked her down and raped her. In the complaint, Rebecca Goodrich related to the court that Matthews had told her daughter that "he had gotten her with child."[87] He pleaded not guilty to both charges, but was convicted of a capital crime in October 1693. In the Court of Assistants, three of the assistants granted a reprieve. It is surprising that a condemned child rapist was granted a stay of execution, but witchcraft hysteria in Salem and Connecticut at the time may have produced a sense of caution in capital cases. With the aid of two confederates, Matthews later escaped from the Hartford jail. He was recaptured and almost certainly hanged.[88]

In sum, the death penalty for sexual infractions had distinct seventeenth-century characteristics. Excluding Ruth Briggs and the adulterer of unknown identity in 1650, nine males were hanged. The four executions for bestiality, three for sodomy, one exclusively for adultery (Briggs was convicted of adultery and infanticide), and one for incest were the last of their kind to occur in Connecticut. The delisting of adultery as a capital crime in 1672 further marked the reluctance to execute for these violations. As the spiritual fervor of the founding generation waned over time, rape remained the only sexual offense for which anyone was executed after 1672, the year that Thomas Rood was hanged for incest. With the notable exception of homicide, lessening religious zeal undercut the basis for biblical retribution.

Eight of the hangings occurred in New Haven, with its broad-ranging proscriptions.[89] Of the seven executions for bestiality and sodomy, six were in its jurisdiction. No one of elite standing was convicted. Nicolas Sension, a well-to-do resident of Windsor, escaped execution despite a long history of predatory homosexuality. There was, however, no such toleration for John Knight, a servant in New Haven, who was convicted of sodomy for two liaisons.

If fortuitous eyewitnesses to illicit acts were not forthcoming, officials sought to coerce confessions through intense interrogation. William Potter's son and wife caught him copulating with domestic animals, and a fisher-man spied Walter Robinson servicing his sheepdog. Under intense question-ing from officials, the swineherd George Spencer confessed to bestiality with a sow, an act that may not have happened. Thus, the first execution of a white person in what is now Connecticut was the outcome of a coerced con-fession, an ominous precedent for death penalty proceedings.

Witchcraft

In seventeenth-century New England, religion and folk culture overlapped on the evil of witchcraft. Exodus 22:18 instructed, "Thou shall not suffer a witch to live."[90] A supernatural world, it was assumed, existed. Cunning folk probed the preternatural by astrology, casting spells, conjuring, and for-tune telling. Magic might be benign or malevolent. Personal and social rela-tions in a close-knit Puritan village during the first decades of settlement on the frontier were intense. Fear, jealousy, and animosity might, particularly after a quarrel between neighbors and heightened by religious and political strife, set the stage for accusations of witchcraft against vulnerable residents. As John Davenport warned his New Haven congregation in 1652, a discon-tented mind was "a fit subject for the devil to work upon."[91]

Spectral evidence of witchcraft was particularly nebulous and elusive ac-cording to standards of judicial proof. "It is very certain," Boston's Cotton Mather opined, "that the devills have sometimes represented the shapes of persons not only innocent, but also very virtuous."[92] No other capital crime so challenged routine standards for admissible evidence. Some magistrates and ministers sought to harmonize the law with folk culture through the re-lentless coercion of confessions, which aided and abetted witch hunts. Other officials were cautious and skeptical; creative solutions short of death—fines, bonds for good behavior, probation, banishment, and warnings—were employed to good purpose. New Haven executed no one for the crime de-spite some highly charged cases during the 1650s. Connecticut, after much contention, hanged the last of eleven witches in 1663, and authorities blocked anyone else going to the gallows, including convictions that were over-turned in 1665, 1668, and 1692. In 1692, William Jones, a deputy governor of Connecticut, cautioned "jurors, etc. not to condemne suspected psons on bare prsumtions without good and sufficient proofes."[93]

The accused witch was typically an older woman of low status and hum-ble means who had an unsavory reputation. A virulent misogyny projected anxiety about sexuality and reproduction upon aged women, who were the antithesis of fecund maternity.[94] At times of acrimony, villagers (sometimes possessed adolescent girls) singled her out as the agent of malevolence. She had unnatural proclivities and upset the normal balance of things. Accused and indicted, the defendant was confronted with sworn testimony affirming her *maleficium,* her devilishness. Officials might have the defendant inspected for intimate witch marks or subject her to the water test. Villagers and officials, especially ministers, coerced her to confess. A confession was double-edged: by admitting her guilt, she called on divine mercy to save her eternal soul, but at the same time legitimated the protocol that condemned her. If she was found guilty, she was hanged to purge the community of evil.

As shown in table 8, eleven people were hanged for witchcraft in Connecticut in the seventeen-year period from 1647 to 1663. With two exceptions, executions occurred in the greater Hartford region, the place of greatest settlement. Excluding two spouses who were guilty by association, all were white women of English origin. Three convictions overturned by the magistrates were also women, which means that of fourteen people sentenced to die, twelve were women. In fact, of the nineteen women who were executed for any crime over the entire history of both colonies and the state, nine were these women. This mid-seventeenth-century period is the only time that more women than men were executed, almost twice as many.

TABLE 8
Convictions and Executions for Witchcraft, 1647–1692

	Year of Execution or Reversal	Name	Location of Crime	Outcome
1	1647	Alse (Alice) Young	Windsor	Hanged
2	1648	Mary Johnson	Wethersfield	Hanged
3	1651	Joan Carrington	Wethersfield	Hanged
4	1651	John Carrington	Wethersfield	Hanged
5	1651	Goody (Goodwife) Basset	Stratford	Hanged
6	1653	Goody Knapp	Fairfield	Hanged
7	1654	Lydia Gilbert	Windsor	Hanged
8	1662	Mary Sanford	Hartford	Hanged
9	1663	Rebecca Greensmith	Hartford	Hanged
10	1663	Nathaniel Greensmith	Hartford	Hanged
11	1663	Mary Barnes	Farmington	Hanged
12	1665	Elizabeth Seager	Hartford	Reversed
13	1668	Katherine Harrison	Wethersfield	Reversed
14	1692	Mercy Disborough	Fairfield	Reprieved

They were not the gentle sort, people of high or even substantial middle rank. African Americans and Indians played no direct role in these events. Excluding twenty people executed in the extreme situation in Salem in 1692, eleven of the sixteen people executed for witchcraft in New England (Massachusetts was the only other New England colony to do so) were in Connecticut. In sum, witchcraft figured in some fifty-two cases in Connecticut and New Haven colonies, resulting in fourteen convictions, with the verdicts of three condemned women set aside.[95]

Although witchcraft remained a capital crime in Connecticut until 1750, a constellation of factors limited its full implementation after the last execution in 1663. The great expectations of the first generation contributed to sectarian strife. With tensions heightened because of schism, ministers, particularly Hartford's Samuel Stone, were assiduous in pursuit of witches as if to confirm that diabolical means were behind the confounding of the biblical commonwealth that he and his deceased friend Thomas Hooker had done so much to create. Stone died in the midst of the witch panic in 1663, just after his sixty-first birthday. The passing of the founders, the exodus of dissenters, and the expansion of the colony all helped dissipate tension.

Key officials, through critical interpretation of the rule of law, particularly the validity of spectral evidence, undermined the capital crime of witchcraft. John Winthrop Jr., long-term governor of Connecticut (1657, 1659–1676), blocked executions for adultery and witchcraft. Historian Walter Woodward argues that Winthrop Jr. and the Reverend Gershom Buckeley, physicians and students of alchemy, questioned not the existence of witchcraft per se, but found satanic compacts beyond the meager means of colonial rustics.[96] Winthrop Jr. on his return from England after negotiating the empowering Charter of 1662 and Buckeley on his appointment to the pulpit in Wethersfield in 1666 acted to calm troubled waters.

No witchcraft cases reappeared in the river towns, where the phenomenon had run its course by 1670, but the fateful year 1692 saw seven indictments for witchcraft concentrated in the southwest coastal region, particularly in the border villages of Fairfield. The Fairfield environs had not been burned over by previous incidents, and a full generation had elapsed in the colony since the last panic, a convenient interval for a revival. The events in Connecticut predated the notorious Salem trials, and local conditions in both were precipitating factors. Bitter interfamily disputes were at the heart of the matter in Connecticut.

Controversy over the nature of the colony's legal relationship to England contributed to the decision of authorities to reprieve Mercy Disborough, the

last convicted witch in Connecticut. In the aftermath of the Glorious Revolution of 1688–1689, the General Assembly on May 9, 1689, reaffirmed its
commitment to the liberties of the Charter of 1662. Disborough's death
sentence was appealed. Samuel Wyllys, William Pitkin, and Nathaniel Stanley, three members of the Court of Assistants who had not presided at her
trial, boldly granted a reprieve and stayed the execution until the General
Court could review the matter at its May meeting in 1693. While Disborough remained in jail, Buckeley, a powerful patron, came to her aid in December. Disborough had, to her great fortune, been his servant in New
London some thirty years earlier.

Now living in Glastonbury, Buckeley called the death penalty proceedings "a great scandal." He endorsed his fellow clerics who concluded, in his
words, that the evidence was "not sufficient to convict any person of witchcraft." He added that the substitution of one juror for another who had traveled to New York was a serious violation of procedure, yet the plight of his
former servant was but a telling example in a broader, political polemic,
"Will and Doom or the Miseries of Connecticut By and Under an Usurped
and Arbitrary Power." Buckeley was a Jacobite, a diehard supporter of the
Stuart reign. He had served as justice of the peace for Hartford County during
the brief regime of Edmund Andros that, like the Stuart dynasty itself, had
been unseated in New England's analogue to the Glorious Revolution. He
argued that the restoration in 1689 of the colonial Charter of 1662—formally
revoked in 1687 by Andros, King James II's agent—was illegal. The current
Connecticut government, Buckeley continued, had established its own laws,
contravening English hegemony. "That not only our estates and bodies," he
railed in ironic Lockean terms that had been used to justify Parliament's
coup d'etat against James II, "but our lives also, are at the disposition, not of
the King and his laws, but of this pretending, usurping corporation, and in
what hazard they are." Disborough was the case in point. Buckeley applauded the reprieve of her hanging as preventing "a mischief" even as he
questioned the Court of Assistants' authority to do so. "Rebellion against
the King is immediate rebellion against God," Buckeley said. He concluded,
"And it is like the sin of witchcraft," a damning accusation of the present
government who had sentenced Disborough to death for that very crime.
For Buckeley, Disborough's fate was the result of not only incompetent jurisprudence, but illegitimate rule.[97]

Buckeley's tract raised troubling issues for Connecticut's officials, particularly about the legitimacy of the Charter of 1662 that Governor Winthrop
had carefully negotiated with King Charles II. The hanging of a witch, the

first since 1663 in Connecticut, coupled with twenty executions in Salem might attract the mother country's critical review of what was going on in post-Dominion New England. The excesses of the witchcraft panic in Fairfield and particularly in Salem produced a cautionary reaction. On October 3, 1692, Increase Mather published "Cases of Conscience Concerning Evil Spirits" in which he instructed, "It were better that Ten Suspected Witches should escape, than that one Innocent Person should be Condemned."[98] In May 1693, an amnesty in Massachusetts freed all those convicted of witchcraft. No more witches would ever be executed in Massachusetts or any part of New England.

At the same time in Connecticut, the magistrates Wyllys, Pitkin, and Stanley explained to the General Court that they had acted within their authority to reprieve Disborough so that "this Capital Court" could rule on the matter. They were convinced for two major reasons "that the sentence of death passed against her ought not to be executed." First, they agreed with Buckeley's legal argument that "one man altered the jury is altered" and thus a violation of " 'the birthright of the King's subjects.' " The assistants' concern with the "due form of law" was judiciously balanced with political obeisance to royal rule. They added, "If one juror may be changed two, ten, the whole may be so and solemn oaths made vain," which was Buckeley's compelling point. They direly warned the General Court that if it carried out the sentence, "they bring themselves into inextricable troubles and the whole country[.] Blood is a great thing and we cannot but open our mouths for the dumb in the cause of one appointed to die by such a verdict."[99]

Second, the three cited authoritative opinion, including Increase Mather, that the evidence against the defendant was not "sufficiently convictive of witchcraft." There was no confession because Disborough steadfastly maintained her innocence. There were not "two good witnesses" who corroborated diabolical acts. In addition, witch marks, water tests, and spectral evidence after quarrels or threats were "abominated by the most judicious as to be convictive of witchcraft." They pointed to the abuse to which spectral evidence had been put in Massachusetts. In words that may well serve as an epitaph for an era, they concluded, "Those that will make witchcraft of such things will make hanging work apace and we are informed of no other but such as these brought against this woman."[100] The General Court concurred, and Disborough was set free.[101]

After a disruptive witch panic during the early 1660s, key magistrates and ministers in Connecticut sought to contain an often capricious procedure. Officials had not set out to debunk witchcraft, but close attention to the rule of law rendered this capital crime a dead letter. Such an official was William Jones, a deputy governor of Connecticut at the time of Disborough's trial. His surviving, fragmentary notes on witchcraft indicate the need to adhere to the rule of law.[102] Restraint in New Haven Colony and the judiciousness of Governor Winthrop barred the way to the gallows. Defiant defendants, the women (such as Disborough) who refused to confess, and their allies spurred conscientious officials to adopt a systematic standard that rendered execution problematic. As the legal culture changed, so did the social structure and religious mandate that had fueled the misogyny of witchcraft. The years 1692 and 1693 were the finale of this capital crime in New England.[103]

2

THE EMERGENCE OF YANKEE JUSTICE
1700–1772

The foregoing Act [for punishing capital offenders] requires great consideration,
and tho' it be chiefly taken from Scripture, will want much alteration.

Francis Fane, 1733

The fewer capital crimes there are the better.

Anonymous, *Connecticut Courant,* August 11, 1768

The Government of Connecticut have always been remarkably
tender of putting persons to Death.

Noah Hobart, *Excessive Wickedness,* 1768

THE DISCORD that had bedeviled the Puritan errand into the wilderness after the mid-seventeenth century became manifest during the eighteenth,
well before the onset of the American Revolution.[1] Demographic growth
and economic development played a dynamic role in reshaping institutions
and expectations, to which the shattering religious revivals of the 1740s
were a major response. Francis Fane, counsel to the British Board of Trade
and Plantations, was correct that the capital laws of Connecticut that he reviewed in 1733 "will want much alteration." The revised Connecticut Code
of Laws of 1750 not only eliminated a number of capital crimes, but for the
first time omitted an accompanying scriptural imprimatur. Previously, only
treason had stood alone. Now, idolatry, witchcraft, man stealing, and offenses of rebellious offspring disappeared from the books. The vestigial exception was blasphemy.

British officials, such as Fane, also sought to make an independently
minded colony more attentive to the needs of the mother country. English
common law impinged on biblical injunctions; property and commercial
concerns intruded on moral and religious mandates. The tight-knit community of saints evolved into a more worldly society of Yankees. Corporal

punishment and shaming remained, but were increasingly directed toward economic crimes, such as counterfeiting, horse stealing, and theft.[2] Offenders were seen more as criminals than sinners. Juries were reluctant to sentence defendants to death, except as a tacit racial, gender, and class protocol applied. Executions fell disproportionately on African Americans and Indians. Poor and marginal women were subject to a more pronounced double standard than had existed in Puritan times, with the exclusion of witchcraft. The punitive 1699 statute on infanticide is a case in point.[3]

This period encompasses the pivotal transformation of the legal culture from divine terms to a secular ethic, including the effect of the evolution from Puritan to Yankee on capital laws and who was executed.[4] Expanding population and extensive commerce increased opportunities for advancement. New markets and bustling towns enticed farmers, manufacturers, and merchants with the promise of profits. The possibility of worldly advancement in eighteenth-century New England that had earlier been the lot of a fortunate few now seemed available for the many.[5] Small storekeepers sought wealth; frugal farmers engaged in land speculation.

As the North American colonies prospered, the British ministry had compelling reasons to regulate its far-flung empire and centralize its administration. During the seventeenth century, Connecticut was largely autonomous under the Fundamental Orders of 1639 and Charter of 1662. The British Board of Trade and Plantations after 1700 sought to end benign neglect and to integrate its once insignificant colony into a global network. Commercial entrepreneurship within an imperial framework altered the legal landscape from a Puritan emphasis on morality and orthodoxy to one emphasizing commercial law, property crime, and religious toleration. In addition, the Great Awakening that swept intensely over Connecticut during the 1740s radically challenged the Congregational order. Itinerant preachers impugned the settled clergy, communal churches were rent, and the individualistic logic of Protestantism was emphasized as never before. With traditional religion shattered and people loosened from ancient bonds, Connecticut enacted the most substantial modification to date in its capital laws since the settlement of southern New England more than a century earlier.

From Puritan to Yankee

Significant change in the death penalty before the American Revolution was foreshadowed as early as the mid-seventeenth century. The last executions for sodomy in 1655 and for bestiality in 1662 occurred in New Haven Colony.[6]

Connecticut hanged its final witches in 1663,[7] and Thomas Rood in 1672 was the only person who went to the gallows for incest.[8] In the latter year, adultery was dropped from the capital code.[9] Death by hanging for marital infidelity was regarded as excessive, especially as the law might apply to abandoned wives who remarried. In 1717, the General Court addressed the problem in a law that stated that after a seven years' absence of a spouse a marriage was "null and void."[10]

In addition to legal caveats, the emergence of a more worldly society led to revision of the capital laws. Religious orthodoxy and isolated village life were at the heart of Puritan Connecticut. Dramatic population growth complicated social dynamics and expanded people's expectations. From 1700 to 1772, the number of colonists increased more than sixfold, from 30,000 to 200,000. Self-sufficient villages became market towns that economically linked the rural interior to coastal and river ports. On the eve of the American Revolution, New Haven, New London, Hartford, Middletown, and Norwich were commercial centers connected to Boston and New York City. New Haven's population of 8,000 was the colony's high.[11] Connecticut schooners plied the Atlantic. The trade included an exchange of West Indian slaves, sugar, and rum for European manufactured goods and Connecticut farm products.[12] Merchants prospered in these five cities where hundreds of businesses thrived, while licensed peddlers sold their wares in the hinterland.[13] Indigenous industries appeared in silk, cloth, clock making, iron production, and shipbuilding.[14] The shrewd Yankee merchant, who, as legend has it, foisted wooden nutmegs on the unwary, had come of age.

Not all prospered. With a growing population, land became more expensive, and speculation in real estate was rampant. Some could not afford to buy. By the era of the Revolution, 10 percent of adult males had never owned land in the town of Kent, which had been founded in 1738.[15] The consequences of a rural proletariat were numerous. Family life was delayed and premarital pregnancy increased, adding burdens on low-status women. Adult sons pressured their fathers about the urgency of awarding an inheritance that would give them property. Rootless young men and women enrolled as day laborers and servants or wandered to cities to seek their fortune. Their wages were low. Adding to the problems, agricultural production stagnated as an ecological plateau between land, population, and farm practices was reached. By the end of the century, a vast exodus from Connecticut to New York, Ohio, and other points west in search of cheap, fertile land would occur.[16]

Commercial downturns, part of a fluctuating market economy, reverberated throughout the colony. Public officials confronted the issue of what to do about marginal groups. A 1699 law made the estate of the insane or mentally retarded liable for their support; a 1727 addition permitted their commitment to a workhouse, if not otherwise provided for.[17] A sense of disorder is spelled out in requirements in 1706 that towns erect stocks and in 1707 that towns ban transients.[18] A law passed in 1737—for "Suppressing punishing rogues, vagabonds, common beggars and other Lewd, Idle, Dissolute and disorderly persons, and for setting them to work"—pointed to those displaced by the changing economy. The legislators worried about the wandering poor who "are strowling to and fro in this Colony, begging, and committing many insolences." In 1772, officials at Saybrook, for example, reported the brutal murder of a vagrant "with his face much mangled" by another transient who fled to Long Island.[19] Vagrants could be committed to a workhouse. If they proved recalcitrant, their supervisor could place them in fetters and shackles, whip them not more than ten stripes per session, and restrict their food allotment.[20] Following Hartford's lead, where a house of correction was erected in 1729, the New Haven town meeting in 1767 appropriated £100 for "Building a work house."[21] For the first time in the colony, institutions were designated to discipline labor.

The General Court placed special restrictions on Native Americans and African Americans. Like all the thirteen colonies, Connecticut enslaved racial minorities. The 1642 capital law against man-stealing applied only to whites and was no deterrent to racial bondage. During the seventeenth century, the Indian population was decimated in bloody wars and the survivors closely regulated. At the turn of the eighteenth century, the black population was only 700 out of a total of 38,000. By the time of the Revolution, however, Connecticut had the largest number of slaves (6,464) in New England. New London County was the most populous slaveholding region with 2,036 slaves, including those who worked on large farms. Ten percent of the town of New London was of African descent. Between 1756 and 1774, the slave population in proportion to the free grew by 40 percent in the colony. One-half of all ministers, lawyers, and public officials owned at least one slave, as did many prominent families. Most African Americans—slave, indentured, or free—were relegated to menial work as farm laborers, domestics, servants, and in maritime employment. Although the population of African Americans was less than 4 percent, the increase in the number of blacks, especially in port cities, heightened racial tensions.[22]

Systematic discrimination began even before the African American population was numerous. A proscription in 1708 barred slaves from selling goods to
whites; the fear was that the goods were purloined. The previous year, slaves in
New London were charged with repeatedly stealing corn from their master
and selling it for cider and money.[23] A court could punish servants or slaves
who struck a white with a whipping of thirty lashes. Legislators worried that
"negro and molatto servants or slaves are becoming numerous in some parts of
this Colonie, and are very apt to be turbulent, and often quarrelling with white
people to the great disturbance of the peace."[24] In 1717, New Londoners sought
to prevent free blacks from living in town and owning land. The General Assembly extended the prohibition throughout the colony and barred free blacks,
even retroactively, from owning land or going into business without permission of the selectmen. A law in 1723 restricted the movement of Indians and
blacks after dark and required slaves to have a pass from their master when
outside their normal confines.[25] A 1730 law made speech or a publication by
a slave that contemned a white subject to whipping.[26]

In addition to class and racial tensions that weighed heavily on the death
penalty, the erosion of religious orthodoxy contributed to the secularization
of the capital statutes at midcentury. Puritans assumed that the well-being
of civil society rested on the uniformity of religion. Connecticut officials
bound state and church through the Cambridge Platform of 1648. As long as
unanimity prevailed in the church, all was harmonious. Divisiveness, however, created factions that undermined clerical control and threatened civil
contention. By the time of the second and third generation of settlers, the
utopian fervor of the founders had diminished. The Half-Way Covenant,
first proposed at the Ministerial Convention of 1657 at Boston, allowed a
partial church membership: the children of unconverted members could be
baptized, but they could not receive communion or vote for ministers. Half-
way members had to make a public pledge to obey church rulings and raise
their children as Christians. Opponents saw a dangerous dilution of faith in
this liberal revision of the Cambridge Platform.[27]

At Hartford, Wethersfield, Windsor, and Stratford, critics formed separate churches or left for new regions. The debate roiled the colony and provided the fundamental tension that facilitated the Hartford witch hunt of
1662–1663. Over time, the distinction between full and partial membership
blurred, and dual membership in the common faith was accommodated. As
early as 1679, the influential Solomon Stoddard from his pulpit in Northamp-
ton, Massachusetts, argued for further modifications that reverberated
throughout the Connecticut River valley. He taught that baptized persons,

who made a public profession of faith, should be admitted to communion. The goal was to extend the sacrament to the doubtful many, not just the few who were certain of their worthiness.[28]

Accompanying doctrinal innovations that broadened membership was a corresponding movement toward centralization along Presbyterian lines. The Saybrook Platform of 1708 provided for county "consociations," or regional associations of ministers and colony-wide delegations of ministers, to rule on ecclesiastic matters, including the power to withhold public funding from incompliant churches. The result was the creation of a religious hierarchy of powerful clerics that set dogma and enforced conformity. In governance, sovereignty passed from the people to the pastors and from the congregation to consociation. In theology, a rigid formalism replaced intense soul searching. In less than a century, once autonomous societies of saints had evolved into a religious establishment that united the ministers of the various churches and embraced the entire colony.[29]

The trend toward religious uniformity was challenged on several fronts. After more than a century of brutal religious wars, Enlightenment thinkers, such as John Locke in *A Letter on Toleration* (1689), reasoned that freedom of religion and liberty of conscience were consonant with social stability. In that same time of the Glorious Revolution, England granted toleration to dissenters. Anglican England had long regarded the Puritans as nonconformists and lent support to dissenters in New England. Connecticut had blocked the formation of Anglican, Baptist, and Quaker churches. Queen Anne in 1705 annulled a Connecticut law of 1657 against "Heretics, Infidels and Quakers."[30] New Haven had particularly harassed Quakers, such as Humphrey Norton, who was whipped, branded on the hand with the letter *H* for heretic, and banished, but no heretics were ever executed in either colony.

Mindful that no colonial law in Connecticut could be repugnant to the law of England, a provision for toleration was included in the Saybrook Platform to permit "any Society or church that is or shall be allowed by the laws of this government."[31] Quakers, Baptists, and Anglicans, but not Roman Catholics and Jews, had an official right to worship. They were still taxed to support the Congregational Church. The radical Rogerenes, disruptive followers of John Rogers in New London, were actively repressed.[32] Anglicans converted four Congregational ministers in 1722 and established their first church in the colony at Fairfield in 1724. Seeking to remove the discriminatory tax, they petitioned the General Assembly that British law forbid one exclusive church and that the Episcopacy stood equal to Congregationalism in maintaining Christian faith. Begrudgingly, the legislature exempted

Anglicans in 1727 and Baptists and Quakers two years later from paying the tithe to the Congregational Church.[33]

The relative small number of Anglicans, Baptists, and Quakers might be contained, but the Great Awakening of the 1740s shattered the consensus of the Saybrook Platform.[34] Fundamental alterations in society—population growth, expanding towns, commercial growth, erratic markets, depreciated money, landlessness, delayed marriages, generational conflict, premarital conception, and epidemic disease—exposed the whole population to unsettling apprehensions. Steady economic growth during the first thirty years of the seventeenth century, which had produced a substantial middle class of people, was set back during the next twenty, with the worst times coinciding with the awakening of the 1740s.[35] Emotionally wrought revivals offered solace to guilt-ridden thousands who had abandoned pious practices and broken social taboos in the pursuit of profit, power, and pleasure.[36]

The intense piety of the revivals was in contrast to the dry dogma of the Congregational establishment. Itinerants such as the electrifying George Whitefield in Connecticut during 1741 spread the gospel of redemption. Powerful preachers such as George Tennant and James Davenport intruded into existing parishes, captured congregations, and challenged the authority of settled ministers.[37] The awakening shattered communal churches, severed old religious bonds, and stressed radical individualism. Under siege, Old Light opponents to the new measures used their majority in the General Assembly to legislate against New Light evangelicals. These struggles divided the colony between the more recently settled eastern region of the state, which was very receptive to revivals, and the longer inhabited areas, which were more wedded to the status quo. Battles on the local level over installation of ministers and questions of doctrine split the New Lights themselves into factions. The breakup of Congregationalism encouraged an exodus of followers to join the Anglicans and Baptists.[38]

The outcome was that the established church and ministry lost power to the laity. Religious liberty and denominational diversity were enlarged. The Church of England lobbied for the freedom of the Episcopal societies in Connecticut. The unitary bond between church and society was ruptured: sectarian affiliation was voluntary, and religious persuasion was a matter of private judgment. The Reverend Elisha Williams, a prominent Connecticut legislator, in *The Essential Rights and Liberties of Protestants* (1744), argued that liberty of conscience was a natural right. Recognition grew, as the Reverend Noah Hobart put it in an election sermon of 1750, that the acceptance of religious liberty was a prerequisite for civil tranquility.[39] At the same time, the scriptural rationale for the capital statutes was dropped, and several biblically based crimes disappeared from the books.

Secularization of the Capital Laws

The substantial modification of the 1750 Connecticut Code of Laws was preceded by incremental changes in the legal system from the beginning of the eighteenth century. The legal component of the transformation from Puritan to Yankee was in essence a shift from scriptural mandates to English common law. As the economy expanded, there was less interest in moral enforcement and more concern with legitimating commercial, financial, and property relationships. A more formal, impersonal system supplanted the informal, communal protocol of the previous century. The law provided the rules and regulations for the working of the market economy and the hegemony of capital obligations. The colony licensed attorneys and restructured the judiciary, and adjudication and the appeals process were standardized. Court decisions were written and compiled.[40] Prosecutors were first appointed on an ad hoc basis, and in 1704 the General Assembly appointed a standing attorney for the Queen in each county.[41] Although justices of the peace were authorized in 1700 to hold court for minor crimes in each town, the Court of Assistants was replaced in 1711 by a separate Superior Court that met annually to hear serious crimes, including death penalty cases.[42]

Connecticut's capital laws of 1702 (table 9) were the same as the previous revision in 1672, with some noteworthy exceptions. First, incest was dropped.

TABLE 9
Connecticut's Capital Laws, 1702

1. Idolatry	11. Conspiracy against this colony
2. Blasphemy	12. Arson (death optional)
3. Witchcraft	13. Cursing natural parent
4. Murder (killing with malice or cruelty)	14. Smiting natural parent
5. Murder through guile	15. Rebellious son
6. Bestiality	16. Burglary (third offense)
7. Sodomy (male)	17. Robbery (third offense)
8. Rape	18. Murder of bastard children
9. Man stealing	(infanticide)
10. False witness (to take a life)	19. High treason

Source: *Acts and Laws of His Majesties Colony of Connecticut . . . [1702]* (Boston: Bartholomew Green and John Allen, 1702), 12–14.

There was a biblical injunction to punish the crime of incest with death, but the Hebrew concept of consanguinity was complex and not relevant to family practices in New England. Also in the same year, adultery disappeared from the capital code. Although branding and whipping were part of the severe punishment of those convicted of adultery and incest, the deletion of these two sexual infractions foreshadowed the elimination of other moral crimes from hanging offenses. This behavior was still highly condemned, but execution was considered excessive.

Two additions, exclusively English in provenance, document the trend toward the alignment of colonial practices with imperial standards. "An Act to present the destroying and murthering of Bastard Children" that was added in 1699 copied a Massachusetts statute of 1696 that in turn had been adopted from a Jacobean code. The king's law had the clarity that unelaborated scripture lacked. The law condemned mothers, a burden that fell heavily on young women on the social margins, who concealed the death of an illegitimate infant as guilty of murder. After the Disborough exoneration in Connecticut and the Salem debacle in Massachusetts during the 1690s, the misogyny that fueled witchcraft was displaced, as it were, on the "many lewd Women that have been delivered of Bastard Children to avoid their shame."[43] The other installment was "An Act against High Treason" that, among other things, capitalized anyone who "shall compass or imagine the Death" of the royal sovereign. The Board of Trade in London pressured Connecticut lawmakers to provide for the death of traitors, as Massachusetts had done three years earlier.[44]

The trial of Daniel Garde in 1712 at New London marks the further Anglicization of the law. As the result of a quarrel in Stonington with William Whitear, a stranger to town, Garde challenged Whitear to fight *mano a mano,* in which Garde delivered what turned out to be a mortal blow to his opponent. The Queen's attorney brought a charge of murder against Garde, but the jury demurred. The colony did not have an applicable statute on manslaughter, and the jury's intent may have been to drop the case because they thought that Garde had not committed murder, a crime of premeditation. The Superior Court appealed to the General Assembly to consider the application of the common law of manslaughter, a crime lacking clear intent of doing harm.[45] A similar situation had arisen in the conviction of Thomas Rood for incest just before the revision of the 1672 Connecticut Code of Laws. The code of 1650 did not deal with incest, and the matter was put to the General Court for resolution. In "defect of a law," the General Court ruled, "such persons as are proved to be guilty of Incest, they ought by the lawe of God and or lawes as now they stand be put to death."[46]

In striking contrast to the reliance on scripture forty years earlier, the General Court decided that the Superior Court may apply "the rules of the common law."[47] The point was that biblical guidance was not instructive, whereas English law was. The jury found Garde guilty of manslaughter. His punishment was to stand on the gallows for one hour with a noose around his neck and the other end tossed over the gallows and then to be whipped the scripturally mandated thirty-nine stripes; he was also assessed court costs. With religious codes not relevant to a changing standard, the Superior Court had with the General Assembly's guidance expanded the homicide provision in an extralegal fashion. Unlike the Rood case, in which incest was directly added to the 1672 capital code, the common law of manslaughter did not appear in the revised laws of 1715 and was not "enacted" until 1719. The punishment was expanded to include the confiscation of the convicted person's goods and altered to substitute a branding of the letter M on the hand in place of a symbolic hanging. Branding may have been substituted to more readily identify malefactors, as was the case for burglary and robbery, at a time of expanding population.[48]

After a seven-year delay in officially passing the manslaughter law, the General Court in 1719 now felt confident to bring to public light the irregular procedure that the courts, not only in the Garde case but in others, were relying on common law as a standard. In 1717, the General Assembly resolved that "wherein no rule can be found in ye express Acts of this govᵀ nor in ye word of God . . . ye Judges shall determine ye matter by the laws of England known by ye Books to be then in force."[49] Courts were still bound to follow scripture and colonial acts, but, if these traditional sources were not pertinent, the common law prevailed.

England's goal was "a dutiful Colony, attentive to the Interest and Welfare of the Mother Country."[50] In 1702, the secretary of state directed the colony to enter into regular correspondence of its affairs with London. During his long tenure from 1708 to 1724, Governor Gurdon Saltonstall further moved Connecticut into the British orbit, including support for Queen Anne's War (1702–1713). Nonetheless, the request of the British Board of Trade and Plantations in 1698 that the colony submit copies of all acts and laws was not substantially met until 1731. Connecticut was jealous of its exceptional power of self-government that was distinct in North America, but its autonomy was limited. In a bitter inheritance dispute involving Connecticut's prominent

Winthrop family, the Privy Council in 1728 overturned a colonial statute and the ruling of Connecticut courts as "contrary to the laws of England . . . and not warranted by the charter of that colony." Governor Joseph Talcott in 1731 protested the decision of *Winthrop v. Lechmere,* but the question of the validity of colonial statutes and imperial oversight was not fully resolved until the American Revolution.[51]

In the wake of the *Winthrop* controversy, the Board of Trade directed its attorney Francis Fane in 1732 to see if Connecticut's laws "are repugnant to the Laws of this Kingdom."[52] In addition to broader imperial concerns, the board was aware that Connecticut had a capital code that was at variance with British practice. Fane's report was delayed until 1741 because colonial agents lobbied members of Parliament to maintain colonial prerogatives. His review of the capital code of 1715,[53] which had been unchanged since 1702, was highly critical of Puritan influence. Fane noted that the capital code "requires great consideration, tho' it be chiefly taken from Scripture, will want much alteration."[54] Indeed, he found the religious prescriptions of the Puritans antiquated and contrary to good jurisprudence. He judged that idolatry was "at present needless" with no current relevancy and that blasphemy, which might include cursing, "seems too hard to make it a capital offense." Witchcraft "would be much better left out . . . especially considering the great abuse that has been made in New England of the laws against witches, and that many innocent people have thereby lost their lives."[55] He opposed the death penalty for man stealing, bearing false witness, and rebellious children based on pentateuchal penalties. He objected to execution for robbery and burglary. He also found "the stigmatizing or branding persons and obliging them to wear a public mark of infamy is more liable to make them incorrigible than to reform them."[56] He noted that the section on rape ought to formally extend the death penalty to the violation of a female under the age of ten years as was the case in England.[57] The statutes would also benefit by being more specific and determinate so that judicial latitude would be restricted. Although Fane's opinions appear not to have been directly presented to colonial officials, they foreshadowed the major revision of the capital code in 1750.

Imperial pressure, religious pluralism, and commercial expansion undermined the Puritan legacy that had linked the capital code with Hebraic literalism since the inaugural statutes of 1642. A quarter century before the upheaval of the American Revolution, the transition from Puritan to Yankee led to the secularization and diminution of the capital code. Along with adultery (deleted in 1672) and incest (omitted in 1702), idolatry, witchcraft,

TABLE 10
Connecticut's Capital Laws, 1750

1. Conspiracy against this colony	7. Blasphemy
2. Bestiality	8. Burglary (third offense)
3. Sodomy (male)	9. Robbery (third offense)
4. False witness (to take a life)	10. Rape
5. Arson (death optional)	11. Murder of bastard children (infanticide)
6. Dismemberment	12. High treason

Source: *Acts and Laws of His Majesty's Colony of Connecticut . . . [1750–1783]* (New Haven: Thomas and Samuel Green, 1769), 68–69. See pp. 18 (burglary and robbery for the third offense), 171 (murder of bastard children), 197 (rape), and 244 (high treason).

man-stealing, false witness, and rebellious children disappeared from the list as shown in table 10. With the glaring exception of blasphemy, the most egregious aspects of the Puritan legacy, at least the ones to which Fane had objected, were gone. The inclusion of blasphemy was a sop to piety, but not enforced to the maximum. In 1752, the General Assembly spared the life of John Green of Norwalk, who, while drunk, "uttered horrible words of blasphemy." The commutation from hanging to a mild sentence of standing in the pillory, a fine, and posting surety for good behavior is an important measure of the diminution of penalties for religious and moral infractions.[58] The number of offenses shrank from nineteen in 1702 and 1715 to a dozen in 1750.

Punishment and Executions

After 1750, crimes that had formerly been capital, such as adultery and incest, were punished with symbolic hanging, branding, wearing a halter, and whipping rather than death. Traditional corporal punishment and shaming techniques were employed as deterrents. The shift from a religiously based commonwealth to a commercially driven economy led to a decrease in the prosecution of crimes such as Sabbath breaking, lascivious carriage, cursing, drunkenness, fornication, night walking, and other violations of the moral order. After 1770, fines, rather than whipping, were common for such offenses. In a surging market economy, corporal punishment—whipping, branding, mutilation, and the stocks—was directed toward property crimes such as counterfeiting, horse stealing, house breaking, burglary, and robbery.[59] There was one instance, as we will see, of the hanging of an obdurate thief. A study of whipping and branding between 1764 and 1784 showed that these punishments were overwhelmingly directed at economic culprits, particularly transients and lower-class incorrigibles. In 1768, a counterfeiter was punished by standing in the pillory for one hour and then publicly whipped twenty lashes.[60] For stealing two watches from a Windsor house, two men were whipped fifteen times, were branded with the letter *B* on the forehead, and had their right ears cropped. One of the men almost bled to death from the maiming.[61]

Homicide

From 1700 to 1772, ten people were executed for homicide, excluding infanticide (table 11). The data show an unmistakable racial dimension. Of the ten who went to the gallows, seven were Native Americans and two were African Americans. Minority men, especially Native Americans, were mostly likely to hang. No white man and one white woman were hanged. At a time when the number of blacks and Indians was not much more than 5 percent of the total population, 90 percent of those hanged were nonwhite. The disproportionate execution of minorities reflected a society based on white supremacy. The identification in the legal records, for example, of the Negro Cuffee and the Negress Hannah with a racial tag and only a first name marks their inferior status and dehumanization.

In a history of New Haven, the Reverend Timothy Dwight, president of Yale, recorded tersely that three Indians, "probably Qunnipiacks," were hanged in 1700 at New Haven for murdering a colonist in the East Haven woods.[62] Significantly, no white man has ever been judicially executed for killing an Indian in Connecticut. In separate events, Solomon Andrews of

TABLE 11
Executions for Homicide, 1700–1772

	Year of Execution	Name	Race	Gender	Weapon	Location of Execution
1–3	1700	Three unidentified men	Native American	Male	Unknown	New Haven
4	1708	Abigail Thompson	White	Female	Scissors	Hartford
5	1711	Young Squamp	Native American	Male	Knife	Hartford
6	1711	Waisoiusksquaw	Native American	Female	Knife	Hartford
7	1720	Negro Cuffee	African American	Male	Gun	Fairfield
8	1731	Negress Hannah	African American	Female	Knife	New Haven
9	1768	John Jacob	Native American	Male	Hatchet	Litchfield
10	1772	Moses Paul	Native American	Male	Club	New Haven

Hartford in 1706 and Samuel Boston of Milford in 1708 were charged with the murder of Indian men, but all-white juries did not find the indictments warranted. The only penalty for Andrews and Boston was to pay the cost of prosecution.[63] Not all Indians accused of murdering whites were convicted, however. Indians who were suspected of killing David Lane of Stratford were acquitted in 1726.[64] Cupacosson, an Indian, was found not guilty of murder in the death of John Everest at Guilford in 1705. In an act of violence attributed to insanity, Everest entered a wigwam, slit the throat of an infant in a cradle, and wounded the attending grandparents. Cupacosson, who was nearby, heard the cries of distress and shot the perpetrator in the head. An all-white grand jury found Cupacosson "blameless."[65]

Two "Indian Murtherers" were tried together in 1711 at Hartford for the murder of other Indians that occurred in English, not tribal, jurisdiction. Young Squamp, "of his premeditated malice," mortally stabbed Mantoshoes at Hoccanum with a knife in the chest. Waisoiusksquaw "with malice afore-thought with a long Sharpe pointed knife" stabbed to death her husband at Stonington. Both the grand and petite juries were liberally composed of twelve whites and six Indians, and translators rendered the proceedings into tribal language for the defendants, yet without legal representation, the ac-cused failed to mount a meaningful defense. On the afternoon of May 15, a cart carried the twosome to the gallows in Hartford. Relatives and friends retrieved their bodies for burial.[66]

In some cases of intraethnic Indian murder, the General Assembly turned over the defendant to tribal authority "so the Indians may have the opportu-nitie to execute on him as they shall determine."[67] The unspecific "crimes of high nature" involving "a trial for Life" of John Jefferie in 1704, a Branford Indian, presages the alternative of incarceration and rehabilitation to hang-ing. Jefferie was placed in the Hartford jail "under Such discipline until there is good hopes of his Reformation or Sufficient bond given for his Civill behavior for the future."[68]

In 1768, the Litchfield County Superior Court sentenced John Jacob to death that November for the hatchet blow to the side of the head of James Chokerer, a fellow native. Jacob was visiting Chokerer and his wife in their wigwam where he attacked the victim. The context of the murder is un-clear, except that some sort of quarrel arose. Jacob's stated reason for the murder was ethnic hatred, that "James was a d——d Skatacook." The Rever-end Timothy Pitkin preached an execution sermon, a didactic tract adver-tised for purchase.[69] Despite the secularization of the capital code of 1750, the sermon was replete with scriptural justification that "it is the statute of heaven, it is the law of the great God, that a murderer shall be put to death."[70] Turning to the condemned man, the preacher exclaimed, "Prisoner, attend! You deserve to suffer the eternal pains of hell."[71] In Christian eschatology, even the murderer at the gallows might hope for redemption. *"Without repentance,"* Pitkin exhorted, *"there is no remission of sin, and without faith in Christ, there is no justification, nor salvation."*[72] Pitkin preached as much to the white audience as to the Indian, affirming a divine mandate for the death penalty. The ritualistic notice that the sermon was "Preached upon the Desire of the Criminal" further legitimated the proceedings.[73] Dissemination of information about an execution expanded with the printing of the sermon and coverage by the colony's emerging newspapers.

The most notorious situation was that of Moses Paul in New Haven in 1772. Paul was probably a Wampanoag, a tribe in southeastern Massachusetts, that had been Christianized, as his first name indicated, shortly after English contact. At age five, he was apprenticed to a white man in Windham, Connecticut. Over his fifteen years of apprenticeship, he became literate and was instructed in Christianity. As a young man, he served in the Connecticut militia, perhaps fighting in Detroit under Colonel Israel Putnam to suppress the Pontiac revolt. He then took to the sea, where as a sailor he traveled to the West Indies. After army and maritime service, he returned to Connecticut. He was drinking heavily and was a transient. Official documents indicate that he was intoxicated on the evening of December 7, 1771, when he entered a tavern in Bethany looking for a drink. The tavern keeper's wife evicted him. Accounts differ as to who started the quarrel, but a fight ensued between Paul and Moses Cook, a white lodger, outside the inn. According to Paul, Cook attacked him, threw him into a snowbank, tied his legs, whipped him, and called him a "drunken dog." Paul made his way back into the tavern to retrieve some clothing. Cook threatened him with a cane, and Paul struck his opponent on the head with a club. Cook died five days later, and Paul was charged with murder.[74]

Paul pleaded not guilty, but on December 31, after a nine-hour proceeding, a jury in New Haven County Superior Court sentenced him to death.[75] The execution was scheduled for June 17, 1772. William Samuel Johnson, a distinguished lawyer, appealed the verdict to the General Assembly, which delayed the execution. Johnson presented a different version of events than what had transpired at the trial. In the original proceedings and as reported in the press, Paul had in an act of calculated revenge waylaid Cook as he left the tavern and killed him with an iron bar.[76] Johnson sought sympathy for his client, a "poor distressed Indian prisoner, now bound in chains and fetters of iron." What the "poor ignorant memorialist" had failed to explain earlier was that Cook was also inebriated and had acted in "a threatening manner." Paul had defended himself not with an iron bar but a wooden club, and he did not lay in wait for his antagonist. Most important, he acted in passion and anger, not with malice aforethought. Johnson had revised the stereotype of the drunken Indian to his client's advantage in describing a melee of manslaughter, not murder. The General Assembly was, however, not persuaded and set the execution at New Haven for September 2, 1772.[77]

For the first and only time, an execution sermon was preached by an Indian. A "great concourse of people" attended the sermon of the celebrated Samson Occom, a Mohegan, Presbyterian minister, and missionary to the Indians.[78] After a long, eloquent account of sin and redemption, he turned to "My poor unhappy Brother MOSES," whom he identified as "an Indian, a despised creature." There was no escape from the quintessential divine decree for the death penalty, claimed Occom, quoting Genesis 9:6: "Whoso sheddeth man's blood, by man shall his blood be shed." On a more hopeful theme, Occom explained God's free offer of grace to sinful humanity by stating, "O, poor Moses! hear the dying prayer of a gracious Savior on the accursed tree,—Father forgive them for they know not what they do."[79]

Occom finished with words to "the Indians, my bretheren and kindred according to the flesh." He inveighed against "the devilish sin of drunkenness that we suffer every day."[80] Occom knew about what he spoke because he had publicly confessed in 1769 that he was a recovered alcoholic.[81] On this day, he spoke directly of the ravages of alcohol on his people: debased living standards, irrational behavior, neglected children, immodest women, shameful men, breakdown of community, and sacrilege. "When a person is drunk, he is just good for nothing in the world," he intoned.[82] In a brief but provocative political statement, he explained the plight of indigenous people: "Though you have been cheated over and over again, and you have lost your substance by drunkenness, yet you will venture to go on in this most destructive sin." Occom was damning Indian inebriation, but the worst of it was that these "fools" were in no condition to redress the oppression of being "cheated over and over again." In a veiled but pointed phrase, he was alluding to the white conquest, which included the destructive introduction of hard liquor into Indian culture. "Break off your drunkenness," he concluded.

Paul, however, did not die in vain. Occom's arousing sermon went through nineteen editions. He was the premier Indian minister and was in great demand, including in white congregations. His message, however, was to Indian peoples. His son-in-law, Joseph Johnson, a Mohegan, also published a

Christian message of hope to the condemned Paul.[83] In 1773, in an extension of his powerful execution sermon, Occom called for a proto-nationalist, Indian movement of renewal. The Brother Town community was an effort to promote racial solidarity and Christian ethics apart from the corruption and subjugation endemic in white-dominated society. A large number of Indians, many of whom had been converted during the Great Awakening and perhaps one-half of the total native population in Connecticut, joined an exodus to Oneida territory in New York in search of their own Canaan.[84] The General Assembly's rejection of Paul's petition was not only the end of the rope for him, but, as Occom pointed out, in a larger sense it was the end for indigenous people as a whole.

A counterpoint that highlights a double standard of racial justice involves a similar drunken fight between white men. At Norwich in 1761 during an altercation, Ebenezer Rude wounded John Knight with a sword, who in turn stomped his antagonist to death. The New London Superior Court sentenced Knight to death for murder, but on appeal the General Assembly granted him a new trial. Knight was then found guilty of the lesser offense of manslaughter and was not executed.[85]

Two African Americans were hanged for homicide. Both involved domestic violence. In the first case, Negro Cuffee murdered another slave, Negress Mary, as court records racially identified them, in the household of Hezekial Talcott, a squire in Durham. The context of the violence is not documented, but it was typical for successful farmers to own a few black slaves. Mary likely was employed about the house, and Cuffee was a field hand. Cuffee fled into Paugusett territory, where he shot to death an Indian with a gun he had taken from his master. Cuffee appears not to have been represented by counsel. He was hanged at Fairfield on March 15, 1720.[86]

In the second case, Negress Hannah attacked two young, white women with a knife as they slept in the household of Moses Atwater, a squire in Wallingford. The reason for the assault is not given, but one woman died of a cut throat. The screams of the victims in the night awakened the Atwaters, who discovered Hannah with a bloody knife and blood on her person. The murder raised a nightmare vision of slave violence. The accused apparently did not have a defense attorney, and the sheriff hanged her on July 3, 1731. A bill included in the court documents indicates that the sheriff was responsible for building the gallows; carting the condemned person to the execution site; digging the grave, which probably abutted the gallows; and the actual hanging itself, for which "ye executioner" received £6. Because the hanging took place in New Haven, a large group of spectators was probable.[87]

Hannah was hanged for killing a woman of English ancestry, but no white person has ever been judicially executed for the murder of a black person. How typical was the grand jury that acquitted a white man of "killing a certain Negro boy" in Fairfield in 1705? The defendant, John Sloss, was only assessed court costs.[88] Another example openly points to a racial double standard. Because his mulatto slave boy, Sharper, stole and ran away repeatedly, James Rogers III nailed the boy's ear to his house wall, forced a corn cob in his mouth, and bound his hands and feet so that the boy could not move. The master kept the slave in that posture for twelve hours. The king's attorney in 1753 charged Rogers at county court in Norwich with "torture" and placing a life in "eminent danger" without just cause.[89] In addition, the prosecution said that Rogers "exercised great cruelty on the bodies of two more of his servants, Negro men (viz.) Cato and Simon." Rogers, a man of social standing, hired counsel. His attorney demanded that the court void the charges, arguing that Sharper, Cato, and Simon were "slaves for life" and "absolute property" and that the defendant therefore "is not holden by law to answer thereto." The court discharged the case, and Rogers was only assessed court costs.[90]

Abigail Thomson was the second female and the only white person, male or female, to be hanged for homicide during the period. On December 14, 1705, violence occurred at a home in Farmington when Abigail in anger flung an iron tailor's shears at her husband. A point of the tool penetrated the skull of the victim near his ear, and Thomas Thomson died of the wound on January 2, 1706. Abigail pleaded not guilty, and the court assigned her an attorney. She maintained that she had not intended to kill her husband and that he had previously struck her with a broom. Neighbors and relatives testified that Abigail had been physically abusive toward her husband.[91] "And I asked my mother," her son testified, "if she was not ashamed to beat her husband, and She said she was not, and Said he was an old devil, and She would be the death of him."[92] Others indicated that Abigail on several occasions had threatened to kill her spouse. The all-male jury found that she had acted maliciously in throwing the shears that killed her husband. Her attorney appealed to the General Assembly, which reprieved her death sentence because it was "attended with great difficulty."[93] Were her vocal threats to kill her husband more bravado than a premeditated intent to do harm? The General Assembly was not persuaded that the violent act constituted manslaughter and upheld the murder verdict. It may be that the male legislators found that Abigail's behavior was so far from expected gender norms that they finally allowed the death penalty to stand. She was hanged in Hartford on May 27, 1708[94]

Connecticut continued to exclude from the death penalty a homicide if committed under demonstrable mental incapacity, a practice reaffirmed by William Blackstone's authoritative *Commentaries on the Laws of England* (1765–1769). Such was the case of Roger Humphrey, a veteran of the French and Indian War, who had become "delirious and distracted." In such impairment, he killed his mother, but the Hartford County Superior Court in 1758 found him not guilty because of insanity. Eventually, Humphrey's father, with a government subsidy for the unfortunate veteran, cared for his son, whom he confined to a "small place" at home. The court ordered the matricide held there under "constant confinement during his natural life."[95] These conditions might well have been particularly oppressive.

Infanticide

The mid-eighteenth century brought profound cultural changes. Commercial growth included a shift from wealth in land to cash assets and an erosion of inheritance traditions between parents and children. Instead of arranged marriages, which were more about the transmission of the family farm than a love match, economic pressures delayed unions, facilitated romantic liaisons, and altered sexual practices. With a dramatic drop in the standard of living during the 1740s, the number of rootless youth expanded. Premarital conceptions increased,[96] and the elite expressed concern with the number of poor women bearing children outside of wedlock. Because of hard times, the old solution of compelling fornicators, especially those with few resources, to sanctify their unions was less a possibility. The courts singled out low-status women for illegitimacy and immorality. The exemption of their better-off sisters and philandering men from prosecution during the eighteenth century marked a Yankee double standard, unlike the Puritan practice of holding sinners—male and female, rich and poor—to a single, divine standard.[97]

Executions for infanticide, not unlike the religious revivals, cluster in a fifteen-year period that coincided with profound cultural changes (table 12). Alarm over fornication had brought into law in 1699 "An Act to prevent the destroying and Murthering of Bastard Children." That statute, like its Massachusetts counterpart of 1696, copied a severe English law of 1624 that made concealment of the death of a newborn bastard presumptive evidence of murder. It asserted that "many leud Women" out of "shame" and "to escape punishment" of an illegitimate birth hid in various ways the death of the infant. If a dead infant were found, officials suspected that the

TABLE 12
Executions for Homicide (Infanticide), 1700–1772

Year of Execution	Name	Race	Gender	Weapon	Place of Execution
1	1738	Katherine Garrett	Native American	Female	Block of wood	New London
2	1743	Negress Kate	African American	Female	Curtain sash	Hartford
3	1745	Elizabeth Shaw	White	Female		Windham
4	1753	Sarah Bramble	White	Female		New London

mother's claim of miscarriage might mask a murder. To avoid the charge of infanticide, the mother needed at least one witness to corroborate that a stillbirth had occurred. An unassisted birth, to which a frightened, unmarried woman might be prone, meant that there would be no supporting witnesses.[98]

Of twenty-five infanticide cases before 1790 in Connecticut, nineteen came before the courts after 1740, with five of those during the 1750s.[99] The willingness to prosecute, however, was not matched by the inclination of juries to impose the death penalty. Juries were hard pressed to determine if there had been a live birth or not and whether there was criminal culpability. In an early application of the law in 1702, a jury found Sarah Moore not guilty of infanticide. Her situation was unusual because she was married to a Windsor selectman. She was charged with murder through neglect shortly after birth of a child whose father she refused to name. Perhaps the jury believed that adding a hanging would do little for justice in a scandal involving adultery, illegitimacy, and infanticide in a prominent family.[100]

A number of women suspected under the statute, even those of marginal status, had their cases discharged. In 1747 at Stonington, an infant's corpse was found concealed near a fence. Betty Kiness, an unmarried Indian servant, had given birth unassisted. By the letter of the law, she was guilty of infanticide. The court, however, dismissed the case because the jury of inquest could not determine if Kiness had caused the death.[101] In a 1750 case, Peg, an Indian slave, also gave birth alone in Saybrook. She was suspected of causing the death of her illegitimate offspring through neglect, but not violence. She was chronically ill, and the New London County Superior Court dismissed her case. In additional cases, Abigail Wilson, a transient, and Lucretia Smith, "very poor," were not found guilty of infanticide at New London in 1760 and 1764, respectively.[102] Other women not found guilty under the statute include Jane Thompson of Union in 1754[103] and Phebe Elderkin of Goshen in 1763.[104]

That some accused women escaped execution highlights the circumstances under which four did not. The inconsistency in the application of the death penalty is striking. Most juries freed defendants; only a few sent them to the gallows. Katherine Garrett was the first person executed under the 1699 law and in 1738 was the first person hanged in New London. Unmarried, she was a Pequot born on the North Stonington reservation and had been employed as a servant by the family of the Reverend William Worthington and his wife, Temperance, in Saybrook. The Worthingtons testified that their servant secretly and with no assistance gave live birth on January 4, 1737, in the barn to an "Indian male child." The cries of the baby alerted the Worthingtons, who found the infant with a fractured skull, buried in hay. The infant died after ten hours despite the ministrations of a midwife.[105] Garrett pleaded not guilty, but she later confessed the deed to a jury of inquest. A special Superior Court found her guilty of "murthering her bastard child" with a block of wood.[106] With overwhelming evidence presented by a prominent white family against an Indian servant who lacked counsel, the decision was not unexpected.

Garrett's execution on May 3, 1738, was the occasion for an execution sermon by the Reverend Eliphalet Adams, a Harvard graduate and eminent New London minister. The publication is the earliest one of its kind extant for Connecticut. The text follows a narrative of sin and redemption. "But I would especially warn persons," Adams preached the morning of the execution, "against the *lust of uncleanliness,* those *sins against our own bodies.*"[107] Then turning to the Indian woman, he sought her approbation, saying "that as a poor unhappy sinner *you may patiently submit to the justice of this sentence,* to take *away by your death* the guilt of blood from the land."[108]

During more than a year of incarceration, Garrett, isolated and bereft, was relentlessly proselytized by the clergy, who gained her profession of Christianity and baptized her. The sermon text gives sensational attention to her last day. That morning, she "was exceedingly overwhelmed and cast down"; she fainted several times during Adams's address.[109] In the afternoon, she left prison for a mile-long procession on foot, accompanied by ministers and other officials, to Town Hill. A huge crowd, including substantial figures such as Joshua Hempstead,[110] thronged the gallows. She was too frightened and incoherent to speak clearly, so a minister read "The Confession and Dying Warning of Katherine Garrett" to the spectators. The last words were not her own, even though they were purported to be, because they were redolent of the pulpit: "Oh! Beware of all sin, especially of fornication; for that led me to murder." In a paraphrase of Saint Paul's injunction, so revered by the ownership class, the minister read, "I would also warn servants, either whites or blacks, to be obedient to your masters and mistresses."[111] With the coffin before her and the rope about her neck, the sheriff hanged her, a sinner "against God." This final message of Christian triumph and racial supremacy exclaimed, "Particularly, may all her *country people,* in their several tribes, wither round about us or farther off, hearken diligently to the offers and proposals of the gospel that are made to them!"[112]

In the second case of infanticide, the record of Negress Kate's conviction is sparse. She was a slave, identified by race and a first name only, on the Wethersfield estate of Thomas Belding. She was an unmarried woman, accused of strangling her "Male Negro Infant" baby with a curtain sash and hiding the corpse on April 28, 1743.[113] Daniel Wadsworth, a prominent pastor in Hartford, in a conversation with her in jail on May 26, noted, "She denies ye fact" of her crime.[114] The Hartford County Superior Court, however, found Kate guilty on September 12. Wadsworth regularly attended to her and Negro Jack, a convicted rapist, in jail, praying, "O Lord have pity on those poor creatures."[115] On November 16, the Reverend E. Whitman of First Church of Christ at Hartford preached the execution sermon. At 3:00 p.m., officials in Hartford expediently executed the two African Americans together. "May it be a warning to others," Wadsworth wrote in his diary.[116]

Elizabeth Shaw was the first white woman executed under the 1699 law and the first person hanged in Windham County. On July 4, 1745, residents found the corpse of an infant boy in bushy woods on the ground; the body was by the side of an old log, covered with bark, several hundred yards from the house of William Shaw, an established resident of what now is Hampton. Investigation, including a gynecological examination of the nineteen-year-old Elizabeth Shaw by twelve women, indicated that she had given birth, left the infant to die, and concealed the corpse. Shaw was unmarried and lived with her parents before she was committed to the Windham jail. She pleaded not guilty, but was sentenced to death. On November 18, 1745, after an execution sermon, a large crowd followed the cart that carried the distraught young woman to a gallows erected for the occasion at the intersection of a road from Windham to Mansfield. There the sheriff hanged her.[117]

A local historian writes that Shaw was mentally deficient and that her stern father had turned her over to authorities.[118] That may explain why she was the only one of four women hanged for infanticide who was not of low status or a racial minority.[119] Her situation soon became part of local lore.

In 1772, a broadside judged her in Christian doggerel as an immoral woman: "Satan found her on his ground and did her soul ensnare." The author included the folk belief that a murderer who touched the corpse of the victim caused it to bleed anew:

> She was commanded with her hand
> to touch the infant's flesh,
> Which when she came to touch the
> the [sic] corps did bleed afresh.

The final refrain was a familiar warning:

> O may we all who hear her fall
> a timely warning take:
> Let's not delay another day,
> before we sin forsake.[120]

The execution of Sarah Bramble, a servant, on November 21, 1753, was a demarcation point in capital punishment in Connecticut. She was the last white woman executed in Connecticut, the last woman executed for infanticide, and the only white person executed in public in New London. Unmarried, she gave birth alone to a girl on March 21, 1752. The concealed corpse was found burned and bruised. Bramble claimed a stillbirth. There were no witnesses to the birth other than the mother. That was prima facie evidence under the 1699 statute for guilt, but the jury in September 1752 deadlocked. Although appalled by the crime, some were reluctant to hang her. While Bramble was imprisoned for more than a year, a second trial found her guilty. The mistrial was not considered a violation of the English common law of double jeopardy. On the day of her execution, she defiantly refused to attend the execution sermon. Ten thousand people from miles around surrounded the gallows at a high point on the main road outside of town.[121]

Rape

The reluctance of juries to convict for infanticide was paralleled by a disinclination to enforce capital punishment for rape. For a fifty-year period (1694–1742), no one went to the gallows for that crime. There was no statute for attempted rape until the 1770s; before then, plaintiffs and juries were faced with an all-or-nothing situation: acquit or hang. For the first three-quarters of the eighteenth century, only two men, both African Americans, were hanged for the crime (table 13). The prosecuted were generally on the

TABLE 13
Executions for Rape, 1700–1772

| 1 | 1743 | Negro Jack | African American | Hartford |
| 2 | 1749 | Negro Cuff | African American | New Haven |

social margins. In sixteen rape prosecutions from 1700 to 1772, six were black, one was Indian, and nine were white. Typical among whites was Charles Wilson, a transient, jailed in 1770 on suspicion of the rape of a "young woman" in Bolton, but freed for lack of evidence.[122] White perception of black men as sexually aggressive, a threatening underclass, was ubiquitous, especially during the eighteenth century. No man of any race was executed for raping a black or an Indian woman. White women were the plaintiffs in both rape cases that resulted in an execution.[123]

The law stated, "If any Man shall forceably and without consent, Ravish any Maid, or Woman, by committing carnal Copulation with her, against her consent, he shall be put to death." Although not explicitly stated, the statute was extended in practice to females of any age. The complaint had to be made "forthwith" upon the assault, and the understanding was that there must be "actual penetration."[124] Delay in bringing charges, the need to prove penetration, and the validity of the woman's word as opposed to the man's worked against convictions.

The proverbial caution about the credibility of women who claimed to have been sexually assaulted was raised in the spurious accusation of a white woman who accused a black man. Hannah Beebe, a single woman of Lyme, charged on May 13, 1756, that Bristo, a slave of the Reverend George Beckwith of the same town, had "by force threw her on the ground and pulled up her clothes and attempted to lie with her and she then fell into a fit, and no further knowledge what was done till afterwards and when recovered, supposed said Bristo had committed copulation with her against her will." The New London County Superior Court in late September 1756 sentenced the defendant to hang. Upon learning that Beebe had "openly and freely declared said Bristoe [variant spelling] to be innocent of said crime,"[125] however, Governor Thomas Fitch reprieved the execution in a special order on November 29, 1756,

Depositions presented to the General Assembly in January 1757 revealed a conspiracy to use the emotionally laden charge to gain financial reward, if not to cover up some sexual misconduct or plot revenge. Beebe, for unspecified reasons, was preparing a "lascivious carriage" against Bristo when Thomas

Tozer, a white man from East Haddam, convinced her, as her father reputedly said, that "the court would give his daughter a considerable sum of money" if Bristo were convicted of rape. They also thought that Beckwith might pay as much as £800 not to have his valuable slave hanged. Two witnesses, Beebe's mother and Wait Wright, a mulatto youth, added false testimony that Bristo raped Beebe, and she apparently had pangs of conscience about sending an innocent man to death, feelings with which her parents concurred. The mother admitted that she was "mistaken" in her account, and in Wright's recantation he said that "Bristo never touched said Hannah." The General Assembly ordered Bristo, who maintained his innocence, freed of the charge, but he remained a slave. Whether the instigators made overtures to the minister or received money from him for not pressing the rape complaint is not documented. There is no indication that Tozer, who hatched the plot, Hannah, and others who abetted the malevolence suffered judicial penalties.[126]

No doubts marked the proceedings against Negro Jack, a slave of a New York man. On June 8, 1743, when Hannah Andrews, a married woman, became lost on horseback south of Middletown as she returned home from visiting friends, she asked directions of Jack. He threatened her but let her go. He then caught up to her and pulled her off the horse. Her complaint, filed the next day, stated that he had "uncovered my nakedness and I cried out for help but he with force did enter by body with his private part and had as I suppose emiting [sic] of his seed into my body and then told me I would have a black bastard." She attempted to escape, but the assailant caught her again, clubbed her, and stomped her about the head, leaving her for dead in the woods. After several hours, she regained consciousness and crawled to the road, where she was found. The explicit statement of the life-threatening assault—which detailed force, the victim's resistance, sexual penetration, and ejaculation—was promptly deposed and crafted to match the statutory definition of the crime. Jack was captured before he could flee to New York, the victim identified him as the rapist, and he admitted his guilt at the arraignment.[127]

Newspapers from Boston to Philadelphia reported that "a Negro Fellow was lately committed to Gaol there [Hartford] for a Rape committed on the Body of a white Woman and afterwards beating her in so barbarous a Manner as to leave for dead in the Woods."[128] She was bedridden for three weeks. In October 1743, Hannah Andrews's husband, Ephraim, received £30 compensation for his wife's medical expenses. His petition to the General Assembly spoke of "the barbarous, cruel, violence of an inhuman Negro." Jack had no attorney, nor was there an effort to mitigate the capital sentence passed by the Hartford County Superior Court a month earlier.[129] Jack and Negress Kate, who had been convicted of infanticide, were executed on November 16, 1743, the only time in Connecticut that two African Americans were hanged simultaneously.[130]

On that Wednesday in Hartford, another African American was punished for a crime fraught with racial tension. Authorities charged that on May 12, 1743, in Middletown, Negro Barney, a sixteen-year-old slave, led his six-year-old master's son, Thomas Allyn, to a remote field, stripped him, and violently forced him to the ground. There, with a knife, Barney "cut one of the said Thomas's testacles [sic] from his body and cut the skin of the other and laid the same open and cut and mangled his penis." The perpetrator left the victim where he lay until he was discovered eight hours later. Thomas survived; Barney was arrested.[131] Although the motivation for the sexual maiming is not known, the emasculation challenged white male dominance.

In September, the grand jury of the Hartford County Superior Court endorsed the indictment of malicious maiming, to which Barney pleaded guilty. The defendant was not represented by counsel. The court asked for guidance of the General Assembly because there was "no special provision in any law of this Colony for the punishment of such crimes."[132] The governor and legislature empowered the judges of the court to fix an appropriate punishment. On November 15, Roger Wolcott, the chief judge of the court and future governor, and four assistant judges sentenced Barney to an unprecedented retribution the next day to which there was no appeal. The timing was purposeful because it provided the opportunity for officials to force Barney to watch the execution of Jack and Kate, fellow slaves. Barney was ordered to sit on the same gallows for an hour with a rope around his neck, taken to the whipping post to incur thirty-nine lashes on "the naked body," and branded with a "hot iron" on the forehead with the letter C for castrator.[133] The public punishment of three African Americans, two of whom had committed violent acts against whites, made an emphatic statement.[134]

The court ordered Barney back to jail. After twenty-eight days, he was brought forth to be publicly whipped with thirty-nine stripes. The ritual was repeated once more with the addition that he "shall be further punished by castration and having both his testicles cut out, and then be from the said gaol discharged."[135] How well Barney endured the excision in January 1844 is not clear, but the court's intent was the law of the talion, gonad for gonad, not a death penalty per se. If he survived, he was visibly marked by the brand on his forehead and rendered a eunuch, incapable of reproduction. He was the first person, and significantly an African American slave, judicially castrated in Connecticut. Dismemberment was made a capital crime in 1750.

In contrast to punishment of Jack and Barney who pleaded guilty, the death sentence for the Negro Cuff was contested, albeit unsuccessfully. Benjamin Pardee complained to the justice of the peace that Cuff, a slave of a militia captain, had raped Diane Parish, an orphan and his fourteen-year-old apprentice, in East Haven on October 2, 1748. The next day, she told under oath that as she was walking alone on a road Cuff had "violently" seized and "threatened to kill her." Despite her "Screaming and Striving," "he entered her Body with his Private Member," statements that legally defined the crime. After the rape, he let her go. Arriving on the scene was a fifteen-year-old boy on horseback, who attested that he had seen the last stages of the assault. He rode the girl to his mother, who with another woman determined through a physical examination that she "had been entered by some man." Confronted with these accusations, Cuff confessed his guilt and was jailed pending the convening of the New Haven County Superior Court.[136]

The court assigned two attorneys for the defendant. In the past eleven years, four people had been hanged—three for infanticide and one for rape—and a fifth had been castrated for dismemberment. None had been represented by counsel, three were slaves, and Jack's guilty plea put him on a fast track to the gallows. The castration of the Negro Barney for dismemberment in 1744 raised substantial issues about procedure. There were also questions about whether infanticide and rape should warrant capital punishment. Cuff's plea of innocence did not persuade the jury, which convicted him. His attorneys sent to the General Assembly "the humble supplication of a condemned malefactor lying in the New Haven gaol begging for his life," which delayed the impending February 1749 execution. They significantly argued for equality under the law: "Some may think and talk that the life of a slave may be treated other than the life of another." They also raised technical challenges about the inapplicability of biblical law on the rape of a woman who was not "betrothed," the need for two witnesses to a crime, and the credibility of the youthful victim. Most important was that the petition asked for a nonlethal punishment for a capital crime, a commutation to "whipping branding transportation or Castration any or all." The General Assembly denied the attorneys' request, and the defendant was likely hanged in the spring of 1749. Nonetheless, the officials had ensured that there would not be a rush to judgment, even in a rape case involving a black slave and a white girl.[137]

Race played a pivotal, but not exclusive, role in the commutation of the death sentence in 1760 for rape of Vanskelly Mully, the first white man so convicted since 1693. He was a French soldier captured in Niagara and held in a Fairfield jail during the Seven Years' War in North America. The father of a ten-year-old girl promptly reported that on August 16, at Greenwich, that prisoner had sexually assaulted his daughter. Mully was found guilty of rape in Fairfield County Superior Court and was sentenced to hang on November 4. On October 9, he petitioned the General Assembly to commute the sentence. On investigation, the legislators found reasons to spare his life. A repentant Mully contended that he was not aware that his crime was "so high and aggravated" as to be warranted with death. He had been brought up in the French provinces ignorant of the law, illiterate, and "deprived of the Bible." The morning he had encountered the victim, Amy Palmer, he had drunk a "quantity of strong liquor" before breakfast and had been overcome by the "power of temptation." He admitted that "his conduct and behavior toward the girl was abusive, injurious, and glaringly sinful." Community members added that a sexual assault, but not a rape, was the more likely event. The victim's account was suspect, and she was seen nimbly riding a horse astride after the event. There was also compelling evidence that Mully had never sexually penetrated the victim. The men who searched him found his shirt stained with semen and supposed "he fumbled about." On reflection, the parents concurred and only asked for "proper punishment according to the merit of the offence."[138]

The General Assembly was persuaded that a sexual penetration had not occurred and so commuted the death sentence for rape for the first time. The sexual assault by a drunken enemy soldier on a young girl was not, however, taken lightly. Mully was symbolically hanged for one hour, was whipped thirty-nine times, had his right ear nailed to a post and cut off, was whipped again after confinement to jail, and was banished from the colony.[139] If Mully had been black, would the community have supported the commutation? In any case, after 1693 only black men were executed for rape, all of white females.

Burglary

The first and last time anyone was executed in Connecticut for a purely economic crime was that of the inveterate burglar Isaac Frasier (table 14). Frasier's hanging on September 7, 1768, also marked the first publication of

TABLE 14
Executions for Burglary, 1700–1772

1	1768	Isaac Frasier	White	Male	Fairfield

an execution sermon, the earliest pamphlet describing the convict's criminal career, and the initial occasion for a systematic criticism of the death penalty. The long-standing capital statute for "Theft and Burglary" was a three-tier schedule of punishment that was further spelled out in 1735. The first offense involved the branding of the culprit with the letter *B* on the forehead, one ear nailed to a post and severed, and fifteen stripes on the "naked body" while tied to a post. The second offense led to another branding, the remaining ear cropped, and twenty-five stripes. The third offense mandated death.[140] Population growth and commercial expansion provided the stage on which rootless young men engaged in various forms of thievery. Officials routinely identified them as outsiders: vagrants, transients, tricksters, the Irish, and Welsh, who often bore stigmata for prior crimes.[141]

Frasier's exploits were a sign of the times. A professional criminal, his thievery was incessant, numbering dozens of instances—sometimes several break-ins per night—ranging over southern New England and nearby New York. A New Haven newspaper that tracked his activities for its readership called him "a notorious offender."[142] A half dozen times he broke jail, using smuggled tools and burning down the lockup. Well branded and without ears, he finally met his match in Fairfield, where the Superior Court ordered that "he should be loaded with chains" and guarded every night until, as the *Connecticut Courant* put it, he "was turned off" on September 7 before a huge throng.[143]

T. S. Green, the printer, sold two editions of *A Brief Account* "from his own mouth"[144] of the twenty-eight-year-old's life that were marketed on the day of execution. The pamphlet was a prototype of sensational crime literature. The cover featured a skull, an hourglass, and a candle, all images of the ephemeral nature of life. Unlike the Gothic literature that would soon emerge, *A Brief Account* was emphatically moralistic.[145] In a personal statement, the condemned felon sought "to inform my fellow men of my execrable wickedness, in house-breaking, and stealing, hope by my example and untimely end, may be a means to deter others from the like heinous iniquities." Born in "low circumstances" in Kingston, Rhode Island, his father died in the Louisburg campaign.[146] An honest but poor mother was unable to keep her son to a straight and narrow path. Illiterate and unchurched, he endured a miserable apprenticeship to a shoemaker and at age sixteen enlisted in the French and Indian War. "Extremely desirous to be rich" in a covetous time, he soon took to stealing, escapades the text abundantly details.[147] The picaresque adventures are countered with a somber finale. Frasier warns of a wanton life that dates from his juvenile apprenticeship and gives the obligatory instruction to avoid drink, swearing, and profaning the Sabbath. He is quoted as affirming the legitimacy of the death penalty, the leniency of the judicial system, and the kindness of the ministers, including two who prayed with him on the gallows. There was a four-month delay between the sentence and the execution, but during the interim the General Assembly rejected his petition for a nonlethal outcome.[148]

Yankee entrepreneurship is seen in the published execution sermon, whose preface is an advertisement for *A Brief Account*. The burden of the Reverend Noah Hobart's homily was to sanctify the death penalty. "The civil magistrate," the Fairfield minister intoned, "has a just right in some cases to inflict capital punishments, or to take away the life of a malefactor."[149] The General Assembly was correct in not commuting the sentence, he stated. Turning to the condemned prisoner, Hobart rebuked Frasier's "excessive wickedness," a sin identified in Ecclesiastes 7:17: "Thus have you, though often reproved, hardened your neck, and now you see the consequence, you are to be destroyed and that without remedy."[150] As the prisoner stood before "an endless eternity," the minister told him to accept pardon and salvation in "The Blood of JESUS CHRIST."[151]

A remarkable challenge to the ethics of the death penalty for "any species of theft" was, however, raised by an anonymous author in four full columns of the *Connecticut Courant* on August 22, some two weeks before Frasier's execution.[152] The essay was a closely argued piece that drew knowledgably upon Enlightenment thought, particularly John Locke's *Two Treatises on Government* (1689) and Marchese Cesare Beccaria's *On Crimes and Punishments* (1764). "Penal laws . . . ," the Italian nobleman wrote, "are still so imperfect, and are attended with so many unnecessary circumstances of cruelty in all nations, that an attempt to reduce them to the standard of reason must be interesting to all mankind."[153]

The anonymous essayist posited that natural law, social compact theory, and scripture provided no rational basis for the execution of theft. "The community therefore, as they can have no power but what they receive from individuals have no right to take our lives from us for the crime aforesaid, either with our consent, or without it," he stated.[154] Beccaria's sentiment was similar, for he found it absurd to make "a sum of money equivalent to a man's life."[155] The essayist, however, was not a complete abolitionist. He found that natural law and the Hebrew Bible sanctioned execution for murder. "Whereas each individual in a state of nature, had a right to destroy the murderer," he reasoned, "they now give up this right to the community, that the community may take away the life of that man who has forfeited it, and has a right to the enjoyment of it no longer." Statutes that equated theft with homicide were illogical, subverted the sense of justice, and encouraged lawlessness. He concluded: " 'Tis probable therefore, that as the number of capital crimes are increased, the instances of murder will be multiplied. For this reason the fewer capital crimes there are, the better."[156]

Although the learned argument did not benefit Frasier, the essay was a prologue to fundamental change. Through printed sermons, biographies of the condemned, and newspaper articles, dissemination of information about capital punishment widened. The transition from Puritan to Yankee provided the opening for a major revision of the death penalty statutes. In 1750, the biblical citations disappeared from the books, much as Fane recommended. Alteration of the statutes had already been occurring piecemeal. Criminal jurisprudence had become more concerned with economic than with moral crimes, and English common law crowded out Puritan practice. The last witch was hanged in 1663. Adultery was decapitalized in 1672 and incest in 1702. No one was executed for sodomy or bestiality during the eighteenth century. The 1750 capital code still included blasphemy, but the General Assembly blocked an execution in 1752, rendering it a dead letter. Juries were reluctant to hang young women for infanticide, and the year 1753 marked the last such event. Popular opinion did not support the death penalty for rape, at least for white men after 1693. Frasier's hanging for theft was a turning point in 1768. With the opening of Newgate Prison in 1773 and new concepts of retribution, theft and rape, among other crimes, were punished with incarceration. The anonymous essayist was prescient, a harbinger of Enlightenment reforms. After 1768, executions were limited in practice to homicide and racially based rape.

3

THE ERA OF NEWGATE PRISON
1773–1827

Beccaria and other writers on crimes and punishments had satisfied the reasonable
world of the unrightfulness and inefficacy of the punishment of crimes by death.

Thomas Jefferson, 1777

The punishment of murder by death, is contrary to reason,
and to the order and happiness of society.

Benjamin Rush, 1792

Beccaria's endeavor to have capital punishment abolished has had beneficial effects.
Even if Joseph II nor the French ever succeeded in entirely abolishing it, still we
have begun to see which crimes deserve the death penalty and which do not.

G. W. F. Hegel, 1821

THROUGHOUT THE Western world during the late eighteenth century, Enlightenment intellectuals challenged the death penalty. This pivotal period,
which culminated in the American, French, and Haitian revolutions, was
characterized by what one scholar has called the "inventing of human
rights."[1] Connecticut too was part of the international ferment in criminal
justice. Over the course of seven months in 1786, the *New Haven Gazette* reprinted the entire English translation of twenty-eight-year-old Cesare Beccaria's influential *On Crimes and Punishment* (1764). "Is it not absurd, that the
laws, which detest and punish homicide, should," the Milanese count asked,
"in order to prevent murder, publicly commit murder itself?"[2] Readers might
not embrace the abolition of capital punishment, as did Benjamin Rush in
Philadelphia, but since the late seventeenth century juries and officials had,
with significant exceptions, been restrictive in the imposition of capital punishment. Much of Beccaria's agenda for just laws, prevention of crime, proportionate punishment, and rehabilitation of offenders resonated with similar
sentiment in Connecticut. An editorial endorsement of the Italian reformer

in the *Gazette* instructed citizens that "a mild penal system is a political advantage," a measure of good government.[3]

The promise, but also limits, of the new humanitarian sensibility was represented by the opening in 1773 of Newgate Prison, which today in East Granby is the only remaining colonial prison in the United States. Inmates were expediently housed in the subterranean depths of an abandoned copper mine, a Dantesque innovation that did not exist at its notorious London namesake. More a holding pit than a correctional facility, Newgate nevertheless allowed for incarceration, not execution or corporal punishment, of felons. During the half century of its troubled existence, incorrigible robbers, convicted rapists, and other desperados went not to the gallows, but to prison. The hanging of Isaac Frasier, the inveterate thief, had in 1768 highlighted the need for an alternative. Over the course of these decades, the number of capital laws was significantly reduced. The stocks and pillory, the cropping of ears, branding, wearing of emblematic letters, symbolic hanging, and flogging (with three exceptions) were eliminated. By 1828, when the model penitentiary at Wethersfield opened, homicide was the only capital crime for which anyone would be executed. This era, in its concern with bodily integrity, penology, and diminution of capital punishment, was an important transition to current assumptions about criminal justice.

The Changing Legal Culture

Beccaria's influence was not the sole factor in reforming the law.[4] In the previous century, Puritan scruples with due process were a cautionary check. New England did not embrace the Bloody Code of the old country or the judicial torture of the European continent.[5] A worldlier mind-set contributed to the secularization of the Connecticut Code of Laws in 1750. The decline of biblical literalism reduced the number of hanging offenses and rendered others, such as blasphemy, moot. By the mid-eighteenth century, Yankee juries were reluctant to convict in death penalty cases, with the exception of homicide and the rape of white women by black men. Revolutionary fervor quickened the impetus for change. "The cause of America," Thomas Paine famously claimed, "is in a great measure the cause of all mankind."[6] The death penalty and corporal punishment defined corrupt monarchies, not virtuous republics. In Virginia, Thomas Jefferson in 1778 introduced "A Bill for Proportioning Crimes and Punishments," which posited that "cruel and sanguinary laws defeat their own purpose."[7] So too in the early republic the emergence of the Second Great Awakening premised on divine benevolence fostered hope for the regeneration of sinners.[8] Enlightenment thought, republican ideology, and a theology of salvation contributed to a humanitarian sensibility.[9]

An aversion to public rituals of shaming, maiming, and hanging rested on the belief that they were cruel, excessive, and debasing. For example, a deserter from the British army at New York in 1772 was convicted of burglary in Fairfield County. Officials were prepared to whip, crop, and brand him according to the law, but British General Thomas Gage protested that "such a mark of infamy and disgrace put upon him would render him unfit to be taken again into his majesty's service."[10] The legislature agreed to return him to his unit without mutilating him provided he stayed out of Connecticut. With a similar concern about violent protocols of honor among gentlemen, the General Assembly in 1779 outlawed dueling.[11]

In postrevolutionary Connecticut, three prominent figures—Joel Barlow, Zephaniah Swift, and Timothy Dwight—argued from different perspectives about the need to reform the death penalty.[12] Barlow, a deist and a Jeffersonian Republican, took the most extreme position. While in London, he wrote to the National Convention of France in 1792 urging that "the punishment of death shall be abolished." Perhaps, with his home state in mind, this lawyer observed that "punishments in modern times have lost all proportion to the crimes to which they are annexed." He called for government to correct misbehavior through "instruction" and "gentle reproach." Reflecting the revolutionary euphoria of the time, he called for the "total regeneration of society."[13]

Swift and Dwight, Federalists, did not so fully share the Enlightenment embrace of sensational psychology and the malleability of human behavior. Although prominent members of the Standing Order (Connecticut's elite), they were not diehard conservatives. The Yale-educated Swift was the state's leading jurist and the person most responsible for the major reform of Connecticut's judicial system during the period, including the separation of the courts from the legislature in the Connecticut Constitution of 1818. During 1795–1796, he published an impressive compilation of the laws with an erudite commentary in which he acknowledged an intellectual debt to Beccaria and Baron Charles-Louis Montesquieu. Instead of "sanguinary measures," Swift endorsed "the principle of punishing a certain class of crimes, by confinement to hard labor and coarse fare. For this purpose, New-Gate prison was created."[14]

Swift observed that the criminal law was currently divided into three parts. First were the capital crimes: homicide, treason, rape, sodomy, bestiality, dismemberment, and arson that involved the loss of life. He editorialized that this list was too long; he argued, "The dreadful punishment of death ought only to be inflicted on treason and murder."[15] In fact, since the Revolution, no one has been executed for treason in Connecticut. A second tier was infractions that led to the state prison, including robbery, burglary, forgery, counterfeiting, arson (without loss of life), attempted rape, perjury, and aiding escape from Newgate. The third tier was lesser offenses that resulted in fines or corporal punishment; the latter applied in effect to the lower orders who did not have pecuniary means.

Swift approved a revision in practice, but not in statute, of the bastard infanticide law that might in a rigid construction cause "an innocent woman to suffer death, who only attempted to conceal her disgrace, by concealing the death of a bastard child, which was born dead." Now in Connecticut, it was not essential to produce a witness if the appearance of a stillbirth was clear. Further mitigation of the law in practice required evidence that the infant was born alive, not simply an assumption that infanticide had occurred. Swift was concerned that the existing statute was oppressive.[16]

A grandson of renowned theologian Jonathan Edwards, Dwight was from 1795 to 1817 president of Yale, which he made a center of religious revivalism. Along with his student Lyman Beecher and his appointee Professor Nathaniel William Taylor, he sought to make Congregationalism more appealing in an age of voluntarism and rationalism, deism and Unitarianism. The New Haven theology gently opened the door to Arminianism, the doctrine that human efforts toward salvation are compatible with God's sovereignty. Dwight tentatively explained, "In my apprehension, it is never true, that the attempts of the concerned, towards the attainment of salvation, make no difference as to the event."[17] His cautious hope extended to efforts to meliorate conditions in this world.

In 1813, Dwight lectured to the Yale senior class on the question, "Ought Capital Punishments ever to be inflicted?" He praised Beccaria's contribution, but found his reasoning specious. Despite a revised soteriology, Dwight was Calvinist enough to believe that human nature was seriously flawed by original sin. He did not support, as Barlow did, the abolition of the death penalty. Although he was not specific, he appeared, like Swift, to find execution appropriate in certain situations. It was a necessary restraint on the propensity to sin. "We fear death," he preached, "because we know it is the passage to eternal punishment or endless happiness: to heaven or hell."[18] Scripture was not, however, a sure guide to criminal law unless the situations meshed, an emphatic recognition of the secularized capital code of 1750.

Where Dwight, the "pope" of Congregationalism, and Barlow, champion of Paine's *Age of Reason* (1794–1795), found common ground was surprisingly quite broad. The number of capital crimes ought to be limited, punishment must be commensurate to the crime, and correction of the criminal was imperative. The "great object," Dwight told the students, was to redeem the criminal. Current prison experiments "are not calculated to reform offenders." That was all the more reason, he stressed, "to try the experiments on the plan of humanity to the utmost." He recommended that prison officials distribute religious tracts, preach the gospel, and separate the youthful inmate from the hardened convict. With missionary zeal, he exhorted, "No expense should be spared."[19]

The General Assembly in 1773 took the initiative for reform. Following the recommendation of a committee appointed in May, the legislators that October purchased a nineteen-year lease to the isolated mines at what then was Simsbury for £60. A room fifteen feet by twelve feet was prepared at the bottom of a seventy-foot shaft into the copper mine and sealed with an iron door. Another shaft was opened for ventilation. During the day, the inmates mined the ore, and at night they descended a ladder to the subterranean depths until morning. The plan was simply to provide a secure place for long-term incarceration for which the county jails were not designed. Sequestration at Newgate was "in lieu of the infamous punishments in divers cases now appointed."[20] Those convicted of burglary, robbery, counterfeiting, and horse stealing, all economic crimes, might be sentenced to hard labor of no more than twenty years at Newgate. Except for the last offense, a second conviction, at the court's discretion, might be for life. This provision replaced the death penalty for a third conviction of burglary and robbery.[21]

What is missing from the scant records is any mention of rehabilitation, which Barlow and Dwight later emphasized. There were at first no chaplains or Bibles distributed. The criminal was removed from society to "a public gaol and work house." A "master" with three assistants was hired by the colony to keep the prisoners "profitably" at work. The recalcitrant or unruly might be placed in fetters and shackles or be whipped no more than ten times. These punishments occurred entirely within the prison, where such a spectacle would not coarsen public morals. The colony employed overseers to audit the balance sheets and establish regulations for running the institution. They were also responsible for providing food, clothing, and tools as well as instruction in mining to the inmates. Frugal Yankees planned to have convict labor pay for financial outlays, which proved to be elusive.[22]

Besides being grim, conditions at Newgate for the first decade were far from regular. Over a ten-year period, one-half of the inmates escaped and prisoners torched the facility three times. The first inmate escaped shortly after detention, establishing a precedent of jail breaks. Air shafts were secured, blockhouses erected, stockades mounted, and armed guards employed, but the prison remained far from secured. The situation became even more perilous with the confinement of Tories and British prisoners of war during the Revolution. In the spring of 1782, twenty-eight men, mostly Tories, overpowered guards, killed one, and fled. That fall, after major arson during another breakout, officials closed the prison. The remaining prisoners were transferred to the Hartford jail, and Newgate was not reopened until 1790.[23] An Episcopalian minister, the exiled Tory Samuel Peters, sarcastically summed up Connecticut's penology in 1781: "In a few months, the prisoners are released by death, and the colony rejoices in her great humanity and the mildness of her laws."[24]

An exception to the limits on capital crimes was the expansion of treason during the Revolutionary War. With a 114-year tradition of self-government under the Charter of 1662, Connecticut Colony declared its independence in 1776 based on "the sole authority of the people hereof, independent of any king or prince whatever."[25] The "provisions state" was a logistics center for the war. Tories and British incursion created alarm. In October 1776, acts of disloyalty to the state or the United States, including destruction of war materiel, were made capital crimes.[26]

In the spring of 1783, with peace and independence assured, the General Assembly repealed many wartime measures. Treason, however, remained on the books. The social disorder and economic dislocation after the war led at the same time to a draconian revision of the code on burglary and robbery. A person convicted of committing such crimes while intending violence or threatening harm with a dangerous weapon could be sentenced to death. If a superior court found no aggravated circumstances of "personal terror, force, and violence," the defendant was subject to a whipping of not more than forty stripes and imprisonment in a workhouse or jail at hard labor for not more than ten years. For a second conviction, "he shall suffer death." No one was ever executed in this revision, but the concern for property and personal protection was clear. In addition, the temporary closure of Newgate Prison influenced the decision because incarceration was not a viable alternative.[27]

The following year, the state began a movement toward an independent judiciary. Members of the executive and legislative branches were prohib-

TABLE 15
Connecticut's Capital Crimes, 1784

1. Bestiality	7. Murder
2. Sodomy	8. Presumptive murder of bastard infant
3. False witness, life threatening	9. Rape
4. Arson, life threatening	10. Treason
5. Destroying war materiel	11. Burglary and robbery,
6. Dismemberment	life threatening

Source: *Acts and Laws of the State of Connecticut in America* (New London: Timothy Green, 1784), 18, 83–84, 179, 214, 268.

ited from simultaneously serving on a superior court. The General Assembly also created a new Supreme Court of Errors to hear lower court cases on a writ of error.[28] The separation from the legislature was not complete. Death penalty crimes were first heard in a superior court, but were now subject to appeal to this new supreme court.

The state of Connecticut first enumerated its capital crimes in 1784 (table 15). Since the last compilation in 1750, there had been no fundamental change in the transition from colony to state. The crime of destroying war materiel was a legacy of the Revolution, and the renewal of the death penalty for violent thievery was a response to postwar fears and economic dislocation. Blasphemy, which had maintained a vestigial appearance in the capital statutes, was reduced to a whipping of no more than forty stripes and one hour in the pillory.[29] For the first time since the founding of the settlements, no religious offense was a capital crime. The persistence of bestiality and sodomy, although biblically proscribed, were more commonly seen as sexual perversions, crimes against nature, than violations of divine decree.

The reopening of Newgate Prison in 1790 provided for better security and the opportunity to make incarceration an option to other punishments. The legislature appropriated a substantial £750 for the state prison, ten guards were added, and an extensive fence now enclosed the facility. A "prison house" was constructed over the mine shaft, and jail breaks were mostly frustrated. Disobedient prisoners could be placed in fetters and shackles and whipped no more than ten stripes per offense. Conviction for burglary, robbery, counterfeiting, and horse stealing was given graduated punishment: for the first offense, three years at hard labor; for the second, six years; and for the third, life imprisonment. In addition, burglary or robbery with clear "violent intentions" was no longer a capital crime, but replaced with life imprisonment at hard labor.[30] Two years later, nonlethal arson, perjury or its subornation in noncapital offenses, and attempted rape of "any Female" were for the first time punished with imprisonment. At the superior court's discretion, the sentence for rape could be for life.[31] Women convicted of an imprisonable offense were in 1793 confined in the county jail or workhouse, not the notorious Newgate.[32]

The contradiction between a lenient judicial practice and the punitive act "to prevent the destroying and murdering of bastard children" came to the fore in 1808. There had not been a conviction for this crime since the execution of Sarah Bramble in 1753.[33] Clarissa Ockry, "a black woman," of Preston gave birth on September 6, 1807, to an illegitimate male child who was subsequently found dead and whose death was allegedly concealed. The state's attorney charged her with murder under the 1699 statute.[34]

Adding to the drama, Zephaniah Swift was the presiding judge in the Superior Court at Norwich in 1808. He instructed the grand jury in Ockry's case that courts had adopted a "milder practice" in applying the capital law. Before convicting the mother of murder on the concealment of the infant's death, he explained, proof was needed to show that the child was born alive. "For it is a principle founded in humanity," he instructed, "that it is better that the guilty should escape unpunished, than to convict them by rules of evidence that will endanger the innocent." If the appearance of the corpse indicated a stillbirth, the charge of murder was dismissed. Swift emphasized that the "mild humane, and benevolent construction of the Statute has removed all grounds of complaint, and the innocent are no longer exposed to a conviction by a literal, and rigorous construction of the Statute." He nonetheless reminded the twelve men of the jury that it was "the highest duty of Government to restrain by every possible method, the crimes that result from an improper intercourse of the sexes; for they lead to the destruction of the dearest interest of Society."[35] In other words, as the law read, to avoid the "shame" of pregnancy outside of marriage, "lewd and dissolute" women might conceal the birth and death of such a child so that "it cannot be known that they were not murdered."[36]

Despite the cautionary precedents, Ockry was convicted on February 6 and sentenced to die on June 10. The trial record is incomplete, but the defendant's petition for relief to the General Assembly in May showed that her admission of infanticide was forced by prominent whites who "repeatedly urged her to confess."[37] While held in the Norwich jail, she found herself under extreme mental stress. She was under the misimpression that an illegitimate birth itself was a capital crime and that if she did not admit fully to her guilt, she would be condemned to hell. As "a woman of colour" on the margins of respectability, she was badgered to admit her guilt.[38]

Under great duress, Ockry testified that she had given live birth. The prosecutor seized on the admission to charge that she did "choke [,] stifle and smother and suffocate her said male bastard child." Having murdered the infant, she then hid the corpse "so that it might not come to light whether said Child was born alive or not but be concealed." The state's attorney applied the statute literally and closed the escape hatches that Swift had highlighted. The jury was persuaded that the letter of the law had been met.[39]

At this time, to ensure justice, capital defendants were represented by counsel. Having lost the verdict, Ockry's skilled attorney, Calvin Goddard, mounted an effective rebuttal in May to the legislature, which had the power of redress in criminal convictions. The stressful circumstances of the trial and the anguish of the defendant had apparently not permitted Ockry to present a full account of events, even to Goddard, or to summon witnesses on her behalf. The petition directly challenged the prosecution's assertions: Ockry never stated she killed the infant, but that "her child was feeble and lived but a few moments"; she denied "any direct agency in *terminating its existence*"; and she duly confessed her sins and "impudence" in a solitary delivery of what was a *"premature birth,"* but "she cannot accuse herself of deliberate murder."[40] Two days before the scheduled June 10 execution, a divided General Assembly agreed to commute the punishment to six months in jail. Having escaped the gallows, an afflicted Ockry died one week later in her cell at Norwich. Her debilitating ordeal had become a virtual death sentence.[41]

The condemned's plea that the infanticide law, contrary to its artful finesse, still exposed "the innocent to suffer with the guilty" led directly to a major revision of the oppressive 1699 law. In 1808, legislators crafted a less draconian statute for the regulation of female sexuality in which the death penalty for murder stood, but there were lesser options for punishment. The three-part revision included a fine of $150 or three months in jail for secretly giving birth to an illegitimate child; to sit on the gallows with a rope around the neck for one hour for hiding the death of a "bastard"; and death for infanticide. The law still punished women for illegitimate births, but the presumption of murder was dropped and more discretion given to juries. Infanticide was now equivalent to homicide, but no woman was ever executed under the revised 1808 statute.[42]

Furthermore, substantial changes occurred in the application of corporal punishment that had been debated three decades earlier but had been left

unresolved. During the October 1815 session of the legislature, the renowned Roger Sherman, at the direction of Governor John Cotton Smith,
headed a committee to review the criminal code. Two years earlier, the
body had discussed whether whipping for property crimes should be altered
to incarceration. Sherman agreed with the governor and most of his colleagues that "the punishment of whipping on the naked body" was "incom-
patible with the decency and humanity which could characterize the code
of a civilized state." In May 1816, punishment for blasphemy by the pillory
and whipping were abolished.[43] The committee recommended incarceration proportionate to the seriousness of the crime. Federalists and Jeffersonian Republicans now shared a broad consensus that corporal punishment
was degrading and debasing.

What provided additional momentum for reform was the conviction of
one Polly Rogers, an Indian, in 1815 at Windham for adultery. She petitioned
the legislature for redress from the punishment of branding with the letter
A on the forehead, wearing a halter with the letter A, and being whipped.
She explained that her abusive husband, Daniel Rogers, had abandoned her
some seven years earlier. After a respectable amount of time, she had assumed that he was dead and had remarried. The Windham County Superior Court, however, found the current relationship bigamous and adulterous. In keeping with the sensibility of the age, she protested the "cruel
punishment of being branded with a hot iron." She never intended to commit a crime and asked for a divorce. The legislators granted her request and
freed her from jail.[44]

The next May, the General Assembly radically altered the adultery law,
whose origins dated to 1672 when the offense was taken off the capital list.
The 1816 revision still defined adultery as that of a man with a married
woman, whereas fornication defined sexual intercourse between a married
man and a single woman. Branding, wearing a halter, and whipping were
expunged. "A punishment fixing such a mark of infamy on the person of the
offender, which could not be effaced by reformation," Swift noted, "was
properly exchanged for imprisonment in Newgate." If convicted, the man
was sentenced to the state prison and the woman to jail for three to five
years.[45] During the same session, the punishment for various felonies that
prescribed sitting in the pillory and whipping was repealed.[46]

In addition, article 2, section 10, of the new Connecticut Constitution of
1818 gave the governor "power to grant reprieves after conviction, in all
cases except those of impeachment, until the end of the next session of the
general assembly and no longer." Unlike most states, the General Assembly

TABLE 16
Connecticut's Capital Crimes, 1821

1. Treason	4. Arson, life threatening
2. Murder	5. Dismemberment
3. Perjury, life threatening	6. Rape

Source: *Stat. Conn. 1821*, 95–96.

retained the general pardoning power, a legacy of the Charter of 1662. The legislature exercised this function, including in capital cases, until creating the Board of Pardons in 1883.[47]

The last major revision of the capital code during the Newgate era occurred in 1821, three years after the adoption of the new state constitution (table 16). During the early republic, capital offenses had shrunk from eleven in 1784 to six in 1821. The former death penalty crimes of bestiality, sodomy, and destroying war materiel were now punished by incarceration at the state prison. Former capital crimes of violent burglary and robbery were made imprisonment offenses in 1790, and the presumptive murder of a bastard child was fundamentally altered in 1808. In practice, after the last execution for rape in 1817, homicide was the only offense for which anyone would be executed in the state. The creation of Newgate Prison as well as the expansion of jails and workhouses made incarceration a substitute for more extreme retribution.[48] Swift added that the Beccarian goal of the criminal code of 1821 was "to proportion the punishment according to the nature and grade of the crime, so that every man may know when he violates the law, and what punishment he is liable to suffer for it."[49]

Treason

Near the end of the Revolution, the General Assembly authorized superior courts to remove alleged traitors from military custody by a writ of habeas corpus for trial in civilian courts as the chief judge thought appropriate. Although the act was purportedly to expedite the trial of traitors, the effect was to assert the predominance of "the laws of this State."[50] In sum, a long tradition of the rule of law, republican ideals, and the availability of Newgate Prison acted to check the number of wartime executions of any type. Indeed, George Washington early in the conflict set the precedent that the use of torture and gross mistreatment of prisoners of war was a violation of the humanitarian ideals of the Revolution.[51]

Moses Dunbar is the only person ever executed for "high treason" in
Connecticut's courts. A convert to the Church of England, Dunbar was an
outspoken supporter of Great Britain, for which he was mobbed, jailed, and
forced to sign a patriotic statement. He fled to Long Island, where he accepted a captain's commission from General William Howe to recruit for
the royal army. Imprudently, he returned to Waterbury to be married and
was arrested. The Hartford County Superior Court convicted him of treason. He escaped jail, but was caught and hanged before a "prodigious Concourse" of spectators.[52] With pervasive counterrevolutionary activity near
the New York border, officials made an example of the notorious turncoat.
At Dunbar's execution on March 19, 1777, at Hartford, the Reverend Nathan
Strong preached, "The man who injures his country, and will not be restrained by considerations of duty, justice and gratitude, must be cut off
from the earth that others may be safe."[53]

Homicide

From 1773 to 1827, the state hanged a dozen people for homicide (table 17).
Except for a mixed-race girl only twelve years old, all were men. Seven of
the perpetrators were white, and five were African American, Native
American, or of mixed race. During this period, the black population was
no more than 3 percent of the total Connecticut population, and Indians
constituted less than 1 percent. The number of nonwhites hanged for
homicide is greatly out of proportion to their ratio in the general population. Although young people were convicted of capital crimes, so were
middle-aged men. Assailants and victims were all acquainted and of the
same racial composition, that is, if paired as white or nonwhite. Domestic
violence took a high toll, including men killing four wives or companions.
Five children, including three siblings, under the age of eight were murdered. Friends also attacked friends. Alcohol was involved in at least five
incidents. Revenge, anger, and rage figured in all cases except for that of
Davenport, whose purpose was robbery. No firearms were discharged;
instead, bludgeons and cutting implements were employed as weapons of
convenience.

The situations of Hannah Occuish in 1786 and Peter Lung in 1816 are
most distinct. The former is exceptional for the age of the mixed-race girl,
and the latter prompted a constitutional contest over separation of powers.
The cold-blooded murders committed by Barnett Davenport in 1780 show
how late-eighteenth-century society reacted to wanton cruelty.

TABLE 17

Executions for Homicide, 1773–1827

Name	Race	Gender	Age at Execution	Year of Execution	Weapon	Victim	Location of Crime
1 John Dennis	White	Male	Unknown	1777	Hoe	Male coworker (white)	New London
2 Barnett Davenport	White	Male	19	1780	Clubs/ arson	Five family members (white: man, woman, three children)	Washington
3 Thomas Goss	White	Male	52	1785	Ax	Wife (white)	Barkhamsted
4 Hannah Occuish	Mixed race	Female	12	1786	Stones	Six-year-old girl (white)	New London
5 Richard Doane	White	Male	45	1797	Battering	Male friend (white)	East Windsor
6 Thomas Starr	White	Male	43	1797	Knife	Male friend (white)	Middletown
7 Caleb Adams	White	Male	18	1803	Ax/knife	Six-year-old boy (white)	Abington
8 Samuel Freeman	Mulatto	Male	25	1805	Beating/ knife	Female companion (Indian)	Ashford
9 Harry Niles	Indian/ black	Male	Unknown	1807	Club	Wife (Indian)	Lisbon
10 Miner Babcock	Mulatto	Male	19	1816	Knife	Stepfather (African-American)	Preston
11 Peter Lung	White	Male	49	1816	Beating	Wife (white)	Middletown
12 George Henry Washington	Indian	Male	Unknown	1824	Beating	Wife (Indian?)	Hebron

On July 21, 1786, authorities examined the corpse of six-year-old Eunice Bolles covered by a makeshift pile of stones along the road to Norwich outside New London. Her skull was fractured, and her limbs heavily bruised, and fingerprints marked her throat. After giving a false lead, Hannah Occuish, a not quite twelve-year-old servant of mixed race, confessed the next day. The overt reason for the brutal attack was revenge because Eunice, a white girl, had gotten Hannah in trouble in June for taking the younger child's strawberries. As one observer lamented, "Such an instance of deliberate revenge and cruelty in one so young, has scarcely a parallel in any civilized society."[54]

The legal convention was that juveniles between seven and fourteen years old were, as Swift later explained, in a "doubtful period" regarding the ability to discern good and evil. Before age seven, a child was "supposed to be totally incapable of committing a crime." After age fourteen, for matters of jurisprudence a youth was an adult. In instances such as the present homicide, "the malice supplies the want of age,"[55] and "such evidence of premeditated malice" persuaded the jury to find Occuish guilty despite a plea of not guilty. The aptly named Judge Law, who presided, feared that without the threat of lethal retribution, "children might commit such atrocious crimes with impunity."[56]

The defendant's attorney, Timothy Larrabie, who was appointed by the New London County Superior Court, petitioned the General Assembly to spare Occuish's life. The burden of Larrabie's argument was that the eleven-and-one-half-year-old girl did not understand the consequences of her actions or the significance of the trial. She naively told officials that if she was not whipped, "she would do so no more." Her education was so deficient that she was "totally ignorant of a supreme being that punishes evil." Larrabie continued that she had "no other idea of death than it will free her from the service of her temporal master which hath been severe."[57] On the morning of the murder, Hannah had been fetching water for her master, while Eunice was on her way to school. Lost on her white interlocutors was that her short life was based on exploitation. Instead, what the criminal justice system understood was that Occuish was the daughter of "an Indian squaw" and an "African" who had incomprehensively murdered a white girl half her age. The General Assembly refused to commute the sentence of this dark-skinned defendant.

Twenty-six-year-old Reverend Henry Channing, a tutor at Yale, gave Occuish's funeral oration on December 20 in the new Congregational Church at New London. The young preacher confronted the question of evil in traditional, theological terms: "Wherefore has our land been thus stained with crime, which, with all its painful circumstances, it has never known before?"[58] His answer was that Occuish's brutality was "striking evidence of the depravity of human nature."[59] Channing's "indefatigable" ministry to Occuish after her conviction made her fearfully aware of her fate.[60] The girl became especially distraught when asked how long she had to live. The minister catechized her to *"Repent* and *believe* in Christ" to avoid eternal damnation. At the conclusion of the sermon, Channing addressed her directly, saying, *"Hannah,* the time for you to die is come."[61] The girl was crying, as was most of the audience. After a two-hour interlude, the sheriff, guard, and ministers walked her to the gallows behind the old meetinghouse. Eyewitnesses reported that she appeared "greatly afraid" and said little, but to thank the sheriff, part of gallows' etiquette condoning the rite of death.[62] She is the youngest person hanged in New England, if not the United States, and the last female executed in Connecticut.[63]

Within a decade, an uncannily similar murder played out with different results. In 1795, Ann Negro, the twelve-year-old slave of Samuel Clark of Pomfret, quarreled over some toys with Clark's five-year-old daughter Martha in the master's absence. With a sharp knife from the buttery, the slave girl slit the throat of the younger girl to the bone in revenge. Upon her master's return, she told him that a stranger had done the bloody deed, but she soon confessed and was jailed at Windham. A jury in the Windham County Superior Court ruled that it was "willful murder by the hand of the negro girl."[64] Unlike Occuish, Ann was whipped thirty-nine times, branded with the letter *M* on the hand, and confined to the vicinity of the jail for life. It appears that the earlier hanging of a girl precipitated an unofficial ban on the execution of females altogether.

Article 5 of the state constitution of 1818 that separated the legislature and judiciary for the first time was incongruously prompted by a drunken husband, fifty-one-year-old Peter Lung, battering his forty-eight-year-old wife, Lucy, to death. The Lungs, soused spouses with a large family of nine children in a rough neighborhood in Middletown, frequently quarreled. An inebriated Peter again turned violent in a dispute over who should prepare dinner on Sunday, July 31, 1815. The common laborer pummeled his wife, who died sometime Monday night. A jury of inquest concluded that "her death was occasioned by violence and repeated blows upon her head and body, given by the hand of her husband."[65] In lieu of the sitting superior court that had adjourned, Zephaniah Swift, now chief justice of the state's supreme court, called a special session of the superior court to hear the case at Middletown on August 29. The jury ruled on September 1 that Lung was guilty of murder, and Judge Baldwin sentenced him to hang on November 25.[66]

On September 6, the defendant petitioned the legislature for relief, including a new trial. Lung's counsel complained on several levels: that he had not had time to prepare an adequate defense, that the special court had been convened irregularly, and that procedural unfairness occurred during the trial. Agreeing that the convicted man should have the chance to produce testimony on his behalf, the General Assembly in October annulled the judgment and ordered a new trial.[67] The General Assembly in asserting its long-standing judicial oversight shunted aside the Supreme Court of Errors. The action had grave implications for the rule of law.[68]

Meanwhile, the requested second trial convened in Haddam. A grand jury on December 19 heard the same evidence and again indicted Lung for murder. Despite the assistance of four attorneys for the accused during a three-day trial with many spectators, the verdict was that Lung had killed his wife "in a scene of savage barbarity."[69] Judge Trumbull sentenced Lung to hang on June 20, 1816, for the "murder of a weak and defenseless woman."[70]

By early February 1816, Swift's angry response to the General Assembly's annulment appeared in a fifty-page pamphlet.[71] His *Vindication* was a defense of the narrator's actions and a warning against the excess of popular assemblies. Swift was outraged by the imputation that by seating a special court he "proceeded to arraign, try, convict, and sentence a man to death."[72] The rebuke was "the most painful occurrence of my life," for it suggested "usurpation, an illegal exercise of power, so flagrant as to require to be resisted by legislative interference."[73] A staunch Federalist, the erudite Swift feared the volatility of the people. At first, popular sentiment embraced the unfortunate victim, but, he wrote, "in capital cases—when the awful sentence of death is pronounced, then a sentiment of compassion begins to operate in favor of the unfortunate convict."[74] A travesty of justice, he sarcastically concluded, was "the singular result from the exercise of Legislative Benevolence."[75]

In mid-March, an anthology of letters written by Lung after his second conviction went on sale.[76] The *Brief Account of the Life of Peter Lung* marked a first in death row publication in Connecticut.[77] The compilation was purportedly written by the convict and not told to an interviewer, nor was it the genre of sin and redemption authored by a minister to instruct public morality. The text was instead a series of letters primarily to family members. Although Lung stated that they were to be read after his death, these personal letters went on sale more than two months before the June 20 execution. Intimate family relations were available for all to read, for a price. Crime literature had an entrepreneurial quality that whetted an appetite for the unseemly and salacious. The primary incentive, however, was to create sympathy for Lung's forthcoming petition to the General Assembly. Lung maintained, "If I was the means of my wife's death, I did not intend it."[78]

The chief justice's withering criticism in his *Vindication* set the tone when the General Assembly convened in May, and the reconvicted Lung unsuccessfully sought a pardon. As the June 20 execution date approached, Lung was visited in the Hartford jail by his children for a last time. Preceding the execution on Thursday at Middletown, the Reverend David Field of Haddam preached a sermon at the Presbyterian Church appropriately entitled *Warning Against Drunkenness.*[79] Turning to Lung, he scolded, "In a fit of intoxication, you inflicted upon her wounds, marks of which she carried to the grave."[80] He warned the large assembly, *"take heed then."*[81]

After the public religious exercises, "an immense crowd" gathered in the afternoon at the gallows.[82] A military escort cleared the way through as many as 12,000 people. As he made his way on foot, Lung conversed with chaplains and said that he was ready to die. He ascended the gallows, and a final prayer was offered. Dressed in grave clothes, he told the spectators to learn from his example and bid them farewell. An eyewitness observed, "No trembling appeared in his voice or limbs, and when the platform was struck from under him, he expired without a struggle."[83]

Lung was the next-to-last white man in Connecticut executed in public. It was clear in 1816 that the traditional venue was outdated and inappropriate; the spectacle was brutalizing and degrading, incongruous for a republic. Swift's caution, grounded in the high Federalist perspective of the well born and able, of the volatility of popular passion is a key insight. Public opinion had become democratized, as had the politics represented by the triumph of the Toleration Party in 1817.[84] As time passed, sympathy for the unfortunate murder victim passed to the fate of the condemned perpetrator. Lung's adjudication became a media event covered widely in newspapers. For the first time, a series of pamphlets competed for attention: Swift's *Vindication,* Lung's *Brief Account,* and Field's *Warning Against Drunkenness.* Field's work had a secular addendum, "Sketch of the Life and Hopeful Repentance of Peter Lung," that provided readers with a riveting account of the criminal up to his last moments.

Hundreds attended the funeral of Lucy Lung, and thousands watched the "affecting execution" of her husband.[85] Newspapers reported on "the deep interest the public mind had taken in the event."[86] As Swift had anticipated, there was empathy for the condemned criminal. The *Middlesex Gazette* noted, "The behavior of the unfortunate sufferer on this trying occasion was such as to attract the tenderest sympathy of every rational behavior."[87] The middle-aged murderer appeared resigned, repentant, and respectful. The military "preserved the strictest disciple and decorum," and the law officers "performed their painful duty with all that tenderness and precision which the occasion demanded."[88] All had gone well on the surface, yet the military was present to preserve order. There was no riot, but what of the carnival atmosphere, with families in attendance with children and vendors selling refreshments on a fine day in June? A footnote, the very last words, in the "Sketch of the Life," raised the unsettling question, "How he would have lived had he been reprieved, is unknown."[89] The execution forestalled the possibility of rehabilitation, a position that would soon gain greater currency. What was directly answered in 1818 in reaction to Swift's *Vindication* was that, for the first time in Connecticut's history, a formal separation of the legislature and judiciary was incorporated in the new constitution. a constitution that also disestablished state-supported religion.[90]

During the American Revolution, Barnett Davenport, a teenager, became the first to kill purposefully by arson. His home invasion was, in the words of the *Connecticut Courant,* "a series of the most horrid murders, ever perpetrated in this country, or perhaps any other."[91] Newspapers from Boston to Philadelphia carried news of the mayhem committed on February 3, 1780, on an unsuspecting family in Washington, Connecticut.

After his arrest and commitment to the Litchfield jail on February 10, Davenport, a nineteen-year-old deserter from the Continental Army during the American Revolution, confessed to the deeds. The publication of his account is the first narrative of a capital offender in Connecticut told ostensibly in his own voice. An unknown jailhouse interviewer rendered the sensational story with public consumption in mind. The reader learns that the perpetrator was a wayward youth who had committed numerous thefts from an early age. He was prone to violence: he had planned to kill one employer, and while in the army he had burned down a looted house. Davenport, who had been born in New Milford, had taken a job as a hired man under a fictitious name with Caleb Mallery and his wife. As Davenport admitted, "I determined upon the murder of Mr. Mallery and his family, the first opportunity and this, merely, for the sake of plundering his house: without the least provocation or prejudice against any of them."[92]

After the Mallerys and their three grandchildren went to bed for the night, Davenport set his plan in motion. He repeatedly bludgeoned the sleeping grandparents and a seven-year-old girl who was in the same room until they were mortally wounded. Two other children, ages six and four, awakened in fear in another room. He ordered them to stay in bed. Meanwhile, he stole money and other items. To obscure the crime, he set the house ablaze, a fire that burned to death the two youngest children. Despite an effort at flight with assistance from his brother, he was soon apprehended.

There were two major ways that society came to terms with the horrific murders of five people in one family. One was the published confession of the criminal, which appeared in the newspapers. This *Brief Narrative* told of Davenport's dysfunctional family, impiety, and lack of education that contributed to, as one commentator put it, one "young in years, but old in crimes."[93] For a life of "wickedness," Davenport affirmed, "I must (most justly) suffer a violent death, and I greatly fear, everlasting burning, horror and despair."[94]

On April 25, Davenport was convicted on capital charges to which he pled guilty. On May 8, officials in Litchfield hanged him in public before a large crowd. The *Connecticut Gazette* at New London exhorted, "May the sordid life, the unheard crimes, and fearful end, of this poor wretched malefactor, be a warning to parents and children."[95]

Davenport's brother Nicolas, who assisted his escape, was compelled to sit on the gallows for an hour with a rope around his neck, was whipped thirty-nine times, and was sentenced to ten years of confinement at Newgate Prison. In addition, he probably was forced to watch his brother's execution.[96]

In the dozen executions for homicide during the period, no victims were strangers to their assailants. Such was the situation in the African American household of Miner Babcock, a nineteen-year-old "mulatto" at Preston. An ongoing dispute with his stepfather, London Babcock, led the youth on October 11, 1815, to stab the older man seven times, partially disemboweling him. Although he initially denied involvement and hid the knife, the younger Babcock maintained that he was protecting his mother and that the situation was manslaughter. The New London County Superior Court appointed the underage defendant a guardian to secure his interests, and he was eventually found guilty. A local newspaper reported that on June 6, 1816, at Norwich the youth was "launched into eternity" as "several thousands witnessed the awful spectacle."[97]

In this same period, spousal violence was high, with men killing five female intimates. Samuel Freeman, a twenty-five-year-old itinerant of African and Indian parentage, was accused of murdering Hannah Simmons, a recent Indian companion, on May 12, 1805, at Ashford. According to a jailhouse interview, they had quarreled. Her battered corpse with deep stab wounds to her jugular veins was discovered in a pasture under circumstances that implicated her companion. Despite claims of innocence, a jury found Freeman guilty of murder. He denied that he had intentionally killed Simmons, but confessed to a variety of shocking sins, including sexual promiscuity, attempted bestiality, striking Simmons, and the beating of his pregnant wife, who, as a probable result of the abuse, had miscarried and subsequently died. Although great concern was shown with observing the rule of law, no non-white testimony, except for the defendant, was solicited. Clergy, cavalry, and infantry accompanied Freeman to the gallows erected adjacent to the Windham courthouse. After he prayed for divine pardon before a "large assembly," he "was launched into the eternal world."[98]

The penultimate public execution in Connecticut was for wife murder. The Tolland County Superior Court found that a patriotically named George Henry Washington, an Amerindian, had beaten his wife to death in Hebron on March 19, 1824. He denied that he killed her, but eventually confessed. There was no appeal to the General Assembly. After the ritualistic sermon on June 1, a company of light infantry and cavalry escorted the condemned man to the gallows erected not far from the Tolland courthouse. A "vast concourse" of 10,000 spectators observed what a newspaper described as the stereotypical "proud spirit and stout heart of an Indian." Washington defiantly thanked no one, clergy or sheriff, as was customary. Despite the multitude, the hanging concluded with "perfect regularity," and "no unfortunate incident occurred."[99]

Alcohol was an instrumental factor in at least four homicides during this period. Drinking hard liquor throughout the day at home, the tavern, and work was routine in preindustrial America. A drunken quarrel in East Windsor on July 4, 1796, between two friends from Scotland, Richard Doane, a stonecutter, and Daniel McKiver, a shoemaker, led to the former pounding the latter to death. Doane denied that he was guilty of willful murder. He was, however, a forty-five-year-old itinerant with an unsavory reputation. In a final message before the hanging on June 10, 1797, Reverend Strong warned from the steps of the new statehouse, "Almost every violence that takes place in civilized society, and family unhappiness may be traced to intemperance as their cause."[100] Upward of 10,000 people at Hartford watched as the scaffold was dropped under Doane. One commentator ruefully reflected, "Had this man, in due time, received the correction of the work house, it might have saved him from the halter."[101]

Homicide and Mental Competency

Although substantial questions about mental competency were raised in two murder trials during this period, both times the defendants were hanged. Thomas Goss, a fifty-two-year-old father of six, in the early morning on February 17, 1785, at Barkhamsted split open his wife's head with two ax blows as she slept with three young children, including a babe at her breast. The father carried two of the blood-smeared children to a neighbor's house, where he expected to be commended for his deed. He maintained that his wife had been a witch possessed with the spirit of the devil and that he had been directed by a band of angels who persuaded him that the children be spared. Despite "wild opinions" and a plea of insanity, a Litchfield County Superior Court jury found him "guilty of willful and premeditated murder."[102]

For several reasons, Goss was not found non compos mentis. The crime was horrific domestic violence that evoked strong emotions, including retribution. Judge Law in pronouncing sentence was through "delicacy of sentiment" reduced to tears.[103] Although Goss denied rumors that he had committed other murders, including one of his own children, he was tainted by an unsavory reputation. Most of all, as a newspaper report put it, "it is difficult to determine whether he is insane or not."[104] At times, Goss seemed very eccentric, but otherwise he had worked his middling farm and attended church in a regular fashion. One observer indicated a pattern of behavior that slipped in and out of madness. Goss had appeared "irrational" before trial, but after the verdict "was very composed for a considerable time." Three weeks before the execution, Goss acted like a "deluded wretch." He announced that he was the brother of Jesus, and he abused the clergy and refused to listen to the final sermon. His last words on November 7 at the gallows were that divine intervention would prevent his hanging, a prophecy that the sheriff soon disabused.[105] The evidence indicates that officials hanged a madman.

A grisly murder on September 13, 1803, at Abington raised similar questions about the sanity of the perpetrator. Caleb Adams, eighteen years old, killed Oliver Woodward, age six, with whom he lived. Reuben and Cynthia Sharpe, a childless couple, had taken the boys in because both had deceased parents. Adams resented the younger boy, who was a more recent addition to the household. After incidents in which the young Oliver antagonized Adams, the older youth lured the child to the woods, bashed his head in with an ax, and slit his throat with a knife. The bloody implements were left next to the corpse. Adams fled to an uncle's house, where he soon confessed.[106]

Various reports offered different perspectives on the assailant's motivation. One newspaper account described Adams as "a strange child" with "capacities of his mind . . . not equal to lads in general of his age."[107] Another observer concluded, "In none of the powers of the understanding was he deficient." This assessment maintained that the defendant was instructed by an "evil advisor" "to pretend to be ignorant and stupid" so as to escape punishment. If Adams were engaged in a ruse, it did not work. His words— "After I determined to kill him I never once thought of any thing, but how I should do it; I did not think of the consequences to myself"—convinced the jury that the defendant was not a simpleton but a malicious murderer.[108] No pardon was forthcoming from the General Assembly.

In the late morning of November 29, the day of execution, a crowd of 10,000 gathered outside the courthouse at Windham for the religious service. Elijah Waterman, pastor of the local church, spoke of the condemned youth's difficult upbringing: "Few ever commit capital crimes, but those, who from want of family instruction and proper restraint, have their consciences easily defiled, by lesser sins, till by degrees being hardened, they give loose to all the corruptions of the heart."[109] Later, on the scaffold, the Reverend Moses Welch of Mansfield invoked the divine declaration, "*Whoso sheddeth man's blood, by man shall his blood be shed.*"[110] A penitent Adams was baptized and kneeled to pray twice on the gallows. With a final ministerial message of Christian redemption, "the criminal was launched into eternity."[111] Observers declared the crowd "very orderly and solemn."[112]

Other juries found defendants accused of homicide not guilty by reason of insanity. The clergy and physicians played some role, but community standards were uppermost. The circumstances of the case, courtroom arguments, and composition of the jury also affected judgments. A man "disordered in mind" in 1778 at Wallingford shot to death Moses Tyler, but was not convicted of a capital crime.[113] A mother in "a fit of lunacy" killed her three young children and attempted suicide in 1779 at Killingworth. She "was confined to prevent her destruction," but not prosecuted.[114] Elisha Witter of Preston in 1781 "in a fit of distraction" killed his sister, her infant, and his own child." The Superior Court at Norwich acquitted him of the crime because he was "likely to remain delirious to the day of his death." Witter was kept "closely confined" and maintained by his father.[115] Anna Gilbert of Derby in 1813 killed her infant, but she was not convicted in the New Haven

County Superior Court.[116] The determination of who was irrational was not arbitrary, but it was ambiguous.

What to do with the criminally insane posed additional problems. An increased concern to monitor "lunatics and other Insane Persons, who are dangerous and unfit to go at large," was the subject of a 1793 statute.[117] The law was prompted by the acquittal of Ezekiel Case in the Superior Court at Hartford. Case was a hired man who worked in the shoemaking shop of the Ackley family in Windsor. On July 20, 1792, without warning, he killed his proprietor's three-year-old daughter with hammer blows to the head. A number of witnesses testified that Case had been "in a state of insanity for a number of years."[118] That October, the General Assembly charged a committee "to prepare a bill for the disposition of lunatics acquitted of murder." Legislators ordered town selectmen to confine the "dangerous" insane to a "suitable place" such as the county jail.[119] The 1793 law was repealed, probably because of town protests over the cost, four years later. In effect, what happened was that the violently deranged were closely confined and chained in homes and outbuildings. It would be decades before the state developed a systematic policy on housing the criminally insane.[120]

Rape

Three African Americans were executed for rape during the 1773–1817 period (table 18). All the victims were white girls and women. The concentration of black men hanged for rape reflected the profound racial tension of the times.

The era of the American Revolution brought to the fore the contradiction between freedom and slavery. On the eve of the Revolution, Connecticut had the largest number of African Americans in New England, an underclass of 6,500 people (about half of whom were enslaved) in a population

TABLE 18
Executions for Rape, 1773–1817

Name	Race	Year of Execution	Victim	Place of Execution
1. Joseph Mountain	Free black	1790	White, age 13	New Haven
2. Anthony	Free black	1798	White teenager	Danbury
3. Amos Adams	Free black	1817	White, married	Danbury

of 190,000 whites. The Reverend Levi Hart of Preston in 1774 scolded a Farmington congregation, "Who can count us the true friends of liberty as long as we deal in, or publicly connive at slavery?"[121] In the same year, the General Assembly passed an "Act Prohibiting Importation of Indian, Negro, or Molatto [sic] Slaves" into the colony.[122] Like other New England states, Connecticut provided for gradual manumission in 1784, but chose not to enact entire abolition a decade later. Dwight, then president of Yale, explained the legislature's reluctance: "It is conceded to be *morally wrong*, to subject any class of our fellow creatures to the evil of slavery, but asserted to be *politically right, to keep them* in such subjection."[123]

After 1800, white complaints about dissipated and dangerous blacks were common. Black rapists in Connecticut were a local example of horrific, racial violence in Haiti during the 1791–1803 period. As the number of slaves declined to 310 in 1810, an effort to restrict free blacks mounted. The legislature in 1814 and the constitution of 1818 limited suffrage to "free white male persons."[124] From 1773 to 1827, apartheid in the larger society played out in the criminal justice system, particularly in executions for rape and incarceration in Newgate.[125]

A jury in New Haven County Superior Court "immediately" found that Joseph Mountain, "a transient Negro man," did "ravish and carnally know" thirteen-year-old Eunice Thomson "against her will and without her consent" on May 26, 1790. She was the younger of two sisters whom Mountain had attacked on a thoroughfare two miles outside New Haven. He pleaded not guilty, but eleven witnesses, including the teenaged sisters, testified against the defendant. He had lingered at the scene, yelling abuse at the victim's rescuers. Mountain was soon apprehended and "heavily ironed" in jail.[126] He petitioned the General Assembly for commutation from the August decision that sentenced him to death on October 20. The memorial challenged the "propriety of capital punishment" for rape because it was not "expressly warranted by the laws of God." Instead of death, the petition raised several alternatives: a life sentence at Newgate, to be sold abroad (a violation of state law at the time), or "even submit to be castrated than to face death." The legislature demurred.[127]

The Reverend James Dana of New Haven delivered an execution sermon that was a classic statement for the death penalty.[128] He noted, "The excision of a member of society can be justified only for crimes of *magnitude*." He agreed with reformers that theft should not have the same punishment as murder. "It is a presumptive evidence of the wisdom and lenity of our penal laws, of the just sense our legislators have of the rights of the subject, and the importance of life," he continued, "that capital punishments are very rare with us."[129] International consensus was, however, that murder, treason, and rape were capital crimes. The latter offense was necessary "to protect female honor from violence." Furthermore, Dana posited, "It is *unsafe* and *dangerous,* and therefore *unfit* that such an offender should live" and that "life imprisonment was incommensurate for the morally depraved whose atrocious acts cannot be "cured nor endured."[130] Mountain was such a "hardened and audacious" offender, a career criminal, that the minister concluded that morning with the prescription, "If this spectacle of human depravity and misery should prove a restraint to others from committing any such evil it will not be exhibited in vain."[131] That Wednesday afternoon, 10,000 people watched the execution.[132]

Shortly afterwards, the life story of Mountain appeared for sale,[133] and an extensive readership clamored for the pamphlet. David Daggett, then a young New Haven lawyer and later chief justice of the Connecticut Supreme Court, compiled the account based on interviews with the condemned man. Like Davenport's *Confession* a decade earlier, the sensational story was told in the voice of the criminal. Daggett compassionately directed that profits proceed to the "unhappy" victim. *Sketches of the Life of Joseph Mountain, A Negro,* a substantial and sophisticated pamphlet, marks the coming of age of the death row testimonial as a genre in Connecticut.[134] The account provided an intimate look at depravity, the underside of Christian civility in the new republic.

Daggett's endeavor was undoubtedly spurred by the popularity of *A Narrative of the Life of William Beadle.*[135] Beadle was a prominent Wethersfield merchant who in the hard times of 1782 methodically killed his wife and four daughters and then himself rather than face economic humiliation. The orthodox attributed the "horrid massacre" to the perpetrator's deviant deism. The many editions of Beadle's *Narrative* with morbid illustrations and grim poetry represented a public fascination with monstrous, moral perversion, the leitmotif of the Gothic murder mystery such as the novels of Charles Brockden Brown during the 1790s.[136]

Two other African Americans were hanged for rape, both in Danbury, which marked the only time public executions occurred there. In the case of Anthony, newspapers characteristically highlighted the racial dimension in reporting that a "negro man" raped a "young white woman."[137] The crime occurred on March 7, 1798, on a road in Greenwich in a chance encounter late at night. The assailant and victim apparently were strangers. The Fairfield County Superior Court sentenced Anthony, who was about twenty-five years old, to hang. Anthony had been born to a free, but poor, mother on Long Island; there is no mention of his father. At age twelve, he had been hired out. Unschooled and unchurched, he had moved to Greenwich, where he "spent too much of his time idly with people of his color."[138] He was intoxicated on the night of the assault. Illiterate and poor, he asked for a commutation to life imprisonment at hard labor at Newgate. Unable to write his name, he signed the petition with a mark. The legislature denied his request.

A large crowd gathered for the execution on November 8. The Reverend Timothy Langdon, the local pastor, preached to an overflowing congregation "to pity and pray for the poor criminal" whose hope was for repentance.[139] The execution was just retribution for a life that was "impenitently disobedient and flagrantly pernicious."[140] In the afternoon, another minister addressed the mass of spectators at the scaffold that had been erected on the outskirts of town. The Reverend J. Blatchford of Bridgeport explained, "It is a plain case that the only principle wicked men have of forbearing at any time to evil things is the dread of impending punishment."[141] The sheriff hanged Anthony, whose one named tagged his lowly status.[142]

The last person hanged for rape in Connecticut was twenty-eight-year-old Amos Adams. The *Connecticut Courant* reported that on August 29, 1817, at Weston "a black fellow" committed "the hellish crime of rape." The "fiend" had carried out the "savage deed" on Lelea Thorp at night in her home while her husband was away.[143] In contrast to his earlier antislavery stance, Swift, who presided at the trial, castigated Adams as representative of his people. African Americans were "marked by idleness, dissipation, disorderly and insolent behavior and by the constant commission of petty offenses." Pointing to Adams, he observed that rapes "are commonly committed by men of your color." He warned, "Unless [African Americans] can be checked in their career of vice, there is great reason to apprehend, that the community will be compelled, in self defense, to establish special regulations, to restrain, to control, and to govern them."[144]

The execution sermon on November 13 by the Reverend William Andrews of Danbury further commented on the relationship between race and crime. Andrews noted that a "few" African Americans were "virtuous members of society," but "the rest are engaged in every evil work."[145] He noted accurately that one-third of prisoners at Newgate were black and that one black rapist had already been hanged at Danbury. He ascribed these dire statistics to the imperative for a white man's burden. "There is not any benevolent society to which I could more heartily lend my feeble support," he instructed, "than to an association for the purpose of reforming the morals and improving the condition of blacks."[146] Although Andrews's assessment was less harsh than Swift's, both saw a racial caste system as inevitable.

In addition, Andrews exhorted authorities to suppress vice, which was epidemic in the black community. He warned, "How easy is the transition from fornication to adultery, and from adultery to the crime for which life must be taken!"[147] The biblically named Adams was the epitome of the "sinner" with "depraved inclinations."[148] For black and white, however, "the blood of Christ cleanseth from all sin."[149] With faith in the atonement, the condemned rapist shall pass "from gallows to glory," Andrews preached to an overflowing congregation.[150]

Adams wept as he listened. He sat in a pew in the packed meetinghouse with a halter around his neck and a white cap of execution on his head. During confinement, he had confessed to an attempted rape in Northfield, Connecticut some time earlier. In a procession with two military companies marching in step to a fife and drum, he walked to the execution site at the edge of town. A crowd estimated at 15,000, the largest to ever watch such an event, had started to arrive the previous night. Refreshment stands catered to their needs. Some spectators climbed trees for a better vantage point. Adams knelt at the foot of the gallows for a momentary prayer and unsteadily ascended. Shortly after his arrival at 3 p.m., the platform dropped. After an interval, the sheriff cut the rope with a sword, and the corpse was removed.[151]

Three convicted rapists, including an African American, had their sentences commuted. Their circumstances are a counterpoint to those hanged. James Gibson has the dubious distinction of being the only man castrated for rape and, with Negro Barney (emasculated in 1744 for genital dismemberment of a white boy), of being the only people punished with sexual mutilation for crimes. The Superior Court at Hartford in March 1783 found Gibson, a twenty-two-year-old white deserter from the British navy, guilty of committing "carnal copulation" on a Mrs. Hubbard "against her consent" on December 27, 1782. The complainant was described as a sixty-year-old Middletown "matron of most virtuous character."[152] The sailor had accosted her while she was walking alone during the day on the same road as he was. Gibson appealed the death sentence. He challenged whether there was "sufficient proof" for conviction. At the May session, the General Assembly commuted the white man's punishment to castration. Newgate Prison was shut down from 1783 to 1790, so incarceration may not have been considered an option.

Castration was excoriated in the press. The *Connecticut Courant* applauded the legislature's decision to discharge the death sentence as an "act of kindness" because "the evidence was so full as not to admit any doubt to his guilt." The editors warned, however, that physical mutilation was in keeping with the "conduct of Asiatic Princes," not "a free, sovereign, and independent state." The newspaper continued, "We never can, as free people, be reconciled to their modes of execution."[153] The excision must have occurred in private, for there was no further press account. Sheriff Williams recorded that he "caused the commutation of punishment therein mentioned to be executed."[154] If the emasculation of Negro Barney was followed, Gibson endured a double testiclectomy.

A landmark occurred in May 1805 when the General Assembly mitigated the death sentence of convicted rapist Eli Lyon to hard labor for life at Newgate. The Fairfield County Superior Court in January had found that the transient Lyon, who pleaded not guilty, had ravished Mrs. Jerusha Ferris of Newtown on September 13, 1804. Lyon had a history of derangement, but the victim had testified that the assailant had acted with "reason and cunning."[155] The commutation appears prompted by questions about the defendant's mental competency. In 1819, the legislature granted a petition to free Lyon from incarceration because he "now is in a state of mind little, if any, superior to that of an idiot." After commitment to Newgate, he had rapidly declined. Reduced to an "object of pity," the legislature had rejected a similar memorial the year before, but now freed him to live with his brother in New York under a hefty $2,000 bond and the stipulation that Lyon never appear again in Connecticut.[156]

The reluctance after 1817 to hang rapists, even African Americans, is seen in the commutation in 1822 of Henry Wilson, a transient. Newspapers highlighted that a "black man" had committed the "unnatural crime of rape" on November 19, 1821, "under the most aggravated circumstances" on a "white woman," Mrs. Deborah Webb of Danbury.[157] As a night visitor seeking lodging, Wilson took advantage of the husband's broken leg to get in bed with the couple. After a "terrific struggle," a newspaper luridly recounted, "he finally committed the horrible crime, which his death alone can expiate."[158] Unable to agree initially on a verdict, a Fairfield County Superior Court jury found him guilty.

The illiterate, who pleaded not guilty, petitioned the legislature for mitigation of a death sentence impending on August 1 to life imprisonment. There was "considerable debate" over "some doubts" about the evidence. The alleged rape had occurred in the dark. The defense maintained that another Negro may have been the culprit. In addition, there was no wound on Wilson's face that the victim said she had inflicted. She also charged that a stain on Wilson's shirts was her menstrual blood, which the accused rebutted was tobacco juice. Furthermore, the petition raised the canard, whether accurate or not, that "the character of the said Deborah Webb both as to truth and chastity is at least questionable."[159] The General Assembly in May granted Wilson's request not to hang him.[160] Other states, including neighboring Rhode Island, had decapitalized rape, and within a decade Connecticut would join them. The legislature in 1826, however, rejected Wilson's memorial to free him from Newgate despite his declaration of "I am not guilty." Nine years later, the General Assembly released him after he served thirteen years in prison with good conduct.[161]

Bestiality

In New Haven in 1662, William Potter was the last person to be hanged in Connecticut for the offense of bestiality. As capital crimes except for homicide were eliminated, a conviction for bestiality anachronistically occurred in 1799 in the Litchfield County Superior Court. A dearth of documentation does little to clarify a bizarre situation. Gideon Washburn, an octogenarian farmer, was found guilty in August 1799 of some half dozen acts of "carnal copulation" with cows and mares over the previous five years. Chief Justice Root, who presided, found "the awful sentence of death" justly merited. The distinguished jurist expressed disgust with the "brutal lust" that was "beyond the natural force" of the defendant's advanced years.[162]

Washburn, eighty-four years old, petitioned the General Assembly for a pardon or postponement of the impending October execution. A violation of law occurred, the defense argued, because "no *two* witnesses testified to any one fact, and there was not any corroborating evidence." In addition to pleading not guilty, the defendant was characterized as "very infirm in mind and body" and "debilitated and deranged."[163] The idea that a senile man copulated with livestock seemed preposterous. The jurors, judge, and legislators were, however, persuaded otherwise. One can only speculate about the larger community context. The General Assembly did postpone the execution from October to January. One week before the January 17, 1800, execution, Washburn's children visited the inmate on Friday evening. The jailer found him "stupid and insensible" in the morning. He died on Sunday without gaining consciousness, five days before the scheduled hanging. Whether the timely demise was natural or, as the local newspaper put it, caused by "criminal or desperate means" remains "mysterious."[164] There were those in Litchfield who were convinced that his children brought him laudanum, by which he cheated the hangman.[165]

The Limits of Newgate Prison

The state prison provided an alternative to hanging, corporal punishment, and shaming. The pivotal transition is represented by the treatment of the "notorious" John Brown, a habitual thief and fugitive.[166] A bit of doggerel captures the moment in 1769:

> Before the Bar, poor John was had,
> To hear his sentence—good and bad
> When from the Judge's mouth we hear,
> His sentence was to lose an Ear. . . .
> His sentence likewise to be stript,
> And on the naked body whipt.
> Then branded with the Letter B,
> That every One may plainly [see]
> Burglary, the heinous Crime,
> For which he suffers at this time.[167]

An itinerate immigrant, Brown, twice cropped and double branded, was condemned to death at age twenty-two for a third case of housebreaking in 1772. The General Assembly in October commuted his sentence to imprisonment at Newgate. Despite Brown's blatant defiance of the law, the General Assembly was, four years after the execution of Isaac Frasier, not willing to hang another "burglarian."[168]

Similarly, the New Haven County Superior Court in 1789 sentenced arsonist Joseph Dickerman to a life term for attempted murder.[169] Moses Johnson found himself incarcerated at Newgate for life in 1794 for the attempted rape of two of his daughters.[170] Eighty-seven-year-old Prince Mortimer, a slave captured in Guinea, spent his last days in state prison for the putative poisoning of his master in 1811.[171] Legislators in 1825 mitigated Theresa Mansfield's capital conviction for the murder of her spouse to imprisonment at Newgate, where she was one of few women housed.[172] In 1825, seven inmates were serving life terms at Newgate, including sixteen-year-old David Jackson Jr. of Norwich for bestiality, which four years earlier was a hanging offense.[173]

Incarceration spared inmates from the gallows and various physical indignities. Newgate was, however, a hellhole. "I cannot get rid of the impression," Edward Kendall, an English traveler observed in 1807, "that without any extraordinary cruelty in its actual operation, there is something very like cruelty in the devise and design."[174] During a twelve-hour work day, convicts were heavily ironed with handcuffs and leg fetters. While making nails at the forge, they were chained at the neck. Pork and beef were thrown on the floor of the smithy; the meat was washed and cooked in the water that cooled molten iron. At night, prisoners descended seventy feet down a ladder of the old mine shaft to subterranean cells, where they slept on wooden berths lined with straw. Kendall concluded, "If it be to reform, it is one of the weakest of all human projects; if to punish, it is one of the most barbarous."[175]

In 1810, a legislative committee investigating the state prison concluded that "it is difficult materially to amend a system radically wrong." The committee found Newgate "universally filthy and afflicted with vermin" and recommended a state workhouse, as had another report four years earlier, and new prison.[176] A parsimonious General Assembly postponed action. Other voices, including the *Connecticut Courant,* excoriated those soft on "monsters in vice." As the editors wrote in 1815, "We hope to hear no more regret expressed that we have such a place of confinement as Newgate—and that while it is recollected that none suffer there, but those guilty and depraved wretches who commit the very worst crimes, and the grossest outrages, no exertions will be made from mistaken notions of humanity to substitute a milder punishment."[177] That same year, another legislative committee headed by the august Roger Sherman concluded that there was a pressing need to remove those convicted of lesser infractions from the hardened criminals at Newgate. Sherman called for the need of "proportioning punishments to crimes—conduce to the better management, both in point of economy and humanity, of Newgate prison—and in various other ways subserve the interest of the State, and the important ends of justice."[178] Disagreement among legislators again blocked action.

After another failed recommendation in 1821, a comprehensive report to the General Assembly four years later boldly declared, "The Newgate prison in Granby wholly fails to answer the end for which prison discipline is intended." The committee concluded, "Rather than a school for reformation, it is in effect a seminary of vice." Not only was Newgate inefficient and inhumane, it had been running an annual deficit of $8,000. The committee recommended a new, profitable penitentiary committed to the reformation of the criminal at Wethersfield.[179] In 1826, the indefatigable prison reformer Louis Dwight seconded the commission's recommendations. "I consider [Newgate], on the whole the worst prison, except one," he wrote legislators, "which I have found in traveling about four thousand miles."[180] The state closed Newgate. Great expectations greeted the opening in 1828 of the model penitentiary at Wethersfield, including further reforms in the system of capital punishment and the first mass effort in the state to abolish the death penalty.

4

THE DEBATE OVER CAPITAL PUNISHMENT
1828–1879

Wethersfield, the smallest penitentiary in America, is the best.
Gustave de Beaumont and Alexis de Tocqueville, 1833

Since God has decided that the murderer shall be put to death, for us to
determine otherwise, is to legislate over the Law-giver of the universe.
Reverend Joseph P. Thompson, 1842

We should blot from our statute book that relic of a barbarous age,
and substitute instead therefore imprisonment for life.
Governor Thomas Hart Seymour, 1850

During the antebellum period, the first systematic debate over capital punishment occurred in the northern and midwestern states. In the Old South,
where draconian measures were essential to maintain racial subjugation,
little discussion ensued. Connecticut was no exception to the general rule.
The divide between opponents was passionate and acrimonious, reflecting
antagonistic perceptions of human nature and how to achieve the good
society. Supporters of the death penalty argued that it was essential to the
maintenance of law and order. They stressed sober Calvinist sentiments of
original sin and the divine imperative of the execution of murderers. Opponents responded that the death penalty was brutal and contrary to the Christian message of universal love. They offered the alternative of life imprisonment in the new state penitentiary for the perpetrators of violent crime.

Unlike a few states and nations that eliminated the death penalty, opponents failed to carry the day in Connecticut, but during the mid-nineteenth
century, constraints were imposed nonetheless. Capital punishment was
limited in 1846 to those convicted of first-degree murder, although treason
and arson with intent to kill remained on the books. A dozen men who
were found guilty of premeditated homicide were hanged between 1828 and

1879. After 1831, executions moved from unrestricted observation to "hanging by the neck, within the jail, or within an enclosed yard, so as to prevent public observation."[1] Rather than inspiring fear in spectators, public executions were now seen as dehumanizing and brutish. The General Assembly also commuted nearly a dozen death sentences, and a more sophisticated understanding of mental disorder kept others from the gallows.[2] Critics complained that these refinements merely allowed the process of judicial execution to occur under the guise of humanitarian reform and did not address the core issue of the state's right to impose the death penalty.[3] Central to the continuation of capital punishment were sensational murders that were increasingly well publicized, including those of two wardens and one guard at the state penitentiary. The social dislocation of the growing manufacturing sector, the influx of impoverished Irish peasants, and the Civil War also checked abolitionist sentiment. Indeed, by the 1850s, prisoners of Irish birth rivaled African Americans as the largest group (outside of native-born Protestant whites) incarcerated at the state prison.[4] For many, it seemed axiomatic that the death penalty was essential to keep the lid on a volatile society in the throes of an industrial revolution.

The Promise of the Penitentiary

The opening of the Connecticut State Prison at Wethersfield on October 1, 1828, however, reflected more hopeful, even utopian, assumptions about penology. Not only had Newgate run a total deficit of some $80,000 over the last decade, but its regimen acted, officials concluded, "to corrupt and debase the convict, rather than reclaim him." In contrast, the directors reported in 1829 that the new prison had "exceeded our highest anticipation, both as it respects [its] moral and pecuniary character."[5] In place of sullen disorder at Newgate, a British visitor marveled only a few months after the opening of Wethersfield that "such appears to be the simplicity of all parts of the system that everything has fallen into its place with the precision of habitual order."[6] Gustave de Beaumont and Alexis de Tocqueville, who inspected prisons in the United States during 1831 and 1832, offered an important distinction between Newgate and Wethersfield. "The abolition of the punishment of death was confounded in America with the penitentiary system," the young French noblemen explained. "People said—instead *of killing the guilty, our laws put them in prison, hence we have a penitentiary system.*" The substitution of incarceration for capital punishment was a necessary but not sufficient condition in penology. In other words, Newgate substituted imprisonment for the gallows and corporal punishment, but offered no program for rehabilitation. Instead, the mingling of desperadoes provided a school for crime. "It is," the inspectors continued, "further necessary, that the criminal whose life has been spared, be placed in a prison, whose discipline renders him better."[7]

Wethersfield adopted such a plan, known as the Auburn after the eponymous New York prison. Prisoners worked together during the day, but were placed in solitary confinement at night. There was supposed to be no communication between prisoners at all times. This "silent" system was a popular modification of the more severe "separate" system adopted in Pennsylvania in which inmates were completely isolated from one another. Environmental determinism was well rooted in Enlightenment thought, notably dating to John Locke's influential *Essay on Human Understanding* (1690). The penal application was intended to quarantine prisoners from evil influences and to encourage spiritual regeneration. The proverbial image of the prisoner was that of a penitent alone in a sparse cell reflecting on the Bible.

The rationale, as Beaumont and Tocqueville accurately noted, was "essentially religious," a transformation of character in keeping with the spiritual enthusiasm of the Second Great Awakening. In words that contrasted Newgate and Wethersfield, they summarized: "The inflexible severity of a uniform system, the equality of punishments, the religious instruction and the labor substituted for the system of violence and idleness, the liberty of communication supplanted by isolation or silence, the reformation of the criminals instead of their corruption; in the place of jailors, honorable men who direct the penitentiaries; in the expenditure, economy, instead of disorder and bad management." The small scale of Wethersfield allowed the superintendent and chaplain to be "thoroughly acquainted with the moral state of each individual, and after having studied his evil, they endeavor to cure it."[8] The French visitors recommended the Connecticut model for their country.

Officials in Connecticut anticipated a profitable operation, low rates of recidivism, and, in place of criminality, civility. The new institution had a utopian quality. A penitentiary was, the word suggested, a place for penance, reflection, and reform. One observer pronounced that Wethersfield "is almost the beau ideal of a perfect penitentiary."[9] The directors expected "to instruct and reclaim these men," "to restore them to society." They wished "to substitute in the treatment of these men, so far as it should be practical, the law of kindness, for that of severity."[10]

The penitentiary remains the paradigm for penology, but ominous problems soon appeared that indicated that it was not a panacea. Two years after its opening, the directors warned that the courts were flooding Wethersfield with "the idle, the intemperate, the imbecile, and the unprofitable members of society." There were more prisoners than cells, and some prisoners were doubled up. "The practice," they alerted, "is at variance with the whole system of discipline which has prevailed, and will ultimately subvert and destroy it, if it does not endanger the safety of the prison."[11] A subsequent jailbreak resulted in a murdered guard, for which two inmates were hanged. In 1833, another incident, a mutiny "approaching anarchy" among the prisoners, was attributed to maladministration.[12] A survey of 200 inmates by the chaplain in 1835 indicated profound social problems among the convicts. Only 10 owned real estate, 37 could not read, 50 could not write, 48 were African Americans, 100 did not live with their parents after age ten, 106 were urban dwellers, 107 were not natives of the state, and 150 abused alcohol.[13] There were also challenges in housing female prisoners and the criminally insane. Issues of profit, sanitation, hygiene, disease, heat, ventilation, diet, and education were endemic over the decades. Nevertheless, the crusader Dorothea L. Dix, who visited the prison several times in 1845, found that with some qualifications, "Everything is in order." Generally ignoring the social causes of crime and the limits of incarceration, she and state officials remained persistent in their commitment to individualistic change through the silent system. They were adamant, if naive, in the expectation that "in proportion as we extinguish the *terrors* of the law, we should awaken and strengthen the *control* of the *conscience*."[14]

After the Civil War, Nathan Mayer, a prison inspector, questioned the assumption of romantic reform based on moral suasion. A Jewish physician, he was not as inclined to accept the cure-all of Christian penance as Dix and other Protestants. He found that the blanket imposition of noncommunication among the prisoners created an "evil." Rather than uplifting, isolation produced "moral and mental decay," emotional breakdown caused by sensory deprivation. Convicts slept, ate, and relieved themselves in monastic cells that were eight feet by four feet wide, six-and-a-half feet high, and barred by a heavy plank door with an iron grate. One bathtub served two hundred inmates. "To keep warm," Mayer reported, "some prisoners move about constantly, having the aspect of wild beasts in cages." He recommended that antisocial feelings could be counteracted through opportunities for constructive conversation at times of instruction and recreation. He urged, in keeping with Jewish emphasis on education, schooling of the numerous illiterates. "By leaving instruction out of its prison system the State abandons one of the most powerful means of reform," he alerted.[15] In some ways, not unlike state mental hospitals and poorhouses, prisons over the course of the nineteenth century became more warehouses than places of rehabilitation. Despite naive assumptions, Wethersfield after 1828 provided an alternative to all forms of capital punishment except for premeditated homicide.

Degrees of Murder

The ideal of rehabilitation contributed to a diminution and refinement of the number of capital crimes. In 1830, the legislature made rape and dismemberment crimes punishable with life imprisonment.[16] As Governor Gideon Tomlinson observed, "Perpetual confinement, therefore, should only be inflicted in a few extreme cases, and for such high offenses as demand exemplary but not capital punishment."[17] At the same time, the General Assembly sequestered the gallows within the jail so "as to prevent public observation."[18]

An observer of the last public execution, that of Oliver Watkins in 1831, agreed, saying, "We are persuaded that executions should be done in private." His sense of "humanity and propriety" was offended by "the large number of females present." Their "refinement and delicacy" were "degraded" by such "barbarous spectacles." On the whole, the 10,000 or more spectators behaved well, encouraged by several companies of riflemen and cavalry, but as evening approached, "there were painful scenes of riot and intemperance." In the wake of a carnival atmosphere, this anonymous reporter no longer accepted the axiom of an earlier age that public executions put the fear of the Lord into sinners. Instead, he was convinced that more "evil" was done and more people were "hardened."[19]

Treason remained a capital crime, but no one was executed for the offense even during the Civil War.[20] In what was the most substantial restatement of the murder statute in two centuries, the legislature in 1846 classed murder into different levels of punishment. The legislators explained that "the several offences, which are included under the general denomination of murder, differ so greatly from each other, in the degree of their atrociousness that it is unjust to involve them in the same punishment."[21] The effect was to create legal hurdles on the path to capital punishment. As the revision stated, "willful, deliberate, and premeditated killing" and the taking of life involving "any arson, rape, robbery or burglary" constituted first-degree murder. "All other kinds of murder" were classed as second degree. First-degree murder brought the death penalty. Second-degree murder—along with arson and perjury that endangered life, dismemberment, and rape—brought "imprisonment in the Connecticut state prison during [the convict's] natural life."[22]

The jury in its verdict stipulated the degree of murder. In a refinement in 1870, the jury could find the defendant "guilty of homicide in a less degree than that charged."[23] In other words, if the jury found a second-degree murder, the defendant was spared execution. Such was the situation in the sensational trial at New Haven in 1871 of Lydia Sherman, whom the press called "the arch murderess of Connecticut" for allegedly poisoning members of her family.[24] The jury found that circumstantial evidence was not beyond reasonable doubt and thus opted for murder in the second degree. In addition, if the accused confessed, the court examined the witnesses to determine the degree of murder and sentenced accordingly.

Connecticut's Supreme Court of Errors clarified the murder statute in several noteworthy cases. In *Connecticut v. Potter* (1846), the tribunal defined what constituted an impartial jury. The situation arose over whether jurors who had read about a murder in the newspapers could be disqualified because their judgment had been unduly influenced. The high court decided: "Where a juror has a settled opinion in the case, and has declared it, he ought not to sit. But where it is a mere impression, arising from facts supposed to exist, of the truth of which he has formed no opinion, or where the opinion is upon a point so free from doubt, as to lay no foundation for a dispute, there can be no ground to infer hostility or prejudice, and so the juror must be considered indifferent."[25] Otherwise, with the abundance of journalistic coverage of murders, no citizen would qualify to sit on a jury, even if the person had not formed a set opinion. In an earlier capital case, *Connecticut v. Watkins* (1831), the court affirmed, "If testimony is competent and relevant, it must be admitted; and confidence must be put in the jury, that they will legally apply it." The defense in this case had sought to exclude the proposition that the adulterous affair of the prisoner provided a motive to kill his wife. The court disagreed because justice required the presentation of "pertinent and material evidence."[26]

The Supreme Court of Errors also clarified the process of fixing the severity of a murder conviction in *Connecticut v. Dowd*. In 1849, Solomon Dowd and Lucina Coleman challenged their conviction on second-degree murder for the fatal poisoning of Niles Coleman, the defendant's husband. Their counsel argued that murder by poison was classed by statute as one in the first degree and that the jury's verdict of the lesser offense therefore "amounts to an acquittal of the offense charged." The court unanimously disagreed, stating that "the lesser crime is manifestly included" in the greater. The justices also noted that the 1846 law explicitly empowered a jury to determine the degree of guilt, which it did. They concluded, "Such a construction operates against the greater severity" of first-degree murder. They did not "feel authorized, in the construction of a statute like this, involving the life or death of the person accused, to make an exception where the legislature made none."[27] The Supreme Court then affirmed the power of juries to convict murderers in the second degree, an option short of the gallows, even if the indictment had been in the first degree, a capital offense.

Similarly, the high tribunal in 1873 explicated the construction of "willful, deliberate, premeditated killing" that defined capital murder. The New Haven County Superior Court found one John Robert Johnson guilty of murder in the first degree for killing Johanna Hess at Meriden in 1872. The defense maintained that Johnson was a chronic alcoholic, a "dipsomaniac," whose judgment was so besotted at the time that "he is guilty of no higher crime than that of manslaughter." The Supreme Court found that the jury likely misunderstood the judge's instructions that "drunkenness does not excuse a party from the consequences of a criminal act" to mean murder in the first degree and the punishment to mean capital punishment. The bench ordered a new trial in which the jury was to weigh whether there was a deliberate intent to take life. "Intoxication is admissible in such cases, not as an excuse for crime, not in mitigation of punishment," the justices explained, "but as tending to show that the less and not the greater offense was in fact committed."[28]

Johnson appealed his subsequent conviction on second-degree murder because there was no criminal intent due to intoxication. At best, the defense claimed that "the jury could convict him of [no] crime higher than manslaughter." The Supreme Court denied a new trial this time. Although first-degree murder was defined by express malice, the justices made clear that second-degree murder was defined by implied malice that could be deduced from the circumstances of the homicide. "Intoxication, which is itself a crime against society," all the justices concurred, "combines with the act of killing, and the evil intent to take life which necessarily accompanies it, and all together afford sufficient grounds for implying malice." They concluded, "Intoxication is no excuse for crime."[29] The Superior Court had properly instructed the jury, which in turn had found malice in the circumstances of the crime that rendered the verdict second-degree murder, not manslaughter. The application of the murder statute of 1846 barred Johnson from the gallows, but not from prison.

Connecticut's Supreme Court also played a critical role in a capital crime involving the contentious issue of the insanity defense. John Andersen, known as the Wallingford murderer, was a poor and combative Swedish immigrant of questionable mental stability whom the New Haven County Superior Court sentenced to hang on April 20, 1876, for first-degree murder. The high court heard his case on appeal because "where human life is at stake, justice, as well as humanity, requires us to pause and consider." In a narrow three-to-two opinion, Justice Elisha Carpenter, who wrote for the majority, stressed that the irrational circumstances of the homicide raised the pressing question whether the defendant "is a proper subject of capital punishment."[30] At a new trial, medical experts further debated the nature of criminal responsibility and mental disorder. The verdict the second time around was for second-degree murder, and Andersen was sentenced to the penitentiary for life. The oversight of the Supreme Court stayed the hangman's rope.[31]

The Abolitionist Campaign

Revisions of the capital code fell short of the goal of an extensive, grassroots campaign to abolish the death penalty altogether. Not unlike the antislavery movement, opponents in Waterbury castigated the gallows as what they called "that relic of barbarism."[32] The debate in Connecticut reached a crescendo during the 1840s and early 1850s in which hundreds of residents petitioned the General Assembly. The death penalty was challenged but not undone. The most articulate voice in favor of capital punishment came from the orthodox clergy, a bastion of the status quo. Just as mainstream ministers denounced the radical antislavery movement, they castigated opponents of the death penalty. The Reverend Leonard Bacon, minister of New Haven's First Church and prominent advocate of the American Colonizationist Society, wrote, "The haunters of dramshops—the frequenters of brothels—those whose oaths shock you as you pass along the street—are generally in favor of the abolition of capital punishment."[33] At a critical moment in 1842 when much of the legislature and Governor Cleveland Chauncey, the first to do so in that post, backed repeal, the Reverend Joseph P. Thompson, pastor of Chapel Street Congregational Church in New Haven, sought to turn the tide. Chauncey was a Democrat, a party less concerned than the moralistic Whigs with governmental regulation.

Thompson spoke on three successive nights on the topic "Right and Necessity of Inflicting the Punishment of Death for Murder" to audiences that included legislators meeting that year in New Haven. The premise was, *"Since God had decided that the murdered shall be put to death, for us to determine otherwise, is to legislate over him, the Law-giver of the universe."* Thompson made clear that, anticipating the 1846 capital code, he was speaking of premeditated murder, which must be "clearly proven" and did not extend to the insane, who theologically speaking lacked free will. The "unenlightened benevolence" of abolitionists undermined *the prevention of crime by the support of the law.* Not unlike his progenitors, the minister saw biblical mandates such as the oft-cited Genesis 9:6 ("Who so sheddeth man's blood, by man his blood be shed") as the foundation of civil society. Legislators had already set aside the Sabbath and had expanded women's grounds of divorce. Thompson implored, "Shall we throw off one by one the restraints of the bible, till all are gone?"[34]

"No" was the enthusiastic response of the *New Englander,* an organ of traditional values. The New Haven journal credited Thompson's lectures with persuading members of the House of Representatives to vote in favor of the current law by a two-to-one margin. The editorial argued at length that the capital code was just, fair, necessary, and "a *requirement of God.*"[35] The next year, the Reverend Jonathan Cogswell, a professor at the staid Theological Institute of Connecticut, published *A Treatise on the Necessity of Capital Punishment.* He characterized Beccaria, the Milanese reformer, as "a corrupt magistrate" who purveyed a "weak, sophistical argument." In keeping with his conservative colleagues, Cogswell warned, "Let the community go on much longer, lowering the standard of morality, without any check and there will no barrier against the inroads of vice—and no protection for life and property."[36] In addition, the *Hartford Daily Courant,* a partisan Whig organ and defender of traditional moral strictures, denounced the "sickly humanity" and "gross absurdity" of the agitators.[37] "No Christian legislature, who acknowledge the Divine author of the Scriptures, and the obligations of the law of God, can abolish the punishment of death for the crime of *murder,*" the newspaper editorialized.[38]

Debate in the General Assembly over capital punishment was intense during the 1840s. The African American press hailed the "progress" to ban the death penalty in the state.[39] Not unlike antislavery petitions that flooded the Congress, Connecticut residents systematically lobbied their representatives. The argument was severalfold: divine law did not mandate the death penalty, executions did not reduce crime or improve society, and the gallows was a "relic of a less refined and less enlightened age." Petitioners urged the substitution of "perpetual imprisonment" for the "positively injurious" practice.[40] A tally of petitions from 1843 to 1854 indicates that more than 1,700 residents protested the death penalty. Most signatories were men, probably because women could not vote.[41]

Despite the support in 1842 of Governor Chauncey, a Democrat, the Senate by a narrow vote of 11 to 10 and the House by overwhelming 107 to 56 defeated a ban on the death penalty. Supporters had hoped "to wipe off the last remaining drop of blood from the statute book,"[42] but the majority stated, "Death is the only equal or just penalty for murder."[43] A similar outcome occurred the next year, with the Senate voting 11 to 9 and the House 122 to 50 against repeal. The argument that capital punishment was "legalized murder" did not persuade those who saw it as "the only penalty proportionate to the offence."[44] In 1850, Governor Thomas H. Seymour, like his Democratic predecessor, called for abolition. He concurred with the sentiment of petitioners that "this reform is demanded by every consideration that is dear to the heart of the patriot and the Christian."[45] Opponents again carried the day with the caveat that "the security of society" is at stake.[46]

The next year, Governor Seymour retold the General Assembly that with effective laws and the penitentiary, "the death penalty ceases to be necessary, and is therefore unjust."[47] In 1852 and 1853, the Senate, by voting twelve to seven and twelve to eight, respectively, endorsed repeal.[48] Abolitionists pointed to an unseemly incident at the sequestered execution in 1844 of Lucian Hall in Middletown. To placate a passionate crowd, the sheriff allowed men, women, and children to parade by the warm corpse as a military band played "Yankee Doodle Dandy." "Is it the most refined and amiable who go to gallows exhibitions?" they asked. Abolitionists pointed also to the repeal of capital punishment in parts of Europe as well as in Michigan and Rhode Island. Maine, Vermont, and Massachusetts had placed limits on its use. Universal abolition, they predicted, was "a mere question of *time*, not *fact*." The proposed legislation would make convicted murderers serve life terms without hope of pardon or commutation. Such prisoners would be secured in a dual set of cells so that they would not be in physical contact with prison officials, whom they might harm.[49]

The House voted no, convinced that repeal violated "the dictates of enlightened reason, the plain principles of retributive justice, and the distinct and positive authority of the supreme law of God."[50] There was no bicameral reconciliation. In 1854, by a vote of 146 to 39 in the House, a compromise bill was indefinitely postponed. The compromise was to permit the execution of convicts who committed murder while imprisoned for life. A pardon was possible for all others serving life terms, but only with two-thirds votes of both houses.[51] The effort to ban the death penalty had run its course; a grassroots petition campaign had ironically swayed the elite Senate, but not the populist House. Public attention turned away to the more pressing issues of Irish immigration and the expansion of slavery in the western territories.

The Executed

Despite a qualified death penalty, twelve men were executed during the first fifty years of the state penitentiary (table 19). Because of voluminous superior court records in each county, it is not practical to compare them against those indicted for murders who were not executed. A profile of the dozen nonetheless shows some distinct characteristics. Their crimes were violent, lethal, and judged to be premeditated given the circumstances. Six of the twelve were racially and ethnically not members of the white, Protestant majority: one was an African American, another Native American, and four were Irish immigrants.

In sheer numbers, the influx at midcentury of thousands of famine Irish created a new underclass that overshadowed blacks and Indians. In Hartford, the Irish population tripled from 2,000 in 1850 to 6,000, or 20 percent of the population ten years later.[52] Widespread antipapist and xenophobic sentiment led to the formation of the American party. These so-called Know-Nothings elected Chauncey Jerome mayor of New Haven in 1854 and William T. Minor governor the next year. Minor successfully sponsored legislation that restricted ownership of ecclesiastical property to congregations (not bishops), required a literacy test for voting, forbade state courts from naturalizing aliens, and disbanded foreign-born (Irish) militia companies. The bias that "no Irish need apply" was commonplace.[53] During the height of ethnocentrism from the 1850s through the early 1870s, four men of Irish origin were hanged.

Among the executed, occupational attainment and educational skills were limited. Most were laborers; some were itinerants. Caesar Reynolds, an African American, was a professional thief. Henry Leander Foote and Albert Starkweather were born into families with some means but were ne'er-do-wells. They were mostly young men: one was seventeen years old, five were in their twenties, and five were in their thirties. James Wilson, a seasoned burglar, was the oldest at forty-six. What distinguished them from their peers was the use of deadly violence as a means to an end. The impulsiveness of youth was also a factor in a majority of cases. A varied mix of social circumstances and personal qualities predisposed them to murder.

The victims of homicide included two wardens and one guard of the state prison. Revenge figured in the former, a jailbreak gone awry in the latter. Murder accompanied four robberies and one rape. Male aggression against women was a common theme. Domestic violence inordinately took the lives of women: two wives, two mothers, one sister, and one niece. Overall, nine women, compared with five men, died. Except for one Indian woman

TABLE 19

The Executed, 1828–1879

Year of Execution	Name	Race	Age at execution	Birthplace	Occupation	Victim	Weapon	Crime Site
1831	Oliver Watkins	White	35	Ashford	?	Wife	Strangled	Sterling
1833	Caesar Reynolds	Black	30	Unknown	Burglar	Ezra Hoskins (prison guard at Conn. State Prison)	Iron bar	Wethersfield
1833	William Teller	White	28	New Jersey	Counterfeiter	Ezra Hoskins (prison guard at Conn. State Prison)	Iron bar	Wethersfield
1834	David Sherman	Indian	36	Unknown	?	Wife and baby	Ax	Norwich
1844	Lucian Hall	White	26	Unknown	Burglar	Lavina Bacon (robbery)	Knife	Middletown
1846	Andrew Potter	White	23	Hamden	Railroad hand & oysterman	Lucius Osborn (robbery)	Pike	New Haven
1850	Henry Leander Foote	White	38	North Branford	Painter & itinerant	Niece (rape), mother	Knife and hammer	Northford
1850	James McCaffrey	White	36	Ireland	Itinerant	Charles and Ann Smith (robbery)	Ax and handgun	Hamden
1854	Michael Jennings	White	17	Ireland	Laborer	Esther Bradley (robbery)	Knife	New Haven
1862	Gerald Toole	White	24	Ireland	Salon keeper	Daniel Webster (warden at Conn. State Prison)	Knife	Wethersfield
1866	Albert Starkweather	White	24	Hartford	?	Mother and sister	Ax and knife	Manchester
1871	James Wilson	White	46	Ireland	Burglar	William Willard (warden at Conn. State Prison)	Knife	Weathersfield

slain by her Indian husband, all the victims were white. In all but probably one case, the perpetrator and the victim knew each other. Knives, axes, and bludgeons—common household and work implements—provided the weapons. Oliver Watkins strangled his wife with her necklace, and James McCaffrey shot one person he robbed before delivering death blows with an ax. Handguns were the exception.

Violence directed at women took different forms. Juries convicted Watkins and David Sherman of murdering their wives. Watkins pleaded not guilty to killing Roxanne, his wife and the mother of his children. She died at Sterling on March 22, 1830, and the trial concluded before the legislature mandated the end of public executions at its May session. After having been found guilty in Superior Court at Brooklyn, Watkins petitioned the General Assembly for relief, which suspended his death sentence from May to June. Unaware of the reprieve that occurred only days before the original execution date, several hundred men and women gathered in Brooklyn for the anticipated hanging only to be, as the *Windham County Advertiser* sarcastically commented, "disappointed." The newspaper castigated public hangings as encouraging a "sickly appetite." In addition, it warned that a pamphlet circulating in the area that denounced Watkins was "directly calculated to injure the public morals and prejudice the public mind against the prisoner." Although Watkins might be guilty, the local paper editorialized for an "impartial trial."[54]

The General Assembly granted Watkins another trial and moved the execution date to November to accommodate the proceedings. In October, a special session of the Superior Court in Brooklyn with a new jury and with a packed house found him guilty again. In his sentence, Judge Thomas Scott Williams pointed to "that fatal mark of your guilt."[55] The telltale "mark" was what the prosecution asserted were the bruises of strangulation that Watkins had inflicted about Roxanne's neck. The defendant countered with Doctor Josiah Fuller, who suggested that the deceased had died of seizure, not murder. For that medical opinion, state's attorney Arthur Judson charged the physician with perjury, for which Fuller was eventually acquitted. Watkins's death date was set for August 1831 so that the prisoner could appeal his case to the Supreme Court of Errors, which was to next meet in Windham County in July 1831.

At the hearing, the high court was not persuaded by the challenge. The defense contended that the state's evidence of Watkins's extramarital affair was inadmissible because it "did not conduce to shew that he murdered his wife." There was no direct evidence linking the defendant to the killing of his wife. Nonetheless, the prosecution offered testimony that Watkins was engaged in "adulterous intercourse" with one Mrs. Waity Burgess, "a woman of lewd character," offering that the sexual liaison was the motive for murder: "The prisoner's wife stood as a barrier between him and the gratification of his adulterous propensity. The death of the wife would remove that barrier." The tribunal ruled that although the adultery did not prove murder, it showed an "alienation of affection" between husband and wife.[56] The Supreme Court allowed the evidence (which was instrumental for the jury to find Watkins guilty of murder with malice aforethought) to stand and denied the motion for a new trial.[57]

After a much delayed sentence, at eight o'clock on the morning of August 2, 1831, the sheriff took Watkins from his cell in Brooklyn. The early hour may have been to provide ample time for the large crowd that had thronged the town the night before to dissipate over the course of the day without any untoward incidents. A carriage conveyed Watkins, who sat on his coffin and was guarded by four military companies, to the gallows. Three ministers solemnized the event with prayers and sermon. A local dignitary read a statement in which a subdued Watkins still proclaimed, "I now solemnly declare that I am entirely innocent of the Charge, and as ignorant of the cause of my wife's death as any person now before me." An observer remarked on the convict's "calmness and perfect composure." A sense of uncertainty attended this last public hanging in the state. "Whatever he may have thought and felt, he died with scarcely a struggle" as "the Drop fell, and in an instant all was over." Thousands of spectators watched solemnly. Toward night, although a rowdy atmosphere prevailed among the lingering crowd, the early time set for the execution worked toward preventing any actual disturbances.[58]

In addition to wife murder, domestic violence took a deadly toll on the distaff side, for which male relatives were hanged. Henry Leander Foote in 1849 killed his niece and his mother, and Albert Starkweather in 1866 murdered his sister and his mother. For the first time in a capital case, Foote, in a feat of self-publicity, published a lengthy pamphlet of his life that appeared shortly before his hanging.[59] This imaginative murder story was an amalgam of autobiography, travelogue, lurid tales, temperance tract, confession, and sermon. In anticipation of Anthony Comstock and the purity crusade, Foote drew on familiar Christian themes of temptation, sin, and redemption. Like Comstock, he was a Connecticut farm boy, but one who abandoned the virtues of the village for the demimonde of New York City. During his incarceration, the thirty-eight-year-old Foote employed a fluid style, including a fancy for verse, to memorialize himself in the mid-nineteenth-century equivalent of what Andy Warhol famously called fifteen minutes of fame. His profile on the cover shows a dapper, dark-haired man with fashionable side whiskers but an oddly recessive chin. A bold title makes clear that the subject is not some civic worthy but a convicted rapist and murderer.

In the pamphlet, the reader learns that the young Foote quickly took to the strong drink and evil company that flourished in the saloons, theaters, and brothels of New York City, a boat ride away from his home on Long Island Sound. Abandoning a widowed mother and a sister in bucolic Northford, the wayward son set off in 1835 from the burdens of farming and school teaching. He served three years in the cavalry, a "school of vice," fighting in the brutal Seminole War and then lived some years in Brazil, where he nearly died of what may have been malaria. After further travels, he married and had a child in Charleston, South Carolina. He attributed their sudden deaths in 1840 to his "subsequent wild career."[60] After seven years, the prodigal arrived home to rejoin his mother, who was raising an orphaned twelve-year-old niece, Emily Cooper. On September 14, 1849, drinking heavily and sexually aroused, Foote drugged his cousin with a potion from a brothel and raped her. Fearful of the consequences of his impetuous assault, he decided to kill the entire family, including himself. He cut Emily's throat with a pocketknife, pummeled his fifty-eight-year-old mother in the head with a hammer, and cut an artery in his arm. He survived; the others died.

The moral of the tale, as Foote understood it, was that intemperance and licentiousness had placed him "entirely in the power of Satan." In keeping with the "free pardon" of revival religion, he repented his sins, confident that the "Savior" had made him "a monument of his longsuffering mercy" and ensured "blessed immortality beyond the grave." The pamphlet is a curious mixture of promotion, prurience, and piety, one in which titillation and moral instruction mingle. The countryside contrasts with the city, rootedness with roving, austere New England with sensual Brazil, purity with corruption, and the ideal woman with "bewitching female satans."[61] Foote was a man out of place and out of control in a changing world.

Two additional pamphlets skewered Foote. A nearby resident in Branford reported that the neighbors thought that Foote's intention was to murder both, burn the bodies with the house, and collect the insurance, but he was detected before he could complete his nefarious mission. This tract carried an emphatic temperance message to young men who wandered off the Christian path:

> Like him when in your cups, you may,
> The widow and the orphan slay
> Another murderer then appears,
> Another village all in tears,
> Another Sheriff call'd to hang,
> Another of the drinking gang,
> A monster though in human shape,
> *Guilty of murder and rape.*[62]

Foote's drunken outrage in 1849 heightened an already compelling prohibition movement. The Reverend Lyman Beecher at Litchfield in 1825 delivered six lectures that called for a temperance crusade, and four years later the newly formed Connecticut Temperance Union attracted thousands of members. In 1841, a Norwich paper declared its purpose in its name, *Total Abstinence.* Then, four years after Foote's execution, the Whig party in its concern for moral regulation sponsored the state's first prohibition law, part of a trend that had begun in Maine in 1851. The restrictive legislation was in part a response to drunken male violence against women.

The notoriety of Foote's crimes was furthered by a detailed account of the convict's last sixteen days. William Goodwin, a relative by marriage of the ill-fated Emily Cooper, was the author. His purpose was to inform the public of "the feelings, preparation and behavior of that culprit," for which there was a ready market. "It is to be regretted," Goodwin observed of Foote's professed piety "that upon the whole it turned out to be anything but religious." Rather than moral anguish, exemplified by a demonstrative Irish Catholic, James McCaffrey, who was hanged at the same time, Foote maintained a "stoical indifference." The prisoner went through the forms of spiritual contrition, but paid more attention to the worldly aspects of his death. In addition to meeting with clerics, Foote wrote about himself, had his portrait painted, ordered his meals, contracted for a walnut coffin, arranged for a marble tombstone, and hired a carriage to convey mourners, particularly "any ladies," to his gravesite.[63] He conveyed the 160-acre family farm to his married sister. He sold his publications and portrait to curious visitors who trooped by his cell; the proceeds paid for his funeral arrangements. He worried that it might rain on the day of execution, which it did. To Goodwin's amazement, Foote slept soundly the night before the execution.

That morning, the convict bathed, shaved, and perfumed himself. He requested that Goodwin—by this time a confidant—comb his hair and clean his fingernails after he was dead.

Goodwin's death watch was supplemented by an explicit description of the execution that the New Haven newspaper rendered the next day for the excluded public. Some 300 spectators gathered within the prison yard about a gallows' platform eight feet high and eight feet square. Two ropes, one for Foote, the other for McCaffrey, were attached to a beam above the platform and ended in nooses. Military guards were deployed within and without to maintain order. A large crowd that had gathered outside the jail spread onto the green and adjacent streets. A number of women were present, gathered, it may be assumed, in solidarity with the female victims, if not curiosity. No disturbances occurred.

Led by the sheriff and followed by clergy and deputy sheriffs at 10:45 a.m., each convict was covered in a loose, white garment from his neck to above his feet, wore a white cap, and had his elbows pinioned behind him. The two walked up the stairs to the platform, and an Episcopalian priest (Foote's choice) gave a brief prayer in which he spoke of "just punishment" and the "forgiveness" of Jesus Christ. The sheriffs adjusted the nooses about the men's necks with the knot beneath the left ear and tied each leg together to minimize the thrashing of the death throes. In a "tremulous voice," Foote spoke briefly of his hope for salvation and referred listeners to his final comments that were in the second edition of his pamphlet.[64] At 11:01 a.m., the officers drew the caps over the faces and pulled the bolts to the trapdoors, and the prisoners fell six feet. Three physicians attended. They reported that Foote's physical struggle ceased after seven minutes, his pulse stopped after eight and one-half minutes, and there was no heartbeat after ten minutes. Blood and mucus from Foote's mouth stained his white hood. This explicit account of a hanging may well have fueled abolitionist sentiment as well as morbid interest.

The bodies were taken down at 11:45 a.m. and laid out in the jail. Foote's corpse was enshrouded and placed in a coffin. A hearse accompanied by two carriages—with two ministers, Foote's sister and brother-in-law, Goodwin, and Foote's publisher—took the remains to Northford for internment. At 3:30 p.m., the entourage arrived. Before a sizable assembly, the casket was opened and the face, which appeared normal, was uncovered for all to see. The body was buried appropriately some distance from that of Foote's mother's. After the burial pit was filled, a tombstone was erected. In the marble were carved Foote's name, date and age and a biblical message of redemption. When Goodwin returned to the New Haven jail to retrieve a prayer book, he found that Foote had left him a lock of his hair and a verse of farewell to a "good friend."[65]

Burglars murdered two matrons who surprised them while looting their homes. The modus operandi in these two cases was similar: both assailants had chosen the Sabbath to rob the residences of wealthy men and had anticipated that no one would be home. Indisposed, the women had unexpectedly remained alone. Because they knew the men, they were killed to eliminate witnesses. Such was the situation on the late morning of September 24, 1843, in the outskirts of Middletown when Lucian Hall, a twenty-six-year-old ex-convict, broke into the home of Ebenezer Bacon, a prosperous farmer, who was known at times to keep large sums of cash. After breaking in through a kitchen window, Hall rifled through a desk in the front room only to be unexpectedly confronted by the wife, Lavina. As she tried to defend herself, Hall knocked her down with a wooden chair and beat her about the head with the heavy furniture. She was prostrate and wounded, but alive. Hall took a butcher knife from the buttery and stabbed her several times in the chest and stomach. "I did this," he confessed, "to make sure she was dead." The murder was incidental to the robbery because as Hall put it, "I knew I was recognized by Mrs. Bacon."[66] He took the money and fled, leaving a mangled corpse behind.

Hall was a ready suspect who was arrested three days after the murder. He had already served time at Wethersfield for house breaking. Authorities found blood on his clothes, his hand had a recent wound from a knife, and some people saw him in the vicinity of the Bacon farm. During the investigation, two other men with unsavory reputations implicated themselves in the murder. Perhaps out of a desire to please authorities or other emotional duress, William Bell and Bethuel Roberts responded to questions about the crime that indicated that they were participants. Both knew the Bacon home well. Roberts, a chronic alcoholic who suffered delirium tremens, appeared on the verge of a confession and indicated that Bell had struck the first blow. Several people testified that they had seen blood stains on Roberts's shirt, for which at the time no chemical test existed. A grand jury indicted the threesome for murder on March 8, 1844.

During the course of the trial at Middlesex County Superior Court, presided over by Chief Justice Williams, it appeared to the defense counsel, E. A. Buckley and E. Spencer, that Bell and Roberts, who now maintained their innocence, had not been involved. As the case prepared to go to the petit jury, it appeared, however, that all three might be found guilty. Buckley and

Spencer urged their clients, if guilty, to confess and not condemn the innocent to death. With this prompting, Hall declared on March 16 to counsel, "I AM THE GUILTY ONE; Bell and Roberts are INNOCENT." The lesson, an anonymous commentator concluded, was that "very little confidence is to be placed in the statements even of innocent men, which are made while they are under the heavy accusation of a capital crime."[67]

Bell and Roberts were acquitted, but Hall was hanged on the afternoon of June 20 at the Middletown jail. Dressed in white, the prisoner was attended on the scaffold by Episcopal and Baptist clergy, the latter of whom had played a role in his dramatic confession. After the white cap was pulled over his face and the noose adjusted, Hall uttered, "Oh, Dear Me! God Almighty have mercy on me." Eleven minutes after the platform fell, doctors pronounced him dead.[68]

On July 24, 1853, Michael Jennings, a seventeen-year-old Irish immigrant, broke into the home of his former employer, Brazillai Bradley, in New Haven for the purpose of securing through robbery disputed wages. Jennings unexpectedly encountered Esther Bradley, the wife, who because of illness had not attended their Baptist Church that morning with her husband. Jennings stabbed her dozens of times with a pocketknife, and she bled to death on the floor of her sitting room. The house was ransacked, and Jennings left with more money than the disputed wages. He had been seen in the area, his clothes and knife were bloody, and his alibi that he had attended mass at the time did not hold up. As he tried to escape on the railroad, his suspicious behavior led to his apprehension. Newspapers reported that an "Irishman" had "most horribly mutilated" the victim.[69] A state newspaper concurred with the finding of the jury in New Haven County Superior Court that "the guilt of Jennings was so conclusive."[70] Chief Justice William Wolcott Ellsworth sentenced the defendant, who showed no emotion, to hang on July 11, 1854.

Almost a dozen petitions of more than 160 male citizens, including Jennings's father in Brooklyn, New York, asked the General Assembly to commute the youthful convict's sentence to life in prison.[71] A majority of the joint select committee on capital punishment concurred. They agreed with the father that the murder was not premeditated, but part of an effort to reconstitute lost wages that went terribly wrong. "Jennings dead would be soon forgotten," but "in the awful silence of a solitary cell, his example would be a continual warning to the young." These seven members hoped that in prison he might reform through "the discipline of the prison, the teachings of religion, and the silent-but-effective workings of conscience." They concluded that the certainty of punishment is more of a deterrent than "a thousand scaffolds."[72] A minority of two concluded that his guilt admitted "no reasonable doubt whatsoever." Their opinion that there was "no reason whatever for interfering with the judgment of the court and jury" carried the General Assembly, which indefinitely postponed consideration of commutation.[73] Officials hanged Jennings, who never confessed, in the yard of the New Haven jail. An observer dismissively noted that the prisoner showed the "emotion of cowardly fear, rather than the contrition of a true penitent."[74] Sufficient police were employed; there was no protest by Irish immigrants. Jennings was one of the youngest people ever hanged in Connecticut.

Juries in New Haven Superior Court convicted two men of capital murder in separate robberies in the city. They were the first executions there for decades, and they produced a great deal of soul searching. The trial of twenty-three-year-old Andrew Potter in 1845 raised troubling questions about why a youth from a pious family had lured a friend to a lonely section of railroad tracks for an assignation with prostitutes only to kill him for his expensive pocket watch. Potter beat and stabbed Lucius Osborn to death on a secluded railroad trestle with an iron-tipped pike on February 9. He threw the weapon into the river and left the corpse so that it might appear that Osborn had been hit by the train. The working-class youth further forged a promissory note that stated that he had loaned Osborn $100 in return for the gold watch. He then sought payment from the victim's father. His arrest was prompted by witnesses who saw him along the railroad tracks and by the bogus note, which misspelled the victim's name. Potter on February 11 fingered a black man and a day later two white men for the killing. The prisoner's father and uncle prompted him to tell the truth. Potter confessed on February 17 that he had been the sole perpetrator and that he had planned the crime weeks in advance.[75] The jury decided the defendant was depraved, not demented, and found him guilty of first-degree murder. He was sentenced to hang.

One month after the murder, Thompson, who had been Potter's pastor at Chapel Street Church, asked why the son of "respectable and pious parents" had committed a "deliberate and awful malignity." The Congregationalist cleric's answer in good Puritan fashion was that a decline of morality in New Haven was the cause. He noted that Potter had frequented brothels, "houses of hell," in the city. There young men and women were degraded and corrupted. In the sermon *Lewdness and Murder,* Thompson preached, "They have lost the sense of shame; lost almost the sense of right and wrong; lost all moral power against temptation, and all repugnance to crime." New Haven had become larger, more impersonal, a port city where pockets of lewdness flourished. He damned "the low and filthy hovel or cell, where different races mingle in scenes of vice and ribaldry that make night shudder."[76] In addition to citing the brutish lust of West Africans, Thompson implicated blacks in New Haven with the unsavory sex trade. Only a few years earlier, the Reverend Bacon, the distinguished pastor of First Church in New Haven, observed that "the outcast negro" kept "harlots for the convenience of his customers."[77] Temptations of the flesh had led Potter to leave the church, to take up drink, to use profanity, to seek out whores, and ultimately to murder. Thompson, a supporter of capital punishment, called for a vice crusade that would close "houses of ill fame," suppress "immoral books," and regenerate New Haven.[78] Potter's downward descent was a harbinger of the subversion of civilization itself.

The murder galvanized the community. Goodwin, the New Haven publisher, distributed a pamphlet, *Trial and Confession,* which depicted on the cover Potter spearing a prostrate Osborn. The illustrated crime genre, with an additional portrait of Potter, could now be readily disseminated at low cost with the technology of the steam press. During the trial in October, a plot by Potter to escape jail was foiled.[79] In May 1846, the legislature weighed a commutation of the death sentence. A petition from Jabez and Almira Potter, the parents, asked the legislators "to save the life of their son." They suggested, as had his attorneys, that he was mentally ill and at the time of the crime "labored under a delusion." They added, as did some 1,000 other petitioners, men and women, "All the purpose of punishment will be insured by such commutation." A minority of the committee on commutation concurred, but their recommendation was rejected by the larger body.[80] The Supreme Court of Errors at its July 1846 session refused to grant a new trial. The justices found that the jurors had not been improperly influenced by newspaper reports of a "horrid murder" and that Potter's confession was voluntary, not coerced.[81] Officials hanged Potter shortly thereafter on July 20 in the New Haven jail.

Homicides committed by inmates against personnel at the state penitentiary led to four executions. The perpetrators revolted against the oppressive, silent system. As Caesar Reynolds, an African American convict, put it, "The idea that men are made better, or in popular language reformed and made penitent by confining them in State Prison at hard labor, degrading them in their own eyes and in the eyes of the world, and taking away pride and ambition, is altogether a mistaken one." Born in Rhode Island, Reynolds turned early to theft in the greater Hartford region. For him, crime was a means of survival as a member of an "unfortunate and degraded people."

Resourceful and relentless in robbery, he was nevertheless sentenced in 1819 to two years at Newgate, where he came out "tenfold worse than when he went in."[82] Caught again in 1822, he and three white men escaped from the Hartford jail. A $30 reward was posted for the return of the "stout, thick set, very black" fugitive about five feet eight inches in height.[83] Apprehended and convicted of a second larceny, Reynolds returned to Newgate for a six-year term, where he ironically labored to build his future abode, the prison at Wethersfield. After another series of break-ins, Hartford officials arrested him, but he again escaped from jail only to be recaptured. At the September 1829 term of the Hartford County Superior Court, Judge John Thompson Peters sentenced the three-time felon to life in prison at hard labor. Reynolds despaired of this "infamous slavery" and welcomed a "prospect of escape."[84]

In 1833, the thirty-year-old Reynolds joined with a white criminal, twenty-eight-year-old William Teller, another escape artist who conceived a plot to break out of the model Wethersfield prison. Born in New Jersey, Teller had grown up in lower Manhattan, where he became a full-time burglar and sometime seaman who supported a mistress on ill-gotten gains. One step ahead of the police, he escaped from jail and went on a criminal foray in Albany. He was, however, caught in another crime spree in Manhattan in 1826 and served three years in a New York prison. After his release, on what was to be a one-day outing on August 12, 1830, to Hartford to unload counterfeit bank notes, an alert teller sounded the alarm that led in September to a sentence of fifteen years hard labor at Wethersfield. In despair, Teller kept mentally alert in the gloomy solitude of his cell devising plans to escape.[85]

Despite the ban on communication between inmates at Wethersfield, Teller conspired with other prisoners to make a double-ended master key that would open their cells and a kitchen door to the outside yard. From there, they planned to scale the walls and flee. On the night of April 30, 1833, Teller unlocked his cell and that of three other inmates. Ezra Hoskins, a sixty-seven-year-old guard, was the single officer on night patrol on their block. The plan, Teller and Reynolds emphasized at the trial, was not to kill Hoskins, but to subdue him. Teller snuck up behind the partially deaf Hoskins, struck him with a slight blow on the head with a steel bar, and then hit him with his fist. As Reynolds and the others attempted to gag him with a bedsheet, Hoskins, more vigorous than anticipated, resisted and cried out for help. Meanwhile, Teller had in the tension of the moment broken the wrong end of the skeleton key in the kitchen door, foiling the escape. A flustered Teller hit the struggling Hoskins, whom Reynolds was holding, twice with the steel bar, fracturing his skull and causing profuse bleeding. Teller returned to the door, but was unable to force it open with the steel bar. One of the convicts announced that Hoskins was dead. Trapped, the four retreated to their cells and attempted to lock themselves in. The tumult awakened women in the nearby female block, who alerted the guard. The prison was quickly secured, and the four culprits were apprehended.[86]

A legislative committee investigating the "outrages in the State Prison" contradicted Teller's and Reynolds's assertions about the assault on Hoskins. The legislators concluded that "the ferocious and desperate villains" had attempted "by means of the murder of the guard" to carry out their escape. After a two-day trial packed with spectators, the jury at a special session of the Hartford County Superior Court found on May 16 that only Teller and Reynolds were guilty of first-degree murder. On May 18, the day of sentencing, a crowd of hundreds watched as the deputies brought the heavily ironed prisoners from the jail to the courthouse. Both men maintained that they were not guilty of premeditated murder. Reynolds admitted that his clothes were bloody, but "it has not been proved that I participated in the felony [murder] in the least degree,"[87] and Teller said that he had not committed willful murder. In pronouncing sentence, Chief Justice David Daggett countered that "twenty-four disinterested and impartial citizens" in the grand and trial juries had concluded that "having broken the doors of your and their cells, it became necessary, in your view, to kill Ezra Hoskins."[88] He sentenced them to hang on June 28.

Both men on May 21 petitioned the legislature for a commutation. Reynolds again stated that "he did not inflict the fatal blow." He added more generally that "sanguinary punishments are contrary to the genius and spirit of the country."[89] Teller emotionally pleaded, "Life, Life, spare me, this is the last prayer of a most wretched prisoner, but yet a human being."[90] A separate petition with forty-four signatures opposed capital punishment. Instead of death, solitary confinement for life would allow for the men to "become sensible of their transgression and repent."[91] An animated debate ensued in the House of Representatives, but by a large majority the commutation was voted down.[92] One commentator damned commutation as "a miserable apology for crime."[93] The attorneys for the condemned men then asked for a reprieve; the legislature postponed the execution to September 6.[94] A final legal procedure to block the execution was a writ of habeas corpus claiming that Reynolds and Teller were illegally held because only the governor, not the General Assembly, could constitutionally grant reprieves. Judge Peters of the Hartford County Superior Court, however, ruled against it.[95]

At the very time the habeas corpus challenge was being considered, the two prisoners attempted another escape. Although chained to the floor, ironed at the legs, and handcuffed, on the night of June 25 they momentarily outfoxed their guards and broke loose in the building. A savvy guard threw a nearby key to the bolted, main door out of reach through a grated window into the street. Not unlike their previous failed effort, the two condemned men could not exit the prison. A hue and cry was raised, and they were again taken into custody. Unlike the ill-fated Hoskins, no guards were injured during this failed escape.[96] On September 6 at 9:00 a.m., three dozen people—mainly police, clergy, reporters, and some friends—attended the dual execution in the jail yard that was blocked by enclosure from public view. Forty-five soldiers forestalled any disorder. At the gallows, both men resolutely denied that they were guilty of first-degree murder. A reporter observed that Reynolds was composed but that Teller was agitated. Two hymns were sung, and both men shook hands with the sheriff, who pulled white hoods down over their faces. As one witness wrote, "The drop fell and they were launched into eternity."[97] The cadavers, if not retrieved by friends, were "at the disposal of the professors of anatomy and surgery in the medical institutions of this state."[98]

The dual executions of Reynolds and Teller were the first and last interracial hangings to occur in Connecticut. In their mutual desire to escape incarceration, the two criminals forged a bond that transcended the caste barriers of the day. Teller praised his comrade as "an ingenious and resolute fellow."[99] For the first time, lengthy statements by condemned men in their own voice were published for general distribution. In contrast to penologists who hailed the penitentiary as a reformatory of criminals, Reynolds and Teller rebutted that incarceration hardened convicts and emboldened resistance. For the first time, petitions to the General Assembly for commutation systematically criticized the inhumanity of capital punishment. For the first time, their executions were by statute to occur "within an enclosed yard, so as to prevent public observation."[100] The *Connecticut Courant* editorialized on the landmark event: "Whatever may have been intended or expected from the example of public executions, there can be no doubt that the practical effect of them has been decidedly injurious." Instead of "solemnity of feeling," the numerous spectators tended to "levity, dissipation, and licentiousness" that had "the most pernicious influence on public morals."[101]

Three decades later, an inmate, Gerald Toole, stabbed to death the warden of the state prison, Daniel Webster, which again raised questions about crime and punishment. Toole had settled in New Haven after arrival from Dublin, Ireland, in 1858. Two years later, he had been sentenced to a life term at Wethersfield for the arson of a saloon he owned that had threatened the lives of two occupants residing in an upper level of the building. Although he never confessed, Toole's alleged motive in burning the Irish pub was to collect insurance. The initial reports of the warden's murder on March 27, 1862, characterized the event as a premeditated attack by a revengeful inmate. Based on reports from prison officials, the *Hartford Daily Courant* angrily called for retribution: "His life will pay the forfeit of his terrible crime."[102]

At the trial and in Toole's published autobiography, however, the defendant provided a more complex explanation for his attack. In what twenty-four-year-old Toole called "a true and faithful picture," the supposed model prison was described as a place of dehumanization and brutality. He was one of thirty inmates contracted to fabricate boots for a private contractor. Factory production of footwear had rendered the artisanal craft outdated, except for forced prison labor. Unable to produce the stipulated dozen pairs of boots during what could be an eleven-hour work day, the warden lashed him on his naked back five times with a cat-o'-nine-tails, a whip with multiple braided and knotted strands of horse hide that in Toole's words was "excruciating and piercing beyond conception." The next day, with only ten pairs of boots finished, Toole fatally stabbed the warden three times with a concealed shoe knife rather than be whipped again. Vengeful officials took the assailant to an isolated cell, where they stripped him stark naked and repeatedly whipped and beat him. Toole confessed to the murder, but argued that he retaliated in "self-preservation."[103] Toole believed that his supervisors had harassed him unreasonably—whether for ethnic reasons is not clear—even though he worked as hard as he could. In early May, a jury nevertheless found him guilty of first-degree murder, and Chief Justice Joel Hinman sentenced the prisoner to death.

Efforts at commutation failed to secure approval of the General Assembly.[104] One critic in a letter to a Hartford newspaper did not excuse the crime but suggested thoughtful reforms at the prison. He noted that Toole was "a man stung by a sense of insupportable justice." Instead of physical punishment, he urged rehabilitation through education, employable job skills, and supervised integration for the ex-convict back into society. "Banish corporal punishment and those who retain it. Encourage the prisoner with payment for extra labor," he wrote.[105] A legislative committee, however, failed to alter the status quo. At the gallows on September 19, Toole, who had converted to Protestantism, had his pastor read a statement of protest: "When I reflect, even now, upon the inhuman punishment meted out to such of those as chance to be the objects of the spite of his [Webster's] under officers, I *cannot* say, I *will not* say, because it would be untrue, that I had no justification for my act." He alluded to his autobiography, a lengthy and articulate apologia pro vita with an attractive portrait of the author, in which he maintained, "If there is a hell on earth, it is the Connecticut State Prison."[106]

The execution produced an outpouring of morbid curiosity. During the morning, citizens toured the Hartford jail to see the condemned man behind bars until he complained. That early afternoon, in an evasion on the ban on public executions, several hundred ticket holders watched the death ritual inside the jail compound. The corpse was cut down after hanging twenty minutes and was placed in an open coffin. "A great many," it was reported, went during the afternoon to view the dead man, who looked life-like, roses covering the rope burns on his broken neck. The *Hartford Daily Courant* concluded that Toole, "calm and fearless to the end," endured a "just death at the hands of the law."[107]

Within a decade, another disgruntled inmate, James Wilson, killed Webster's replacement, William Willard. As Willard made afternoon rounds of the prisoners' cells on August 14, 1870, Wilson stabbed the warden in the stomach with a shoe knife fixed to the front of a cane that he stuck through the bars. His intestines severed, Willard died the evening of the attack. Newspaper reports the next day gave favorable play to crowds outside the prison calling for Wilson to be hanged immediately for the death of the popular official. An 1867 law had specifically deterred a rush to judgment in capital cases by barring an execution without a lapse of twelve months after sentencing. A deputy warden called the culprit the "worst man ever confined in the Connecticut State Prison." The forty-seven-year-old Wilson, a Scot-Irish who had immigrated to the United States from Belfast as an infant, was a "notorious convict."[108] Although the latest judicial records identified him by an alias, Wilson's, birth name was David Kentley. Previously, in 1851, the New London County Superior Court had sentenced a transient named John Marshall to three years for burglary. Willard, an officer at the prison at the time, later recognized Marshall as James Wilson, whom the Hartford County Superior Court in 1858 had sentenced to sixteen years at Wethersfield for another burglary. Willard's identification of the professional criminal added considerable time to Wilson's jail time and was part of his animus against the warden.[109]

Wilson, as he was commonly known, claimed to have committed more than eight hundred thefts. He reputedly had escaped from penitentiaries in

New York, New Jersey, Ohio, and Michigan. In the last jailbreak, he had fro-
zen his feet, which were amputated at the insole, impeding his illegal liveli-
hood. After a failed escape in 1870 at the Connecticut State Prison, Willard
put Wilson in a punishment cell for six weeks. These solitary stone "dungeons"
were unheated and without light, and Wilson's rations were restricted; these
cells were also used as morgues until families retrieved the corpses of dead
prisoners. Wilson expressed fear that he would freeze and starve to death.
He became a spokesman for prisoners' grievances, complaining that the
warden forced rotten fish and putrid meat on the inmates.[110] Not unlike
Toole, Wilson justified the murder. As he wrote his sister on October 12, 1871,
"I killed the warden strictly in defense of my own life."[111]

At the fall session of the Hartford County Superior Court, proceedings of
Wilson's capital case unfolded in a dramatic way. The defense had the right
to preempt twenty jurors, whereas the state attorney could exclude anyone
opposed to the death penalty. There was a dispute about the impartiality of
some jurors given the extensive news coverage. Wilson, who pleaded not
guilty, opted at first to plead his own case, but gave up after the court ruled
some questions out of order. Judge William T. Minor assigned two attorneys for the defendant because Wilson was impoverished. An effort to show
that oppressive conditions in the prison warranted reducing the charge to
second-degree murder or manslaughter did not persuade the jury. After deliberation of twelve minutes, the panel found Wilson guilty of first-degree
murder.[112] Given the opportunity to speak, Wilson rebutted, "I have only to
say that I do not feel that I have been tried yet. I am perfectly satisfied with
the result to be hanged. It will be an act of supreme mercy compared to being compelled to live in the Connecticut State Prison, as I have been."[113] The
judge scheduled the execution for October 13, 1871.

After the verdict, Wilson further protested by total abstinence from food
for nine days before voluntarily stopping his fast. At its February term, the
Supreme Court of Errors denied the motion for a new trial. Chief Justice
Thomas Belden Butler argued that "no man can justify the killing of another in self-defense until he has exhausted all other means of safety."[114] In
protest again, Wilson took no food for five days before doctors force-fed
him beef tea through a tube inserted into his esophagus. He told his jailer
that he would not hang.[115] At the June session of the General Assembly, attorneys on either side made their case for and against commutation. The
state's advocate, Henry C. Robinson, said that he opposed the "barbarous
system of capital punishment" but held that Wilson, if anyone did, deserved
death.[116] The petition for commutation failed.

With execution approaching, the condemned man willed his body to the Medical College of New Haven provided that institution sponsor several proposals for legislative action: a restriction on officials striking an inmate except in self-defense; the abolition of punishment by the cold-water shower and the cat-o'-nine-tails; the re-covering of the stone floor in the solitary cell with wood; and allowing visits of the directors of the prison to inmates without prison officers present.[117] These acts would eventually come to pass, but not in the near future.

Although closely guarded, Wilson early in the morning of the hanging pushed a sharpened three-inch wire, one-eighth inch in diameter, into his chest, piercing his heart. He remained conscious and able to function, although mortally wounded and in excruciating pain. Wilson's rationale for suicide was not that he was "afraid to die but because it [hanging] is an unworthy death—a death of a dog and a murderer." Officials decided to continue on schedule, but they limited the number of public attendees to twenty-five instead of three hundred because the hanging might not go smoothly. The sheriff and deputies got Wilson robed and up the stairs to the scaffold, where he unexpectedly put the noose around his own neck. "When a man puts this over his head in the cause of humanity, it is not disgraceful to die," he declared. The chaplain gave a brief prayer, and the prisoner cordially shook hands with the executioners. The sheriff pulled the black cap over Wilson's face and released the bolt as he walked the stairs. Fourteen minutes after the trap fell, his heart ceased to beat. Some 2,000 people—men, women, and children—viewed the corpse in an open coffin at the jail. Wilson, as much as he could, died on his own terms and justified his deadly assault on the warden in humanitarian terms. The local newspaper countered that "Kentley [Wilson] deserved the full legal penalty for his crime" for "it was not William Willard he struck at, but organized society."[118]

Commutations

Almost all death sentences were appealed to the General Assembly. Although the constitution of 1818 separated the judicial and legislative branches, the latter retained the power to reduce or entirely forgive sentences. The governor could issue a temporary reprieve of a death sentence. An advocacy procedure was in place where petitions for or against commutation were presented to an appropriate committee. Records of the trial were made available.[119] In addition, defense counsel and the state attorney made their presentations. The legislature was in effect the court of last resort. In the

TABLE 20
Commutations for Capital Convictions, 1828–1879

	Name	Date of Commutation	Race	Victim
1	John Barnum	1833	White	Father
2	David Sherman	1834	White	Wife
3	John Sharp	1836	White	Unknown
4	John Burke	1842	White	Wife
5	David Abbott	1842	White	Wife
6	Sarah Freeman	1843	Black	Female neonate (mulatto)
7	George Jackson	1849	"Man of color"	"Man of color"
8	Benjamin Balcolm	1851	White	White man
9	William Calhoun	1851	White	White man
10	Henry Mennasseh	1851	Indian	White man
11	Isaac Randolph	1856	White	Unknown
12	Frederick Hall	1871	White	Unknown
13	John Robert Johnson	1873	White	Landlady

case of capital convictions, there were no pardons during this period, but there were a number of commutations (table 20).

All the commutations reduced the death sentence to life in prison. Eight occurred during the height of the debate over capital punishment in the 1840s and 1850s. In all, twelve men and one woman had their sentences reduced. Among these successful petitioners, ten were white, two mixed race (Indian and African American), and one an Indian. Among the victims of the homicides were four women, five men, and one newly born female infant. Domestic violence took the lives of three wives and one father.

Consideration of mental competence figured prominently in two situations. Eighteen-year-old John Barnum, who shot his father in Danbury with a musket, was thought to be insane, and his death sentence was commuted in 1833. Petitions in 1845 and 1851 to have him discharged from the state prison, however, failed.[120] Dr. Amariah Brigham of the Hartford Retreat for the Insane and other physicians diagnosed David Abbott, who strangled his wife with his bare hands at Middlebury in 1841, as a monomaniac who "has been for a long time laboring under a morbid delusion," and his commutation was granted in 1842. The minority protested that "this wife killing is becoming a common offense in the community, and must be punished with condign severity, or there is no protection for those whose inferior strength prevents them from effectually protecting themselves."[121] The editors at the

Hartford Daily Courant similarly deplored "a mawkish sympathy for criminals" and further questioned the propriety of the General Assembly in re-trying the case "as if they were a legal judicial tribunal."[122]

Another homicide raised the question, as Justice Elisha Carpenter of the Supreme Court of Errors put it, "whether drunkenness, as a fact, may be considered by the jury as evidence tending to disprove an essential fact in the case, a deliberate intention to take a life."[123] An injured mason, John Robert Johnson, a Swedish immigrant, was unemployed, and his landlady evicted him. "Under a wild impulse, he struck her a blow which resulted in her death," his counsel Ratcliffe Hicks asserted.[124] Not only at the time on July 8, 1872, of the assault was Johnson drunk, but he was, counsel claimed, a chronic alcoholic, "insane" with the "disease of dipsomania." When the jury found Johnson guilty of first-degree murder, Hicks filed a motion for a new trial. Hicks, a Democrat, was an outspoken opponent of the death penalty. He averred that the judge at the New Haven County Superior Court erred in not instructing the jury on the role of intoxication in the assessment of premeditated murder. The appellate court concurred that "intoxication is admissible in such cases, not as an excuse for crime, not in mitigation of punishment, but as tending to show that the less and not the greater offense was in fact committed."[125] A new trial was granted, and Johnson was found guilty of second-degree murder. Hicks protested that his client's inebriation warranted the lesser charge of manslaughter. The Supreme Court in a unanimous opinion denied a retrial and explained, "Intoxication, which is itself a crime against society, combines with the act of killing, and the evil intent to take life which necessarily accompanies it, and all together afford sufficient grounds for implying malice." "Implied malice" defined second-degree murder and a life sentence, whereas "actual malice" was a capital crime.[126] Manslaughter was a homicide in which there was "no malice." Hicks had triumphed on his major legal challenge to the death penalty. As he wrote, "Hanging brutalizes the community, and too often only attests the inhumanity of mankind to man."[127]

Extenuating circumstances were critical in the determination of other commutations. Sarah Freeman, a black servant, gave birth to a bastard child fathered by a white man who had deserted her. She had concealed the pregnancy and gave live birth. A jury in New Haven County Superior Court in 1842 found that she had willfully killed the infant by smothering and choking it and then casting it into a full privy where death occurred. Based on "the disgusting facts," Chief Justice Williams sentenced her to hang on June 15, 1843.[128] Her petition to the legislature a month before the execution rebutted that "acting under the impression and compelled with a desire to conceal all traces of her shame, with her mind confused, with bodily anguish, grief and fear, she hastily threw into the vault what she thought was a dead body."[129] Legislators were convinced that she had no intention to commit murder and substituted seven years at Wethersfield for the gallows.[130] Without the commutation, Freeman would have been the first woman hanged for infanticide since 1753.

A finding of a lack of premeditation contributed to other commutations. With the children screaming in horror, a violent marital dispute in which both partners assaulted the other turned deadly when the husband struck his wife with an ax to the shoulder and then slit her throat with a knife. The Hartford County Superior Court in 1841 found John Burke guilty of first-degree murder. In a close vote in the Senate, a majority of legislators the next year found that the "act was done in the heat of blood upon a sudden provocation given by the deceased."[131] The death sentence was altered to a life term at hard labor.

At the height of the debate over the death penalty, 775 men and 112 women, including the mother of the prisoner, from towns in New London County, successfully persuaded the General Assembly to spare the life of George Jackson. A drunken quarrel in 1847 led to a fight between two strangers at a house in Ledyard "inhabited and frequented by worthless colored persons."[132] Jackson, "a man of color," struck Edward Nelson, "also a person of color," who died two days later. Even though the homicide involved disreputable "colored" men, apparently of African and Indian background, some prominent whites, including politicians, judges, four ministers, and one doctor, protested the death sentence, which they found extreme for the circumstances. Without dissent, in 1849 legislators concurred and stated that they "in wisdom and in mercy commute the punishment of this wretched man to something less awful and terrible than death," which was life in the state prison.[133]

At the middle of the nineteenth century, the reform impulse was at its height in Connecticut. Slavery was completely abolished in 1848, and in 1854 the state passed its first prohibition act. For more than a decade, a petition campaign to repeal the death penalty gained the support of two Democratic governors and on occasion a majority of the Senate. Although legislative committees recommended the end of the death penalty, substantial majorities in the House went the other way. The parameters of the debate were clearly defined. Opponents of capital punishment argued that it was a violation of Christian ethics and coarsened civil sensibility. The rebuttal was that the death penalty was a divine mandate and an essential retribution for the preservation of society.

The debate was heated, but there was common ground. An 1846 law limited capital murder to cases that included deliberate premeditation with malice aforehand. Twelve men were so hanged for homicides that involved prison assaults, domestic violence, and robbery. (See table 19.) These convicts were generally of low status and included one African American, one Indian, and four men born in Ireland. Even so, an almost equal number had their sentences commuted. Concepts of monomania and irresistible impulse challenged the willfulness at the heart of capital murder. Indeed, juries tended not to convict and the legislature used its power of commutation in cases in which premeditation was not clear.

In the decades bracketing either side of the new century, there was less discussion of the repeal of the death penalty. During an unsettling era of urbanization and corporate capitalism with an influx of new immigrants from southern and eastern Europe, capital punishment for many seemed essential to preserve social order. An ideology replete with eugenics, social Darwinism, and xenophobia sought to contain by strong measures what was called the criminal class.

5

THE MENACE OF THE CRIMINAL CLASS
1880–1929

There was no hitch, no blunder, the judicial killing was a scientific piece of work.

Hartford Daily Courant, May 14, 1880, on the hanging of Edwin Hoyt

You [the state of Connecticut] execute only some poor, unfortunate Italian, negro [*sic*], or Irishman without friends and without money.

Ratcliffe Hicks, March 16, 1893

This hanging men is bad business, all around, but so is murdering; and the purpose is to make those, who might earn the same penalty, stop and think twice before taking that unpleasant risk.

Hartford Courant, Dec. 5, 1894, on the hanging of John Cronin

BY 1900, A DYNAMIC corporate capitalism profoundly dominated the United States. Connecticut was at the heart of the urban and industrial transformation that Civil War spending in the "munitions state" had brought to fruition. Huge factories employed a vast number of workers. Textiles—cotton, wool, silk, and thread—were concentrated in the eastern part of the state and were the largest industry in Connecticut. Hartford, made the sole capital in 1875, dubbed itself the insurance capital of the world. New Haven, the former dual capital, had a variety of manufacturing concerns. Weapons makers in several areas dominated the national market. Large, well-financed corporations outstripped smaller, family businesses. There was also a demographic shift as the importance of agriculture declined. Although by 1890 five times as many people lived in cities than in small towns, a rotten borough system of skewed representation allowed outpaced villages to dominate the legislature. Military production during World War I furthered industrialization. By 1920, a majority of residents lived in cities, and the population of New Haven and Bridgeport each topped 100,000. Hartford had some of the worst slums in the United States for a city of its size, and throughout the state, significant blighted areas contrasted with smaller enclaves of wealth.[1]

Immigrants fleeing poverty, political instability, and anti-Semitism in southern and eastern Europe provided much of the burgeoning, low-wage labor force after 1880. The changing composition of the population was dramatic and a source of cultural tension. In 1910, almost one of three state residents was foreign born. By the eve of World War I, 70 percent of the total population of 1,114,756 were first- and second-generation immigrants. In 1920, 10 percent of the population of Waterbury had been born in Italy; at the same time, 18,000 eastern European Jews resided in the Hartford region; and in 1930, one-quarter of the people of New Britain were of Polish ancestry. By 1920, residents born in Italy numbered almost twice that of any other foreign-born group.[2]

The epic story of the uprooted is well known, but what is not familiar is that the "new immigrants" figured predominately among those judicially executed as well as among the victims of murder. The actual number of people hanged reached an all-time peak in the decades bracketing the new century. The capital code was not substantially altered, and due process of law was observed. The unsettling conditions of urbanization, industrialization, and population movement, however, often inordinately affected newcomers, outsiders, and people on the move. Those on the margins of a capitalistic society marked by extremes of wealth and power were disproportionately enmeshed in the criminal justice system. Old world traditions did not blend neatly with new-world realities. Violence is shocking, often inexplicable, and not always reducible to social and economic circumstances or ethnic tension. Nonetheless, stressful situations, difficult living conditions, and the ready availability of handguns facilitated homicides and first-degree murder convictions as never before or ever since. Authorities worried about the menace of what they termed the criminal class and were attracted to eugenic explanations of evil. In a rationalization of state power, legislators in 1893 mandated that executions occur after the midnight hour before only a limited number of observers in the fortified state prison. Although newspapers reported the graphic details on the front page, the actual execution procedure was isolated and secretive. A new mechanized gallows rendered dozens of hangings routine and efficient, befitting the machine age.

The Legal Context

The capital code did not on its face single out immigrants or any other group. Judicial fairness remained the ideal, although social circumstances skewed the purview of criminal justice. The General Assembly in 1882, 1885, and 1893 extended compensation for defense attorneys involved in death penalty, life imprisonment, and felony criminal cases. Connecticut in 1917 adopted the first statewide public defender system in the United States. The judges of the Superior Court appointed one public defender per county. The restatement of the death penalty statute in 1902 was fundamentally the same as it had been for decades. Any "willful, deliberate, and premeditated killing" or a homicide that occurred in the commission of arson, rape, robbery, or burglary constituted first-degree murder. A new inclusion—homicide involving "any explosive compound"—reflected fears of labor agitation by immigrants associated with the sensational Haymarket incident at Chicago in 1886 for which the state of Illinois hanged four anarchists for a bomb blast that killed seven police officers.[3] Confrontation between workers and management was rife, with public officials supporting capitalists against unionists.[4] The handgun assassination of President William McKinley in 1901 by Leon Czolgosz, a steelworker of Polish descent who was attracted to radical causes, prompted a statute that made an "attempt to cause the death" of the president or a foreign ambassador a capital crime.[5] Treason remained a hanging offense, but no one was executed for "offenses against the sovereignty of the state."[6] In what historian Robert Wiebe called the search for order during the late nineteenth century, Connecticut established a board of pardons in 1883 and centralized the gallows at the state penitentiary at Wethersfield in 1893.[7] Executions were purposefully cloistered. Within twenty days of a death sentence, the prisoner was transferred from jail to the state penitentiary. The place of execution was removed from the county in which the crime had occurred, and the number of spectators was greatly restricted. The time of execution was limited to early morning darkness. Unless there was a reprieve or a stay, the execution was to be carried out not less than one month and not more than six months after sentencing. Punishment was punctual, but some leeway was built in for challenges.

The legislature in Connecticut had previously exercised the power of pardoning and commutation. The governor could issue a reprieve, a stay of execution that allowed a death row prisoner additional time to seek redress. Unlike most states, in Connecticut there was no gubernatorial power to commute or pardon. The editors of the *Hartford Daily Courant* found the legislative process "clumsy and vicious," not to mention subject to political machinations.[8] The legislature concurred and established a board of pardons that consisted of six persons: the governor, a justice of the Supreme Court of Errors, and four other persons, one of whom was a physician. All three branches of government had a role in constituting the board. The General Assembly, and then in 1902 the governor with consent of the Senate, appointed a bipartisan panel whose members served a four-year term. The board oversaw not only releases from the state penitentiary, but also commutations of the death penalty.[9] In its procedures, the board required, among other data, the nationality of the prisoner, a concern that reflected the influx of aliens into the state.[10] The *Hartford Daily Courant* concluded that the new panel "will correct many abuses before the legislature and secure both to the public and the prisoners, equally fair play."[11]

A Profile of the Executed

This chapter now examines a profile of those who were judicially executed in the half century before the onslaught of the Great Depression. They all shared a conviction of first-degree murder, a homicide that was premeditated, committed with malice aforethought, or during a felony such as arson, rape, or robbery. All other murders were second degree, which brought a life term. The criminal justice system had a number of interlocked steps that were meant to ensure the rule of law in a capital crime. The state's attorney brought an indictment against an individual before a grand jury. If this group of twelve jurors found a true bill, a petit or trial jury of the same number was impaneled to weigh evidence presented by the prosecution and defense in an adversarial procedure moderated by a judge. After deliberation, the jury rendered a verdict of not guilty or guilty, which could be in a lesser count than charged. A few defendants opted to plead guilty, in which case statute allowed the judge to examine witnesses and affix the degree of guilt. In the sentencing phase, the judge prescribed death by hanging for first-degree murder and life in the state prison for second-degree murder. The defendant had the opportunity to appeal to the state's Supreme Court. If the appellate court found an error, it ordered a new trial. The defendant could also petition the governor for a reprieve that provided a temporary postponement of the execution. During the limited reprieve, the convict could appeal to the state's highest court for a review and also ask for a commutation, usually to life in prison, from the board of pardons.

Despite these potential hurdles, the state hanged sixty people from 1880 to 1929 (table 21). A decennial indicator records the highest actual number of

TABLE 21
The Executed, 1880–1929

Year of Execution	Name	Age at Execution	Nativity	Religion	Race	Occupation	Crime Site	Weapon	Victim
1880	Edwin Hoyt	38	Conn.	Episcopalian	White	Woodcutter	Sherman	Knife	Father
1880	Henry Hamlin	33	Ireland	Roman Catholic	White	Robber	Wethersfield	Handgun	Prison guard
1882	James Smith	23	Ireland	Roman Catholic	White	Laborer	Ansonia	Handgun	Police chief
1888	Philip Pallidona	24	Italy	Roman Catholic	White	Quarryman	Bridgeport	Handgun	Brother
1889	John Swift	22	Ireland	Roman Catholic	White	Machinist	Hartford	Handgun	Wife
1891	Jacob Scheele	63	Germany	Protestant	White	Innkeeper	New Canaan	Shotgun	Police officer
1892	Andrew Borjesson	32	Sweden	Lutheran	White	Farm worker	New Milford	Knife	Woman/sexual
1892	Angelo Petrillo	25	Italy	Roman Catholic	White	Day laborer	New Haven	Handgun	Brother-in-law
1894	John Cronin	37	Ireland	Roman Catholic	White	Farm laborer	S. Windsor	Handgun	Landlord
1896	Kaspar Hartlein	39	Germany	Roman Catholic	White	Farm laborer	Manchester	Knife	Woman/sexual
1897	Thomas Kippie	41	Scotland	Roman Catholic	White	Brazier	New Haven	Knife	Wife
1897	Giuseppe Fuda	31	Italy	Roman Catholic	White	Laborer	E. Norwalk	Hatchet	Wife
1897	Nicodemo Imposino	24	Italy	Roman Catholic	White	Laborer	E. Norwalk	Hatchet	Woman/sexual
1898	Charles Boinay	33	N.Y.	Roman Catholic	White	Laborer	Trumbull	Handgun	Man (robbery)
1898	Benjamin Willis	21	N.Y.	no religious profession	White	Temporary jobs	Wilton	Handgun	Man (robbery)
1899	Frederick Brockhaus	20	Germany	Protestant	White	Temporary jobs	Wilton	Handgun	Man (robbery)
1900	Charles Cross	17	Brooklyn, N.Y.	Episcopalian	White	Chore boy	Stamford	Shovel	Woman (sexual)
1904	Paul Misik	33	Hungary	Lutheran	White	Quarryman	Newington	Handgun	Man (coworker)
1904	Joseph Watson	17	S.C.	A.M.E.	Black	House servant	Hartford	Handgun	Police official
1905	Gershom Marx	73	Russia	Jewish	White	Farmer	Colchester	Ax	Farm laborer

1906	Ephraim Sherouk	25	Russia	Russian Orthodox	White	Laborer	Somers	Strangulation	Landlady
1907	Henry Bailey	40	Conn.	Protestant	White	Handyman	Middletown	Ax	Employer
1907	Alexander Herman	40	Poland	Roman Catholic	White	Laborer	Bridgeport	Handgun	Landlord
1908	John Washelesky	28	Poland	Roman Catholic	White	Farm laborer	New Haven	Board	Fellow laborer
1908	Lorenzo Rossi	33	Italy	Roman Catholic	White	Laborer	Hartford	Knife	Saloon patron
1908	John Zett	48	Bohemia	Roman Catholic	White	Farmer	Rockville	Hammer & knife	Wife and granddaughter
1909	Giuseppe Campagnolo	27	Italy	Roman Catholic	White	Farm laborer	N. Haven	Shotgun	Man
1909	Raphael Carfaro	20	Italy	Roman Catholic	White	Farm laborer	N. Haven	Pitchfork	Man
1910	John Zawedzianczek	26	Hungary	Roman Catholic	White	Laborer	Glastonbury	Knife	Man (dispute)
1912	Andrea Tanganelli	25	Italy	Roman Catholic	White	Bricklayer	New Haven	Handgun	Woman (sexual)
1912	George Redding	21	Conn.	Christian Science	White	Bookkeeper	Hamden	Handgun	Man (robbery)
1913	Louis Saxon	28	Russia	Jewish	White	Tailor	New Britain	Handgun	Wife (de facto)
1914	James Plew	28	N.Y.	Protestant	White	Farm laborer	Cheshire	Handgun	Man (adultery)
1914	Motejius Rikteraites	26	Lithuania	Roman Catholic	White	Factory worker	Waterbury	Razor	Wife
1914	Joseph Buonomo	24	Italy?	Roman Catholic	White	Pimp	Stratford	Handgun	Prostitute
1914	Joseph Bergeron	40	Montreal	Roman Catholic	White	Tinsmith	New Haven	Handgun	Woman
1915	Bernard Montvid	23	Lithuania	Roman Catholic	White	Criminal	New Britain	Handgun	Priest (robbery); woman
1915	Frank Grela	41	Galicia	Roman Catholic	White	Laborer	Hartford	Handgun	Wife
1916	Isaac Williams	27	Conn.	Episcopalian	White	Burglar	Barkhamsted	Metal axle	Man (robbery)
1916	Harry Rowe	22	N.Y.	Protestant	Black	Dishwasher	Barkhamsted	Metal axle	Man (robbery)
1916	Pasquale Zuppa	27	Italy	Roman Catholic	White	Laborer	Guilford	Rock/knife	Man (robbery)
1917	Joseph Castelli	24	Italy	Roman Catholic	White	(Deaf mute)	New Haven	Iron bar	Wife

(continued)

TABLE 21
(Continued)

Year of Execution	Name	Age at Execution	Nativity	Religion	Race	Occupation	Crime Site	Weapon	Victim
1917	Francisco Vetere	25	Italy	Roman Catholic	White	(Deaf mute)	New Haven	Iron bar	Woman
1917	Giovanni Don Vanso	21	Italy	Roman Catholic	White	Butcher	New Britain	Handgun	Man (vendetta)
1917	Stephen Buglione	21	Italy	Roman Catholic	White	Butcher	New Britain	Handgun	Man (vendetta)
1917	William Wise	23	N.Y.?	Jewish	White	Waiter	New Britain	Razor	Woman (affair)
1918	Carmine Lanzillo	24	Italy	Roman Catholic	White	Laborer?	West Haven	Handgun	Man (robbery)
1918	Carmine Pisaniello	21	Italy	Roman Catholic	White	Laborer?	West Haven	Handgun	Man (robbery)
1918	Francesco Dusso	25	Italy	Roman Catholic	White	Laborer?	West Haven	Handgun	Man (robbery)
1919	Erasmo Perretta	27	Italy	Roman Catholic	White	Cobbler	New Britain	Handgun	Man (dispute)
1919	Joseph Perretta	32	Italy	Roman Catholic	White	Cobbler	New Britain	Knife	Man (dispute)
1919	Nikifor Nechesnook	28	Lithuania	Roman Catholic	White	Laborer	Waterbury	Hatchet	Man (robbery)
1920	Daniel Cerrone	33	Italy	Roman Catholic	White	Quarryman	Hamden	Handgun	Stepdaughter
1921	Elwood Wade	23	Conn.	Presbyterian	White	Milkman	Bridgeport	Knife	Man (re: wife)
1921	John Kaurawskas	36	Lithuania	Roman Catholic	White	Factory work	Milford	Hatchet	Woman (robbery)
1922	Emil Schutte	49	Germany	Lutheran	White	Shop owner	Haddam	Shotgun	Father, mother, and son
1926	Gerald Chapman	34	N.Y.	Roman Catholic	White	Criminal	New Britain	Handgun	Police officer
1927	Chin Lung	32	Unknown	Roman Catholic	Asian	Worker	Manchester	Handgun	Chinese man
1927	Soo Hoo Wing	22	N.J.	Roman Catholic	Asian	Worker	Manchester	Handgun	Chinese man
1929	John Feltovic	19	Conn.	Roman Catholic	White	Criminal	Bridgeport	Handgun	Man (robbery)

Sources: Helpful sources of data include *Executions in Connecticut since 1894* (Hartford: Connecticut State Library, 1972); and the database *Hartford Courant* Historical, 1764–1984, via the University of Connecticut Libraries.

executions that ever occurred in what is now Connecticut. From 1890 to 1899, there were eleven hangings; from 1900 to 1909, there were twelve; and from 1910 to 1919, there were twenty-four. If the rate of execution reflects a broader social pattern, it correlates with the new hegemony of corporate capitalism and the dislocation of vast numbers of people. The bookends of 1880 to 1889 with five people hanged and 1920 to 1929 with eight are historically high, but represent a tapering off from the peak years. It must be emphasized that the first two decades of the twentieth century are the zenith of capital punishment. Nothing comparable in actual numbers of executions occurred during the colonial period, the nineteenth century, or after 1930. After the ten-year high of 1910 to 1919, the rate of capital punishment continued dramatically downward (with the exception of the 1940s) throughout the rest of the twentieth century.

Gender

The sixty people executed were all males. It is axiomatic that men are more prone to violence than women, and there is likely what Edward Wilson might term a sociobiological basis for such behavior.[12] Whatever the predisposition for men to kill, a tacit protocol that had existed since the late eighteenth century worked to exclude females from the gallows. A patriarchal code of honor made it unmanly to hang a woman. Men might place womanhood on a pedestal, but the assumption remained that females were emotional and not entirely responsible for their actions. This gender bias spared women from the death penalty and put the onus on men. The *Hartford Courant* concluded that "a man would have been strung up without respite," but "the idea of hanging a woman is very repulsive."[13]

The most dramatic example of a woman saved from the death penalty was Bessie Wakefield. After two years in an adulterous love affair with James Plew, a farm laborer in his late twenties, the pair plotted to murder her husband, William O. Wakefield, on June 23, 1913. Bessie regarded William, with whom she had three young children, a cruel husband. With Bessie's complicity, Plew chloroformed William while he lay in bed on a Sunday morning. The drug did not have much effect, so Plew marched William into the woods in Cheshire where he shot his victim six times with a revolver and stabbed him with a jackknife. In a transparent attempt to suggest suicide, Plew left the victim with his shoelaces entwined about his neck. The illicit relationship was well known; thus, the motive for what was an obvious murder implicated the couple. Plew pleaded guilty and in one of the first examples of its kind allowed Judge Lucien Burpee of New Haven County Superior Court to interrogate witnesses and fix the degree of homicide. The judge found the defendant guilty of first-degree murder, and the warden of the state penitentiary hanged Plew at 12:02 a.m. on March 4, 1914.[14]

In a separate proceeding, Wakefield claimed that she was not guilty. An all-male jury, however, found her guilty on October 31, and she was sentenced to die on March 4 with Plew.[15] The defense's successful appeal to the state's highest court citing forty-five errors in the trial stayed the execution. The astounding number of errors was an announcement that violation of a taboo against the execution of women must not be allowed to proceed. Wakefield's plight set off an unprecedented storm of protest from the ongoing feminist movement. As reported in the *Hartford Courant,* Katharine Houghton Hepburn, president of the Connecticut Women's Suffrage Association and mother of the later famed actress, argued, "I am opposed to capital punishment and I am sure that I voice the sentiments of the suffragists of Hartford when I say I do not believe Mrs. Wakefield should be hanged." She and other officers of the association added, "No woman should suffer the death penalty when women are barred from participation in the lawmaking function." Elizabeth D. Bacon, president of the Hartford Equal Rights Club, brought a variant perspective. "Capital punishment," she averred, "is all wrong. Humanity demands its abolishment. Nevertheless as long as the present law exists both sexes should suffer equally."[16]

The Reverend Herbert J. White of First Baptist Church in Hartford seconded Bacon's position: "I am opposed to hanging Mrs. Wakefield—not because she is a woman but because she is a human being like the rest of us. Let us rise up and strike out this blot on Christianity and the name of our state." All three opposed capital punishment and supported women's rights but from different angles. In rejecting a double standard even to the point of death, White concluded, "Surely no woman wants to admit society loads woman with 90 per cent of our moral responsibilities, and certainly society cannot spare a woman's life because of her lack of morals."[17]

The sentiment to block Wakefield's hanging overwhelmed the position for equality of punishment. Some 30,000 petitioners from around the nation, unaware that there was no gubernatorial prerogative to commute, sent petitions, pro and con, to the governor. Women around the nation protested. Although the matter was entirely a state situation, a Pennsylvania matron called for Mrs. Woodrow Wilson, the president's wife, to intervene.[18] A ten-year-old New Jersey child wrote, "I am a little orphan girl and please don't kill this lady, and make orphans out of the little children."[19] Most tellingly, the editors of the

Hartford Courant recalled that Wakefield would be the first female hanged since 1786 when Hannah Occuish, a mixed-race girl, was infamously executed. The newspaper correctly observed, "The judicial cruelty of that hanging saved some other women from that fate."[20]

The Supreme Court of Errors in April 1914 granted a new trial. Among other issues, the tribunal found that the lower court had erred in not instructing the jury that some of the coroner's testimony was hearsay and ordered a new trial. The five-judge panel unanimously concluded, "We think that the defendant was harmed by the court's failure to give such instruction."[21] That summer, in the glare of national publicity, the second trial found her guilty of second-degree murder. Judge Joel H. Reed of New Haven County Superior Court sentenced her to life in prison.[22] At that time, the *Hartford Courant* called for the abolition of capital punishment, at least for women, because "man-made law" excludes participation by women.[23] Ironically, feminist arguments combined with patriarchal protection to endorse an unofficial ban on the execution of women that had existed in Connecticut since 1786, in southern New England since 1789, and in northern New England since 1905. As an afternote, the Connecticut Board of Pardons freed Wakefield from prison in 1933 after her eighteenth appeal. Women's groups persisted on her behalf, arguing that she was an ignorant, young woman victimized by older men.[24]

Age

Among those executed, young men figured prominently. More than half of the total were younger than thirty. Three teenagers were executed, the last ever to suffer that fate in Connecticut. Age fourteen was the statutory age of reason at the time, but no one younger than seventeen was hanged during this period. And only two men over age fifty—one age sixty-three and one ten years older—were executed. Never again would men of those advanced years be sentenced to death.

The murders committed by youths and elderly men were seen as irredeemable proof of a hardened criminality not worthy of commutation. On March 7, 1900, the Fairfield County Superior Court at Bridgeport found seventeen-year-old Charles Cross, a chore boy from a hardscrabble background in Brooklyn, New York, guilty of first-degree murder of his employer, a frail sixty-year-old resident of Long Ridge, during a rape.[25] The day before Cross's execution on July 20, the *Hartford Courant* concluded in an editorial titled "Misplaced Sympathy" that "the public will be safer in its homes" because "murderers in Connecticut are punished for their crimes and not for their years."[26]

Four years later, seventeen-year-old Joseph Watson shot Henry Osborn, Hartford's former police commissioner, to death in his home. The African American youth, who had arrived in the city from the Deep South two years earlier, had been Osborn's house servant. A dispute over wages and racial disrespect led to the homicide on August 5, 1904. As Watson put it, "I wanted revenge on Mr. Osborn for the way he treated me."[27] Anti-black tensions were high, and a crowd of 1,500 white people milled about the courthouse during the late September trial. During the proceedings, the indigent Watson, a school dropout at age ten, was represented by two attorneys. He pleaded not guilty. The able Hugh O'Flaherty challenged potential jurors about racial prejudice and argued that his client had come to reason with, not to kill, Osborn. "Can't we do something with the boy other than break his neck?" O'Flaherty asked the all-white jury.[28] After only twenty-eight minutes of deliberation on September 30, the foreman returned a unanimous verdict against Watson. Significantly, there was no effort to stay the execution of November 17 as there had been with Charles Cross, a white teenager. As the local press put it, "It is doubtful if there was ever a more unprovoked murder here or one that caused so much horror in the community."[29]

The oldest person executed in Connecticut was seventy-three-year-old Gershom Marx, a farmer in Colchester of Russian Jewish background. Authorities on April 8, 1904, dug up a dismembered body on Marx's property. Officials charged that Marx had killed Pavel Rodecki in a dispute over wages. They also suspected that Marx had similarly disposed of a "Hebrew peddler" and another immigrant farmhand.[30] An additional employee, a Polish man, claimed that Marx had tried to poison him. With the threat of arrest, Marx shaved his beard, donned new apparel, and fled to Paterson, New Jersey, where he was preparing to leave the country by steamer. With a hefty $3,000 posted for his apprehension, he was returned for trial in October, found guilty, and sentenced to hang on January 20, 1905. Governor Henry Roberts issued a reprieve to May 18, but neither Connecticut's Supreme Court nor its Board of Pardons intervened on the convict's behalf. A largely reticent Marx did not confess to the attending rabbi or any official. He took the warden of the state prison by the hand and said shortly before his execution, "Don't forget I always said I was innocent. Goodbye."[31] Marx's failure to admit guilt, even at the point of execution, raised unsettling questions about the righteousness of capital punishment.

None of the men at the extremes of the age spectrum was a native-born Connecticut Yankee of Protestant background. They were all in some way outsiders. Charles Cross was from poor circumstances in Brooklyn; Joseph Watson was a black youth from the Deep South; and John Feltovic was the son of Roman Catholic immigrants in the Bridgeport slums. Jacob Scheele, a beer-drinking German Protestant, and Marx, a bewhiskered Russian Jew, were born outside the United States. Of these five, three of them used firearms to commit homicide, and the other two employed bludgeons.

Nativity

At least forty-five of those executed in Connecticut were not born in the United States. Another three were either born outside the country or were probably the native-born children of recent arrivals. If one takes the higher number, 80 percent of those hanged were closely connected to overseas immigration. The twenty men born in Italy—one of three hanged—far exceeds any other place of nativity, including the United States. In fact, during the 1897–1920 period, a high point of new arrivals, twenty of forty-three people hanged—almost 50 percent—were born in Italy, yet those born in Italy in 1920 among the general population made up less than 20 percent of the foreign born in the state.[32] As early as 1897, the press observed after the execution of Nicodemo Imposino, an immigrant laborer, "The recent developments in this state seem to show that it [murder] runs among Italians of the lower class."[33] Although political boundaries were subject to change during an era of revolution and war, a significant number—seventeen—hailed from various parts of central and eastern Europe: four from Lithuania; three from Russia; four from Germany; three from Poland and Galicia; two from Hungary; and one from Bohemia. The handful from northwestern Europe reflects the shift in population away from that region at the start of the twentieth century. Of the four men born in Ireland, one in Scotland, and one in Sweden, all were hanged during the early part of the demographic shift. The last, Thomas Kippie, born of Irish migrants to Scotland, was executed in 1897. Thus, of six men hanged from northwestern Europe, five were actually Irish. Because a few places of nativity are not certain, as many as sixteen men or as few as fourteen were born in the United States. Only six were born in Connecticut. Geographic mobility, especially foreign-born status and notably nativity in Italy, characterized those executed.

Old-world traditions contributed prominently to some first-degree murder convictions. The practice of vendetta, what the newspapers called an
"Italian feud," played out on the night of September 25, 1917, in New Britain.
Giovanni Don Vanso, a twenty-one-year-old butcher in New York City,
learned that Raffaele Simonelli, who had allegedly killed his maternal uncle
in Nola, Italy, was living in Bridgeport. With Stephen Buglione, a fellow
worker of the same age, Don Vanso confronted their victim, whom they
shot three times in the back of the head with revolvers. All three men had
been born in Italy. After lengthy discussion with their counsel, both Don
Vanso and Buglione pleaded guilty. Their confession meant that Judge William S. Case of New Haven County Superior Court examined witnesses and
determined the degree of the crime without a jury. Judge Case found that
the young men's traditional act of vengeance "falls far short of removing
from the crime the elements which brand it as murder in the first degree."
The press described a "wild scene" in the courtroom as the death sentence
for November 16 was pronounced for the defendants. With Don Vanso in
tears, there was a "high state of hysterics" as female relatives screamed, tore
their clothes, stomped their feet, and fell to the floor.[34] The culture clash not
only of vendetta but unrestrained emotionalism worthy of a Verdi opera
was acted out in a normally staid New England courtroom. At their dual
execution, one after another, at the penitentiary, Don Vanso and Buglione
were attended by a Roman Catholic priest who gave them last rites and held
a crucifix to their lips moments before they were hanged. A flagging Don
Vanso's last words were mumbled in Italian.[35]

Ethnic hostility among diverse populations also led to executions. A
gang of five young Italian immigrants, including two brothers, on the night
of November 27, 1916, in West Haven shot to death Morris Goldstein in a
robbery. Goldstein, himself a new arrival to Connecticut, ran a secondhand
clothing store. He was also a peddler who bought old clothes, mended
them, and resold them at his business. Among these five scheming Roman
Catholics, rumor, building on centuries of anti-Semitism, had it that the
Jewish Goldstein carried $1,000 with him. Although Goldstein may have
seemed an easy mark, the victim resisted, and the assailants, armed with
revolvers, killed him. After an involved effort to determine guilt, various
punishments were ordered among the quintuplet. Carmine Battiata was
convicted to serve 3–15 years for manslaughter, and Luigi Lanzillo had a life
sentence for second-degree murder. The remaining three—Carmine Lanzillo, Carmine Pisaniello, and Francesco Dusso—were found to have been

directly involved in the actual homicide. Yankee dispatch was brought to their executions, which occurred on June 17, 1918. The trio was hanged within an hour of one another after midnight using the same knotted hemp. All the inept assailants found on the supposedly rich Jew was a watch, which they took. Goldstein had no money on him.[36]

Lithuanian self-help societies sought to distance themselves from Bernard Montvid and an accomplice, Peter Krakus. Montvid was convicted of having shot and strangled to death Father Joseph Zebris and his housekeeper, Eva Gilmanaitis, in a robbery at a Roman Catholic rectory in New Britain in 1915. All were Lithuanians. Adding to the outrage was that Father Zebris had baptized Montvid in the old country. Furthermore, the press reported that radical literature was found in the possession of Montvid and Krakus. Not only were the duo professional thieves and murderers, they were "socialists of the most rabid type," a correlation that explained for some the dangerous inclinations of foreigners.[37] In another venue, Krakus was executed in Delaware for killing a policeman. Two weeks before twenty-three-year-old Montvid was hanged, a spokesman for Lithuanians, Joseph Neviackas, wrote an open letter to the press stating that the two convicts never belonged to immigrant organizations. "We have," Neviackas wrote, "always urged our fellow countrymen to become citizens of this country and to obey the constitution and laws of this country."[38]

Race

Fifty-six of the sixty people executed in Connecticut during this period were of European background; the exceptions were two African Americans and two men of Chinese ancestry. All the victims of these homicides were white except for one Chinese man killed by other Chinese. No whites were hanged for killing anyone of another race, whereas two blacks were hanged for murdering whites. Seventeen-year-old Joseph Watson's murder of a prominent Hartford official in 1904, discussed earlier in another context, was one of the most sensational murders of the era. The issues of age and class, and especially race, made it so. Having lived in several areas in the Deep South, Watson was a recent arrival to the capital city, where he joined several relatives. Segregation, sharecropping, disfranchisement, lynching, and rioting against blacks characterized this nadir of racial relations in the South and border states. A well-established system of apartheid existed elsewhere, including Connecticut. In Hartford, the African American population was

about 1,500 people, or about 2 percent of the total 80,000 residents. According to a long-standing racial caste system, the vast majority of blacks worked
in menial jobs, primarily domestic service. Competition with the burgeoning number of "white" immigrants from southern and eastern Europe
worked to exclude blacks from more productive jobs.[39] A school dropout at
an early age, Watson worked as a "houseboy." A jaunty cap and assertive
air compensated for his low status. He owned a revolver and frequented
pool halls, a venue condemned by the better sorts.

   Watson's bloody murder of his employer, fifty-seven-year-old Henry Osborn, pivoted on the axis of race. A dispute over unpaid wages was complicated by the dominance of an older, powerful white man over a subordi-
nate, but defiant, black youth. Watson explained that Osborn "got mad and
called me names and said he wouldn't pay me a damn cent,"[40] so "I decided
to shoot him or pay him back somehow."[41] Whites, including Osborn, routinely referred to Watson as "Nigger Joe," a moniker that identified his inferior position.[42] A mortally wounded Osborn told an attending physician,
"The nigger shot me."[43] As word spread that Watson had shot Osborn but
had not been caught, a crowd of 1,000 whites gathered outside the victim's
fashionable row house on Capitol Avenue. Squads of police searched "the
negro [sic] quarters of the city" in a show of power and intimidation.[44] Nine
hours after the early morning shooting, police eventually found the culprit
hiding under a mattress in the victim's basement. "There is the nigger,
cover him with your gun," one arresting officer ordered another.[45] The
crowd cheered as Watson was led out, and there were some shouts of "lynch
him." The news account discounted the threats as not "serious," but in
"fun." With white mobs lynching blacks at an all-time high in the United
States, however, the call for extrajudicial justice was anything but light-
hearted jest. A "mob" was described milling about the police station where
Watson was held. Illustrations and photographs of a solemn-looking Watson after his arrest appeared prominently in the press. In keeping with eugenic descriptions of the criminal class, the *Hartford Courant* made clear that
"Watson's hair is very kinky . . . His features are of the pronounced negro
[sic] type." Front-page headlines pointed to a "Negro Murderer."[46]

   The police, however, acted to prevent any vigilante violence.[47] African
American spokesmen quickly disassociated the minority community from
the suspect and the homicide. William B. Edwards, "one of the leading colored men in the city," expressed "deep regret" that "a member of his race
should have been guilty of such a crime." He remembered Osborn as "a

friend of the colored race." He added that all "colored men" emphatically condemned the crime.[48] Similarly, the defense attorney Hugh O'Flaherty and state's attorney Arthur F. Eggleston avoided blaming a group for the wrongdoing of an individual. Flaherty sought to spare the defendant's life. Eggleston pressed for a first-degree murder conviction, but elegantly stated the ideal of impartial justice: Watson "is not here as a negro [sic]. He is here as a subject amenable to the law. The state knows no race or color."[49] The Reverend Aetius A. Crooke of African Methodist Zion Church ministered to the condemned man. In a Sunday sermon titled "The Lessons and Life of Joseph Watson," Crooke told a packed congregation that the youth had repented and had "died a converted man."[50] White officials and black spokesmen had in their own ways avoided a racial conflagration like those that occurred in a number of cities during the Jim Crow period. Retribution was allowed to unfold through established capital procedures. Given the mores of the day, Watson was buried in a segregated section of Spring Grove Cemetery.[51]

Rivalry between tongs—immigrant Chinese societies—made a New England appearance with the murder of Ong King, a Hip Song member, at a Manchester laundry on March 24, 1927. Two On Leong tong men from outside of Connecticut, Chin Lung, age thirty-two, and Soo Hoo Wing, age twenty-two, were sentenced to death for what appeared to be an assassination. A distinguished defense team, which included a former state attorney general, raised questions about Wing's culpability. They argued futilely before the Connecticut Board of Pardons that the only evidence against the younger man was a fingerprint on the handgun. As the chief defense counsel, Homer S. Cummings, forcefully put it, "There isn't enough evidence to hang a dog on, let alone a human being."[52]

Newspaper accounts reflected occidental stereotypes about the unfamiliar Asians. Although both men were described as "inscrutable," the press reported that the convicts broke into tears on learning that the Board of Pardons turned down their petition. The convicts were Baptists, but Wing's distraught wife of Japanese ancestry persuaded the death row inmates to convert to her religion, Roman Catholicism. After both men were hanged on November 8, 1927, the On Leong society in Hartford's Chinatown sponsored an elaborate funeral that mixed Eastern and Western traditions.[53] Unlike the fear and rage surrounding a black youth's murder of a white official, the intraracial killing of a Chinese man was more of a tragic curiosity. The Chinese were perceived as an exotic minority, small in number and inwardly focused, that was not a threat to the dominant culture.

Religion

A century after the disestablishment of the Congregational church in Connecticut, the religious affiliation of the sixty executed men reflected the changing demography of the state. Of forty-five men who were not Protestants, forty-one were Roman Catholics, three were Jews, and one was Russian Orthodox. Of those hanged, 75 percent were non-Protestants and 68 percent were Roman Catholics, mostly from Italy. The denominational transformation that the famine Irish had begun at midcentury was completed by the new immigrants. The descendants of Puritans, who once persecuted Roman Catholics, Jews, and other Protestants, were a minority during the twentieth century in the general population as well as in the execution chamber. The sequestration of executions within the confines of jails during the 1830s rendered the hortatory execution sermon to the assembled populace obsolete. Spiritual consolation became a private matter between clergy and convict, especially on death row at the penitentiary. A growing Irish population after 1850 made priests essential in the penitentiary and at the scaffold.

Twenty-three-year-old James Smith, who in a drunken rage shot to death the chief of police in Ansonia in 1880, was accompanied by three priests at his execution in the New Haven jail on September 1, 1882. Smith was administered last communion by Father McGuiney of Saint Mary's, appropriate attendance for a man born in Ireland. As he walked to the scaffold, the convict wore a crucifix over his black suit. After hanging for thirty minutes, officials cut down the body and gave it to the priests for burial. The press reported "great excitement among the Irish residents" in Ansonia.[54] In a line that stretched for a mile and a half, 10,000 people took a last look at the corpse that lay in state at Saint Assumption Church. In the funeral sermon, the priest warned about the evil of strong drink, a proverbial affliction of the Irish.[55]

As coreligionists of other nationalities emigrated, they found cultural and linguistic barriers to attendance by priests of Irish ancestry. Such was the case of the first Italian immigrant, Philip Pallidona, to be hanged in Connecticut. Pallidona, identified in the press as the "Italian murderer," shot his brother to death in a bitter financial quarrel in 1887 at Fairfield. Although Pallidona at first did not want to be attended by a priest, he came to accept the ministration of Father Leo of Winsted, the only Italian priest in Connecticut. He walked to the scaffold accompanied by the priest and a "countryman." Before Pallidona was hooded to be hanged, the priest held a crucifix for the condemned man to kiss. After Pallidona was executed at the Bridgeport jail in 1888, attending doctors wanted to experiment on the corpse with electric stimulation. An indignant Father Leo tolerated no such sacrilege and had the body buried within an hour. Ironically, it was Italian scientists Luigi Galvani and Alessandro Volta who had popularized galvanism or electrophysiology.[56]

Three Jews, two immigrants and one probably of the second generation, were executed. Although attended by Rabbi C. Hoffenberg of congregation Ados Israel, seventy-three-year-old Gershom Marx refused to confide in his spiritual counselor. The aloof Marx had no contact with relatives and invited no one to his execution. The rabbi dutifully attended the execution, but was, as the press reported, "unnerved by the ordeal"[57] on the early morning of May 18, 1905. A Jewish undertaker took the corpse for burial at Bris Abraham cemetery.[58]

Jewish organizations rallied on behalf of Louis Saxon. No one doubted that a jealous Saxon, a tailor from Russia, had shot to death Anna Spelansky in New Britain at her place of work on the night of November 27, 1912. Jews sought, however, to clarify misunderstanding of their traditions and to ensure due process. They mobilized speakers, legal talent, and political influence, including that of Herman Kopplemann, a state representative. A circular was sent for funds to the "Hebrew people" of the state. Attorney Jacob Schwolsky sought to correct reports that Saxon was not married to Spelansky, with whom he had three children and from whom he subsequently separated. Schwolsky explained that in Russia the czarist government recognized the legitimacy of marriage officiated by "any good Jew," rabbi or layperson.[59] On another front, prominent figures such as Dr. Louis Blumer and Rabbi Koma Rosenbaum testified that Saxon was non compos mentis. As Schwolsky put it, "An insane person should not be hanged."[60] An appeal to the Connecticut Supreme Court, supported by money from Russian Jews, came to naught. Authorities hanged Saxon on June 27, 1913.[61]

Coreligionists sought a commutation for William Wise, a waiter, who was convicted of killing Anna Tobin, a married gentile woman with whom he was having an affair in New Britain in 1917. The incriminating evidence, however, seemed persuasive. Wise's account to the police that "the Jews did it"—slashed Tobin's throat and wounded him—appeared the statement of a desperate man.[62] He was defended by attorney Albert Greenberg. A rabbi and Wise's sobbing sister pleaded unsuccessfully with the Board of Pardons to spare his life. After Wise's hanging on December 14, 1917, the United Jewish Charities arranged for his burial.[63] There was nothing comparable in Connecticut to the lynching by prominent citizens in Marietta, Georgia, of the falsely accused Leo Frank in 1915 for the rape and murder of thirteen-year-old Mary Phagan, an outrage that led to the founding of the Anti-Defamation League.

Social Status

By any measure, almost all the men hanged were at or near the bottom of society. No one of the upper class and few that might be termed middle class were executed. None matriculated at college, and few attended high school. Overall educational attainment was marginal. After Paul Misik, a Hungarian quarryman, confessed to the shooting death of another man in 1903 in Newington after a drunken quarrel in a saloon over thirty cents, the press commented on "the prevalence of ignorance among immigrants."[64] Incomes were limited, residences humble, living standards modest. The overwhelming number worked in blue-collar or manual labor, arduous but not very remunerative employment. A typical job was a factory operative, day laborer, farmhand, quarryman, tinsmith, handyman, dishwasher, house boy, milkman, cobbler, waiter, tailor, butcher, or woodcutter. Some—including Henry Hamlin, Bernard Montvid, Isaac Williams, Harry Roe, and John Feltovic— were engaged in systematic burglary and robbery. Joseph Buonomo was associated with organized crime, particularly prostitution, in New York City and Chicago.[65] Chin Lung and Soo Hoo Wing took on the role of assassins for their tong. The most notorious criminal was a national gangster of the 1920s, Gerald Chapman, a fugitive from federal prison who pulled off a multimillion dollar heist.

The individual who had the highest social ranking was Emil Schutte, a German Lutheran immigrant. A robustly built man with a bristling mustache, he was known as a "prosperous businessman" in Haddam who owned a general store and farm. While a constable, he arrested a neighbor Joseph Ball, a ne'er-do-well with whom he had a feud. His rage built to such a point that in the early morning darkness of December 10, 1915, he set fire to the Balls' home (Schutte called it a "shack"). As the parents and a son fled the house in panic, Schutte blasted them with a shotgun. Aided by his sixteen-year-old son Julius, they dragged the bodies back into the conflagration, where they were consumed by fire. Authorities later sifted through the remains and found the buckshot.

A stern patriarch of eight children, Schutte had once chased his wife with a revolver across a field after a quarrel. Four of his children, including Julius, eventually testified against their father, who was found guilty in 1921 of the murder of the Ball family. A defiant Schutte declared, "The Balls were beasts. I'd do it again if I had to," although he officially maintained his innocence.[66] His children added that he had also killed a hired man and cremated his corpse, a crime for which he was not charged. A reprieve by the governor, two appeals to the Connecticut Supreme Court, and a petition to the Board of Pardons only delayed his execution to October 24, 1922. There was little likelihood for a commutation for what the press called "one of the most sordid and horrible stories."[67] The day before the execution, the father forgave and kissed his children, including Julius, who had testified against him. As officials hanged the forty-nine-year-old murderer, he clutched roses in his hands.[68]

Weapons

During the urban industrial era, handguns were for the first time the predominant weapon used by those hanged for murder. In these incidents of homicide that led to execution of the convicted perpetrators, firearms of all types, especially handguns, were the cause of most victims' deaths. Samuel Colt had patented the revolver in 1836, but the arsenals of the Civil War expanded production of armaments of all types. Although a 1915 law penalized the carrying of concealed weapons without a permit and eight years later sales of pistols to "aliens" were restricted, handguns were plentiful, accessible, cheap, and deadly. The pistol that Joseph Watson used to shoot Henry Osborn several times was bought in 1902 by the then fifteen-year-old African American youth for $5 in Savannah, Georgia.[69] A jealous Frank Grela, a laborer from Galicia, obtained a revolver and cartridges in Hartford in 1915 shortly before he shot his wife several times in the head as she slept at night with their nine-month-old baby.[70]

The readily available handgun was the weapon of choice in robbery, especially for the professional criminal. Of thirteen capital robberies in which executions resulted, eight involved gunplay. Although the pistol facilitated robbery, the situation could irrevocably turn lethal. A thirty-three-year-old laborer, Charles Boinay, and his brother-in-law David Weeks in the night of 1897 invaded the farm home in Trumbull of sixty-four-year-old George Marcus Nichols, expecting to find some $2,000. In the confusion of the darkness in which there was an exchange of gunfire, Nichols was shot to death and his sister wounded. Little money was found. Boinay, who had served eleven years in prison for burglary in New York, hanged for the new offense.[71] In an audacious daytime robbery, a masked twenty-one-year-old Benjamin Willis and twenty-year-old Frederick Brockhaus broke into the home of the Lamberts, who headed the Wilton Academy for boys. While Dr. David Lambert (a Yale graduate and pillar of the community) was absent, the culprits chloroformed his wife and ransacked the house for valuables. When the husband unexpectedly returned, the two drunken assailants shot him a half dozen times. The wife later identified Willis as a former student whom the Lamberts had mentored but later expelled for unruly behavior. Both youths, from impoverished backgrounds in New York City, were hanged separately, in 1898 and 1899, for what the press called "one of the most unprovoked and brutal" crimes in Fairfield County.[72]

Handguns also facilitated premeditated murder for the purpose of robbery. A fledging actor, twenty-one-year-old George Redding, sought funds to marry an older woman. As he bluntly put it, "I was broke and needed some money."[73] He lured a young New Haven peddler, Morris Greenberg, to a farm in Hamden to buy produce in 1912. Thinking that the Jewish vendor would be carrying a substantial amount of cash, Redding shot him twice in the back. While the victim pleaded for mercy, the robber shot him twice more in the chest, only to find that the dealer had no money on him. Redding confessed and was hanged the same year.[74] An epidemic of handgun murders had led a decade earlier to a recommendation by the press: "Suppose the police should take fifty men at random in the saloon district and search them, how many would be found unarmed? The policy of not searching until after the deed is done would be amusing, if it were not fatal."[75]

Firearms were the weapon that caused the death of law enforcement officials for which four men were hanged. Henry Hamlin, an inmate, was executed in 1880 for shooting a guard in a futile effort to escape from the penitentiary.[76] James Smith was sentenced to death in 1882 for killing the chief of police of Ansonia with a pistol while on a drunken binge.[77] Jacob Scheele blasted a constable who sought to enforce the temperance laws with a shotgun at New Canaan in 1888.[78] And the notorious gangster of the early 1920s Gerald Chapman shot to death a patrolman who surprised him during a department store heist in New Britain.[79]

Victims

Of the crimes for which men were executed from 1880 to 1929, there were about three male victims for every two females. Men were hanged for killing other men for a variety of provocations, including barroom insults, sexual rivalry, job disputes, robbery, vendettas, and resistance to police officers. The men executed for murdering women had a specific pattern of violence. In extradomestic violence, most homicides involved sexual matters. In domestic violence, ten females were victims. Two were minors; the remaining

eight men (all immigrants with low-paid jobs) went to the gallows for killing their wives.

Of the wife murders, the situation of John Swift highlighted the debate
over capital punishment and women's safety. A legislative commutation of
Swift's death sentence for the murder of his estranged wife provoked a pa-
ternalistic reaction in favor of capital punishment to protect women. A
drunken twenty-two-year-old Swift, who had threatened to kill his wife,
Katie, shot her in the back as she walked to work in downtown Hartford in
1887. Swift petitioned the judiciary committee that inebriation was reason
to reduce his punishment to life in prison. A passionate debate over the issue
ensued. As the scheduled execution approached on April 15, 1889, a majority
of both bodies of the legislature sided with the convict, the House by 118 to
100 and the Senate by 14 to 8. Governor Morgan G. Buckeley vetoed the
commutation and issued a reprieve to April 18 to allow time for a possible
override of the veto.[80]

A demand to execute Swift developed. Katie Swift's dying words—"John
knew what he was doing"—confirmed the threat against her life, for which
she had previously sought police protection.[81] It was contended in sparing
Smith that "drunken husbands will be strengthened in their brutality."
Swift was characterized as "a professional sot, a bar-room loafer, a married
man familiar with the lowest haunts and lowest women of town, unfaithful,
vile in body and vile in mind."[82] An editorial denounced the legislative commutation: "Womankind all through the state—patient, suffering and to a
large degree defenseless women—have in the commutation of his sentence
something to think of with wonder, not to say terror." Reacting to the outcry against the wife killer, the legislature failed to override Buckeley's veto.
On April 18, the sheriff hanged the native of Ireland; the press concluded,
"The law is vindicated."[83]

Reportage

Newspapers dominated the coverage of capital punishment as never before.
With the isolation in 1893 of executions within the penitentiary, journalists
were among the few allowed to witness the proceedings. Mass literacy and
Linotype production made newspapers cheap and readily available to an
expanding urban readership. Crime stories are of perennial interest, and the
press provided comprehensive coverage. The newspaper so dominated the
reporting of capital crimes that the earlier pamphlet literature was largely

superseded, although lurid crime thrillers thrived. With abundant publicity, death row inmates no longer published their own accounts, as they had earlier. There was plenty of sensation to be had in the penny press.

The *Hartford Courant,* the nation's oldest continuously published newspaper, substantially expanded its reporting of death penalty cases. By the 1890s, drawings of defendants first appeared regularly. The portraiture usually depicted the person in formal dress with a placid visage, not a berserker in a homicidal rage. Such was the drawing of Thomas Kippie, who wore a tie, sported a trimmed mustache, and had neatly parted hair. Kippie, a Scottish immigrant of Irish Catholic parentage, was, however, a chronic alcoholic who in 1896 had stabbed his long-abused wife repeatedly during a quarrel at their New Haven home. Because he raved and tore about the courtroom, officials chained him.[84] So too Nicodemo Imposino was shown very proper in a bow tie, yet the twenty-four-year-old Italian immigrant had hacked his wife with a hatchet in East Norwalk in 1897 after suspicions arose about her fidelity.[85] In the illustrations, at least, there was no effort to play on ethnic stereotypes.

Such was not the case for Joseph Watson. If working-class immigrants, nicely dressed and groomed, looked like respectable white folks, Watson's depiction clearly showed that he was African American. The racial boundary was fluid enough for the Irish, Italians, and Jews to become white, but blacks remained black. Whites in Hartford commonly referred to Watson, before and after the murder, as "nigger Joe," a racial tag that set the youth apart. As the story about the arrest of the "Negro Murderer" put it, "His features are of the pronounced negro [sic] type."[86] The newspaper also ran a photograph of the victim, Henry Osborn, and the bedroom in which he was killed, a broadening of visual interest beyond the columns of words. So too photographs of female victims of male violence were now displayed. Frank Grela and the wife he had shot to death in 1915 in a Hartford tenement, and William Wise and Anna Tobin, his married girlfriend whose throat he slit on the streets of New Britain in 1917, all appeared, looking their best.[87] Although the writing was explicit, illustrations never showed a corpse, including those whom the state hanged.

The exploits of the national gangster Gerald Chapman, who shot to death a New Britain patrolman in October 1924, became a media event in Connecticut. The *Hartford Courant* alone carried 350 stories on Chapman during a two-year period. Not as well known today as some gangsters, Chapman was described in the press as "a figure of mystery," a "legend," and "the master criminal."[88] Born in the Irish slums of New York, he turned to crime to lead the high life. Skilled in the use of nitroglycerine to crack safes, the stylish brigand was most notorious for having organized the robbery of a mail truck in Manhattan that transported more than $2 million in cash and security. Convicted to serve twenty-five years at the federal penitentiary at Atlanta, he escaped twice. While at large, he killed Officer James Skelley who interrupted a burglary at a New Britain department store, and fled. The police in Muncie, Indiana, eventually captured him in January 1925 after a gun battle.[89]

Despite various appeals to the United States Supreme Court and President Calvin Coolidge, federal authorities turned Chapman over to Connecticut authorities to be tried for felony murder. Governor John H. Trumbull reluctantly granted three reprieves to allow further redress from the original execution date of June 25, 1925. Chapman maintained his innocence and garnered voluminous support with his celebrity status. The governor's archives on Chapman contain numerous petitions, letters, telegrams, and postcards from across the land. Most opposed the execution, and hundreds, if not thousands, signed petitions to that effect. The motivation appeared mixed. Some were conscientiously opposed to capital punishment; others thought Chapman was innocent. A few were eccentric, containing death threats to the governor, last-minute evidence that exonerated Chapman, and confessions that they had committed the murder. Those supporting the execution took the position espoused by a Presbyterian minister in Missouri. The Reverend M. H. Kerr wrote, "Unless we have many executions of this kind, our nation is in peril and our civilization threatened."[90] An editorial comment from the *Hartford Courant* added that Chapman's cold-blooded murder of the Irish-born cop and family man raised "a knotty problem for those who cry out against capital punishment."[91]

Events surrounding Chapman's execution were sensational. A crowd of 700 gathered outside the penitentiary for the execution that occurred shortly after midnight on April 6, 1926. Several hundred convened at the funeral home in Hartford that received his corpse. Death threats were made against the governor and Hugh M. Alcorn, the state's attorney who had prosecuted Chapman. Rumors flew that gunmen planned to bomb the penitentiary with dynamite. Extra state police patrolled the area. Adding to the tension, the Ku Klux Klan, popular during a wave of anti-immigrant and black bigotry during the 1920s, coincidentally burned fiery crosses in Wethersfield, site of the execution, and gunshots were heard throughout the night.[92] As much as Chapman was hyped by the media, there were some critical reflections. The *Hartford Courant* observed, "He appealed to the bourgeois intellect that craves excitement as release from boredom in following with unending interest and passion chronicles of lust and violent death."[93]

The Technology of Capital Punishment

As of 1830, state law mandated that executions be excluded from indiscriminate view, but some things remained the same as before. Crowds of several hundred ticket holders were still admitted to the spectacle; others less privileged sought vantage spots for a look inside or milled about outside. On occasion, the public paraded through the jail to behold the corpse lying in a coffin. There were technical problems. Local sheriffs were not experienced hangmen. Some jails needed elaborate screening to block the sight from unintended viewers. Gallows, expensive and functional, had to be erected. Officials feared a botched hanging. By 1880, a portable, well-constructed gallows was hauled by wagon to jails around the state to obviate these problems. Edwin Hoyt, an alcoholic Civil War veteran convicted of stabbing his aged father to death, was the first to die on this apparatus, on May 13, 1880. The sheriff issued four hundred passes for the event at the Fairfield County Jail in Bridgeport, but the voices of hundreds denied admission could be heard from the outside. A twenty-foot enclosure was constructed to block the view from outside the jail. A five-eighth-inch rope on pulleys ran to a crossbeam over the four-foot-square drop. The sheriff had earlier simulated an execution with a sandbag. If the rope stretched and allowed the man's feet to hit the ground, the neck would not be broken, "adding," as one commentator remarked, "torture to judicial killing."[94]

After reading the death warrant to Hoyt, the sheriff at 11:30 a.m. led the thirty-eight-year-old convict, followed by an Episcopal priest, deputies, and physicians, from inside the jail to an enclosed scaffold. The convict was dressed in a black suit and tie, and his arms were tightly pinioned behind him with leather straps. He mounted the steps to the drop and stared out from the railed platform at the spectators, including newspaper reporters seated at tables in front. He sat on a chair as a deputy strapped his legs at the ankles. The sheriff ritualistically asked the prisoner if he had anything to say about why the sentence should not be carried out. There was no response. The priest read a brief burial service and in a parting benediction lay his hand on Hoyt's head. A deputy adjusted the noose with the knot tightened high under Hoyt's left jawbone, and another pulled a black hood over his head. The sheriff in an emotion-laden voice bade him farewell and in a parting gesture squeezed the prisoner's hand. He moved to the front of the platform, where a low screen hid the rod that released the bolt holding the trap. The sheriff exclaimed to the audience, "I now proceed to execute the sentence of the law."[95] Since he was standing with other deputies behind the screen, it was not possible for spectators to see who actually released the bolt. The executioner remained anonymous and symbolically absolved of premeditated murder at state command.

The whole protocol from entering the courtyard to that moment took only minutes. At 11:33 a.m., the trap fell and Hoyt dropped heavily. The spectators watched in rapt silence. His feet barely touched the ground before the rebound of the stout rope lifted him several inches clear. His head twisted to the right and raised the hood, revealing where the rope abraded the neck and drew blood. The president of the Fairfield County Medical Association went to the dangling figure to measure the pulse at intervals, which another physician recorded. The initial tremors of the body ceased, and after twelve minutes there was no pulse. Deputies unbound Hoyt's arms and opened his vest. A physician pressed his ear to Hoyt's chest; no heartbeat was heard.

After thirty-five minutes (allowing for extra time to make sure death had occurred), the corpse was lowered onto the lid of a black-shrouded coffin. The sheriff, clergyman, and physicians returned to the jail, with five deputies carrying the deceased. The physicians examined the body and concluded that death was caused by the dislocation of the cerebral vertebrae; in other words, Hoyt's neck was broken. Nearly an hour after death, the doctors applied a galvanic battery to the body that produced some electrophysiological reactions. That afternoon, Hoyt's steadfast sisters took possession of their brother's body for burial. A witness of the hanging concluded of the precise procedure, "No unnecessary pain was inflicted, every arrangement was perfect, admirable decorum was preserved."[96]

Over the next fifteen years, the gallows was trundled over hill and dale to claim seven more convicts. Most were, as that of the cop-killer James Smith in 1882 at the New Haven County Jail, "creditably managed" and transpired with "due solemnity."[97] There were problems with the mechanics of death, however. Andrew Borjesson, a Swedish immigrant who had slit the throat of the woman who rebuffed him, was scheduled to die at Litchfield County Jail in 1892. Two horses pulled the gallows northward from its New Haven home base, but the local facility was not suited for the gallows, so authorities erected a temporary structure nearby.[98]

Besides the technical problems, the emotional stability of the death row inmate presented a challenge. Angelo Petrillo, who shot his brother-in-law to death on the streets of New Haven in 1891, was the first immigrant from southern or eastern Europe to be hanged. Attended by priests, including the Italian-born Father Leo, and two Sisters of Mercy, the twenty-five-year-old husband and father nevertheless suffered a breakdown. From his cell, he yelled for help and cried out "murder." He was carried bodily on the death march to the scaffold, where he continued screaming until the very last moment. Guards had to hold an agitated Petrillo over the trap.[99]

Problems plagued the mode of the death penalty at the dawn of the twentieth century. The spectacle of a traveling gallows was a macabre statement on New England culture. Flustered sheriffs were besieged by hundreds of requests for admission to a hanging. The hysterics of Petrillo—"one of the most harrowing in the records of the state"—forced the issue.[100] In response, the General Assembly in 1893 made a landmark change. The place of execution was made exclusively within the state penitentiary, itself an armed fortress. The warden was sole executioner, and, unlike the county sheriffs, became adept at his trade. The moment of death was hidden in the night—"before the hour of sunrise on the designated day"—as a means to further isolate the event and to render the paradox of judicial killing less apparent. Spectators were restricted to two dozen or fewer, and mostly officials at that. In addition to prison staff, the sheriff from the county in which the prisoner was convicted, the prisoner's clergyman, and not more than three adult males designated by the prisoner were authorized to attend. Women and children were excluded; death was man's business.[101] The 1893 legislation institutionalized, centralized, and professionalized capital punishment as it had never been before.

Further innovation occurred in 1894 with the mechanization of the gallows. There was some attraction for the application of electricity that in the age of Thomas Edison seemed à la mode. "The best proposal ever made was that of the *Scientific American,* perhaps of others previously," the *Hartford Courant* enthused, "that a great electric spark be applied to the victims and they be shocked to death. It is sure, instantaneous, and uniform."[102] Although New York State had three years earlier first employed electrocution at Auburn prison, cautious Connecticut legislators appropriated $3,000 to refine what was familiar.

An isolated room at the penitentiary was set aside for the death chamber. The chief engineer of the prison modified a contraption used with great success in Colorado and widely adopted elsewhere. Ironically, a former inmate, a skilled carpenter, implemented the plans. Warden Jabez L. Woodbridge patented the device in 1910. The same automatic gallows was used for all fifty-five hangings at the penitentiary from 1894 to 1936.[103]

No longer did the convict just fall to his death, but his body was suddenly jerked upward and then dropped downward. Not only was the combination deadly, but there was less chance in the jerk upward that the noose would come unadjusted. A pulley system bolted into a substantial beam conveyed the rope and noose. The other end was affixed to a 300-pound counterweight (later increased to 450 pounds). Once the condemned man, his arms pinioned, stepped on a metal plate beneath the noose, his weight activated a noiseless mechanism (constructed by Pratt and Whitney) attached to the counterweight. Three well-trained guards quickly played their parts: one strapped the legs above and below the knee; the second adjusted the black hood; and the third fixed the knot of the noose tight to the left jaw. At that moment, the cylindrical counterweight was timed to plunge through a circular opening in the floor, lifting the prisoner suddenly six feet toward the ceiling. Strangulation and dislocation of the neck were produced by the upward pull and then subsequent fall to within two feet of the floor. The warden, facing the condemned man from across the room, could override the mechanism with a lever, which, if uninterrupted, would drop the counterweight at the end of forty seconds. A dial, emblazoned grimly with a skull and crossbones, above the door to the death chamber registered the expended time. If necessary, the warden could at any point stop the mechanism or drop the counterweight by hitting a red lever.[104]

The state board of charities that oversaw various public institutions protested what was called the new automatic gallows. There was concern that the prisoner activated the mechanism when he stood on an iron plate, thus adding suicide to the crime of murder. The legal opinion was, however, that there was no violation of the 1893 statute because "the condemned man dies by the application of the law of gravity."[105] In addition, medical opinion concluded, "The gallows adopted is certainly more humane in that it raises the man from the ground, giving the blow of death at once instead of at the end of a drop." The physicians added that "the condemned in no sense commits suicide, as he in no sense executes any voluntary motion towards its end."[106] An illustration from 1926 shows the warden depressing a plunger with his right foot that activates a lever that controls the counterweight, which is hidden behind a partition.[107]

Thirty-seven-year-old convict John Cronin, an Irish immigrant who was born in Wales, was first. In an act of revenge, the drunken tobacco worker shot his former landlord in the back in South Windsor in 1893 as he ate breakfast with his young daughter. As the execution date of December 18, 1894, approached with a rejection from the Board of Pardons, the warden moved the convict to the "death cage," a room next to the execution chamber in the "death house." The cage was made of hardened steel that neither saw nor file could cut. In further precautions, guards strip-searched Cronin and gave him new prison garb before confining him. A Roman Catholic priest and two Sisters of Mercy visited him. Despite the dehumanizing aspects, officials stressed the amenities of the "iron cage." There was a soft mattress, a feather pillow, carpet, a toilet, running water, and a reading lamp, under which he perused religious literature. Personal items and a rosary lay on a table. He conversed with guards and a reporter. The warden's wife sent him flowers and candy, a practice that faded as impersonal, institutional rigor dominated.[108]

In preparation for the execution, the warden closed the prison, locked down the four hundred inmates, and posted guards. Shortly after midnight, the warden awoke Cronin and read the death warrant. In an act of absolution for his role as executioner, the warden concluded, "I bear you no ill will. I am simply doing my duty," and Cronin replied, "I bear no hard feelings toward you, warden."[109] Two priests administered last rites in the iron cage. The warden returned to the main building and led a procession of officials to the death house. Nineteen people—prison staff, clergy, physicians, and reporters—were present in the execution chamber. Cronin had not invited anyone to attend. One hundred fifty people had applied to be present, not aware that the 1893 statute excluded the public.

At 1:00 a.m., all was ready. Guards pinioned Cronin's arms behind him and led him the few paces from the iron cage through an unbolted oak door to the execution chamber. The priests, chanting prayers, followed Cronin. An engineer stood ready in case of a problem with the apparatus. Reporters lined the back wall. The warden took over control of the levers of the automatic mechanism. Cronin stepped on the plate and was quickly strapped, hooded, and noosed. With a high sign from a guard, the warden hit the red lever, dropping the counterweight, and twenty seconds later at 1:02 a.m. Cronin was yanked up and then fell down, just as planned. Physicians seven minutes later detected no pulse and four minutes after that no heartbeat. As a *New York Times* reporter concluded, Cronin died with "no struggling or other repulsive feature to the execution."[110]

After that milestone, Connecticut executed dozens of men in an almost routine manner. With floodlights illuminating the death house, the whitewashed execution chamber with its specialized personnel and technical apparatus had a clinical atmosphere. Speed and predictability were of great importance. An official timer measured to the fraction of a second the extinction of life. Motejius Rikteraites, twenty-six-year-old Lithuanian immigrant, slashed his wife's throat in 1913 in Waterbury. Within twenty-four seconds of entering the death chamber shortly after midnight on May 8, 1914—before he could take in the scene—he was hanged. Twenty-seven-year-old Pasquale Zuppa had killed a fellow Italian immigrant for his money in Guilford in 1915. On March 10, 1916, he entered the death room at 12:05:02 a.m., and in a record-breaking fifteen seconds, even giving time to kiss a crucifix held to his lips by Father Francis Bonforti of Saint Anthony's in Hartford, the trap was sprung. In less than twelve minutes, a doctor pronounced him dead.[111]

Even mass production was possible. Multiple hangings on the same hemp rope, ad seriatim, within minutes of one another included Giuseppe Campagnolo and Raphael Carfaro in 1909;[112] Isaac Williams and Harry Roe in 1916;[113] the only deaf mutes executed, Joseph Castelli and Francisco Vetere, in 1917;[114] Giovanni Don Vanso and Stephen Buglione in 1917;[115] Carmine Lanzillo, Carmine Pisaniello, and Francesco Dusso in 1918;[116] and the only brothers ever executed, Erasmo Perretta and Joseph Perretta, in 1919.[117]. Eleven were Italian immigrants; Williams and Roe were an interracial duo.

The more automatic, the more dehumanized execution became. Daniel Cerrone in 1920 cried out desperately as the noose tightened, "Mama! Mama!"[118] The unclaimed body of Ephraim Sherouk (aka Frank Sherrie), a native of Russia, was buried on the penitentiary grounds in 1906.[119] Nikifor Nechesnook's corpse in 1919 was lowered into a basket and shipped to Yale Medical School for dissection.[120] An observer noted in 1926 that the notorious gangster Gerald Chapman, strapped for execution, looked "far from a heroic figure."[121] Tong member Chin Lung, one year later, was described at the point of death as "an ungainly human package."[122] Reporter John Kelly called the youthful John Feltovic's hanging in 1929 a "rocket trip to the high ceiling."[123] Feltovic gasped a dozen times, clutched at his coat, kicked free of his leg straps, and twisted to and fro on the rope. Several days after the execution, the editors justified Kelly's explicit content: "If capital punishment is to be retained as a deterrent of murder—the widest possible publicity should be given to the methods of its application."[124]

An Enthusiasm for Eugenics

At the turn of the twentieth century, the new technology of death was, along with eugenics, a response to a broadly perceived threat by a dangerous underclass. The unequal distribution of power and wealth in the capitalist system generated the self-serving ideology of social Darwinism: those at the top were superior, and those at the bottom inferior. The pseudoscience of eugenics lent itself to elite efforts to restrict, segregate, and eliminate the supposed defectives, all in the name of improvement of the human race, while legitimating the privilege of the better sort. Connecticut in 1895 enacted the nation's first law penalizing marriage and fornication if a partner was mentally retarded, an epileptic, or a pauper.[125] Sterilization statutes in 1909 and 1918 established procedures at the state prison and public hospitals for the insane if those inmates might "produce children with an inherited tendency toward crime, insanity, feeble-mindedness, idiocy, or imbecility." The 130 ayes to 28 nays in the House showed overwhelming support. By 1932, 8 males and 150 females had been legally sterilized.[126] Simeon Eben Baldwin, chief justice and Democratic governor (1911–1915), believed whipping, which had been abolished a century earlier, to be an effective deterrent for some crimes and supported castration as a punishment for rape.[127] "Stop the supply of the vicious, the weak, the no-willed people," a pamphlet written around the same time warned, "who cannot support themselves in the community—of the criminals and prostitutes and paupers, by cutting off the supply at its source, namely—by providing adequate custodial care of the feeble-minded of the State."[128] The pamphlet, written by the state medical superintendent of the mentally retarded, was characteristic of the desire to restrain the dangerous classes.

In its description of first-degree murderers, the press employed similar language. The assumption was that if these convicts had genetic traits that predisposed them to violence, their executions were necessary to preserve law and order. The argument for biological determinism obviated examination of the social and economic context of crime. Eugenics in this sense offered an apology for capital punishment, not unlike some predestined sinner of Puritan times destined to hellfire.

Ironically, an Italian Jew, Cesare Lombroso, developed the concept of criminal anthropology, that body types posited biological determinism.[129] Yankee observers regularly characterized executed immigrants as subhuman. Philip Pallidona, the "Italian murderer," had a "sullen" countenance. Moreover, "his head is small, and narrows toward the top in a manner which would cause the ordinary observer to set him down as of inferior intellect." He was "the lower class of his nationality" with a "repulsive face, low forehead, short chin and neck."[130] Giuseppe Fuda was "low-browed, swarthy and ignorant."[131] Similarly, John Cronin had a "heavy shoulder" and a "chuck neck" and walked with a "shamble." The Irish immigrant was "an undoubted degenerate, the last of a dying family, and had little or none of those sensibilities which form the distinction between man and the lower order of animals."[132] Another Irish Catholic, Thomas Kippie, "inherited vicious and degenerate traits."[133] With Hungarian quarryman Paul Misik in mind, the *Hartford Courant* deplored the concealed weapons, saloon culture, and "prevalence of ignorance among immigrants."[134]

Native-born murderers of the lower class also shared defective inheritance, as reported in the press. The ancestors of the young Charles Cross were drunks, epileptics, prostitutes, and the insane. He himself was "a liar and thief from childhood, addicted to immoral habits, and a cigarette fiend."[135] Dark-skinned Joseph Watson's hair was "very kinky," and his features were of "the pronounced negro [sic] type."[136] Handyman Henry Bailey bore the "hereditary taint" of drunkenness from his mother.[137] Most emphatically preordained to murder was farm laborer James Plew, who was allegedly related to the notorious Jukes, a family to which criminologist R. L. Dugdale in 1877 traced generations of criminals. The press concluded, "The shadow of the gallows was upon him when he was born—he now awaits the fate of many of his blood."[138]

Although the attraction for tough-minded solutions to social problems subverted efforts to abolish capital punishment, a minority of voices called for abolition. Francis Wayland, a professor at the Yale Law School, made the case in 1883 at the American Social Science Association, of which he was president. In an early use of forensic statistics, he found that between 1850 and 1880 ninety-seven people were tried for first-degree murder. Of that number, thirteen were convicted in the first degree. Seven were executed, but six had their death sentences commuted to life in prison. Forty-two were found guilty in the second degree, and seven were acquitted on grounds of insanity. He concluded that juries were often reluctant to impose the death penalty, even in some blatant situations. Rather than continue a law that was not consistently enforced, he urged its repeal. In its place, he urged life in prison without the possibility of release. "Hanging does nothing more than put him out of the way," he said, adding, "Does imprisonment for life do less?"[139]

Abolitionist sentiment momentarily surfaced in the General Assembly a decade later. Ratcliffe Hicks stressed that capital punishment was "imperfect": "You have never executed in this State a man worth $10,000 and never can, no matter what kind of a murder he commits," he inveighed. "I plead for the same laws and the penalties for the Vanderbilt and wandering beggar in the street."[140] Representative Walter S. Judd added that execution was no deterrent to murder, and notable public figures such as Henry Ward Beecher, Charles Sumner, Horace Greeley, and Wendell Phillips were abolitionists. A majority of the judiciary committee, however, supported the status quo. Typical of the entire period, the bill to abolish the death penalty was overwhelmingly rejected.[141]

6

THE WANING OF EXECUTIONS
1930–1960

The state just cannot kill off the problems it can't handle.
Attorney Thomas McDonough, 1946

Capital punishment is not a deterrent. It is not a punishment. But in certain
situations it is like putting out a fire, or killing a mad dog.
Editorial, *Hartford Courant,* Feb. 19, 1957

I detest capital punishment. This is a sad and repugnant business. None of us
will be the better for the taking of a human life this night.
Mark Richman, Warden of the Connecticut State Prison, May 17, 1960

FROM THE GREAT Depression through the immediate post–World War II era,
several crucial turning points occurred in Connecticut's policies affecting
capital punishment. After almost a half century of hanging the condemned
at the penitentiary, the state adopted electrocution in 1937, well after its implementation elsewhere. Officials saw electrocution as efficient and up to
date. Influenced by humanitarian impulses after World War II, legal maneuvers blocked executions from 1949 to 1954 in Connecticut. In 1951, the legislature adopted a statute that for the first time allowed juries in verdicts of
first-degree murder to recommend life in prison instead of execution. With
Democratic Governor Abraham Ribicoff ready to sign a bill outlawing the
death penalty, the General Assembly after momentous debate failed to de-
liver such legislation during the spring of 1955. The moratorium was broken
that summer with the electrocution of three men whose death sentences
had been held in abeyance. During the winter of 1955–1956, Joseph Taborsky and his subservient sidekick, Arthur Culombe, carried out a series of
execution-style murders that created public panic. Taborsky, who had earlier been freed for a conviction of a murder in 1950, died in the electric chair

in 1960. His wanton killing garnered widespread opposition to abolition, and the death penalty remained on the books.

Electrocution

In 1935, the General Assembly passed legislation that made electrocution "the method of inflicting the punishment of death" for capital crimes.[1] Fifty-five men had been hanged since 1894 by the mechanized gallows at the penitentiary. The board of directors at the penitentiary unanimously endorsed the change that was actually begun in 1937. The process was well established: New York electrocuted the first convict in 1890, Massachusetts adopted the method in 1900, and during much of the twentieth century it was the prevalent means of execution.[2] Implementation was inexpensive and straightforward. Much of the work was done by prison labor. The electric chair was installed in the same high-ceilinged chamber where the gallows had been. Electrocution was faster and, it was believed, less gruesome than hanging, a position affirmed by the United States Supreme Court in 1890.[3] A hanging usually killed in fifteen minutes, but the body was left suspended for an equal amount of time to make sure death had occurred. The electric chair did its job within five minutes.[4]

One critic of capital punishment complained, however, "We have simply substituted one brutal savagery for another."[5] In a more indirect way, warden Charles S. Reed protested. Already uncomfortable in activating the mechanized gallows, he demanded that a professional executioner be hired to operate the electric chair. The 1935 law provided for such a person for the first time in three hundred years. The executioner had no official position with the state. Connecticut distanced itself from the immediate act of killing by hiring an outsider on a voucher system. In 1960, the time of Taborsky's electrocution, the state paid the executioner a fee of $800, up from $150 in 1937. It was expected that the executioner be skilled "in the application of electric current to the human body." In what was a male ritual, no woman witnessed a hanging or electrocution at the Connecticut State Prison. This electrical expert demanded strict anonymity for personal protection from retribution. A previous executioner had quit because of death threats and low pay.[6] Both were also executioners at Sing Sing.

The warden at the time explained the macabre job description at length:

> Immediately prior to performing an execution the executioner tests all the electrical equipment and he rehearses step by step the procedures to be fol-

lowed with the members of the prison staff who will assist. At the time of the execution he checks the condemned man to see that the straps are properly attached, that the electrodes are properly fixed and so on. He then steps to the electrical panel, pulls the switch and regulates the flow of current for specific intervals of time. He is in the same room with the person being electrocuted and watches this person closely to determine the reaction of the electrical current. He wears no special clothing or uniform in the performance of his duties.[7]

The lack of "special clothing or uniform" was to render the executioner as unidentifiable as possible. His name was not disclosed, and executions took place at night. Because of the ordeal, prison guards involved received time off. Obscurity shrouded the increased technical sophistication. Joseph McElroy, an Irish immigrant in his mid-forties, was on February 10, 1937, the first person electrocuted by Connecticut. In a drunken rage the previous summer, he had nearly decapitated with a knife and razor his estranged female companion of some years, a New Haven nurse. He had threatened her on several occasions. As the state's attorney argued persuasively for first-degree murder, "He saw her go out with another man. Why any woman should be butchered for that is beyond my comprehension."[8] Officials were particularly anxious about making the execution a success. The law required the warden to carry out the court's sentence within five days after its issuance. To deter crowds from gathering at the front of the penitentiary, the hour of death was kept secret. McElroy was not informed until twelve hours before the time. At 6:30 p.m., guards moved him from death row to the death cell only paces from the updated execution chamber. Unlike the early morning hangings, electrocution occurred around 10 p.m., a more convenient time for officials but one still veiled by darkness. The executioner was Robert Elliot, who performed his job for New York and several other states. Only somewhat later, as anonymity became the norm, did the press not report the name of the executioner.

Twenty-two spectators, including reporters, were searched—a first in Connecticut—for cameras and weapons. In 1928, a photograph of an electrocution—that of Ruth Snyder at Sing Sing—had been illicitly taken by a journalist and created a sensation when it appeared on the front page of the *New York Daily News* with the headline, "Dead!"[9] They watched McElroy—dressed in gray trousers, white shirt, and felt slippers—enter the death chamber shortly before 10 p.m. Elliot supervised five guards who forced the convict into a large oak chair and strapped him down. Electrodes soaked in brine for greater conductivity were applied. One was attached to McElroy's right leg; his pant leg had been slit and pushed above his knee. The second, to complete the circuit, was attached to a metal helmet that held a wet sponge soaked in saline solution on his shorn head and copper wire that ran to an electric board. An ill-fitting black leather mask—the counterpart to the black hood at hangings—was placed over his face to conceal that part of the death agony. The preparation was done in less than two minutes. Ten feet away at the electric board, Elliot threw a switch, a red light went on, and the current hummed. Almost 2,000 volts at 10 amps jolted McElroy, whose body strained against the straps. Three jolts of current were applied in short intervals: the first was expected to kill by stopping the heart, and the other two were to ensure that death had occurred. The electrodes crackled and smoked, scarring the body. After a few minutes, a doctor, applying a stethoscope to McElroy's chest, declared him dead. Guards undid the restraints and removed the corpse. On its own terms, the state's first electrocution went without a hitch.

One veteran journalist reflected, however, that a hanging was less traumatic to watch even though it took longer to kill.[10] Father Joseph Reynolds, Roman Catholic chaplain at the prison, spent the last hours and attended the executions of three men in July 1955 after a suspension of electrocutions since 1949. An opponent of the death penalty, he concluded: "Those assigned to this chore, by reason of duty, treat the condemned person worse than a wild animal. No thought whatever is given to the sacredness of the human body. It is absolutely cruel, inhuman and paganistic."[11] In addition, Gerald J. Demeusy, the state's leading criminal reporter who witnessed all six electrocutions from 1955 to 1960, concurred: "Sights and sounds of each execution—the sudden shriek of electricity, a muffled gasp, the snap of flesh against leather, violent convulsions and flaming leg hair—had been sickening to behold."[12] Witnesses hurried from the execution room to escape the smell of burnt flesh and hair. Demeusy added that officials and reporters walking through the cell blocks to witness an execution were spit upon and pelted with feces by protesting prisoners.[13]

Double electrocutions designed for expediency could have gruesome outcomes. On July 18, 1955, John Donahue and Robert Malm, men of different body weights, were sentenced to death, one rapidly after the other. The executioner had to compromise on the amount of electricity that would kill. There was no time to reset the apparatus. Seated eight feet away on backless, wooden benches in clear sight of the electric chair, Demeusy observed of the lighter man, "Fire flashed, hair crackled and blood gushed from under the black mask as three successive electrical charges of 30-seconds duration struck

Donahue like thunderbolts." Although grotesque, Donahue died quickly. Guards unstrapped the body, placed it in a zippered bag, and wheeled it out. Three jolts of the same current did not immediately kill the heavier Malm, whom it was feared might revive. Only after the prison physician checked Malm's heartbeat with a stethoscope five times was death declared.[14]

Prelude to a Moratorium, 1930–1948

The upheaval of the Great Depression and World War II did not lead to a greater reliance on capital punishment to maintain law and order. Executions continued apace, but the fifteen total for this period were increasingly meted out for particular situations. They included attacks on law officers, robbery, and assaults against females. Homicide during a robbery was the major crime for the death sentence. The ethnocentric legislation of 1924 that restricted entry into the United States of southern and eastern European Catholics and Jews changed the population dynamics of previous decades. Four men born in Italy, Ireland, Canada, and Germany were executed. Although most of those executed were native born, judging from the ethnic names a number of children of recent immigrants figured among the group. Young men continued to predominate. Only one of fifteen was older than thirty-seven, and he was in his mid-forties. Eight were in their twenties; two were teenagers. Handguns were most commonly used; they were the weapon of choice in robbery in which three police officers and three shopkeepers were killed. Four females were victims, and two of these involved sexual assaults by strangers. Only McElroy's jealous vengeance in a love affair gone awry might constitute domestic violence. Those executed were, like those before them, on the margins of society. There were notable examples of low educational attainment and some degree of mental impairment. Indeed, for the twenty-one men executed from 1930 to 1960, only four completed high school.[15] For the first time, recidivism stood out. For ten men, it appeared that the death penalty was the outcome of a youthful life in crime. The issue of the proper response to criminal offenders, especially juveniles, heightened the debate over capital punishment.

Great Depression, 1930–1939

From 1930 through 1938, during the Great Depression when a fourth of the workforce was unemployed, five men were executed (table 22). Three involved murders committed with handguns during robberies, including the

TABLE 22
The Executed, 1930–1939

Date Executed	Name	Age at Execution	Nativity	Religion	Race	Occupation	Crime Site	Weapon	Victim
1930	Frank DiBattista	25	Italy	Roman Catholic	White	Convict	Hartford	Handgun	Man (store owner)
1930	Henry O. Lorenz	25	Germany	Protestant	White	Store clerk	Wethersfield	Handgun	Man (creditor)
1936	John Simborski	28	Conn.	Roman Catholic	White	Criminal	New Haven	Handgun	Police officer
Electrocution Began in 1937									
1937	Joseph McElroy	47	Ireland	Roman Catholic	White	Hospital worker	New Haven	Razor and knife	Former mistress
1938	Frank Palka	25	N.Y.	Roman Catholic	White	Airplane mechanic/ convict	Bridgeport	Handgun	Two police officers

killing of three police officers. The other two were personal disputes: one over a debt and the other an ill-starred love affair. All those executed during this time were white men of lower social status. With the exception of the middle-aged McElroy, they were in their mid- to late twenties. None held a middle-class job or had attained a significant level of education. Frank Palka, a riveter at Sikorsky Aircraft Corporation who shot to death two Bridgeport police officers, had the most sophisticated employment; he was also convicted of rape in New York. John Simborski, who shot to death a pursuing New Haven police office during a robbery spree, was to some degree mentally deficient. Frank DiBattista and Simborski had youthful criminal records. Three of these five were immigrants, and four were Roman Catholics. None was a native-born Protestant white. A journalist described DiBattista, who shot a Hartford grocer in the head, as a "young immigrant boy."[16]

Despite persuasive evidence that led to first-degree murder convictions, there were various challenges to the death penalty. DiBattista, a former elevator boy in New York City, lost appeals to the Connecticut Supreme Court and Board of Pardons. The chief justice, George W. Wheeler, mindful of another recent murder of a shopkeeper by young toughs, opined, "The protection of society against such crimes demands that this class of criminals, when proven guilty, should receive, in penalty, the rigor of the law."[17] Gertrude Stephenson, an outspoken critic of the death penalty, rebutted with the biblical imperative, "Thou shall not kill."[18] Henry O. Lorenz, who was born in Germany, also lost an appeal to the Board of Pardons, and the Hartford County Superior Court judge had earlier rejected an insanity plea. Nonetheless, relatives of the victim, including those in Sweden, asked for commutation to a life sentence.[19] Despite the sordid nature of the crime in which Lorenz shot the victim point blank in the head, the *Hartford Courant* editorialized in 1930 against the death penalty on two counts. First, "hanging is a vestige of an earlier system of justice in which revenge played an important part."[20] Second, "The truth is that the person who murders is either permanently or temporarily incapable of being deterred from crime by fear of the death penalty." The alternative was, "Life in prison would serve to protect society."[21] The defense for Simborski offered medical testimony that the persistent offender, who had spent much of his life in reformatories and penal institutions, had a brutal father and a retarded mentality. Attorney Philip Troup told the Board of Pardons, hours before the scheduled April 7, 1936, hanging, "You would not think of hanging him if he were only eleven and a half years old, no matter what he did."[22] After four gubernatorial reprieves and a review by the Connecticut Supreme Court, the Board of Pardons rejected his appeal. As Justice John W. Banks explained the high tribunal's rejection of Simborski's plea, "There is no escape from the conclusion that the killing was willful, deliberate, and premeditated and with specific criminal intent and was therefore murder in the first degree."[23] Except for unusual circumstances, there was a reluctance to mitigate the death sentence for those convicted of killing police officers and prison guards. Simborski was the last person hanged by the state.[24]

Although Palka was found responsible for shooting to death on September 30, 1935, two Bridgeport police officers, a jury found him guilty of second-degree murder because he was very drunk at the time. The state's attorney appealed to the state's highest court, which found that the Fairfield County Superior Court had erred in instruction of the nature of premeditation. With new evidence entered during the second trial, another jury on October 15, 1936, convicted Palka of first-degree murder and sentenced him to death on February 15, 1937. The defendant appealed to both the Connecticut and U.S. Supreme Courts that he was tried twice for the same crime. Neither court found that his constitutional rights had been violated.[25] Two and one-half years after the crime, Palka was led, as one witness described, "white and trembling" to the electric chair.[26] The *Hartford Courant* protested, "The indefinable 'ends of justice' would have been served as well had Palka's sentence of life imprisonment been upheld. Burning him in the electric chair will not restore to life the policemen he killed."[27]

Several men during the 1930s had their death penalties reduced either through commutation or retrial. Mental competency, childhood experiences, age, and the plausibility of evidence were critical. A three-judge panel sentenced cousins Tony Klim and Vito Petraitis, both little older than twenty, to a double hanging on November 17, 1931. Klim confessed that he had shot to death the manager of a grocery store in Windsor during a Saturday night robbery. In early November, the Board of Pardons commuted the sentences to life in prison. Both men were deemed mentally deficient; a psychiatrist labeled Klim a "high grade imbecile."[28] The culprits had experienced extreme poverty, and Klim had dropped out of school after sixth grade. The board agreed with the public defender that the pair were not fit subjects for capital punishment. The *Hartford Courant* editorialized that the outcome was "merciful and just." Although the two knew the difference between right and wrong, "Their crime was so directly a result of their environment and other conditions over which they had no control at all, that it seems unduly harsh to execute them."[29]

At the middle of the decade, two additional men were spared the gallows. The Board of Pardons during July 1935 changed William H. Dodez's sentence to life in prison. Dodez, a sixty-six-year-old railroad engineer from Bridgeport, had shot a former best friend who had married his divorced wife and allegedly mocked him. He had also lost his job due to failing eyesight, which convinced the board, chaired by Governor Wilbur Cross, that his emotional state and advanced years warranted life in prison. In a retrial granted by the Connecticut Supreme Court, the first-degree murder verdict against Dominick Santella was reduced to fifteen years in the penitentiary. The state contended that twenty-nine-year-old Santella had blasted a seventeen-year-old youth with a shotgun in a robbery of a dice game at Norwalk. The prosecution's lead witness implicated the defendant, but other testimony rendered the accusation doubtful. Santella, who maintained his innocence, reluctantly pleaded guilty to manslaughter, but escaped execution.[30] Governor Cross appointed a special panel of three psychiatrists to examine John Palm, whom prison officials had deemed insane. The convict was awaiting execution on March 30, 1938, for the shooting of a New Haven policeman during a holdup. Palm was declared incompetent, the death sentence was suspended for the duration of the affliction, and he was transferred to Norwich State Hospital. The Board of Pardons subsequently commuted the punishment to life in prison.[31]

World War II Era, 1940–1948

The execution of ten men during the World War II era doubled that of the Great Depression (table 23). The spike upward needs to be qualified, however. Two crimes alone counted for five of the ten hanged. Two carnival workers were convicted of killing a grocer during a robbery. They represented the state's first dual electrocution. In addition, three inmates were sentenced to death for killing a prison guard. The trio was the state's only triple electrocution. In multiple executions, the condemned went to the same electric chair one after the other.

There are several exceptions to the profile of these ten men compared with those of the Depression. There was only one immigrant but three African Americans among them, and handguns figured in only two killings. Two of the men had murdered their victims after raping them. The men were thirty-seven years old or younger, including two teenagers. All were at the lower level of society in terms of social status, education, wealth, and

TABLE 23
The Executed, 1940–1948

Date Executed	Name	Age at Execution	Nativity	Religion	Race	Occupation	Crime Site	Weapon	Victim
1940	Vincent Cotts	32	Conn.	Unknown	White	Carnival worker	Middletown	Handgun	Grocer
1940	Ira A. Weaver Jr.	35	N.C.	Protestant	White	Carnival worker/ criminal record	Middletown	Handgun	Grocer
1943	Peter Gurski	26	Penn.	Roman Catholic	White	Machinist/ criminal record	Plymouth	Strangled	Rape (woman)
1943	Wilson H. Funderburk	28	S.C.	Roman Catholic	Black	Itinerant/convict	Hartford	Scissors	Rape (girl)
1944	Carlo J. DeCaro	19	Conn.	Roman Catholic	White	Machinist	Thompsonville	Handgun	Man (robbery)
1945	Nicolas Rossi	32	Canada	Roman Catholic	Black	Writer	Plainville	Iron pipe	Woman (robbery)
1946	James McCarthy	21	Conn.	None	White	Convict	Wethersfield	Wrench	Prison guard
1946	Arthur Tomaselli	24	Conn.	Roman Catholic	White	Convict	Wethersfield	Club	Prison guard
1946	Raymond Lewie	19	Conn.	None	White	Convict	Wethersfield	Iron pipe	Prison guard
1948	Robert Bradley	37	Not Conn.	Protestant	Black	Criminal	East Haven	Ax	Three black men

occupation. What is striking about this group as well as the earlier one is that seven of the ten had prior criminal records. A life history of lawbreaking facilitated the path to the death chamber.

Three white convicts at the penitentiary—James McCarthy, Arthur Tomaselli, and Raymond Lewie—who killed a guard in a failed escape attempt on March 9, 1945, are such examples. In more than a century of the existence of the Wethersfield institution, no inmate convicted of murdering a guard escaped the death sentence. In their late teens and early twenties, the three had a long history of infractions. McCarthy, the ringleader, and Lewie were serving life terms for second-degree murder. Tomaselli was a convicted burglar. The trio beat the guard to death with various bludgeons, including his own club. As state's attorney Hugh Alcorn put it, "Every step of the plan had a potential murder in it."[32] After deliberating for three hours, a jury that included nine women (who were now regularly participants on the panel) found all three guilty of first-degree murder. Despite three reprieves issued by Governor Raymond E. Baldwin, the Connecticut Supreme Court and the Board of Pardons turned down the defendants' pleas. Remarkably, the teenaged Lewie, a product of state reformatories who had not been charged in the killing, volunteered that he had struck the guard with an iron pipe. Lewie fatalistically explained his self-accusation to the judge, "I want to burn,"[33] and the trio did, on the night of October 1, 1946, all within thirty minutes of one another. Lewie's attorney, Thomas McDonough, protested that his client was intent on "legal suicide."[34] Lewie believed that God was angry with him for trying to escape execution.[35] In an additional act of expiation, Lewie donated his eyes to blinded war veterans and willed his body to Yale Medical School.

In addition to Joseph Watson at the beginning of the twentieth century, three other African Americans were executed during the 1940s. These four were the total for their race during that century. Critics of the death penalty correctly pointed to the disproportionate number of blacks on death row, particularly in the South. In Connecticut, the pattern does not hold for the 1940s. The three black men were electrocuted for killing five victims, of which four were black. Their crimes were more egregious—shocking and bizarre—than anything else.

Wilson H. Funderburk was a twenty-eight-year-old itinerant barber from South Carolina whose criminal record began at age fourteen. He had traveled to Hartford, where he enticed an eleven-year-old Negro girl on April 7, 1942, to a secluded area. After he raped her, he stabbed her several dozen times in the chest and stomach with barber scissors.[36] Nicolas and Robert

Rossi were half-brothers from Montreal. For several years, Robert, a transvestite, successfully assumed the role of Nicolas's wife. In that role, she gained employment as the maid for a sixty-year-old white woman in Plainville. In September 1943, Nicolas struck the employer over her head with an iron bar in a robbery. The half-brothers fled in the dead woman's car, where in Missouri an alert police officer discovered the gender ruse. The siblings confessed. The interracial killing undoubtedly heightened tension. Nicolas Rossi was convicted of first-degree murder and electrocuted on June 18, 1945, and Robert Rossi received a life term.[37]

Robert Bradley, who had a criminal record in several states, worked with an African American accomplice, William Lisenby. The two tricked black men to a remote area in East Haven for an assignation with white women. While they waited for the nonexistent liaison, the men were instructed to dig a barbeque pit for the festivities, which turned out to be their graves. Three men were axed to death on separate occasions and robbed, and their cars illegally sold. A mushroom picker discovered the shallow graves in the woods. In return for a life sentence, Lisenby testified against Bradley. Denied a review by the U.S. Supreme Court, Bradley told the Board of Pardons that he would rather die than serve a life term. Defiant to the end, he cheated the prison chaplain, with whom he refused to pray, with a marked deck of cards as they passed his last hours in the death cell. He was executed on April 12, 1948, the last African American to suffer that fate in Connecticut.[38]

Vincent Cotts, Ira A. Weaver Jr., Peter Gurski, and Carlo J. DeCaro—all whites—were also at the low end of the social spectrum. Cotts and Weaver were carnival workers who lived in a rundown Middletown tenement. Weaver, who hailed from North Carolina, had a long criminal record. The duo shot to death a local grocer in a robbery that netted them $6. Although Weaver first confessed to being the shooter and then accused Cotts, both men were executed on April 30, 1940.[39] Gurski on February 23, 1943, was the fifth man to go to the electric chair. He was sentenced to death for the rape and murder the previous July of a retired sixty-six-year-old schoolteacher in Plymouth after she had tragically missed a nighttime bus. A machinist, he had dropped out of school in fifth grade and had been arrested five times previously.[40] A jury of six women and six men that deliberated less than three hours found DeCaro, a nineteen-year-old machinist, guilty of premeditated murder. He confessed to shooting an older neighbor repeatedly in the head in Thompsonville and burying him alive in a robbery of $1,500. The defense attorney failed to get a "merciful judgment" for a youth who he claimed was somewhat mentally retarded. The executioner sent five charges of current through the obese DeCaro on May 3, 1944.[41]

Gubernatorial reprieves, review by the Connecticut Supreme Court, and appeals for commutation to the Board of Pardons were now routine. In these petitions, defense attorneys, usually public defenders, attempted to mitigate the death sentence. During the 1940s, women regularly served on juries and on occasion made up a majority. The common wisdom was that women were less in favor of the death penalty than men. Although the evidence was overwhelming that DeCaro had committed first-degree murder, several female jurors were in tears as the guilty verdict was pronounced.[42] In addition, African Americans also served on juries, but in lesser numbers than women. The Reverend Julian Taylor, an African American from Ansonia, was foreman of the jury that pronounced Bradley guilty.[43] With the exception of the DeCaro and Bradley outcomes, the appearance of women and African Americans on juries introduced a constituency that on the whole was less than enthusiastic for the death penalty.

Abolition opponents also kept their position in front of the public via letters to newspapers. Even when convicts McCarthy and Lewie, already serving life terms for second-degree murder, killed a prison guard, one critic wrote, "It is possible that if the jury that passed sentence were obliged to shave the head, fasten the electrodes, strap the victim in the chair, turn on the current, and then to remove the body, and console the broken hearted parents I doubt their ever passing another death sentence."[44]

In addition, the Board of Pardons commuted some prominent death sentences during the war era. Leonard Richards, a nineteen-year-old war worker in Bridgeport, clubbed to death a coworker in a robbery. Because of Richards's mental deficiency, the board in April 1943 agreed with the prosecution and defense that a life term was more appropriate than execution.[45] In the same year, John Moon, an African American in Hartford, escaped electrocution for the shooting of his wife.[46] In Fairfield County Superior Court, two sixteen-year-olds, Raymond Lewis and Edward Barrow, were allowed to plead guilty to second-degree murder in the shooting of a New Britain shopkeeper. The state's attorney thought that the crime was clearly first-degree murder but concurred with the public defender that Lewis's and Barrow's youth and troubled past warranted a life term.[47] The board was persuaded to commute Robert Rossi's death sentence in June 1945 because, as the public defender argued, his half-brother Nicolas did the actual killing and dominated his transvestite sibling.[48] Governor Baldwin was persuaded

by the plea of a sailor in the Pacific theater of the war during 1945 to recon-
vene the Board of Pardons that had rejected a commutation for his brother,
Royal Petersen. The latter had been sentenced to death in 1945 for the murder of a Manchester jeweler. Meeting that August shortly before the scheduled electrocution, the board, upon hearing in detail about the disruptive
home life of the Petersens, reversed its earlier decision.[49]

An Unofficial Moratorium on Capital Punishment, 1949–1955

At midcentury, Connecticut was part of an international effort to abolish
the death penalty. Atomic annihilation, the Holocaust, bombing of civilian targets, and tens of millions dead galvanized support for the United
Nations, the World Court, the Universal Declaration of Human Rights, and
the 1949 revisions to the Geneva Convention. In a changing moral climate,
intellectuals weighed in on ethical issues. Albert Camus's essay "Reflections
on the Guillotine" and Arthur Koestler's *Reflections on Hanging,* both first
published in 1957, offered pointed criticism.[50] Camus assessed capital punishment as "an odd law, to be sure, which knows the murder it commits and
will never know the one it prevents."[51] In the United States, the American
Civil Liberties Union, the National Association for the Advancement of Colored People, and major religious denominations magnified opposition to
the death penalty. Of particular concern were the number of African Americans executed under dubious circumstances, a double standard that Swedish sociologist Gunnar Myrdal exposed in the acclaimed 1944 book *The
American Dilemma.*[52] The debate in Connecticut gained clarity after Bradley,
who appeared unafraid of the electric chair, was sentenced to death in 1947.
His attorney, Charles Henchel, former Democratic leader of the state assembly and well-known abolitionist, had taken a stand against the death penalty
when as a recent law school graduate he heard an eyewitness account of the
1928 electrocution of Ruth Snyder in New York.[53] He asked the judiciary
committee in 1947 to outlaw what he called "the horrible and revolting" act
of judicial killing itself.[54] The next year, Bradley's public defender, Elliott R.
Katz, pointed out the issue of "unequal punishment" to an unpersuaded
Board of Pardons. Bradley's accomplice, who testified for the state, received
a lesser sentence.[55] An unofficial moratorium existed from Bradley's execution in 1948 until 1955.

There was mounting reluctance of juries, augmented by women and
blacks, to hand down death penalties. At the state level, gubernatorial re-

prieves, Connecticut Supreme Court reviews, and petitions to the Board of Pardons were virtually automatic. As Ernest A. Inglis, chief justice of the state's highest court, put it, "If there is any chance of a man being entitled to a new trial because of fresh evidence that chance ought not to be cut off because of lack of a due hearing."[56] Federal courts, including the U.S. Supreme Court, were more receptive to review capital cases. There was growing concern with the rights of criminal defendants, particularly regarding coercive police interrogation of suspects. The civil rights movement heightened public awareness of inequities of race and class as to who was executed, a position shared with the political left. Empirical evidence that the death penalty did not deter homicide, which often occurred at a flashpoint of unreasoning rage, was more widespread. Southern states with the highest rates of execution contradictorily had the highest murder rates. The fear that an innocent person might be condemned also gained traction. In addition, religious advocates of the social gospel emphasized "thou shall not kill" over the revengeful "eye for an eye." Connecticut's de facto suspension mirrored an international trend.[57]

State Senator Jacob Fishman in 1951 reintroduced Henchel's bill to end the death penalty after a close vote in the General Assembly in 1950. There was vocal support by Aaron Cohen, a wealthy real estate developer in West Hartford, and Sara R. Ehrmann of Brookline, Massachusetts, whose campaign against capital punishment spanned four decades.[58] Despite the abolitionist impetus, a reservoir of support for the death penalty existed. The state's attorney general, warden of the penitentiary, and police commissioner rebutted that the death penalty was "sparingly used" and was essential for public safety, including at the state prison.[59] The *Hartford Courant* cautioned that the death penalty was necessary for "protection," not "retaliation," against a minority of hardened criminals who "constitute a menace to society as long as they are alive, in prison or out of it."[60]

Henchel's bill to abolish capital punishment was the catalyst for compromise between those on either side of the argument.[61] The result was a major revision of the first-degree murder statute in 1951. Following the lead of other states, including Massachusetts in the same year, Connecticut adopted for the first time discretionary capital punishment. Instead of a guilty verdict mandating a death sentence for premeditated killing, the jury could recommend a life term without pardon or parole.[62] Both sides in the debate had their positions validated. The arbitrator in good democratic fashion was the twelve-member jury, a microcosm of the people themselves. Some of the burden of affixing life and death was taken from the Board of Pardons. In the switch from mandatory to discretionary death sentences, Connecticut experienced for at least the next several years a decline in the homicide rate, whereas the Massachusetts rate remained the same. It seemed that a restriction on capital punishment did not lead to an increase in homicide.[63]

The 1951 statute was not unchallenged. Two years later, William R. Ginsberg, a Yale law student, argued that the law was unconstitutional in several ways. For one, it delegated sentencing to the jury, not the judge. Also, by imposing an irrevocable life sentence, the law denied the possibility of rehabilitation and infringed on the oversight role of the Board of Pardons.[64]

Wallace M. Walters, who was convicted of stabbing to death a woman in a Hartford parking lot in February 1956, similarly questioned the reform. In accord with the 1951 statute, the jury's binding recommendation was that the convict serve a sentence of imprisonment for life without pardon or parole. Walters argued that his due process rights and equal protection of law had been violated. If he had been convicted of first-degree murder, Walters pointed out, the Board of Pardons might commute his sentence. With the commutation, he would then be eligible for parole after serving twenty years. The inequity was that the 1951 law stipulated that no pardon or parole was ever possible. Two other men had been similarly sentenced, and the Board of Pardons had no purview of their situations. The Connecticut Supreme Court, however, ruled unanimously that there was nothing unconstitutional in the 1951 act.[65] Up until 1958, juries had sentenced eight men to death, but, as Walters had predicted, the Board of Pardons commuted some of those crimes and the convicts became potential recipients of pardon or parole.

In anticipation of Walters's challenge, the *Hartford Courant* in 1954 raised more far reaching questions about "the shapeless attitude toward prison and parole." The editors noted the variety of convicts at the penitentiary: the one-time murderer, the psychopath, the gangster, the thief, and "all other non-descripts that fill the cells." What was the goal: punishment, deterrence, public safety, or rehabilitation? The paper pointedly inquired, "Should persons be returned to society when they have been 'punished enough'; when they have been made an example of; when then they stop being objectionable and dangerous; when they have become rehabilitated?"[66] Although no policy recommendation was offered, the journalists raised fundamental questions about the purpose of the criminal justice system that underlay the debate over capital punishment.

With seven men on death row, the effort to abolish the death penalty reached a crescendo during the 1955 legislative session. With a new governor and legislature, it was not clear what the outcome would be. With a coalition of backers, Attorney Henchel of New Haven submitted another anti–capital punishment bill. In January, he urged Democratic Governor Abraham Ribicoff to reprieve those scheduled for execution until the disposition of the General Assembly was known in "the great moral question involved in the taking of life by the state or any individual." He recalled that his predecessors Chester Bowles and John Davis Lodge, a Democrat and a Republican, respectively, were relieved that no executions had occurred during their terms.[67] Governor Ribicoff complied, reprieving William Lorain and John Donahue, whose executions were scheduled for January 21. Although applauded by some, one juror wrote that the reprieve of Lorain, who had shot to death the driver in a carjacking, "was most unsettling to me," and she complained that "not one of the jury felt that he was entitled to any leniency or further consideration."[68]

To clarify issues in anticipation of the spring legislative session, the *Hartford Courant* ran a series of eight articles written by Roger Dove during February and March on the provocative theme entitled "Should the State Kill?" Sophisticated and serious, the discussion, which Governor Ribicoff commended, pointed to the central role that the state's largest circulation newspaper had in shaping public policy. The editors observed that since the last execution in 1948, four men had been reprieved within hours of their scheduled execution. Three had had their heads shaved, pant legs slit, last meals, and papers signed for the disposition of their corpses. In the most extreme situation in 1953, the defense attorney informed Governor Lodge of new evidence at the last moment. Governor Lodge reprieved the condemned man, George Dortch, only minutes before the planned execution. He sat in suspense in the death cell with a chaplain for an additional twenty-five minutes before the emotionally overwrought warden remembered to notify them. Asked about the ordeal, Dortch replied, "I'm grateful. But I hope I never have to go through that again." The chaplain was irate. A tense guard commented ruefully, "Dortch has paid his debt to society. He died tonight."[69] In addition, the Board of Pardons initially turned down two condemned men (Frank Smith and James Buteau), for whom the governor had issued last-minute stays and the board subsequently commuted. As the newspaper correctly observed of the postwar years, "Connecticut justice in the last seven years therefore has been neither swift nor sure as it was in the past."[70]

Conditions on death row for the seven men in early 1955 in the rundown, century-old penitentiary were stark. Because of the extended appeals process, executions that had earlier occurred within a year or so now were indefinitely postponed. Dortch had been the longest on death row, five years. Death row was in a segregated, punishment block on the east side of the penitentiary. It was a short walk through an oak door to the electric chair. The condemned men were in separate, adjoining rows of cells, nine feet square, that had a sink, toilet, and bunk. Radios (until 1955) and shoes were forbidden because they were potential weapons. Two guards watched the continually lighted area twenty-four hours a day. The men exercised alone for twenty minutes a day in a restricted yard with twenty-five-foot-high walls. They could read, write, and smoke, but only the guards could light the cigarettes. Family visits were limited to twice a month, and conversation occurred through a screen. Silence was mostly observed. Bradley and Taborsky vowed that they had rather die than endure life in prison. Both got their wish.[71]

The emphatic support of police officials and prosecutors for capital punishment had an important effect on public opinion and politicians. As police commissioner Edward J. Hickey put it, "I want to ask you what are we to do with the hardened killers."[72] Connecticut police chiefs concurred that the death penalty was a deterrent to murder and that its elimination threatened the lives of police officers and prison guards. They demanded the execution of Frank Wojculewicz and John Donahue, who had shot to death police officers in 1951 and 1953, respectively. As the police chief of New Britain, where Wojculewicz had committed his crime, told legislators, "Capital punishment is not only a protection to my men it's a protection to every man, woman, and child in Connecticut."[73]

Prosecutors endorsed the position of the police. As one stated, "If you kill one of our police officers, you'll die for it." Another, speaking of the sexual predator Robert Malm who killed in 1953, asked, "Why should we feel sorry for a beast who attacks a little girl, rapes her and then kills her so she can't identify him?"[74] Judge Vine R. Parmalee, clerk of the Board of Pardons for three decades, argued that the death penalty was only applied in extreme cases. He noted that there were important checks on capital punishment from the trial by a jury or panel of three judges to automatic review by the Connecticut Supreme Court and a clemency hearing by the Board of Pardons. "The growing move in Connecticut to abolish capital punishment," he concluded, "is unnecessary so long as the Board of Pardons remains as it is now constituted."[75]

In contrast, the clergy of the major faiths urged repeal. The Reverend Doctor Russell H. Stafford, president of the Hartford Seminary Foundation, averred, "Permanent incarceration protects society as effectively as destroying a man's life." The archbishop of Hartford, the Reverend Henry J. O'Brien, acknowledged the authority of the state to take life, as Roman Catholic doctrine would have it; personally, however, he urged abolition. Rabbi Abraham J. Feldman of Temple Beth Israel commented succinctly, "We do not have a right to take a life." And the Reverend Louis M. Hirshon, dean of Christ Church Cathedral, rejected the law of the talion: "If we accepted that as a standard for today, we would be going back almost 3,000 years." All the clergymen morally opposed the death penalty and added that there was no empirical evidence that it was a deterrent, even to the killing of policemen and prison guards.[76]

The newspaper series also pointed to the downward trend nationwide in executions. In 1954, there were 12,800 homicides, but only 83 executions, 71 for murder and 12 for rape. Three southern states—Georgia, Texas, and South Carolina—along with California accounted for 45 percent of the total. The decline had several causes. Juries and judges were reluctant to impose the death penalty. Prosecutors might well settle for a second-degree murder conviction. Appeals and commutations contributed to the diminution. The condemned, abolitionist Henchel pointed out, were on the social margins. African Americans from 1920 to 1950 composed more than half the total. "Any white person of financial means and with friends," he added, "has little need to fear the imposition of the death penalty." Aaron Cohen, a persistent critic, declared, "The state has no right to take human life."[77] Contrary to the assertion by police officials and prosecutors, Rhode Island, Maine, New Hampshire, Minnesota, Michigan, and North Dakota, which had abolished or restricted the death penalty, had few police officers or prison guards killed. Crime rates in those states were equal to or lower than Connecticut's.[78] The occurrence of atrocious crimes, however, prompted popular outcry for a reinstatement of the death penalty in states where it had been restricted. The abolitionist tide turned back in Kansas, South Dakota, Missouri, Tennessee, Arizona, Oregon, and Washington.[79]

The possibility of rehabilitation complicated the debate. Those convicted of second-degree murder were eligible for parole in twenty years, although the Board of Pardons could act sooner. With its irrevocable life sentence, those convicted of first-degree murder, who were not electrocuted, were, as Ginsberg and Walters pointed out, denied that option. Warden George A. Cummings warned that "a mandatory life sentence is contrary to all the aims of prison rehabilitation" and removed the incentive for inmates' good behavior. He noted that over the course of two decades thirty-nine "lifers" had been released on parole and had committed no crimes. Whether reha- bilitation and parole ought to apply to first-degree murderers raised difficult moral and political issues.[80]

The *Hartford Courant* series ended in early March, shortly before hearings on capital punishment began in the General Assembly. The editors con- cluded, "It is difficult to justify capital punishment." They found "no proof" that it was a deterrent, including against the killing of police officers. In ad- dition, they pointed out "the executioner's victims are largely men—the poor, friendless, and Negroes." Women and substantial citizens were virtu- ally exempt. Those who turned state's evidence were spared, but not their accomplices. Furthermore, there was the possibility that an innocent person might be executed. They recommended a compromise: a trial period with- out the death penalty except for the killing of law enforcement officers. Neighboring Rhode Island, which had not executed anyone for more than a century, provided a model. "And on balance," the editors concluded, "it does seem as though the citizens and law enforcement officials of Connecticut would be as safe without the electric chair as they are with it."[81]

From March to early June, debate ensued over a bill to abolish the death penalty except for the murder of law enforcement officers. Supporters in- cluded Henchel, Cohen, Ehrmann, the Connecticut Association for the Ab- olition of the Death Penalty, and a variety of faith-based organizations. The *Hartford Courant* and *Hartford Times* backed the legislation.[82] Governor Ribi- coff favored the legislation.[83] Police officials and a number of influential politicians on either side of the aisle spoke against it. Norman K. Parsells, Republican leader of the House, stated bluntly, "We need capital punish- ment for the same reason we kill mad dogs and scorpions."[84] Harold E. Bor- den, a Senate Democrat who led opposition, feared that the state would be- come a "sanctuary for New York City murderers."[85] After some success in committee, the bill was overwhelming defeated in the Senate by a vote of 36 to 7 in June 1955. Significant bipartisan opposition and the failure of Demo- crats to rally behind the governor doomed this most far-reaching effort in the postwar era.

Commutations

Although abolition failed repeatedly in the General Assembly, the Board of Pardons blocked the executions of five men during the 1950s, all before the 1956 murder spree of Taborsky and Culombe. Four of these convicted murderers were white, and one was black. Three armed robberies contributed to the deaths of three men by handguns. Two drunken men knifed to death two female companions. None of the assailants was a substantial member of society. Disparate sentencing, war trauma, and delayed notice of a reprieve swayed the Board of Pardons.

James Buteau was sentenced to death for the October 1946 murder of a store manager in Meriden, but his partner in the crime, who testified against him, was given a life sentence. Buteau's two attorneys stressed the unfairness, and the Board of Pardons commuted his sentence in May 1950.[86] The differential was even greater in the case of Filippo Tomassi, who was convicted of shooting to death a New Haven jeweler. Although Tomassi was sentenced to death, his accomplice received three to five years for possession of burglary tools. Age may have also played a role in the mercy shown in December 1950 for Tomassi, who was in his early sixties.[87]

After four years on death row and seven stays, Frank Smith's death sentence was commuted two hours before his scheduled execution in June 1954. As the Board of Pardons put it, "Unusual circumstances surround[ed] the trial and conviction." The testimony of Leo J. Carroll, state liquor commissioner, was critical in exposing the confusion. Five years earlier, Carroll was a major in the state police who had investigated the murder of a Greenwich night watchman that was in question. There was conflicting information about who did the shooting involving Smith and two other men, one of whom accepted a second-degree murder plea. Regarding Smith, whom Carroll had actually arrested, he emotionally told the board, "I'm positive, he didn't kill Grover Hart. I'm not sure he was at the murder." The state's attorney rebutted, "If this is to be decided by an ex-state trooper, and the rulings of the courts disregarded, there wouldn't be much sense in my standing here now." And Smith's public defender responded, "Keep Smith alive, because some day we may know what really happened that night of the Hart murder."[88] Fearful of electrocuting an innocent man, the board, including Governor Lodge, spared Smith. As the *Hartford Courant* editorialized, "The Smith case illustrates the need either of eliminating the death sentence once and for all, or of revising procedures to make unnecessary these long torturous delays, and harrowing last-minute efforts."[89]

Wartime trauma was the reason the Board of Pardons blocked the death of Edward W. Krooner, who had stabbed to death a housewife in a drunken binge after an adulterous affair at Hartford on June 16, 1948. In a three-hour hearing before the scheduled execution on November 14, 1950, several naval officers testified that Krooner, a submarine veteran of World War II, "cracked up" under the stress, particularly during a mission to rescue a downed pilot in Tokyo Bay. The board complied with Captain B. F. McMahon's plea, "Show this man a little mercy."[90]

George M. Dortch was the death cell inmate in February 1953 whom the warden in the confusion of a last-minute reprieve forgot to inform that his execution had been stayed. Dortch had been convicted in 1950 of repeatedly stabbing a former girlfriend in Pawcatuck after she had spurned his attention. His attorney added that Dortch's crime had not been premeditated but had been one of passion committed in a state of "alcoholic amnesia."[91] In addition, Dortch's trial was a year after a 1951 law that allowed juries to recommend life in prison, not death, for first-degree murder. Dortch was African American, but his race was not mentioned as a factor in the July 1955 commutation. His unusual death cell ordeal was the paramount factor.[92] The action of the Board of Pardons in providing clemency for these five men from 1950 to 1955 was a manifestation of the anti–capital punishment sentiment of the time.

The Executed, 1955–1960

The moratorium on executions ended the month after the abolition bill decisively failed in the General Assembly. From July 1955 through 1960, six men were electrocuted (table 24). All were white, and all had extensive criminal records dating back to troubled youth. Except for middle-class-born John Donahue, they were from decidedly lower-class backgrounds. None had attained any education beyond high school or secured white-collar employment. All had committed homicide before age forty, and all but one had been raised a Roman Catholic. Two pedophiles killed their victims by strangulation and stabbing, and handguns figured prominently in all other killings. Excluding the girls murdered in sexual crimes, the other victims, exempting one woman, were men, including two police officers. Domestic violence did not play a role in any of these six cases. The appeals process extended the time from the commission of the murder to execution from one and one-half years for Robert Malm to seven years for Frank Wojculewicz. The crimes were heinous and were thoroughly aired in the mass media.

William Lorain, whom Governor Ribicoff had reprieved to July 11, was the first of three convicts to die that month. He and ex-convict John Petetabella had fled to Hartford on the way to New York City after committing a robbery in their native Rhode Island. In Hartford on August 12, 1952, the two had hitchhiked a ride and killed the driver after he refused to give up

TABLE 24
The Executed, 1955–1960

Date Executed	Name	Age at Execution	Nativity	Religion	Race	Occupation	Place of Crime	Weapon	Victim
1955	William Lorain	34	R.I.	Roman Catholic	White	Criminal	Wethersfield	Handgun	White man
1955	John Donahue	22	Mass.	Roman Catholic	White	Criminal	Trumbull	Handgun	State policeman
1955	Robert Malm	31	Raised in Calif.	Protestant	White	Dish-washer	Hartford	Scarf	Girl
1959	George Davies	41	Conn.	Roman Catholic	White	Tool setter	Wolcott	Stabbed and strangled	Two girls
1959	Frank Wojculewicz	41	Conn.	None	White	Truck driver / criminal	New Britain	Handgun	Policeman and male bystander
1960	Joseph Taborsky	36	Conn.	Roman Catholic to Episcopalian	White	Convict	Several places	Handgun	Five men and one woman

his wallet and punched Lorain in the face. After diligent detective work, both men were apprehended. Lorain confessed to the slaying, but later recanted. Abolitionists used the example of the slaying to point out that the death penalty lacked deterrence: Connecticut had such a statute, but Rhode Island did not. A jury with a majority of women deliberated for four hours before convicting Lorain of first-degree murder with the death penalty. Petetabella, who it was decided did not fire the fatal five shots, was allowed to plead guilty to second-degree murder. At the Board of Pardons hearing hours prior to the scheduled execution, Lorain responded to a question by Governor Ribicoff as to what had happened by charging his accomplice with the shooting. The formerly defiant Lorain, who had made three suicide attempts in prison, broke into tears after learning that officials had refused him clemency. He maintained his innocence, despite five prior confessions, even as the warden led him to the execution chamber. As a priest recited prayers, the executioner, a few feet away, sent three separate charges of 2,000 volts through the condemned man.[93]

Despite the resumption of execution, voices of opposition continued. A Baptist preacher from Rhode Island told the Board of Pardons, "I say let's deal with the causes and not slip these boys into the electric chair."[94] The *Hartford Courant* editorialized, "The citizens of the state might ask themselves whether they and the world are better off for the execution of Lorain." The newspaper pointed to the differential sentences of Lorain and Petetabella as questionable justice, yet a majority of the public and politicians opposed abolition: "For ultimately," the *Hartford Courant* explained, "it is the citizens of Connecticut who have willed the continuation of the death penalty."[95]

One week later, appeals ran out for John Donahue and Robert Malm. July 18 marked the first dual execution for separate crimes since the mid-eighteenth century. Their crimes prompted soul-searching about the causes and prevention of criminal violence. Donahue had been born in what appeared to be a model middle-class family in Arlington, Massachusetts, but quickly acquired a record as a juvenile delinquent. After a highway chase on February 13, 1953, the nineteen-year-old parolee shot and killed a state trooper who had stopped him for speeding in a stolen car at Trumbull. His public defender, echoing Hollywood movies such as *Rebel without a Cause* (1955) and *Blackboard Jungle* (1955), said that his client was a "classic example" of the "modern youth problem."[96] The prosecutor asked the jury to tell all these young men who have no conscience, "You can't shoot our police officers. We'll show you no mercy."[97] Donahue's father offered an apology to the people of the state. Governor Ribicoff excused good parents for an inexplicably bad son. The tearful young Donahue told an unsympathetic Board of Pardons, "For the life of me, I don't know why I did it."[98]

Minutes after Donahue's corpse was wheeled out of the execution chamber, Malm was strapped into the same electric chair. Malm, a dishwasher, was a decorated submarine veteran of World War II, but he had a long history as a sexual predator. On December 9, 1953, two weeks after another assault, he raped an eleven-year-old girl in Hartford and then strangled her with her scarf when she threatened to tell her mother.[99] The state's attorney warned that the defendant was a "sex pervert of the worst kind."[100] The public defender pointed out that Malm had "never received psychiatric help" despite numerous encounters with the criminal justice system.[101] Representative Gertrude E. Koskoff added that "sex offenders cannot improve in prison" and proposed a separate institution that would deal with "abnormal criminals."[102] Similarly, the *Hartford Courant* called for closer surveillance, better record keeping, and psychological counseling for "known perverts."[103] Malm said of the encounter with the girl, "All the time I was kind of confused."[104] He told an interviewer that he did not want to die, but "killing me will kill the monster inside me that made me do what I did to that girl, what I did often before that, and what I probably would do again."[105] The Connecticut Supreme Court concluded unanimously "that he formed a willful, deliberate attempt to kill her,"[106] and the Board of Pardons rejected a mercy petition.

The killing spree of Joseph Taborsky and his mentally retarded partner, Arthur Culombe, which began in December 1955 decisively undermined the political possibility for abolition. As crusader Charles Henchel put it in early 1957, "I think we have now a wave of emotionalism that precludes success for those who want capital punishment abolished."[107] Governor Ribicoff and the *Hartford Courant,* among others, no longer supported abolition. The legacy of the "mad dog killers" has lasted for a half century, making Connecticut distinct in New England.

Taborsky's engagement with the criminal justice system began in the 1940s and spanned the decade of the 1950s. He was the only person to be on death row twice for two different crimes. Born in Hartford in 1925 to impoverished Lithuanian immigrants, he was an incorrigible robber from his youth and was in a state reformatory at age fourteen. His father, who suffered mental disability as did a brother, was absent from the family of two sons and two daughters. Taborsky, the eldest son, formed a strong emotional bond with his religiously devout mother. Detectives gained a confession from him in 1957 only after his mother ordered him to tell the truth.[108]

At that moment, he admitted for the first time that he had shot Louis Wolfson, a West Hartford liquor store owner, in a robbery on March 25, 1950, the fatal culmination of a number of petty holdups. His brother, Albert, who drove the getaway car and was bullied by his elder sibling, told police of the crime in January 1951. Informed of his brother's accusation, Joseph said, "He must be crazy," a sentiment that uncannily proved true.[109] The evidence, however, was contradictory. In dying words to the police, a confused Wolfson described his assailant as a blond, baby-faced teenager of medium height. In contrast, Joseph was older and a muscular, six feet four inches tall with dark hair, deep-set eyes, thin lips, and a massive chin. Nonetheless, on the basis of his brother's statement, Joseph on June 19, 1951, was sentenced to die. Twelve days later, Albert pleaded guilty to second-degree murder.[110]

Within weeks of his incarceration in July, Albert exhibited unmistakable signs of insanity and was committed two months later to a mental hospital, incurably ill. His testimony was legally questionable. After complex litigation and a crowded court docket, the state's highest court ruled in October 1955 that "a new trial will be granted when it appears reasonably certain that an injustice has been done, that the result of a new trial will be different."[111] Because there was no other compelling evidence besides Albert's now-discounted testimony, Hartford County Superior Court in the same month granted state's attorney Albert S. Bill's necessary request to null the Wolfson murder charge. Bill stated with frustration, "I never doubted he was guilty."[112]

Joseph spent fifty-two months on death row, bidding farewell to Lorain, Donahue, and Malm and mopping up the death chamber after their executions. He left prison with the self-righteous air of a wronged man. In an interview with the state's top crime reporter, Gerald J. Demeusy, thirty-one-year-old Joseph painted the demented Albert as a lying ragpicker who sought revenge for fraternal strife by blaming his brother for murder. Joseph told Demeusy that he favored capital punishment but only if it was swift because the condemned "suffer agony in the living grave of a death cell."[113] The two split the profits on an insider essay "My Years in a Death Cell" that appeared in a detective magazine.[114] By the end of 1955, Taborsky had gone on a religious retreat, married a death row correspondent, and moved to Brooklyn to start a new life. Impartial observers might well agree with Joseph's lawyer Nathaniel Bergman's claim of innocence: "I say the state has damned and tortured him enough. He is entitled to be exonerated of the murder and freed."[115]

Not unlike other death row inmates of the era, Taborsky was a recidivist. Unable to hold a job and in an unhappy marriage, he returned in September 1956 to armed robbery on visits to his devoted mother in Hartford. By December, he had teamed up with a former gang member from the late 1940s, Arthur Culombe. Culombe, a mentally slow gun collector and burglar, was someone, like Albert, that the towering Taborsky could easily intimidate. Between December 15, 1956, and January 26, 1957, the twosome committed repeated holdups, sometimes more than one a night, in central Connecticut. Liquor stores were so commonly targeted that the legislature came to mandate early closing hours for public safety. Taborsky and Culombe shot to death six people, five men and one woman, to eliminate witnesses. Several others were severely injured and left for dead. Victims were typically shot in the head as they were forced to kneel, and others were brutally pistol whipped. During a robbery in Coventry, Taborsky ordered Culombe to shoot a three-year-old girl, but his reluctant partner, father of a young daughter, faked the execution. The viciousness of the attacks took on momentum beyond the petty cash of less than $400 stolen in eight robberies.[116]

The notorious "mad dog killings" created widespread public alarm as newspapers, radio, and television highlighted the "terror." An astute Lieutenant Sam Rome, who directed the unprecedented search for the killers, cracked the case based on a clue from a shoe-store owner, Frank Adinolfi, who had survived a savage beating. Adinolfi recalled that one of the robbers asked to look at size 12 shoes, which made Rome suspect Taborsky, who had been spotted in Hartford. Shown a 1950 photograph that included both men, Adinolfi identified Culombe as his assailant. Police took the two into custody on February 23; Culombe confessed three days later and Taborsky the next day, including to the earlier Wolfson murder.[117]

The wave of violence prompted critical reassessment. On February 18, Governor Ribicoff reversed himself on capital punishment after what he called "a recent series of horrible hold-up murders in this state."[118] The *Hartford Courant* also recanted, writing, "Here is proof, if it is needed, of which capital punishment can serve a purpose."[119] The newspaper asked, "Does our reluctance to take human life make our courts too finicky, our prosecutors too lazy; our whole society too squeamish for its own good?"[120] Wolfson's widow, who had moved out of state with her children after the murder of her husband, upbraided Cohen and other abolitionists: "How does it feel to know that you and others like you helped a man commit more murders when you could have stopped him after the first?"[121] John C. Kelly, the state police commissioner, and Elmer S. Watson, the Republican Senate majority leader, opposed efforts to end the death penalty.[122] Stalwarts Henchel, Cohen, and Reverend Lloyd Worley of the Connecticut Council of Churches supported another bill to abolish the death penalty during the spring 1957 legislative session. Representative Gertrude E. Koskoff added, "The Taborsky case only has increased my conviction that capital punishment does not deter murder" and emphasized that Taborsky had been on death row during three executions in 1955.[123] With little support and without debate, the House rejected an abolition bill that May.[124]

Shortly before the trial that month of the two serial murderers, attorney Robert Satter explained in a newspaper essay entitled "Murder and Due Process of Law" that Taborsky had not been acquitted of the Wolfson murder on a "technicality." "We must never think of due process of law as a mere 'technicality,'" he argued, despite the horrible killings that followed. "It is the essential means of achieving justice in our American courts." Without following the rule of law, "it can cause an innocent man to die." He concluded, "That Taborsky and Culombe should obtain a fair trial is of critical significance to all of us."[125]

There was strong public revulsion against a criminal justice system that allowed killers to go free for whatever reason. In addition, as Watson put it, there were "endless delays in punishment" through a lengthy appeals process notable in convicted cop killer Frank Wojculewicz's situation.[126] The *Hartford Courant* captured a persistent sentiment that "when individuals have committed a whole series of murders, each one calculated in cold blood, and needless to boot, society must necessarily feel uneasy so long as that individual is alive."[127]

The debate over capital punishment was further amplified during the trial. After peremptory challenges, eight women, thought by the defense to be less partial to the death penalty than men, and four men made up the jury. Attorney Thomas F. Donough argued that Culombe was "a mental defective; "look at him," he said. He brought one woman juror to tears with, "I can't believe that any American jury would return a first degree verdict and send Arthur Culombe to the electric chair." Public defender Wallace K. Burke challenged the jury on behalf of Taborsky, "It's easy to say here's a criminal, here's a killer—kill him," and noted that the defendant told a psychiatrist, "When I kill another human being, they didn't think it was wrong when they wanted to kill me [in the electric chair]." In Taborsky's perception, his wanton violence was in part retribution for more than four years on death row. State's attorney Bill rebutted that if the duo were not executed, "watch us all scatter." "Don't shrink from your task," he told the jury.[128] They were found guilty on June 27 and sentenced to die on December 16. The *Hartford Courant* summed up, "If ever capital punishment is justified, it is justified for these two."[129]

Both were placed on death row. Taborsky was back in the same cell. He attempted suicide twice. He wrote to Governor Ribicoff to oppose abolition. "It is more humane to kill a convict," he asserted, "than to make him suffer years of imprisonment."[130] In an appeal, the Connecticut Supreme Court unanimously upheld their sentences in March 1960: "A review of all the evidence establishes that the jury could find the guilt of the accused beyond reasonable doubt."[131] The executions were rescheduled for May 17, 1960. The public defender withdrew from the case after Taborsky refused more appeals, including to the Board of Pardons. On the execution night, he had a last meal and was moved at 5:30 p.m. to the death cell, where he received communion in the Episcopalian church, which he had joined. The warden led him the short distance to the death chamber around 10:30 p.m. Taborsky offered no resistance or hesitation. Guards quickly attached the metal helmet on his shaved head, an electrode to a metal bracelet on his right leg, a leather strap across his mouth, and a black cloth over his face. Until the moment that he was gagged and strapped into the solid oak chair, he could have stopped the execution with his right to appeal. He gave no such indication. The warden signaled the executioner, who sent three charges of 2,000 volts of electricity through the condemned man. The prison physician declared him dead within minutes. Guards unshackled the corpse and wheeled it directly to the prison hospital. The thirty-six-year-old mass murderer had willed his eyes to an eye bank and his body to Yale Medical School.[132]

While Taborsky volunteered to die, Culombe appealed on the federal level. The U.S. Supreme Court on June 19, 1961, overturned his conviction based on police violation of his constitutional rights during detention and interrogation. Although the Connecticut Supreme Court was tolerant of questionable police tactics, the U.S. Supreme Court under Earl Warren's leadership created a revolution in suspects' rights during the 1960s. It appeared that Culombe might not be able to be prosecuted successfully on any of the six murders. Relieved not to be executed, Culombe ten days later pleaded guilty to second-degree murder. Despite his public defender's explanation that he might be freed, he believed that he should be punished, and he died behind bars in 1970.[133]

Two other men in 1959 preceded Taborsky to the electric chair. Like Malm, George Davies, a tool setter, had a criminal record as a pedophile of girls and served time for molestation in 1952. He confessed to two slayings within a week of each other in 1956. saying that he had choked and stabbed a nine-year-old girl twenty-two times and a sixteen-year-old girl fifty times. He told a psychiatrist that he preyed on young girls who were of dark complexion and foreign extraction. Davies had been a foster child, had dropped out of school at fifteen, and was a twice-divorced father of several children. He had had counseling during which he received electric shock therapy. After five hours of deliberation, the jury rejected a plea of insanity. Governor Ribicoff granted him two reprieves without avail over three years. Although Davies told the Board of Pardons that he wished to die, he panicked in the execution chamber on the night of October 20, 1959. Guards had to drag the forty-one-year-old to the electric chair and forcibly strap him down while he loudly prayed.[134]

Frank Wojculewicz, an interstate truck driver, also had a well-established criminal record dating to age ten. Two decades later, he had been arrested fifteen times and been incarcerated in four states for robbery, car theft, assault, and attempted rape. In March 1952, after two hours of deliberation, a jury—without applying the 1951 mercy law—convicted the career criminal of murdering a New Britain policeman who had surprised him during an armed robbery in November 1951. Ballistics tests also indicated that he had killed a bystander. During the shootout, police repeatedly wounded Wojculewicz, paralyzing him from the waist down. The judge sentenced the defendant, who appeared in court on a stretcher, to die that July.[135]

Wojculewicz had the distinction of having the longest postponement of his execution to date, some seven years. Some citizens expressed outrage that "this mad dog should not be executed" and at "this ridiculous farce of 'justice and mercy.'"[136] After five appeals to the Connecticut Supreme Court, that tribunal ruled unanimously that despite his medical condition, including incontinence and drug treatment, "he had been accorded a fair trial."[137] One of the few public voices against the death penalty for Wojculewicz was the *Hartford Times,* which suggested, probably incorrectly, that a commutation by the Board of Pardons "would have the approval of a large majority of Connecticut citizens."[138] His public defender told an unsympathetic board, "I know of no case on record of a paralyzed man being put to death."[139] Hours before the scheduled execution on October 26, 1959, guards wheeled the debilitated convict on a mobile stretcher to the death cell. An addled Wojculewicz told the Catholic chaplain that religious preparation was not necessary because God would prevent the death of an innocent man. Around 10:30 p.m., guards pushed him in a wheelchair into the death chamber and lifted him onto the electric chair, which had an oaken extension to accommodate his withered legs. Quickly strapped down in a partially prone position, he was pronounced dead within six minutes of entering the room.[140]

The postwar momentum against the death penalty never gained enough political leverage to abolish capital punishment as had all other New England states except New Hampshire. A major reform occurred in the 1951 compromise in the General Assembly that allowed juries to recommend life in prison, instead of death, for first-degree murder. In addition, from 1950 to 1955 the Board of Pardons prevented the executions of five condemned men. Reprieves and appeals—much to the frustration of the supporters of capital punishment—delayed scheduled executions for years. The General Assembly liberalized decision making of the board in 1959 so that four of five members, not unanimity, were necessary for action. In addition, the executive branch was no longer represented on the board. Instead, the governor now appointed the members: two attorneys, one social scientist, one physician, and one member of the Connecticut Supreme Court.[141]

After the brutal killings by Taborsky and Culombe, political support for abolition eroded. As the *Hartford Courant* put it after the House of Representatives in 1959 voted against abolition 166 to 104, "Let there remain the possibility of executing that amoral animal in human form, the relentless multiple killer."[142] A variety of restrictions—revised statutes, appeals, and judicial review at all levels—subsequently blocked executions, but the death penalty remained on the books. The result was the most recent execution in New England in nearly a half century. The convicted serial killer was Michael Ross, who, like Taborsky in 1960, renounced appeals and volunteered to accept lethal injection in 2005.

7

AN UNOFFICIAL MORATORIUM
1961–2004

Indeed, the only absolute and unmistakable method now of preventing
repetitious murders is through capital punishment.

Hartford Courant, Feb. 27, 1967

The fact that a murder is a grievous wrong does not make it
right to kill the murderer.

Hartford Times, April 29, 1969

EXPANSION OF DEFENDANTS' rights and restrictions on capital punishment
came as a result of rulings by the federal courts.[1] The culmination occurred in the 1972 decision in *Furman v. Georgia.* The United States Supreme Court in a controversial five-to-four opinion found that the arbitrary and inconsistent imposition of the death penalty violated the Eighth
and Fourteenth amendments concerning cruel and unusual punishment
and due process of the law, respectively. The ruling effectively shut down
the death penalty in every state that had it. Connecticut was one of thirty-
seven states to rewrite its capital code to comply with the revised standard.
Under the new law of 1973, the prosecution had to prove that a series of
mitigating factors did not exist. As Joseph F. Gormley, chief state's attorney, complained in 1974, "The chance of successful prosecution under the
present law is zero."[2]

In response to the federal judiciary, Connecticut's statutes and court rulings have provided for a virtual moratorium on executions, but not an out-
right ban. The one interruption since Taborsky's electrocution in 1960, so
far, has been the lethal injection of Michael Ross in 2005. Unlike state courts
in neighboring Massachusetts in 1980 and 1984 and New York in 1995, Connecticut's judiciary has not declared the death penalty itself or its administration racially biased or capricious. It remains constitutional.

Before *Furman v. Georgia*, 1961–1971

The model for a moratorium on capital punishment was established in 1961, well before the *Furman* decision. In that year, the U.S. Supreme Court overturned the first-degree murder convictions of Arthur Culombe and Harold Rogers because of coerced confessions. Unlike Taborsky, who preferred electrocution to life in prison, Culombe's public defender, Alexander Goldfarb, appealed the death sentence to the high court. In February 1960, the Connecticut Supreme Court had unanimously upheld the death sentence of both men, who had contested police procedures. It concluded, "The trial court did not abuse its discretion and properly admitted the confessions in evidence."[3] In contrast to the Connecticut courts, Justice Felix Frankfurter of the U.S. Supreme Court argued in a six-to-three decision that the police in their zeal to arrest the "mad dog killers" violated the constitutional protections of suspects. Culombe, a thirty-seven-year-old father of two, was totally illiterate and mentally deficient, but not insane. He had spent six years in third grade and was twice a resident in an institution for the feebleminded. The Connecticut Association for Retarded Children supported the appeal to the high court.[4] Culombe was particularly vulnerable to intimidation, including Taborsky's threat to kill him if he ever confessed. Despite his protests, police had never informed him of his right to remain silent and denied him access to a lawyer during days of interrogation. In concurrence with the majority opinion, Justice William O. Douglas critically added, "If this accused were a son of a wealthy or prominent person, and demanded a lawyer, can there be any doubt that his request would have been heeded? But [the] petitioner has no social status."[5] Furthermore, authorities had delayed in presenting him to a court, and to solidify their case held him on the broad charge of a breach of peace.

This exchange between defense attorney Thomas McDonough and state police captain Samuel Rome at the original trial in 1957 highlighted the disputed police tactics. Rome directed the manhunt and interrogation.

McDonough: "Didn't I tell you to leave Culombe alone and not bother him anymore?"
Rome: "I don't take my orders from you, Mr. McDonough."
McDonough: "Why did you do that?"
Rome: "I was doing my duty to the people of the state of Connecticut."

Culombe also claimed that the police had kicked and beaten him. The interrogators also brought his wife and children to police headquarters in an effort to elicit a confession. In court, Albert Bill, the state's attorney, asked the defendant to identify his typed confession, but Culombe responded that he couldn't read. Nonetheless, the trial judge admitted the statement of guilt.[6] For these reasons, Justice Frankfurter concluded, "When interrogation of a prisoner is so long continued, with such a purpose, and under such circumstances, as to make the whole proceeding an effective instrument for extorting an unwilling admission of guilt, due process precludes the use of the confession thus obtained."[7] In contrast, the *Hartford Courant* warned, "To set Culombe free is to sign the death warrant of an unknown number of people."[8] Taborsky had been freed from prison in 1954 to kill again. For an outraged Rome and many others, the liberal Court headed by Chief Justice Earl Warren now tied the hands of the police and coddled criminals. A majority of the citizenry believed that Taborsky and Culombe deserved to die. The General Assembly refused, time and again, by substantial margins to abolish capital punishment.

An expedient solution was found to keep Culombe behind bars. The state's attorney and Culombe's public defender with the defendant's concurrence agreed that Culombe would plead guilty to second-degree murder in Hartford County Superior Court. He was convicted in June 1961 and sentenced to a life term. The possibility for parole or pardon was unlikely as Culombe was deemed to be of "subnormal mentality and amoral."[9] The issue was rendered moot because he died in 1970 in prison at age forty-six of natural causes.[10]

A similar but less publicized resolution was worked out for fifty-four-year-old Harold Rogers, an African American who had appealed his death sentence for seven years. The former bricklayer had been convicted for the 1953 shooting of Dorothy Kennedy during a robbery of her liquor store in West Haven. After prolonged police questioning, the suspect refused to confess, until authorities threatened to bring his wife and foster children into custody. The prisoner protested that the police procedure violated his due process rights under the Fourteenth Amendment. The Supreme Court of Errors of Connecticut, however, upheld the conviction.[11] After conflicting judgments in U.S. district courts, the U.S. Court of Appeals for the Second Circuit rejected Rogers's petition. In a March 1961 review, the U.S. Supreme Court invalidated the conviction because the trial judge had used an improper standard in determining whether a confession was voluntary. Justice Frankfurter again rebuked Connecticut:

> Our decisions under that [Fourteenth] Amendment have made clear that convictions following the admission into evidence of confessions which are involuntary, i.e., the product of coercion, either physical or psychological, cannot stand. This is so not because such confessions are unlikely to be true

but because the methods used to extract them offend an underlying principle in the enforcement of our criminal law: that ours is an accusatorial and not an inquisitorial system—a system in which the State must establish guilt by evidence independently and freely secured and may not by coercion prove its charge against an accused out of his own mouth.[12]

The high court remanded the case to give the state an opportunity to retry the inmate. That May, Rogers pleaded guilty to the lesser charge of second-degree murder, for what state's attorney Abraham Ullman called "a most deliberate murder."[13] State's attorney Arthur LaBelle directed that felony suspects be brought to court as soon as possible and advised of their constitutional protections, including the right to an attorney. He directed that alleged murderers be held on a specific charge, not the vague breach of peace.[14] The next year, vocal citizen protest was instrumental in persuading the Board of Pardons to stop the electrocution of Benjamin Reid only hours before the scheduled execution. Reid was the epitome of those who ended up on death row.[15] He was an African American with an eighth-grade education reared in the Hartford slums by a disabled mother, a migrant to the North from the Deep South during the Great Depression. His father, ill and in trouble with the law, had died when Reid was an infant. The minor with subgrade intelligence had been a ward of the state for about half his life. On January 17, 1957, he beat to death Mrs. Florine McCluney, a friend of his mother, with a hammer. The victim reportedly carried large sums of money, but in the bungled robbery Reid failed to take the $2,000 she had on her person. At the time of the murder, he was unemployed and his pregnant wife had left him. He was tried in the same court building and at the same time as Taborsky and Culombe. A jury of seven men and five women sentenced him to death on June 27, 1957. Numerous judicial appeals and seven reprieves stayed the execution until June 25, 1962. During that time, Reid spent five years in solitary confinement in a cell seven feet by seven feet with a light bulb shining and a guard on duty. He had one twenty-minute exercise period a day. Remorseful, he immersed himself in reading the Bible.[16]

Redress did not come from the courts. The U.S. District Court for the District of Connecticut did overturn the conviction on the grounds that the defendant should have had the advice of counsel at the time he confessed. The U.S. Court of Appeals for the Second Circuit, however, reversed the decision. The majority ruled that because counsel had not raised the issue during trial the defendant had waived his rights. In a vigorous dissent, Justice Charles E. Clark called the reasoning "fantastic."[17] The U.S. Supreme Court, however, declined to review the case.[18] In the era of the civil rights movement, Reid's situation became a cause célèbre. Novelist William Styron brought Reid's situation to national attention with an impassioned essay attacking the death penalty in the February 1962 pages of *Esquire*. "To read of his background and career is to read not only of poverty and neglect and a mire of futile, petty crimes and despair," Styron wrote, "but in the end of a kind of wretched archetype: the Totally Damned American."[19] He concluded, "The death penalty, having divested a man not alone of his life but of that dignity with which even the humblest of men must be allowed to face death itself, has achieved its ultimate corruption."[20]

The five-member Board of Pardons, which met the morning of the scheduled execution, was the last resort. Since the 1951 homicide law, the board had not commuted an execution. To do so meant that a commission appointed by the governor would overrule a jury, the will of the people, which had chosen electrocution over life imprisonment. Former Governor John Lodge explained, "How can this board overrule with an act of mercy the jury which originally heard the case and refused to grant mercy?"[21] In addition to Styron, there was extraordinary citizen protest. George Will, the well-known political columnist, was then a student at Trinity College. He was the catalyst for the organization of a committee of administrators, faculty, and students to save Reid's life. Albert E. Holland, cochairman of the group and college vice president, had his commitment shaped by harrowing experiences as a prisoner of the Japanese during World War II. Based on thorough research, the Trinity committee reported that the prisoner's youth, mental deficiency, blighted upbringing, and lack of prior violence made him an exception to the hardened criminals who were indicted for first-degree murder, let alone condemned to death.[22]

The Board of Pardons met at the Wethersfield prison at 10 a.m. on June 25, 1962. Among the first to speak was Robert Satter, a prominent Hartford attorney, who observed that without the furor over the Taborsky-Culombe killings the jury would have likely found Reid guilty of a lesser sentence. Holland stressed the inequality of justice in Reid's conviction compared with other cases. He also called a dozen witnesses who testified to the prisoner's difficult life and his remorse for his actions. Reid's crippled mother pleaded for mercy. Louis Pollak, a Yale professor of law, pointed to the violation of the defendant's constitutional rights. Judge Douglass Wright, the original prosecutor at Reid's trial, argued that mitigating factors ought to have blocked the death penalty.[23] Petitions for the life of Reid flooded the board from groups as diverse as the Junior Chamber of Commerce and Quakers.[24] The *Hartford Times* captured prevailing sentiment: "The issue here is not one of guilt or innocence. It is one of prison or death for a slow-witted young victim of a tangled world who killed and didn't fully know why."[25] Hours before the planned execution, the Board of Pardons commuted Reid's punishment to life in prison with the possibility of parole.

Reid's commutation showed that concerned citizens could stop an egregious execution. As the *Hartford Courant* put it, "Why should Reid be executed when Arthur Culombe, who helped murder six, is serving life?"[26] The Reid case elicited vocal criticism of the state's criminal justice system, which solidified a de facto moratorium on execution and anticipated the *Furman* decision. In May 1960, U.S. District Judge Joseph Smith had notified Governor Ribicoff that prison personnel had held up Reid's mail, had discouraged him from writing appeals, and had lied to him about the outcome of those appeals. Governor Ribicoff ordered a state police investigation, which revealed wrongdoing for which disciplinary action was taken.[27] Styron concluded, "Certainly the law in Connecticut in regard to capital offenders is archaic and monstrous."[28] His point was corroborated by Joseph A. LaPlante of the University of Connecticut Law School in a scholarly essay for the state bar journal. "If the defendants Reid, Rogers, and Culombe did in fact commit the crimes of which they were charged," the professor wrote, "then the people are entitled to demand that their conviction be the result of a prosecution and a trial which can withstand charges of unconstitutionality. The present system as disclosed by the three cases deprives the individual of his rights and society of valid convictions under the law."[29] Connecticut Chief Justice John Hamilton King reflected, "I just don't believe that our truth-gathering means are so good I would be willing to bet someone's life on them."[30]

For the next decade, the baleful shadow of the Taborsky-Culombe murders overshadowed the crusade against the death penalty. Governor John Dempsey, who was expediently noncommittal on the controversial subject, explained in 1962, "A few years ago there occurred in this State a series of brutal crimes which harmed the cause of those who would abolish capital punishment."[31] The next year, the House voted overwhelmingly, once again, to retain capital punishment. Media focus on the Boston strangler, an elusive sexual predator, added to popular support for the execution of hardened criminals. "Unfortunately for the movement in Connecticut," the *Hartford Courant* editorialized, "the memory of Taborsky is still fresh as is the current fear of the Boston strangler. One can hardly blame the public for its feeling that it, too, needs protection."[32] The Reverend Joseph W. Reynolds, a Roman Catholic chaplain who escorted five condemned men to the electric chair, concurred: "Capital punishment should be kept on the books, but used only in the extreme cases where the courts, juries and the Board of Pardons agree a man is beyond correction."[33] In 1965, the House voted by a 100-member margin of 167 to 67 to retain the death penalty. Supporters such as Representative Eva P. Diefenderfer, a Republican from Wethersfield, argued that "to say the death penalty is not a deterrent is ridiculous," and John C. Kelly, the former state police commissioner, characterized abolition as "protection of criminals to the detriment of the people."[34]

Despite the legislative defeats, abolitionists spoke out. A 1961 study by Carroll Brewster, a Yale Law student, of murders and executions since 1930 had showed that of the last twenty executions in the state six men had mental deficiencies and only four had completed high school. No one of high or middle status had been executed. Brewster's findings emphasized that the death penalty fell inordinately on those at the bottom of society.[35] John Boyd, a Republican from Westport, told fellow legislators, "You can't abolish killing but you can stop the willful cold-blooded taking of life in the State of Connecticut by the State of Connecticut."[36] In contrast to other major newspapers, the *Hartford Times* demanded, "Let the electric chair go the way of the whip, the perpetual shackle, the iron collar and other tools of barbarisms. Let's abolish the death penalty in Connecticut."[37] Unitarians, Methodists, Quakers, and members of the United Church of Christ, American Civil Liberties Union, and Women's International League for Peace and Freedom agreed. The Connecticut State Committee to Abolish Capital Punishment distributed a pamphlet signed by twelve Roman Catholic priests that declared, "Born of fear and revenge, it [capital punishment] betrays a startling disbelief in Jesus's message that man is redeemable."[38]

While Governor Dempsey, a Democrat, judiciously avoided a public statement on the death penalty during his ten-year governorship (1961–1971), his Republican successor, Thomas Meskill (governor from 1971 to 1975), threatened to veto any bill for complete abolition.[39] The former mayor of New Britain and congressman declared, "I still think the death penalty is a deterrent."[40] Persistent abolitionists such as Irving Stolberg, a Democrat from New Haven, continued to bring such measures before the legislators. The *New Haven Register* proposed in 1971 a prescient compromise: "Perhaps Connecticut should all but abolish the death penalty by legislation that confines it specifically to those rare cases where the crime is so wanton as to cry out for the extreme punishment."[41]

Events on the national level nudged Connecticut toward such a resolution. In June 1968, the U.S. Supreme Court extended defendants' rights. Justice Potter Stewart delivered the majority opinion that jurors who express doubts about the death penalty could not be excluded by the prosecution during voir dire. The Court warned against a "hanging jury" in *Witherspoon v. Illinois:*

> A man who opposes the death penalty, no less than one who favors it, can make the discretionary choice of punishment entrusted to him by the State, and can thus obey the oath he takes as a juror; but in a nation where so many have come to oppose capital punishment, a jury from which all such people have been excluded cannot perform the task demanded of it – that of expressing the conscience of the community on the ultimate question of life or death.[42]

The three men on death row in Connecticut were not affected by the decision because a three-judge panel, not a jury, had done the sentencing.[43] In that same year, there were for the first time no executions in the United States. The *Hartford Courant,* which spoke of "the vanishing death penalty," observed that "custom and public sentiment" were increasingly opposed to the practice.[44]

The Response to *Furman v. Georgia,* 1972–1988

In 1972, the U.S. Supreme Court in the five-to-four *Furman v. Georgia* decision brought the issue to the fore. With all President Richard Nixon's appointees voting in the negative, a majority of the justices found that unless the death penalty was imposed fairly and with reasonable consistency it was in violation of the Eighth and Fourteenth amendments. At the same time, the Court expressly found in *Delgado v. Connecticut* (1972) that Connecticut's death penalty statute was unconstitutional.[45] With each of the majority writing a separate opinion, however, the ruling was less than uniform. Justice Thurgood Marshall argued that the death penalty was inherently illegitimate. Justice William Brennan observed that a growing reluctance to carry out the death penalty made its imposition arbitrary and unconstitutional. Justice William O. Douglas stressed the role of bias, writing, "It would seem to be incontestable that the death penalty inflicted on one defendant is 'unusual' if it discriminates against him by reason of his race, religion, wealth, social position, or class, or if it is imposed under a procedure that gives room for the play of such prejudices."[46] He pointed to data that showed that African Americans were disproportionately executed for the rape or murder of a white person. Penal laws that were discriminatory, he concluded, violated the Eighth Amendment. Justice Stewart found that so few people were selected for execution that the imposition of the death penalty was capricious, and Justice Byron White concurred that the penalty was imposed in an arbitrary manner. Like contentious rulings in defendant rights, racial segregation, reproductive freedom, and school prayer, critics pointed to an unelected U.S. Supreme Court that usurped the legislative function and contravened the will of the people, a majority of whom backed the death penalty.[47] A Gallup poll at the time indicated 57 percent in favor of the death penalty, 32 percent opposed, and 11 percent undecided.[48] The conservative columnist James J. Kilpatrick wrote: "Many persons who abhor the death penalty, and agree that capital punishment has been imposed irrationally and ineffectually in the past, will rejoice in what the five activist judges have done. But those who love the law, and believe in the separation of powers, will emphatically condemn the way in which they did it."[49] In addition, President Nixon's support for the death penalty resonated with what he called the "silent majority." The Republican call for "law and order" represented a political backlash, not only against the liberal Warren Court, but more generally against the cultural upheaval of the 1960s and early 1970s.

The *Furman* decision was, however, less than it seemed. With each justice writing a separate opinion, the Court expressed a great deal of ambivalence about the death penalty. The Court had not absolutely outlawed the death penalty, but had pointed to circumstances in which it was unconstitutional. Consequently, Chief Justice Warren Burger writing in dissent instructed that states "may seek to bring their laws into compliance with the Court's ruling by providing standards for juries and judges to follow in determining the sentence in capital cases or by more narrowly defining the crimes for which the penalty is to be imposed."[50] Following Chief Justice Burger's direction, Connecticut and three dozen other states revised their capital code to conform to the ruling.

With elaborate strictures, Connecticut's death penalty statute of 1973 sought to pass constitutional muster. Governor Meskill endorsed the bill that the House passed 83 to 49 and the Senate passed narrowly by 19 to 17.[51] It indicated that the jury or court could find the indicted party guilty in a lesser degree than charged if "extreme emotional disturbance" or mental abnormality were present. Legislators spelled out six categories of capital felony: (1) killing a police or corrections officer, (2) murder for hire, (3) having a previous murder conviction, (4) murder while serving a life sentence, (5) murder of a kidnapped victim, and (6) the death of a non-drug-dependent person by the sale of drugs. The death penalty could not be imposed if the jury or court found that the defendant at the time of the crime (1) was younger than eighteen years old, (2) had impaired mental capacity, (3) was under unusual and substantial duress, (4) was criminally liable but played a minor role, or (5) could not have reasonably foreseen the homicide.

If none of these five qualifications applied, the court might sentence the defendant to death if the jury or court determined that (1) a murder occurred during a felony; (2) the murderer had a record of multiple state or federal offenses with sentencing that involved more than one year's incarceration and a crime that inflicted serious bodily injury; (3) the offense involved a grave risk of death; (4) the crime occurred in an "especially heinous, cruel or depraved manner"; (5) the perpetrator had been hired; and (6) the offense had been committed for pecuniary gain.[52] The statute would be interpreted so that the jury must unanimously reject all mitigation to recommend the death penalty.

The new statute was heralded as part of a "crime fighting package," but the mitigating factors made the imposition of the death penalty highly unlikely.[53] The next year, Gormley, the chief state's attorney, glumly commented that "the chance of successful prosecution under the present law is zero."[54] He noted that a multiple murder that had occurred that fall in New Britain was not included within the scope of the new law.[55] By 1976, no one had been indicted under its provisions. Gormley characterized it as "totally useless," a law "designed not to work."[56] Gormley was right. In response to the constraints of *Furman v. Georgia,* the Connecticut legislation had made capital punishment constitutional but rendered it impractical. The outcome was paradoxical: the law was on the books, but only under unusual circumstances could the de facto moratorium be interrupted.

The *Furman* decision also voided the execution of the three men—Arthur J. Davis, Robert Delgado, and Louis F. Cofone Jr.—then on death row at the State Prison in Somers, the successor in 1963 to the antiquated Wethersfield institution. Connecticut's high court ordered that the state's superior courts establish new penalties for the trio. A Korean War veteran, Delgado was a twenty-five-old laborer with a ninth-grade education who had emigrated from Puerto Rico. After Officer Harvey Young arrested Delgado for breach of the peace in Hartford in August 1967, the two fought. The policeman shot Delgado in the chest, but the wounded man wrested the pistol away and clubbed the officer with it. Young collapsed in the street, and Delgado shot him four times point blank. Despite psychiatric testimony that the defendant suffered "acute brain syndrome," he was found guilty and sentenced to die, the first such person of Puerto Rican background so sentenced in Connecticut.[57] Latino organizations asked for clemency "in the name of all Puertoricans [sic] living in the State of Connecticut."[58]

An African American factory worker, twenty-six-year-old Davis was charged with shooting to death six people—two men, two women, and two children—in a New Haven housing complex in a dispute over his girlfriend. All the victims were black. Davis's rampage followed only a few weeks after Charles Whitman had made national news, killing sixteen people, also with a rifle, at the University of Texas on August 1, 1966. In November 1967, a jury found Davis guilty of six counts of first-degree murder and recommended the death penalty.[59]

Thirty-one-year-old Cofone, an Italian American, was an ex-convict who had served time for rape. While on parole, he strangled to death a Wilton housewife, a mother of four, in a botched robbery after she screamed for help. As the public defender pointed out, the jury arrived at the death penalty after learning that the prisoner would be eligible for parole (once again) after serving twenty years of a life sentence.[60]

The three were resentenced to life in prison. A three-judge panel drawn from the New Haven Superior Court gave Davis six life terms so that he would never be released.[61] There was mixed reaction from various officials. Jacob Tufane, president-elect of the Connecticut Police Chief Association, opposed the *Furman* decision. He thought that the death penalty was a useful deterrent to crime. A study of the contiguous states of Connecticut (death penalty), Massachusetts (death penalty), and Rhode Island (abolition), however, did not demonstrate a deterrent effect: "All three states, regardless of their punishment for murder, show a general and gradual increase in homicide throughout the period" of 1963–1971.[62] House majority leader Carl R. Ajello, a Democrat from Ansonia, regretted that the death penalty could not be preserved for the killing of a police officer or prison guard. Abolitionist William Olds, executive director of the Connecticut Civil Liberties Union, praised the ruling as "one of the most important and far reaching in U.S. history." In anticipation of the *Furman* decision, John R. Manson, Connecticut's corrections commissioner, relocated the three death row inmates to the general prison population in May 1972 and made Connecticut the first state to do so.[63]

Four years later, in *Gregg v. Georgia,* the U.S. Supreme Court in a seven-to-two decision reinstated the death penalty. Only Justices Brennan and Marshall dissented from the majority opinion that the death penalty did not inherently constitute cruel and unusual punishment in violation of the Eighth Amendment. The tribunal upheld laws in Georgia, Florida, and Texas that allowed discretion in imposing the death penalty, but rejected mandatory execution in Louisiana and North Carolina.[64] The decision was concurrent with popular opinion at the time. Widespread fear of crime spiked poll data in favor of capital punishment to 65 percent and those opposed to 28 percent with 7 percent undecided.[65] The last execution had been in 1967 in Colorado by gas, and by 1976 more than 600 people were on death row.[66] There were none, however, in Connecticut. The revised law of 1973 met the standards of *Gregg*.[67]

The state's six-year-old law was itself declared illegal by Hartford County Superior Court Judge David M. Shea in December 1979. The ruling came in regard to the impending trial of Gerard Castonguay, a thirty-four-year-old Bristol resident with a long criminal record who had shot a Plainville police officer four times at close range in the aftermath of a house burglary. At issue was *Lockett v. Ohio* (1978), in which the U.S. Supreme Court held that sentencing authorities must have the discretion to consider every possible mitigating factor rather than being limited to a specific list of factors. Judge Shea found that Connecticut's statute did not permit the required "individualized consideration of mitigating factors."[68]

The General Assembly amended the defect in a compromise between opponents and supporters of capital punishment. The revision required that any mitigating factor concerning the defendant's character or background and the history and circumstances of the crime had to be considered. In turn, rape-murder and multiple murders were added to the existing six types of capital felony eligible for the death penalty. As Representative Naomi W. Otterness, an abolitionist Democrat, explained, "If you have to have a death penalty, the one we have (with the new provision on mitigating circumstances) offers the maximum protection for the individual."[69] Democratic Governor Ella Grasso, the state's first female executive and a proponent of the death penalty, signed the legislation that went into effect on October 1, 1980.[70] Several weeks later, the Supreme Judicial Court of Massachusetts struck down its capital code as "impermissibly cruel."[71] The next month, Judge Shea sentenced Castonguay to two twenty-five-years-to-life terms. Castonguay had been convicted that March when the death penalty law was under question, and the judge ruled that a defect in the capital punishment statute meant it could not be applied.[72]

During the next decade, further review by the state courts made the capital code more restrictive. Eight years after the U.S. Supreme Court reinstated capital punishment, Steven J. Wood was the first capital felon in the state to reach the penalty phase. After midnight on April 12, 1982, Wood had ambushed his ex-wife and her male companion in West Hartford. He repeatedly shot the couple, his ex-wife seven times in the face. He then drove her car to their former home, where he shot to death his ex-mother-in-law. He then sexually assaulted his adopted teenage daughter and held her hostage for an hour before shooting her four times in the head. After the state's longest criminal trial, the jury, fifty-four weeks after its selection, found the defendant not guilty of the murder of his ex-wife because of insanity. The jurors, however, declared that the prisoner was guilty of the other three homicides. Multiple murders were a capital felony, but the mitigating factor of an impaired mental condition obviated the death penalty. Given the opportunity to speak before sentencing, Wood declined and failed to express remorse for his brutal behavior. Judge Harry Hammer concluded that "Mr. Wood suffers from a diseased character and a diseased personality and a diseased psyche for which there is no cure" and sentenced the forty-five-year-old man to 120 years for murder. The sensational killings and lengthy trial did little to further public sentiment against capital punishment. Wood's former sister-in-law said bitterly that she wanted him "to be electrocuted."[73]

Kevin Usry escaped execution for the rape and bludgeoning to death with a brick of a New Britain woman on September 8, 1982. The victim was a married Polish immigrant, and the defendant was an eighteen-year-old black youth who had broken into her apartment at night.[74] Although Usry was a special education student of "dull normal" intelligence, he was judged to be mentally competent and duly informed of his Miranda rights. In addition to matching blood tests and pubic hair found on the victim, Usry made inculpatory statements.[75] The jury split seven to five in recommending a death sentence. The judge ruled that the jury had to agree unanimously that no mitigation existed. One dissenting member of a twelve-member jury could stop an execution.

The judge sentenced the prisoner on May 6, 1985, to three concurrent life terms: twenty years for each of three convictions for capital felony, felony murder, and murder. Given the two years Usry had spent in pretrial time and the possibility of parole after serving fifteen years of a twenty-year sentence, he could potentially be released after forty-three years behind bars. Earlier that year, the General Assembly had passed a law, to go into effect on October 1, that made a life sentence "one without possibility of release." Another law eliminated drug dependency as a defense in murder cases. Public defender Gerard Smyth, Usry's attorney, said of the former law, "I hope that change will satisfy most jurors that a death sentence is not necessary since a life sentence will mean lifetime incarceration."[76]

Although still on the books, the death penalty appeared moribund. On June 16, 1984, at about 1 a.m., twenty-seven-year-old Jerry D. Daniels, an unemployed parolee, went to the Norwich home of Christine Whipple, looking for another woman. After he refused to leave and a struggle ensued, he stabbed the twenty-year-old Whipple. He then slit the throat of her three-year-old daughter, nearly decapitating her, after she cried for her mother. He then raped Whipple and stabbed her to death.[77] The jury deadlocked six to six over the mitigating factors of repeated child abuse and mental impairment.[78] On appeal, the Connecticut Supreme Court in November 1988 clarified the procedure, writing that

> the trial court had correctly construed the death penalty statute to impose upon the state the burden of proving one of the statutorily defined aggravating factors beyond a reasonable doubt, and thereafter to impose upon the defendant the burden of proving a statutorily defined mitigating factor by a preponderance of the evidence. We concluded, furthermore, that neither of these burdens can be met without a unanimous finding by the trier of fact. Finally, we held that, if the jury cannot agree on the existence of a mitigating factor, the trial court has discretion to declare a mistrial.[79]

The trial judge acted accordingly to void the death penalty and to impose a life sentence on the defendant for the capital felony conviction.

The Capital Code, 1980s–2005

Not unlike the judicial system, the legislature also kept capital punishment on the books. Furthermore, the U.S. Supreme Court in a five-to-four vote in *Glass v. Louisiana* (1985) affirmed that state-authorized electrocution was constitutional.[80] A 1987 poll showed that 61 percent of state residents favored the death penalty for first-degree murder.[81] In a 1994 dissent, Connecticut Supreme Court Justice Robert Berdon, an opponent of the death penalty, countered:

> Even public opinion polls demonstrate public reluctance and concern over the imposition of the death penalty. While a majority of the public may support the death penalty in the abstract, public support for the penalty drops to below 50 percent when alternative sentences are considered. Given the choice, more people would support life imprisonment without parole plus restitution to the victim's family over the death penalty.[82]

There was other vocal opposition to the death penalty. The Connecticut Civil Liberties Union (CCLU), Connecticut Council of Churches, and Citizens for Better Correctional Institutions, among others, lobbied against the death penalty.[83] William Olds, executive director of the CCLU, denounced it as "the ultimate denial of rights," particularly in its disproportionate application to the poor, uneducated, and blacks.[84] In 1984, Archbishop John F. Whealon of Hartford emphatically endorsed the policy of the 1980 National Conference of Catholic Bishops: "Catholic teaching has always recognized the right of the state to inflict punishment. There is a difference, however, in the possession of a right and its use. Given the circumstances of today, we question whether the use of capital punishment is morally justified."[85] The *Hartford Courant* similarly editorialized, "Murder of a person is a heinous crime, including murder by the state."[86]

William A. O'Neill, Democratic governor from 1980 to 1991 who favored the death penalty for multiple murders and for the killing of law enforcement officials, vetoed a 1986 bill that would have extended capital punishment to some minors and the mentally retarded. Efforts to override the veto failed.[87] Two years later, the U.S. Supreme Court in the five-to-three decision of *Thompson v. Oklahoma* (1988) banned executions of youths younger than sixteen. The Court noted the "evolving standards of decency that mark the progress of a maturing society" as a primary concern in the revocation of the death sentence of a fifteen-year-old boy on grounds of "cruel and unusual punishment."[88] In the General Assembly, staunch proponents of the death penalty sought to revise the provision of the law that permitted a mitigating factor to block execution. Bills that sought to weigh aggravating factors more than the mitigating factors or to balance both equally were unsuccessful. Governor Lowell P. Weicker Jr. (1991–1995), a political independent of the Connecticut Party, vetoed a proposal that would equally consider factors. The bill was fraught, Governor Weicker stated, with "semantic gyrations" that would "confuse rather than improve or further the ends of justice."[89]

A new statute signed into law by Republican Governor John G. Rowland (1995–2004), that went into effect on October 1, 1995, however, facilitated the imposition of the death penalty without obviating the strictures of *Furman*. If aggravating factors outweighed the mitigating factors, "the court shall sentence the defendant to death."[90] No longer did the decision for the death penalty reside on the unanimous rejection by the jury of all mitigating factors. In addition, proportionality review of death sentences during appellate review was dropped from the law. According to this provision, adopted in 1980, the Connecticut Supreme Court was required to affirm a death sentence unless it found that "the sentence is excessive or disproportionate to the penalty imposed in similar cases."[91] The U.S. Supreme Court, however, ruled in *Pulley v. Harris* (1984) that proportionality review was not constitutionally required under the Eighth Amendment.[92] The law also changed the means of execution from electrocution to lethal injection. The new method, it was thought by supporters, was more expeditious and less horrific than the electric chair. Another substantial change was that for the first time the murderer of a child under age sixteen was subject to the death penalty. Governor O'Neill had vetoed a similar bill in 1986 because he thought that it might permit the execution of minors and the mentally incompetent. In turn, Governor Weicker had vetoed several death penalty bills. Governor Rowland (who later would be convicted of corruption, resign his office, and serve time in a federal prison) supported the new legislation as a crime-fighting measure.[93]

The debate over the state's 1995 law had been mirrored in a sharp exchange the year before between Justices Blackmun and Antonin Scalia in *Collins v. Collins*. Justice Blackmun in a passionate dissent against the inequities of capital punishment, particularly racial bias, protested, "It is virtually self-evident to me now that no combination of procedural rules or substantive regulations ever can save the death penalty from its inherent constitutional deficiencies. The basic question—does the system accurately and consistently determine which defendants 'deserve' to die?—cannot be answered in the affirmative."[94] Justice Scalia responded that such sentiment was constitutionally unpersuasive. He added that lethal injection was far less cruel than the suffering inflicted on victims by convicted murderers. He rebutted:

> How enviable a quiet death by lethal injection compared with that! If the people conclude that such more brutal deaths may be deterred by capital punishment; indeed, if they merely conclude that justice requires such brutal deaths to be avenged by capital punishment; the creation of false, untextual and unhistorical contradictions within "the Court's *Eighth Amendment* jurisprudence" should not prevent them.[95]

The opinions of both justices were firmly held and diametrically opposed. Despite the intent of the state's new law to render the application of the death penalty easier, a number of impediments remained. There were nine categories of capital felony for which a person could be sentenced to death or to life imprisonment without the possibility of release. After a defendant was convicted of a capital felony, the jury or court had to state in a special verdict whether one or more of nine aggravating factors, such as the murder of a person under age sixteen, outweighed one or more mitigating factors. Mitigating factors were not an excuse for the crime, but in fairness and mercy provided a rationale for a sentence less than death. The jury or court had to state in the special verdict the existence of any automatic bars to the death penalty and the specific aggravating factors. The four automatic bars to the death penalty were that the defendant (1) was under eighteen years old at the time of the crime, (2) was mentally impaired at the time of the crime but not sufficiently to constitute a defense, (3) was guilty as an accessory to a capital felony but the participation was minor, and (4) could not have reasonably foreseen that the crime for which he or she was convicted would have resulted in someone's death.

Since 1957, the Connecticut Supreme Court automatically reviewed each death sentence. The justices could strike down the sentence if it was the product of passion, bias, or any other arbitrary factor or if the evidence did not substantiate an aggravating factor. In addition, the defendant could seek a direct appeal of any errors at trial. If the direct appeal failed, the defendant could petition the U.S. Supreme Court. If that failed, the defendant could file a state habeas corpus petition that usually claimed ineffective assistance of counsel or a claim of innocence based on the discovery of new evidence. These appeals could be made to the Connecticut Supreme Court and, if denied, to the U.S. Supreme Court. If the prisoner remained unsuccessful at this point, he could file a federal habeas corpus petition on federal issues in U.S. District Court. This claim could be appealed through the U.S. Court of Appeals and to the U.S. Supreme Court. The defendant's case could be returned to the trial court if the Connecticut Supreme Court vacated the conviction or death sentence, if the habeas petition at the state or federal level was granted, or if the U.S. Supreme Court found error. If the trial court again sentenced the defendant to death, the whole process began again.[96] During the appeals process, the courts order a stay of execution. If all appeals were denied, the prisoner could petition the Board of Pardons for a commutation to a lesser sentence or, less likely, a complete pardon. The result of this involved review process was that seven men were on death row in 2000, but no one was yet executed.

The Connecticut Supreme Court continued to turn down constitutional challenges to capital punishment. In 1994, the court ruled against Michael Ross, stating that "our state constitution makes repeated textual references to capital offenses and thus expressly sustains the constitutional validity of such a penalty in appropriate circumstances." Federal constitutional law under the *Gregg* decision did not forbid such a statute, and "courts in the overwhelming majority of our sister states have rejected facial challenges to the death penalty under their state constitutions." The court added that a death penalty was of long standing in Connecticut's legal history.[97] Two years later, the state's highest court reaffirmed that the death penalty was not cruel and unusual punishment under the state constitution, which incorporated all national protections and met federal court stipulations.[98] The court in 1999 again found that the death penalty statute complied with federal constitutional requirements in rejecting a petition of death row inmate Sedrick Cobb.[99]

Although the Connecticut Supreme Court did not strike down the death penalty statute, a controversial restriction was placed on its implementation. In June 1991, Terry D. Johnson, a twenty-year-old man prone to burglary, and his younger brother broke once again into the same gun shop in rural North Windham. Before Trooper Russell Bagshaw could exit his cruiser in the parking lot of the gun shop during a routine patrol, Johnson shot at him seventeen times within seven seconds with a 9-millimeter pistol. One of the hollow-nosed bullets penetrated an armhole in Bagshaw's protective vest, promptly killing the officer in the performance of his duties. In a capital trial, the jury in the penalty phase found one aggravating factor, but no mitigation, and sentenced Johnson to death. Writing for the majority in the defendant's appeal to the Connecticut Supreme Court, Justice Joette Katz, an opponent of the death penalty, ruled in 2000 that the "six seconds of being the target of the defendant's fusillade and up to ninety seconds of consciousness following being struck by one bullet do not suffice to meet the heinous, atrocious or cruel aggravating factor."[100] That is, the victim did not suffer the degree of pain or torture necessary to sustain a death sentence. The court reversed the earlier judgment with respect to the imposition of the death penalty and remanded the case with direction for imposition of a life sentence without the possibility of release.[101] The four-to-three decision made problematic those death sentences from gunshots that killed relatively quickly, including the killing of law enforcement officers.[102]

There was strong reaction to Justice Katz's legal calculus of suffering. "The effect of this piecemeal review is to depict Trooper Bagshaw's suffering as a series of ripples rather than as a wave which, although it crested and broke quickly, was high enough to establish that the killing was especially cruel," wrote Marjorie Allen Dauster, an assistant state's attorney.[103] In 2001, the legislature made killing a law enforcement officer in an attempt to avoid arrest or to stop the victim from carrying out his or her official duties an aggravating factor in determining whether to sentence a defendant to death.

At the same time, Governor Rowland signed a bill to prohibit the imposition of the death penalty on a defendant who suffered from mental retardation.

Connecticut and a number of other states anticipated the U.S. Supreme Court in *Atkins v. Virginia* (2002) that banned such executions.[104] There were now eight aggravating factors and five automatic bars to execution. Legislation signed on July 6 also created a commission "to study imposition of the death penalty in this state,"[105] an effort to assess what had become a legal quagmire. As the *Hartford Courant* editorialized: "State capital punishment laws have been tinkered with for a decade to make them tougher, yet death row is crowded and there hasn't been an execution since 1960. The task of sentencing people to death after sorting out the aggravating and mitigating factors as required by statute has proven almost impossible for juries."[106]

The commission issued its report on January 8, 2003. Significantly, the eight members concurred that the commission's charge was not "to recommend whether death as a punishment for crime is proper or should be abolished."[107] Instead of expressing an opinion on the controversial subject, the commission made recommendations on fourteen wide-ranging issues since the state's revision of the capital code in 1973. Among the most important was that the state pass legislation to bar the execution of a defendant based on a "discriminatory pattern" of race, ethnicity, gender, religion, or sexual orientation.[108] The commission also urged a "proportionality review" of any death sentence to prevent discrimination from one case to another.[109]

National studies since the *Furman* decision have indicated that race influenced capital cases. David Baldus, a professor of law at the University of Iowa, found in a study of 2,500 murder cases in Georgia that blacks had a substantially higher rate of death sentences than whites. In *McCleskey v. Kemp* (1987), Justice Lewis Powell writing for a five-to-four decision of the U.S. Supreme Court denied Warren McCleskey's appeal which was based on the Baldus study. The defendant, an African American, had been sentenced to death for killing a white police officer in Georgia. The majority held that discriminatory effects over the broad range did not constitute discriminatory acts by the state in the individual case. There was no constitutional violation.[110]

In Connecticut, the issue was raised in *State v. Cobb* (1995). Cobb, an African American, was sentenced to death in 1991; he had kidnapped, raped, and murdered Julia Ashe, a twenty-three-year-old white woman in 1989. The defendant moved to enlarge the class of similar cases since 1973 to show that race impermissibly affected capital sentencing. The Connecticut Supreme Court denied his motion, concluding "that the legislature did not intend proportionality review to encompass a comparison with all homicide cases prosecuted since 1973 in which a capital felony could have been charged."[111] The type of detailed fact-finding in *McCleskey v. Kemp* was needed. The court left open the possibility that an evidentiary hearing on the claim could be brought up in the trial court or through a writ of habeas corpus.

In turn, the commission reviewed available data on 166 capital prosecutions provided by the Office of Chief Public Defender. The commission found that minorities (blacks and Hispanics) constituted 60 percent of all capital prosecutions. Of seven men on death row in 2002, three were white, three were black, and one was Hispanic. The most prominent disparity was in the race of the victim of the death row prisoners: six death sentences were imposed in cases that involved a white victim or victims, one involved Hispanics, and none involved black victims.[112] Victims in which the state sought the death penalty also were predominantly women, children, and police officers. Five of the men on death row killed women or girls, and two of these inmates had murdered children under sixteen. No women had been sentenced to death under current law. Without systematic data, the commission drew no conclusions about religion, sexual orientation, and socioeconomic status.[113] The Waterbury judicial district, particularly under the zealous direction of state's attorney John Connolly, had twice the percentage of death penalty trials as the other twelve districts. Of the eight death sentences imposed since 1973, five occurred in the Waterbury district.[114]

Although the commission did not comment on whether the death penalty was proper, its systematic report highlighted disparities—racial, gender, age, and prosecutorial—in its application. It called for additional safeguards during criminal investigation involving videotaping, witness identification, and DNA testing. The report recommended the reinstatement of proportionality review during the appellate process that the General Assembly had eliminated in the capital code of 1995. It was noted that the average annual cost to maintain a death row inmate was $47,000, the same for the 485 other inmates at the supermaximum Northern Correctional Institution where death row was housed.[115] The report found much that was commendable in the state's adherence to the rule of law, such as the competency of the Office of the Public Defender that defended most death sentences. In effect, the report provided a basis for fundamental challenges to the death penalty based on alleged bias and arbitrariness. In 1980, the Massachusetts Supreme Judicial Court had, after all, struck down its death penalty because "such chance and caprice are unconstitutional."[116] Unwilling to upset the status quo on a politically charged issue, the General Assembly did not enact the substantive recommendations from the commission.

Controversy over the death penalty flared in May 2003 when the Connecticut Supreme Court ruled on two distinct issues—prosecutorial misconduct and aggravating factors—in *Connecticut v. Reynolds*. Justice Joette Katz, an opponent of the death penalty on the basis of the Eighth Amendment and the judge in the aforementioned *Johnson* case, charged Connolly, the state's attorney, with deliberate misconduct in the trial of Richard Reynolds. The defendant had been sentenced to death in 1995 for killing Walter Williams, a Waterbury police officer, in 1992 with a pistol shot at point-blank range to the head during a drug arrest. Justice Katz charged that Connolly had repeatedly misled juries about the standard of weighing mitigating factors against aggravating factors. In a lone dissent in *Reynolds,* she concluded: "Past experience has demonstrated that merely to reprimand, once again, a state's attorney who engages in deliberate misconduct that undermines the fairness of a trial does not sufficiently convey disapproval of those tactics. I would conclude, therefore, that nothing short of reversal will deter similar misconduct in the future."[117] An unapologetic Connolly rebutted, "The fact is, Justice Katz is opposed to the death penalty, and I've been successful in five death penalty prosecutions."[118] Although the other justices found some of the prosecutor's statements improper, they determined that they did not constitute reversible error in *Reynolds.*[119]

In the same case, the court conceded that the evidence did not reasonably support the conclusion that the defendant continued to fire at the officer with the intent to torture him psychologically. Justice Richard N. Palmer wrote for the six-to-one majority that it was not plausible to infer that Reynolds's "state of mind changed from an intent to kill to an intent to torture in the brief interval between the point at which the defendant shot Williams in the head and the point at which [he] fired the additional gunshots in Williams' direction while fleeing the crime scene."[120] The ruling affirmed the decision three years earlier in which Johnson shot to death Trooper Bagshaw in a fusillade of bullets. Neither murder constituted the degree of extreme pain or torture necessary to sustain a death sentence under the "cruel, heinous and depraved" aggravating factor. In what may have been the longest published decision in the state, the court upheld the death sentence based on a second aggravating factor. For the first time, the justices found that an out-of-state felony for a similar crime (drug dealing) involved in a capital trial qualified for an aggravating factor. Prosecutor Connolly later commented, "We were fortunate in this case that we were able to prove a second aggravating factor."[121]

That October in *Connecticut v. Rizzo,* the Connecticut Supreme Court clarified the weighing process in a sentencing hearing required by the 1995 amendments to the death penalty statute. The legislature had not specified in the statute what standard the jury must use. The court stated that "the jury must be instructed that it must be persuaded beyond a reasonable doubt that the aggravating factors outweigh the mitigating factors and that, therefore, it is persuaded beyond a reasonable doubt that death is the appropriate punishment in the case."[122] The court ruled that the jury had not been properly instructed on the matter. In addition, the court found, as Judge Katz had earlier argued in *Reynolds,* that Connolly's misconduct "so infected the trial with unfairness as to make the resulting conviction a denial of due process."[123] The court reversed the judgment of the trial court on both points and remanded the matter for a new penalty-phase hearing.

There were further refinements. On October 1, 2004, the General Assembly combined the Board of Pardons and the Board of Paroles. This new Board of Pardons and Paroles expanded from five to thirteen members through gubernatorial appointment. The board retained the power to grant "commutations from the penalty of death." In addition, the governor, who had not been a member of the Board of Pardons since the 1950s, could only issue a reprieve in a death sentence until the next session of the legislature.[124] On March 1, 2005, under the evolving standards of decency test, the U.S. Supreme Court in the five-to-four *Roper v. Simmons* decision blocked the execution of seventy-two men (none in Connecticut) who had committed crimes while under the age of eighteen. One of Connecticut's five automatic bars to the death penalty included such a provision.[125] With that ruling, the *Hartford Courant* urged, "Rather than chip away at capital punishment, the Supreme Court or legislatures should abolish it. Life in prison is a suitable penalty for a capital crime."[126]

Abolition, however, did not appear imminent either at the federal level or within Connecticut despite vocal opposition to the death penalty. The crusade of Sister Helen Prejean, Barry Scheck's Innocence Project, and the Death Penalty Information Center highlighted not only the immorality of capital punishment but the execution of the innocent.[127] DNA evidence exonerated dozens of death row inmates, and, in Illinois, Republican Governor George Ryan's 2000 moratorium on executions pointed to a broken system.[128] Nevertheless, public opinion in Connecticut and throughout the nation still favored the death penalty, especially for horrific crimes.

Despite the persistence of a death penalty statute, the concern for procedural safeguards had blocked executions in Connecticut since 1960. There was not the political will or judicial mandate for abolition. Neither the federal or state courts ruled that Connecticut's imposition of the death penalty was capricious, but there was a reluctance to carry out the full letter of the law. At a minimum, abolitionists could take comfort that no one had been executed in decades. Similarly, proponents of capital punishment had the satisfaction that Connecticut was the only state in New England with men on death row. The commission concluded in 2003 that "it is unlikely that any current Connecticut death row inmate will be executed soon."[129] The next year, Representative Michael Lawlor, cochair of the House Judiciary Committee, agreed because "nobody really wants to do it."[130] The unofficial moratorium, however, would dramatically end in 2005 with the state's first execution by lethal injection.

A Profile of Death Row Inmates, 1973–2005

Between 1973 and 2005, Connecticut prosecuted 194 capital felonies, 69 defendants were convicted, and 28 death penalty sentencing hearings were held.[131] Since 1973, the General Assembly increased the penalty when a defendant was not sentenced to death. An indeterminate sentence of between ten and twenty-five years with a maximum up to life was changed to a fixed term of sixty years for such crimes starting on July 1, 1981. That standard was altered to imprisonment without the possibility of release for crimes starting on October 1, 1985. As of January 1, 2005, there were forty-five inmates sentenced for capital felonies in the custody of the Department of Corrections. Thirty-four were serving life without the possibility of release, and three were serving lesser sentences. By 2005, a total of nine people had been sentenced to die (table 25).[132] These statistics are central to the charge that capital punishment in Connecticut was capricious and arbitrary.

These nine constituted all such persons in New England from 1973 to 2005.[133] No mitigating factors were found to lessen their sentences. They were all men. Of forty-five inmates sentenced for capital felonies in prison in 2005 in Connecticut, only three were women, all of whom were serving life terms. The death row inmates were, with the exception of Robert Breton and Robert Courchesne, young men in their teens and twenties at the time of their crime. Excluding Michael Ross, none had more than a high school education or white-collar employment. Four were white, three were black, and two were Hispanic. Of the victims, most were white, one was black, one was Asian, and one was Hispanic. Courchesne was the only white man who killed an African American. Only black men, Daniel Webb and Sedrick Cobb, were sentenced to death for murders involving interracial sexual assault. Ross killed a Vietnamese American female college student in New York, but he was never prosecuted for that murder. With the exception of a

TABLE 25

Death Row Inmates, 1973–2005

	Inmate	Race	Age at Crime	Date of Crime	Sentenced to Death	Victim	Age	Race	Means of Death	Judicial District	Indictment
1	Michael Ross	White	21–24	1981–84	July 6, 1987	Eight young women	14–25	One Asian, seven white	Strangulation	New London	Kidnap murder sexual assault
2	Robert J. Breton Sr.	White	41	Dec. 13, 1987	Oct. 27, 1989	Ex-wife and son	38 and 16	White	Knife	Waterbury	Multiple murder
3	Daniel Webb	Black	26	Aug. 24, 1989	Sept. 12, 1991	Diane Gellenbeck	37	White	Handgun	Hartford	Kidnap murder
4	Sedrick Cobb	Black	28	Dec. 16, 1989	Sept. 24, 1991	Julia Ashe	23	White	Drowned	Waterbury	Kidnap murder sexual assault
5	Richard Reynolds	Black	23	Dec. 18, 1992	April 13, 1995	Walter Williams	34	White	Handgun	Waterbury	Murder of police officer
6	Todd Rizzo	White	18	Sept. 30, 1997	Aug. 13, 1999	Stanley Edwards	13	White	Sledgehammer	Waterbury	Murder under 16
7	Ivo Colon	Hispanic	18	July 17, 1998	Dec. 5, 2000	Keriana Tellado	2	Hispanic	Beaten to death	Waterbury	Murder under 16
8	Robert Courchesne	White	40	Sept 15, 1998	Jan. 15, 2004	Demetris Rogers	28	Black	Knife	Waterbury	Multiple murder*
9	Eduardo Santiago	Hispanic	20	Dec. 14, 2000	Jan. 31, 2005	Joseph Niwinski	45	White	Handgun	Hartford	Murder for hire

*Rogers had a postmortem live birth, but the infant, Antonia, died six weeks later.

Source: State of Connecticut, "Commission on the Death Penalty," Jan. 8, 2003, Appendices: E. Convictions of Capital Felony Cases Statewide and N. Timeline Sequence for Death Penalty Appeals.

police officer and a middle-aged white man, all the victims were women, juveniles, and infants. Six of the nine were sentenced in the judicial district of Waterbury. The factors of gender, race, age, class, education, and jurisdiction skew who ends up on death row.

Death Row and the Courts, 1987–2005

Today, life on death row at the modern Northern Correctional Institution, a maximum security prison in Somers, entails a methodically structured lack of freedom. The inmates are readily identifiable by their yellow jumpsuits. The group is segregated and closely monitored, but with more amenities and privileges than at the old Wethersfield facility. Most time is spent in individual locked cells, seven feet by twelve feet, with a bunk, desk, stool, sink, toilet, and mirror. A glass slit in the solid metal door and in the concrete wall suffice as windows. There is no set wake-up or lights-out time. All meals are served through a slot in the door and are eaten in the cell. The inmates can purchase televisions and electronic music devices as well as personal goods at a commissary. For five days a week, the men have recreational time and job assignments that get them out of their cells. On weekends, they spend the entire time in the cell. When leaving the cell, they are shackled hand and foot. Leg irons remain on during showers. There is daily mail and attendance by the health staff along with regulated visits and use of the telephone. Unlimited consultation with attorneys in a conference room is permitted. Communication with other visitors is via telephone; no physical contact is permitted.[134] The inmates complain that the extreme isolation and uncertainty of their situation is dehumanizing.[135] The current appeals process can delay their fate for decades.[136] It is from the denizens of death row that the fundamental challenge to the reigning capital statutes has emanated. Public defenders have waged a tenacious effort on behalf of their death row clients, and the state attorneys press for upholding the law. The Connecticut Supreme Court has not only parsed precise points of law, but divided sharply on the morality of capital punishment itself. Several cases are particularly significant.

The first person sentenced to death since the state's revised capital code of 1973 was Michael Ross. On June 28, 1984, an intensive investigation linked his blue car to that of a suspected assailant. Police questioned twenty-four-year-old Ross of Jewett City, who confessed to a series of sexual murders of girls and young women in rural eastern Connecticut. Authorities subsequently charged him with six counts of capital felony (four counts of kidnap-murder and two counts of rape-murder).[137]

The Ross case was exceptional. Between 1981 and 1984, he strangled eight girls and young women between the ages of fourteen and twenty-five, raping all but one according to his account and concealing the bodies in wooded areas. Two victims were murdered in New York, the others in eastern Connecticut. Except for a Vietnamese American student, the victims were white and were strangers to the white perpetrator. In addition, Ross was fined for an assault in 1981 on a woman in Illinois, and he was sentenced to six months in prison for a similar attack on an Ohio woman the next year. In 1984, North Carolina officials charged him with a 1981 rape and attempted murder of a woman in that state. The scope and intensity of this lethal, sexual predation was unprecedented in Connecticut's entire history.[138]

Unlike almost all capital felons, Ross was solidly middle class, although he had acquired a criminal record in his early twenties. At the time of his arrest, he was an agent for Prudential Insurance. He was the only college graduate ever executed in Connecticut's long history. His parents ran a prosperous egg farm in Brooklyn. He was academically successfully at Killingly High School and graduated in 1981 from Cornell University, where he studied agriculture. That spring, after Ross's fiancée broke off their engagement and his parents were in divorce proceedings, he began a four-year killing spree. He confessed in 1987 to killing Dzung Ngoc Tu, a graduate student in one of his classes and his first victim. Her body was found at the bottom of a gorge at Cornell near the fraternity where Ross lived; authorities mistakenly ruled the death on May 18, 1981, a suicide.[139]

As Taborsky was a poster boy for the death penalty during the 1950s, so was Ross for more than two decades. In Windham County Superior Court on November 15, 1985, Ross pleaded nolo contendere to murdering Tammy Williams and Debra Smith Taylor of Brooklyn and Griswold. He surprised his own attorneys that December by asking for the maximum sentence of 120 years, to which he was sentenced. On May 4, 1987, Ross went on trial for the deaths of Robin Stavinsky, April Brunais, Leslie Shelley, and Wendy Baribeault. During the trial, a psychologist testified that Ross had told him in 1984 that he had killed two women in New York. The revelation was dramatic, but at that moment Ross was not being judged on those crimes. Ross pleaded insanity. As he told a British author in 1994: "I used them [his victims]. I degraded them for my own personal pleasure. Which is what I needed to feed my illness."[140] The public defenders argued that Ross suffered extreme emotional disturbance stemming from childhood abuse. Prosecutor C. Robert Satti countered that the defendant raped for pleasure and killed to avoid detection. On June 5, 1987, a jury, deliberating for only eighty-six minutes, found Ross guilty of all six capital felony counts. A statewide poll reported that more than 60 percent of respondents favored his execution. He was sentenced to death on July 6, 1987, which triggered an automatic appeals process.[141]

On July 26, 1994, the Connecticut Supreme Court affirmed the conviction in a four-to-one ruling, but reversed the death penalty judgments and remanded the matter for new sentencing hearings. The reason for the reversal was that the trial judge had improperly excluded evidence of Ross's mental condition from consideration in the penalty phase. The state's highest court found as follows:

> The defendant kidnapped and killed four young girls, and sexually assaulted three of them, in a manner that was especially cruel, heinous or depraved. Imposition of the death penalty requires more, however. Even a defendant who has offered no persuasive legal excuse for his felonious conduct is entitled to have a sentencing jury consider extenuating circumstances that may explain his behavior and mitigate his moral culpability and may therefore counsel against the ultimate sanction of death. Because evidentiary rulings by the trial court impaired the defendant's ability to prove the existence of such mitigating factors, a new sentencing hearing must be held.[142]

In a lone dissent, Justice Berdon argued that "Connecticut's death penalty statute is facially unconstitutional and may not be applied to the defendant or anyone else."[143] Although the U.S. Supreme Court denied certiorari on February 21, 1995, various legal maneuvers continued for another decade.[144]

After Ross, the next man on death row was Robert J. Breton Sr. At about 2 a.m. on December 13, 1987, Breton, a factory worker, drove to the apartment complex in Waterbury in which his former wife and sixteen-year-old son resided. They were asleep. The defendant, wielding a sharp, five-inch knife, beat and stabbed his ex-spouse viciously. She attempted to escape, but the defendant caught her. He finally killed her by thrusting the knife through her neck. Awakened by his mother's cries, the son entered her bedroom, where his father assaulted him. Wounded, the son fled. His father soon caught him and repeatedly stabbed him to death.

The jury convicted the defendant of two counts of murder and one of capital felony. At a separate sentencing, the state claimed that the defendant had committed the dual murders in an "especially cruel manner," an aggravating factor. The defendant claimed thirteen separate mitigating factors, including a long history of child abuse. At the conclusion of the penalty hearing, the jury reported its finding of an aggravating factor and no mitigating factor. The trial court thereafter imposed the death penalty.[145]

On review, the Connecticut Supreme Court found reversible error in the penalty phase. In keeping with *Furman,* the state's high court explained, "Of special importance to this case, a state must avoid defining aggravating factors in an open-ended, subjective manner that would allow the trier unfettered discretion in levying a death sentence and thus create a substantial risk that the trier will inflict punishment arbitrarily or capriciously."[146] The justices found that the aggravating factor, "especially cruel," was too vaguely defined to pass constitutional scrutiny. As they put it, "Our construction of 'especially cruel' rests on our perception that the legislature . . . meant to impose the death penalty at least in those cases in which the trier has found that the defendant intentionally inflicted extreme pain or torture upon the victim, above and beyond the pain necessarily accompanying the victim's death."[147]

Unlike the Massachusetts Supreme Judicial Court, its Connecticut counterpart emphasized, "We have not decided whether the death penalty, per se or as applied, violates any provision of our state constitution."[148] The neighboring states significantly differed in what Chief Justice Warren deemed in the five-to-four decision of *Trop v. Dulles* (1958) the "evolving standards of decency" in determining the "cruel and unusual punishment" clause of the Eighth Amendment.[149] The Connecticut Supreme Court in 1995 (before the new death penalty statute of October 1 went into effect) reversed the imposition of the death penalty on Breton because "the record does not establish definitively that the jury verdict purporting to reject the mitigating factors was the result of the jury's unanimous vote."[150] The court remanded the decision to a three-judge panel for resentencing.[151] Applying the death penalty statute of 1995, the three judges in 1997 still found that Breton had committed the crimes in a cruel and heinous fashion without the existence of a mitigating factor. Merging the murder counts with the capital felony count, they sentenced Breton to death.[152] The state's highest court affirmed the decision in 2003, and in December of that year the U.S. Supreme Court denied the defendant a writ of certiorari.[153] Appeals, however, have blocked his execution to date.

The Connecticut Supreme Court gave important validation to capital punishment in 1996 and 2000 involving a brutal interracial murder. Daniel Webb, an African American, was convicted of kidnapping Diane Gellenbeck, a white bank vice president, from a downtown Hartford parking garage while she was en route to an afternoon meeting on August 24, 1989. He drove her to Keney Park, attempted to rape her, and shot her twice in the back when she tried to flee. As she crawled along the ground calling for help, according to golfers who witnessed the shooting, Webb shot her three more times, once point blank in the face. Webb's 1991 death conviction and sentence were the first to be fully affirmed in Connecticut since 1972, when the U.S. Supreme Court had halted executions nationwide. In the July 1996 decision, the Connecticut Supreme Court found no violation of due process or of cruel and unusual punishment. The court was, however, closely divided, four to three. As Justice Berdon, an outspoken opponent of the death penalty, lamented, "Today is the first time that each of the justices of the Supreme Court of Connecticut has had an opportunity to speak on the issue of whether the death penalty violates our state constitution. . . . The majority's decision today prevents Connecticut from joining those humane and enlightened states and nations that continue to ban the penalty of death."[154] He was joined in dissent by Justices Katz and Flemming L. Norcott Jr., firm foes of capital punishment.

In its 1996 ruling upholding Webb's conviction and sentence, the state's high court permitted him to return to Hartford County Superior Court to challenge lethal injection as the method of execution. Webb was originally sentenced to death by electrocution in 1991, before the General Assembly altered punishment to lethal injection in 1995. In a five-to-two decision, the majority found, "Because we conclude that lethal injection is constitutional under the federal constitution, we similarly conclude that the method is constitutional under our state constitution."[155] They concluded, as did expert witnesses, that the proper administration of the drugs would result in swift and painless death. Justices Katz and Norcott again dissented. (Justice Berdon had retired in 1999 because he had reached the mandatory retirement age of seventy.) As Justice Katz phrased her dissent:

> Accordingly, I would remand this case to the trial court with direction to vacate the penalty of death and to impose a sentence of life imprisonment without the possibility of release. I believe, however, that I have a responsibility to speak out against the death penalty in every case in which this court reaffirms its position that the punishment of death meets contemporary and moral standards of decency.[156]

Connecticut joined ten other jurisdictions that affirmed lethal injection as a humane method of execution. Although the U.S. Supreme Court had yet to rule on it, no appellate court to date had rejected its use. Patrick Culligan, a public defender, protested, "Historically, I think it will be viewed with derision, much as history derides those decisions that upheld the institution of slavery."[157]In December 1999, the state's highest court upheld the conviction and sentence of Sedrick Cobb of Naugatuck in a reaffirmation of the Webb ruling three years earlier. In another sexual murder of a white woman by a black man, Cobb had been sentenced to death in 1991 for the 1989 kidnapping, rape, and murder of twenty-three-year-old Julia Ashe. While Ashe was Christmas shopping at a Waterbury department store, Cobb flattened her tire and, when she returned to her car, offered to help change it. He then asked her for a ride to his own car. Once in her vehicle, he overpowered her and forced her to drive to a remote location, taped her mouth, wrists, and ankles, and raped her. He then pushed her into an icy culvert and watched as she struggled to survive. When she attempted to crawl to safety, he forced her face down back into the water. Her body was discovered two weeks later, on Christmas Day. Two days later, Cobb confessed. He appealed his convictions for capital felony. Writing for the majority in December 1999, Justice David M. Borden rejected all forty-five of Cobb's claims. The Connecticut Supreme Court ruled that there was no error to find aggravating factors and no mitigating factors and that the death sentences were supported by evidence. The death penalty statute complied with due process requirements. The penalty was not excessive under proportionality review.[158]

In both the Webb and Cobb cases, the four-to-three decisions were written by Justice Borden with Justices Berdon, Katz, and Norcott again in opposition. All three dissenters were ethically opposed to capital punishment. They raised the question of racial disparity in death sentences. As Justice Berdon put it, "Although in those prior opinions I have explicated broadly the unconstitutionality of the death penalty, in this dissent I focus on the arbitrariness of its application and the fact that, in practice, the imposition of the death penalty raises serious issues of whether it is driven by racism."[159] Justice Berdon went as far as to violate the confidentiality of the court (for which all his colleagues rebuked him): he revealed that in private discussion he had urged the case be remanded so that the lower court could assess the role of race in the death sentence. Although neither Webb nor Cobb had exhausted federal and habeas corpus appeals, the rulings cleared the way for an execution. Of seven men then on death row, the twosome were the only ones whose death sentences were affirmed by the high court. "I think from what we've seen, there's certainly no predisposition to throw out the death penalty," Gerard Smyth, chief public defender, said in frustration. "Quite the contrary."[160]

In October 2000, the U.S. Supreme Court rejected the appeals of Cobb and Webb in the first challenges to Connecticut's capital punishment law to reach the nation's highest court. Chief state's attorney John M. Bailey commented, "Both of these cases have been thoroughly examined at each step of the legal process, and at each step the original verdicts have been affirmed, as has the capital punishment law enacted by the General Assembly."[161]

Nonetheless, the racial issue would not go away. A legislative panel raised the issue in December 2002. Of seven people then on death row, six had killed whites; the seventh inmate's victim was Hispanic. At the same time, the Connecticut Supreme Court appointed former Chief Justice Robert J. Callahan to serve as a special master to consolidate and oversee the litigation of the issue. Four death row inmates in early 2005 challenged the state's capital punishment law as racially biased. Three of the men—Daniel Webb, Sedrick Cobb, and Richard Reynolds—were African Americans who had been convicted of killing whites. They were joined by Robert J. Breton Sr. and a fifth man, Todd Rizzo, whose death sentence the Connecticut Supreme Court had overturned and who was facing another death penalty hearing in 2005. Breton and Rizzo were white, as were their victims. Cobb introduced data stating that, since 1973, only eleven of the seventy-four capital felony cases prosecuted in the state involved a black victim. In addition, of eighteen capital prosecutions for kidnap-murder, none involved a black victim. Of twelve capital prosecutions for sexual assault–murder, only one had a black victim. Cobb also asserted that twice the percentage of black defendants were convicted of capital felony as nonblack defendants. The five convicts charged that the race of the victim was instrumental in determining who gets the death penalty. Overall, black defendants were disproportionately convicted of capital felonies. The combined challenge could potentially overturn the death penalty.[162]

8

THE EXECUTION OF MICHAEL ROSS
2005

I think this whole case has been uncharted territory.

Thomas Groark, special counsel, April 15, 2005

The defendant, Michael Ross, is, however, no ordinary defendant,
and this is no ordinary case.

Flemming L. Norcott Jr., Justice of the Connecticut Supreme Court, May 9, 2005

This has been a protracted ordeal for the entire state, none more so than for the
families of the victims who have suffered for years and still grieve for their lost
daughters.

Governor M. Jodi Rell, May 13, 2005

MICHAEL ROSS, the inmate longest on Connecticut's death row, did not join
the 2005 suit to review racial bias and other disparities in the administration
of capital punishment in the state. Like Joseph Taborsky, he was a prime
candidate for capital punishment. Both were white men, serial killers of
mostly whites. No racial element, capriciousness, or prosecutorial disparity
was apparent in the convictions for their heinous crimes, which riveted the
state. They preyed on strangers and were caught only after diligent police
work. Both confessed. The crimes were horrific: Taborsky thrilled to gratu-
itous, execution-style shootings during petty robberies; Ross relentlessly
stalked, raped, and strangled vulnerable girls and young women along rural
roads. Unlike the hardscrabble Taborsky, Ross was an aberrant member of
Connecticut's substantial middle class.

The two cases brought to the fore the ethics of capital punishment. As
James Papillo, the state's victim advocate, put it, "So you are left with the raw
morality issue."[1] What was to be done with perpetrators of repetitious homicide against random victims? Were their crimes so brutal that they warranted the death penalty? Didn't Taborsky and Ross get what they deserved?

Or were state-sponsored executions, even limited to the worst of the worst, nothing but legalized murder, cruel and unusual punishment, an evil in itself? Despite numerous safeguards, was the adjudication of capital felonies inherently arbitrary, biased, capricious, and facially unconstitutional? Public policy in Connecticut paradoxically balanced a commitment to capital punishment with a judicial protocol that forestalled its ultimate fulfillment. Why and how was the decades-long moratorium on executions interrupted?

Like Taborsky, Ross was an active agent in shaping the final outcome. A fatalistic Taborsky in 1960 wished to avoid life in prison, but Ross was ambivalent about waiving appeals and volunteering for death. In principle, he opposed the death penalty. At times, he mounted a spirited defense; at others, he purposely sought to end his life.

Two major themes were dominant in the way Ross framed his response. First, he staunchly maintained that he was afflicted with a psychiatric disorder—sexual sadism—that he could not control. He wanted recognition that his psyche had been hijacked by violent obsessions that he later learned medication could suppress. "Basically, I am plagued by repetitive thoughts, urges, and fantasies of the degradation, rape, and murder of women," he wrote in 1998. "I cannot get those thoughts out of my mind." He claimed that chemical castration, for which he lobbied in prison, reduced sexual deviance to a manageable level. "One of the most difficult and painful things for me to deal with today," he averred, " is to know that had I begun to receive just a one-cc injection of Depo-Lupron once a month fifteen years ago, eight women would be alive today."[2]

Second, Ross stated that he wished to spare the families of the victims the anguish that interminable adjudication would bring. He wrote to the prosecutor on September 25, 1994, "I am willing to hand you the death penalty 'on a silver platter' on the condition that you will work with me to get this over with as quickly and as painlessly as possible. There is no need to drag the families of my victims through more lengthy and disturbing court proceedings."[3] Such an expedient conflicted with due process and was invalidated, however. Furthermore, juries in two penalty hearings found no mitigation—no mental impairment—and pronounced him guilty on each of six capital counts. Frustrated at the outcomes, Ross decided irrevocably during the fall of 2004 to choose death and conclude the ordeal for all concerned. The result was an extraordinary legal drama that led to an interrupted moratorium in Connecticut's death penalty.

Exclusion of the Public Defenders

Ross's public defenders presented dozens of objections to his 1987 death penalty. In a three-hundred-page brief filed in the spring of 1992, they claimed that "the death penalty is simply too arbitrary to be enforced."[4] At that time, with four men on death row at the State Prison in Somers, the Connecticut Supreme Court undertook the first significant review of the death penalty in two decades. The tribunal on July 26, 1994, affirmed the death penalty but ordered a new penalty hearing because the New London Superior Court had in 1987 improperly excluded evidence of the defendant's mental state, a mitigating factor.[5] The following May, Ross boldly dismissed his court-appointed public defender and represented himself. He proposed that he be sentenced to death without a hearing so as to spare the victims' families the agony of a new penalty phase that rehearsed the gruesome killings. After several years of negotiation, state's attorney C. Robert Satti, who had been the original prosecutor in the case, agreed on March 11, 1998. New London Superior Court Judge Thomas P. Miano, however, rejected the deal on July 1 because it violated federal and state mandates for a penalty hearing. The next month, Ross reversed his position with the agreement obviated, vowing an active defense against the death penalty. Judge Miano reassigned public defenders to Ross, and the case was essentially back where it had been four years earlier.[6] On November 2, a despondent Ross nearly killed himself in his cell with an overdose of sedatives.[7]After procedural delays of more than five years, the second penalty phase began on February 22, 2000, in New London Superior Court. Psychiatrists for the defense testified that Ross was mentally ill, unable to restrain his violent sexual obsessions without medication. Prosecutor Kevin Kane contended that Ross faked mental illness and willfully committed the crimes. After nine days of thorough deliberation, the twelve jurors on April 6 again recommended the death penalty on all six counts of murder (four kidnap-murders and two rape-murders) in eastern Connecticut. They unanimously found that the crimes were especially cruel, heinous, or depraved; there was no mitigating factor.[8]

The mandatory death sentence on May 12 was highly emotional. The forty-year-old Ross cried as he apologized to the victims' families who crowded the courtroom. He was sorry that he "did not have the courage to take my own life at Cornell, before I allowed my illness to take the lives of others. I realize my apology is inadequate." In turn, Ellen Roode, mother of fourteen-year-old victim April Brunais, stood before the judge to denounce

Ross. "You deserve to die," she said, as the victims' families, who remained unmoved when Ross spoke, openly wept. In sentencing Ross to die on September 15, Judge Miano told the condemned man, "You squeezed the life out of these young women for your own sexual gratification." According to Ross, his public defenders had convinced him to pursue the appeal, which, if successful, would be a major blow to capital punishment. As Ross explained the larger issue, "I realize this isn't about me." Nonetheless, with another emphatic death verdict, he expressed a willingness to die to end the more than sixteen-year ordeal. Dying, he said, "is the least I can do."[9]

During the period of appeals that stayed the execution, a New York court on October 22, 2001, found Ross guilty of killing Paula Perrera, a sixteen-year-old hitchhiker, at Wallkill in 1982 and sentenced him to twenty-five years in prison in New York. He was never prosecuted for the killing on May 12, 1981, of his first victim, Dzung Ngoc Tu, a twenty-five-year-old Cornell graduate student.[10] In Connecticut, which had precedence in the prosecution, the state's highest court on May 24, 2004, upheld the death sentence. A six-member majority found in reviewing twenty-three other capital cases in the state that "there is nothing freakish, arbitrary, wanton, or aberrational about the sentence in this case."[11] Justice Flemming L. Norcott Jr. was the lone dissenter; he again declared that "the death penalty should be abolished in the state."[12]

The now-forty-five-year-old Ross declared on October 1 that he would forgo appeals. The review by the state Supreme Court was automatic, but further appeals to the United States Supreme Court and habeas petitions were not. He dismissed his public defenders, who aggressively sought to prevent his state-ordered death. Instead, Ross retained attorney T. R. Paulding to facilitate his desire to proceed to execution. Paulding had advised Ross during 1994 and 1995 when Ross unsuccessfully sought a death sentence rather than proceed to a second penalty hearing.[13] Five days later, New London County Superior Court Judge Patrick J. Clifford set an execution date of January 26, 2005. When Judge Clifford asked Ross if he would allow anyone else to file appeals on his behalf, Ross responded, "Absolutely not."[14] Despite speculation to the contrary, Paulding said that his client was not bluffing. Within twenty days of sentencing in late October, correction officials moved Ross to the death cell at the neighboring Osborn Correctional Institution as state law required. As the possibility of the first execution in forty-five years loomed, Amnesty International, Connecticut Network to Abolish the Death Penalty, Connecticut Civil Liberties Union (CCLU), and public defenders, among others, sought to stop the execution. The well-known abolitionist Sister Helen Prejean, whose advocacy was featured in the acclaimed movie

Dead Man Walking, met with Ross that autumn. She reported, "I met a human being who is filled with remorse."[15] She discussed his motivations, but, respecting his right to choose, did not seek to dissuade him.[16]

Governor M. Jodi Rell announced on December 6 that she found no legal or moral reason to grant a temporary reprieve. The newly created Board of Pardons and Paroles was the only state agency that had the power of commutation. The popular Republican governor in a predominantly Democratic state added, "I will veto any repeal bill. I do believe there are crimes and actions which are so repugnant to society as to warrant the death penalty."[17] Debbie Dupris, the sister of Ross's victim Robin Stavinsky, exclaimed, "Three cheers for her."[18] The *Willimantic Chronicle,* a newspaper in eastern Connecticut, concurred. "His execution," an editorial read, "will bring some closure for eight families."[19] Ross agreed. He had written to the governor on November 28, "Please do not exercise your power to grant a temporary reprieve, it is the last thing that these families need, especially now with a real execution date less than two months away."[20]

The Battle over Competency

On a motion filed by prosecutors to rule that Ross was competent, Judge Clifford held the first of two hearings for psychological evaluation on December 9. Ross had twice tried to kill himself and was currently taking antidepressants. At a contentious hearing on December 15, Judge Clifford barred the public defenders from intervening on Ross's behalf. The court ruled that Ross was competent and was represented by the attorney of his choice. Public defender John Holdridge rebutted, "That's why he is doing it—to commit suicide."[21] A forensic specialist, Dr. Michael Norko, who had found Ross competent in 1995, told the court on December 28 that Ross had made an intelligent and voluntary decision. At the three-hour competency hearing, Ross bristled at the public defenders who sought to thwart his decision. He accused them of lying that he was incompetent, of harassing him by telling him that the waiving of appeals jeopardized the fate of other death row inmates, and that the victims' families did not have to attend the proceedings. "I'm opposed to the death penalty myself," he said. "I'm very torn up about this whole thing, but I'm doing what I believe is good."[22] He was not willing to drag out the ordeal for years in the quest for an elusive life sentence. As Judge Clifford concluded, "This decision is his right to make."[23]

A litany of voices was raised against capital punishment. The European Union sent a request to block the execution.[24] Michael A. Fitzpatrick, a former co-counsel for Ross in the 2004 appeal to the Connecticut Supreme Court, wrote that in the more than 120 capital murder prosecutions since 1973 the arbitrary nature of who was sentenced to death for atrocious crimes was "beyond rational explanation and clearly contrary to the principle of equal justice."[25] Criminal defense attorney Hubert Santos declared, "The only way to ensure the uniform administration of justice is to abolish the death penalty."[26] Priests urged Roman Catholics to sign petitions in collaboration with the Connecticut Network to Abolish the Death Penalty.[27] Other religious leaders took a similar stand.[28] Dr. Robert C. Goodwin, a psychiatrist who had examined Ross, wrote in the *Hartford Courant* that the medical consensus was that Ross had "an incapacitating psychiatric disorder" that rendered his execution "unacceptable," just as it would for the mentally retarded, schizophrenic, or psychotic.[29] The state's senior Democrat, Bill Dyson, held a one-man vigil in the legislative office building. He wore four red stickers with the slogan "Do not kill in my name," and hanging from his neck was a handwritten sign that said "Abolish the death penalty in Connecticut."[30] The Democratic leadership, however, had agreed to postpone a debate until after the impending execution. In 2001, the last time lawmakers had tried to abolish the death penalty, it had failed in the House of Representatives by a vote of 91 to 55.[31]

As January 26, 2005, approached, there was a flurry of legal efforts to forestall the execution. On December 23, 2004, the Office of the Public Defender filed the first of several writs of error with the Connecticut Supreme Court claiming that Judge Clifford had wrongly barred them from representing Ross at the competency hearings. The public defenders also asked the state's highest court to stay the execution. Five days later, the CCLU on behalf of Dan Ross, the condemned man's father, filed a suit in federal court challenging the constitutionality of lethal injection. Superior Court Judge Stanley T. Fuger Jr. in Rockville on January 3 ruled that public defenders and Dan Ross's attorney had no standing to file habeas petitions on Michael Ross's behalf because he was competent to make his own decisions. The six-hour hearing with a video hookup to the imprisoned Ross was highly charged. Public defender Tammy Pieszak suggested that the judge had predetermined the case. He told her to sit down and lectured, "It is clearly not appropriate to use the judicial branch or the courts of this state as a forum to conduct this debate [over capital punishment]." Paulding accused chief public defender Gerard Smyth of using Ross as a "political pawn" against capital punishment.[32] At the same time the Missionary Society of Connecticut, an affiliate of the United Church of Christ, wrote to the Board of Pardons and

Paroles to demand that a commutation hearing be convened. Gregory Everett, chairman of the board, refused on January 6, explaining that only the convict or his attorney could request a hearing.

U.S. District Judge Christopher F. Droney on January 10 dismissed the Dan Ross and CCLU challenge that lethal injection may bring "excruciating pain." "I believe what's really at stake here," Annette Lamoreau of the CCLU argued, "is the humanity of everyone in this room and the humanity of the state of Connecticut." Edwin Shelley, father of fourteen-year-old Leslie who was killed on Easter 1984, countered: "It doesn't matter to me personally if he suffers. I can't imagine what my daughter's pain was. If his is ten times that, he deserved it."[33] Judge Droney made two points: (1) because Michael Ross was competent, the petitioners had no standing; and (2) the Connecticut Supreme Court had previously decided in a challenge brought by death row inmate Daniel Webb that lethal injection was constitutional.

On January 10, the U.S. Supreme Court rejected a petition for certiorari filed by the public defenders who hoped to block the execution. On January 14 and 19, the Connecticut Supreme Court dismissed writs of error and motions seeking a stay of execution by the public defenders, who that court ruled had no standing in the case. Although abolitionist Justice Norcott concurred with his colleagues, he reminded them that "indeed, a comprehensive statistical study about the influence of race and other factors in the application of Connecticut's death penalty presently is ongoing in the context of consolidated habeas corpus litigation that is being supervised by a special master, former Chief Justice Robert Callahan."[34] Smyth, the chief public defender, added: "There's so much unsettled. It would seem that to do things in a thorough and orderly manner, it would make sense to stay the execution."[35] Hartford Superior Court Judge Robert E. Beach Jr. on January 19 dismissed the protest by the Missionary Society of Connecticut. The petitioner James Wade claimed to represent the interests of society as a whole because "they are killing him in our name—in the name of everyone in the state of Connecticut."[36] Judge Beach supported Everett's position that only a convict or his attorney could seek a commutation hearing. He also rejected Wade's contention that the board's lack of written regulations made it impossible to conduct a meaningful commutation hearing. The state's highest court sustained the lower court's reasoning on January 24.

The previous day, two contrary positions on the death penalty had aired in the opinion pages of Sunday's *Hartford Courant*. John Connolly, the state's attorney for the Judicial District of Waterbury who had put five men on death row, pointed out that the people through the General Assembly had steadfastly over the years maintained the death penalty for crimes committed in an especially heinous, cruel, or depraved manner. Two juries had found Ross guilty. Of thirty-eight states and the federal government with capital punishment, he argued, "Connecticut's law is the most difficult to prosecute under and the most difficult in which to have a death sentence imposed" and concluded that Ross had "exhausted all his appealable claims that have any merit."[37] For Connolly, Ross's execution embodied the will of the people and scrupulously followed the rule of law. In contrast, Michele Jacklin, the newspaper's political columnist, called state execution "murder." "On Wednesday, when that lethal mixture is injected into Michael Ross's arm in the darkness of night," she warned, "we will all be complicit in this death." She added that capital punishment was not a deterrent, litigation was more expensive than life in prison, and lethal injection was horrid; its only purpose in her eyes was vengeance.[38] Connolly and Jacklin clearly expressed the moral divide.

A Stunning Intervention

On January 24, a Monday, Chief U.S. District Judge Robert N. Chatigny boldly stayed Ross's execution in response to a challenge brought by the public defenders working with Hubert Santos, a Hartford attorney. Referring to years of confinement in a maximum security prison, Santos stated, "A government can't say, 'We're going to give you the death penalty, and then put you in conditions that are so unbearable that you don't fight.'"[39] Judge Chatigny ordered a new hearing on Ross's mental competence. He was troubled that previous competency hearings were "quite irregular" because Ross's demurral meant that there was no adversarial process. That is, Ross with his attorney Paulding shared the same position as the prosecutors. "I don't believe a reasonable person," Judge Chatigny explained, "looking at this can say, categorically, the man is competent." He granted the public defenders' "next friend" status so that they could make the argument that the debilitation of years on death row had rendered Ross incompetent.[40]

Ironically, as long as the courts ruled Ross competent, he had the legal right to dismiss the public defenders and seek the death penalty, a proceeding that Judge Chatigny temporarily overturned. In response, chief state's attorney Christopher L. Morano appealed to the U.S. Court of Appeals for the Second Circuit to throw out Judge Chatigny's ruling. Theresa C. Lantz, Connecticut's correction commissioner, moved Wednesday's execution at 2:01 a.m. to the same time on Thursday to accommodate judicial proceedings. On January 25 (Tuesday), the federal appeals court opened the door to consider evidence of Ross's competency at the same time the Connecticut Supreme Court closed it. In a four-to-three decision in Hartford, the majority held that Dan Ross and the public defenders had been given "every reasonable opportunity to demonstrate that Michael Ross is incompetent and have failed to sustain their burden." Jon L. Schoenhorn, Dan Ross's attorney, complained, "I guess the problem is because Michael Ross is not participating, the notion of a lot of state judges is, 'Let's give him what he wants.'"[41] The three dissenting judges would have stayed the execution until the state-ordered review of racial discrimination and capriciousness in the administration of the death penalty was completed.

On the same day, a three-judge panel of the U.S. Court of Appeals for the Second Circuit in Manhattan upheld the stay to allow Judge Chatigny to conduct a competency hearing as soon as reasonable. It pointed out, however, that the judge had acted prematurely to determine "next friend" status for the public defenders before holding the competency hearing that he ordered. Only if the courts determined that Ross was incompetent could the public defenders represent him and potentially block the death penalty, the appeals court stated. State prosecutors appealed Judge Chatigny's questionable intervention, first to supervising Justice Ruth Bader Ginsburg and then to the entire U.S. Supreme Court. Lantz, the state's commissioner of correction, rescheduled the execution to early Friday, January 28.[42]

That Tuesday, the *Hartford Courant,* which provided meticulous coverage with the reportage of Lynne Tuohy and colleagues, weighed in that "the decision whether to execute convicts should not be left to a criminal [Michael Ross]." The state's leading newspaper pointed out that retired Connecticut Supreme Court Chief Justice Robert J. Callahan was a special master appointed by the state currently examining disparities in the prosecution of the death penalty in a consolidated challenge brought by a number of death row inmates. "There is," the editorial concluded, "no compelling reason to execute Mr. Ross now."[43] On January 26 (Wednesday), Judge Chatigny erected a second obstacle, issuing a temporary restraining order in a civil rights challenge brought by Dan Ross. The father claimed that he would be denied the constitutional right to associate with his son if his son were executed before it was determined if he was competent.

The two barriers that Judge Chatigny erected to the impending execution, however, were successfully challenged by the state. First, on January 27 (Thursday), the U.S. Supreme Court in a five-to-four decision vacated the stay of execution. Public defender Smyth lamented: "We're done. The highest court in the nation has denied us the opportunity to present our evidence. There's nothing further we can do."[44] His colleague John Holdridge spoke to the ideological confrontation: "Bush v. Gore again. Apparently five members of the U.S. Supreme Court share [Attorney General] John Ashcroft's radical right-wing agenda to spread the death penalty to New England." He referred to the strong pro–capital punishment agenda of the administration of George W. Bush with five conservative members of the high court— William H. Rehnquist, Sandra Day O'Connor, Anthony Kennedy, Antonin Scalia, and Clarence Thomas—forming the majority in the decision. In a related case earlier in the day that was not within Judge Chatigny's purview, the high court also denied the Missionary Society of Connecticut an emergency stay of execution. Reverend Gordon Bates, the society's anti–death penalty coordinator, lamented: "It simply puts the people of Connecticut on the same level of Mr. Ross—taking the life of a man who can't harm anyone at this point in a premeditated fashion. That's precisely what Mr. Ross did."

Second, on January 28 (Friday), the U.S. Court of Appeals for the Second Circuit dissolved Judge Chatigny's restraining order, but the justices suspended their decision for twenty-two hours. Both sides appealed to the U.S. Supreme Court: Richard Blumenthal, Connecticut's attorney general, asked that the stay be overturned; and Dan Ross's attorneys appealed the dissolution of the temporary restraining order. Blumenthal pointed out that no fewer than four state courts had affirmed Ross's competency. "The U.S. Supreme Court decision today," he noted, "sends a profoundly important message that our state's highest court is entitled to respect and the state is upholding the rule of law, which is a vital public interest."[45] Jim Nugent, co-counsel for Dan Ross, rebutted that "we're looking for a full hearing to determine whether the state has coerced Michael Ross into giving up his appeals."[46] Lantz for the third time rescheduled the execution to January 29 (Saturday) at 2:01 a.m. At 9:55 p.m. on January 28 (Friday), the U.S. Supreme Court vacated the twenty-two-hour stay, clearing the way for the execution within five hours. After two months of furious legal battles, including more than two dozen hearings and petitions for stays of execution, it appeared that Ross would shortly fulfill his death wish.

Earlier that Friday, with the case still docketed in U.S. Distirict Court in Hartford on a habeas appeal filed by the public defender's office, Judge Chatigny audaciously acted to derail the execution. He was prompted by a letter from a prison inmate Ramon Lopez who claimed that Ross had confided to him at Northern Correctional Institution in Somers that he did not want to die.[47] Although the authenticity of Lopez's letter had not been established, Judge Chatigny was alarmed about the quality of Paulding's representation of Ross. It was unusual for attorneys to champion the death of their clients.[48] From his chambers, the judge held a telephone conference at midafternoon with eight of the principal attorneys. For most of an hour, Judge Chatigny berated, cajoled, and threatened Paulding, who was at the Osborn Correctional Institution, to have Ross call off the execution. The judge accused the attorney of ignoring critical evidence that suggested Ross was rendered legally incompetent because of "death row syndrome," an existential despair onto death brought on by years of close confinement and possible harassment. Judge Chatigny noted that his own earlier investigation into charges of abuse by death row prisoner Daniel Webb showed that the allegations might be "well founded."[49] He pointed to the letter of Lopez; a pending affidavit of John Tokarz, a retired deputy commissioner in the Department of Correction who had supervised death row in the mid-1990s; the pioneering study of "death row syndrome"[50] by psychiatrist Dr. Stuart Grassian; Ross's attempts at suicide; and the mental aberration of sexual sadism that raised substantial questions about Ross's rationality. Judge Chatigny faulted Paulding for not bringing this vital information, including written statements in which Ross expressed an unwillingness to die, to the attention of the court-appointed psychiatrist, Dr. Michael Norko, medical director of the Whiting Forensic Institute at Middletown. "I feel strongly," the judge told him, "that you're way out on a limb, and I want to be sure that I discharge my responsibilities as the chief judge of the court dealing with you an officer of this court in making sure that you don't commit a very grave error."[51]

From Judge Chatigny's perspective, a miscarriage of justice was at the heart of the matter. Expert testimony indicated that Ross was a sexual sadist for whom only chemical castration could control misogynist violence. That mental impairment, as Ross argued, should have constituted a mitigating factor that mandated a life term. "I suggest to you that Michael Ross," the judge continued, "may be the least culpable, the least, of the people on death row." He then bluntly told Paulding, "I do not know how anybody in your position could be accepting of his responsibility to proceed in the face of this record to be the proximate cause of this man's death." Instead, a responsible attorney would explain to Ross, who felt trapped, that he did not have to proceed with lethal injection to avoid dragging the victims' families through more hearings. According to the judge, there were alternatives: new evidence might demonstrate incompetence, the Callahan litigation might succeed, or the General Assembly might abolish capital punishment. Judge Chatigny explained that Ross would be punished, as he wished, for his horrendous acts, but short of the death penalty. "We're not in this profession to help people get killed," the judge hectored. As Paulding's colleagues listened, the judge concluded, "What you're doing is wrong." If it turns out that the allegations of death row syndrome and abuse were accurate, he continued, "I'll have your law license."[52]

Not surprisingly, an intimidated and exhausted Paulding promised the judge to explain the situation to his client as soon as possible as the executioners readied themselves and as a vigil gathered outside the prison. Paulding, a former counsel to the House Republican Caucus now in private practice in Glastonbury, was under tremendous pressure. That morning, Sister Prejean had lambasted the beleaguered attorney on the telephone for a half hour for facilitating what she termed state-assisted suicide.[53] Paulding had spent hundreds of hours on the case without pay and thought he was doing the right thing. "When you are a lawyer," he explained, "your singular goal is to do the wishes of your client."[54] Sister Prejean and Judge Chatigny had exploded that rationale.

At about 12:45 a.m. on Saturday, January 29, Paulding called off the execution, scheduled for only a little more than an hour away. "We will seek a full, fair and complete assessment of all the evidence relative to his competence," he announced late Sunday, complying with Judge Chatigny's demand. "Mr. Ross has authorized me to take the steps that make that happen."[55] On Sunday, Dr. Norko, who had found Ross competent a month earlier, signed an affidavit raising doubts about that decision. With new information, including letters that Ross had written in 1998 and 2003 that said that prison conditions made him suicidal, the psychiatrist stated that "it is possible that my eventual conclusions and opinions would have been different."[56] Lantz moved the date for a now uncertain execution to Monday, January 31, at 9 p.m., only hours before the five-day warrant expired. Five execution dates had been set in six days with an overall cost of $289,000, mostly for personnel.[57] On Monday morning, Paulding filed motions for a stay in both state and federal district courts, contending that Ross might have "death row syndrome." He explained that, as an officer of the court, "new and significant evidence has come to light that I simply cannot ignore."[58] He continued, "There is a question as to Mr. Ross' competence."[59] Ross's decision to forgo appeals remained the same, but his client would cooperate in the proceedings. That afternoon, the Connecticut Supreme Court approved the stay and a similar motion lodged by the state. Christopher L. Morano, the chief state's attorney, affirmed, "We will be seeking a new death warrant as soon as practically possible."[60] Months might intervene before proceedings would determine if Ross would be executed.

The reaction to the events Judge Chatigny set in motion was mixed. Seven state prosecutors filed a complaint of judicial misconduct, of which a review panel in July 2006 cleared the judge.[61] Opponents of the execution and the death penalty were supportive. Michael Fitzpatrick, president of the Connecticut Criminal Defense Lawyers Association, said that "in a case where a person's life hangs in the balance, that's no time to mince words."[62] The *Hartford Courant* added, "All this might have been averted had Ross been sentenced to a life term without parole years ago."[63] The newspaper defended Judge Chatigny's unpopular role, including against the state's Republican leadership, which called for a congressional investigation of the Democratic judge.[64]

Those committed to the execution were blindsided. Frustrated, Blumenthal, the attorney general vowed, "We will fight for the criminal justice process to reach finality for the sake of all citizens, but most particularly for the victims' families, who have endured this long ordeal."[65] Joan Stavinsky, whose stepdaughter Robin had been slain by Ross, castigated Judge Chatigny for "sidestepping the laws of Connecticut."[66] An outspoken advocate of retribution, Robert Blecker, a law professor, wrote that "most of us are morally certain he deserves to die."[67] Governor Rell concurred that, as the law permitted, "the state should move forward with his execution."[68] Overall, a poll released on January 12 by Quinnipiac University showed that 59 percent of Connecticut residents favored the death penalty.[69] Not unlike Taborsky during the 1950s, Ross galvanized majority support for capital punishment.

On the same Monday (January 31) that the Connecticut Supreme Court directed Judge Clifford to hold a competency hearing in New London County Superior Court, the legislature's judiciary committee held hearings on the death penalty. The testimony began with a debate between Smyth, the chief public defender, and John Connolly, the state's most successful prosecutor. Smyth emphasized the arbitrary nature of who was sentenced to death, while Connolly stressed that Connecticut had "perhaps the strictest death penalty in the entire country." Almost all the seventy-five speakers supported abolition. They included Robert Nave of Waterbury, head of the Connecticut Network to Abolish the Death Penalty, who said: "This is not a forum on Michael Ross. It is about a system that is not working, about poor public policy." In contrast, Helen Williams, whose son Walter, a Waterbury policeman, had been shot point blank in the head in 1992 by death row inmate Richard Reynolds, opposed abolition.[70] The *Hartford Courant* editorialized the next day that the "Death Penalty Doesn't Work."[71] The legislative hearing indicated that opponents of the death penalty, if not a majority of citizens, were outspoken.

At the same time, the number on death row increased to seven with a Hartford judge sentencing Eduardo Santiago to death. Two additional inmates, Todd Rizzo and Ivo Colon, were awaiting new penalty hearings after courts had vacated their death sentences. On Thursday (February 3), the seven death row inmates at the Northern Correctional Institute announced a hunger strike. They protested that "to endure these conditions of enforced segregation is inhumane and tantamount to psychological torture"[72] and claimed that the isolation in the supermaximum prison produced "death row syndrome," the very issue at the heart of Judge Chatigny's intervention. "We are NOT doing this in protest of Michael Ross' execution," the communication read. "In fact, it is no wonder to the members of death row why he made this decision."[73] They complained that lack of social contact and sensory deprivation made them stir-crazy.

Reopening of the Competency Hearing

There was also drama on February 3 in New London County Superior Court. Judge Clifford and state prosecutor Kevin Kane rebuked the public defenders for seemingly withholding evidence about Ross's mental state until the last moment. Smyth responded that Ross's suicidal letters were available in a packet of material given to the Connecticut Supreme Court on January 10 but that Paulding had ignored them. Under intense pressure, Paulding was granted another week to sort out his moral conundrum: the conflict of interest between representing his client's desire to die and, as an officer of the court, presenting evidence that stymied that goal. Kane added that the state had joined efforts to stop the impending execution because "Mr. Paulding was in no condition to give that advice."[74] Ross, who had endured daily postponements of lethal ejection, explained his frustration. Dressed in prison khakis, he told Judge Clifford that Paulding, not he, had called off the execution at the last hour. "I am competent . . . [but] I agreed that [Paulding] was not in the frame of mind to go forward," Ross explained. "He has been intimidated by the judge [Chatigny] and feels obligated to me to explore things [competency] that I think are meaningless."[75] Wiping away tears, Ross explained that he felt an obligation to protect Paulding, who had represented him well, from losing his law license. Judge Clifford expressed sympathy for Paulding: "The threat of losing your license by a federal judge is a very difficult [position] to be in."[76] The judge bemoaned that it would be difficult to find another attorney to replace Paulding, who worked pro bono and had built a relationship of trust with Ross.

A resolution to the question of representation was worked out within a week. With the blessing of public defenders Smyth and Patrick Culligan, Judge Clifford on February 10 appointed sixty-eight-year-old Thomas Groark as a special counsel to advocate for Ross's incompetence. "In the final analysis, the court has ordered exactly what we were requesting—a full and adversarial competency hearing," the public defenders commented.[77] Groark was a highly regarded trial lawyer and senior partner in the state's largest law firm, Hartford's Day, Berry and Howard, which provided two assisting attorneys (Michael Shea and James Mahanna), all pro bono. In turn, Paulding was retained to advocate for his client's competency and the right to forgo all appeals. "I think this is the ideal resolution of the dilemma I was in and the court system was in," a relieved Paulding said of his former conflict of interest.[78] Kane and Peter McShane represented the state. Judge Clifford also scheduled the tentative execution for May 11, halfway between the minimum requirement of one month and the maximum of six months.

Six days of hearings opened on April 7 with augmented psychiatric testimony. Dr. Norko, the court-appointed psychiatrist, had deemed Ross competent in 1995 when Ross had stipulated for the death penalty rather than go through a second penalty phase. Last December 28, Judge Clifford had ruled Ross competent, based in part on a recent four-hour examination of the prisoner by Dr. Norko. The last-minute intervention of Judge Chatigny, however, had led Dr. Norko to state that he needed to examine new evidence that suggested Ross's incompetence. Paulding hired Dr. Suzanne Gentile, a colleague of Dr. Norko's at Whiting Forensic Institute who had experience in the health care of prisoners. Special counsel Groark hired Dr. Stuart Grassian, a professor at Harvard University Medical School, whose research on "death row syndrome" had raised questions for Judge Chatigny about Dr. Norko's findings. Groark also retained Dr. Eric Goldsmith of New York University Medical Center, an expert on psychiatry and the law, who also expressed reservations about Dr. Norko's assessment in earlier litigation. The state paid more than $100,000 to the four psychiatrists.[79]

Judge Clifford made clear to the attorneys that "no party bears the burden of proof," explaining, "The question is whether, giving full and fair consideration to all of the evidence, from whatever source, the evidence established by a fair preponderance that Ross is competent to waive further appeals and whether his waiver is knowing, intelligent and voluntary."[80]

Drs. Norko and Gentile deemed that Ross was competently making his decision to volunteer for death. Both agreed, as Dr. Norko put it, that "conditions on death row have not had a profoundly negative impact on him." According to the psychiatrists, Ross was actively engaged in writing, correspondence, and overseeing the prison law library. Despite the contention of Dan Ross, of a legal confidant to Ross (Martha Elliot), and of a girlfriend of Ross (Susan Powers), Dr. Norko found that the prisoner had a consistent moral value—dying was the "cost of doing the right thing"—and that Ross primarily did not want to inflict further pain on the victims' families.[81] Dr. Gentile concurred, "He does feel remorse for what he's done."[82]

Doctors Grassian and Goldsmith found Ross incompetent, driven by personality disorders. "Obviously desire to be noble, to die a martyr—a victim—is entirely consistent with his narcissism," Dr. Grassian stressed in comparing Ross to glory seekers Jim Jones, David Koresh, and the Columbine High School murderers. He found "a lot of lies," no moral imperative.[83] Dr. Goldsmith contended that after Susan Powers had jilted Ross in March 2003, he had attempted suicide and had made "the decision not to pursue further appeals." Dr. Goldsmith continued that "his thinking is so inflexible he can't retract from this position."[84] Paulding and Groark echoed their expert witnesses. Paulding asked what was incompetent about seeking redemption "to show people that he is not just Michael Ross serial killer, that he's not just Michael Ross the monster?" Groark rebutted that a "narcissistic disorder," a fear of humiliation, and the need to appear noble compelled Ross to forgo appeals.[85]

With great public anticipation, Judge Clifford issued a "Memorandum of Decision" on April 22. As he first explained, "The court must independently decide the issues at hand because it is a legal, not a medical determination." The U.S. Supreme Court in *Rees v. Peyton* (1966) provided the standard of legal competency for when a death row inmate volunteered for death. As Judge Clifford saw it, the central question was "not whether a mental illness substantially affects a decision, but whether it substantially affects the prisoner's *capacity* to appreciate his options and make a rational choice among them." The four psychiatrists agreed on Ross's mental disorders, but they disagreed on how those disorders affected his decision to forgo appeals. The judge found the analysis of Drs. Norko and Gentile more persuasive than that of Drs. Grassian and Goldsmith. "There has been," he continued, "a constant theme in Ross' communications going back to 1987 of waiving appeals and sparing the families the pain of further litigation. Moreover, Ross has been actively trying to accept the verdict of death for over ten years."

Ironically, "death row syndrome," which had prompted the reconvening of the hearing at Judge Chatigny's instigation, "never materialized in the case." According to Dr. Grassian's own terms, Ross was an active agent, not "dead" in his cell. According to a fair preponderance of evidence, Judge Clifford concluded, "Ross has the capacity to understand his choices and knowingly, intelligently and voluntarily to waive his right to further appeals."[86] Barring unanticipated circumstances, it looked like New England would have its first execution in forty-five years.

The Divisive Politics of the Death Penalty

During March, as the competency hearing was reopened, the General Assembly prepared to vote on whether to abolish capital punishment. To lessen the political repercussions, the majority leadership of the Democratic legislature had scheduled the vote for after Ross's putative January 26 execution. James A. Amann, speaker of the House and a Democrat from Milford, had unsuccessfully sought to block any vote on the controversial issue. He was certain that the largely Democratic effort would fail and would leave legislators in conservative districts vulnerable to defeat. "We worked our tails off to get 99 members," he told his colleagues. "I don't want to come back with 90 or 88."[87] For Amann, it was not the politically smart thing to do with the Ross issue on the front page.

The stay of the execution flummoxed Democrats. A move to strike the death penalty would not only effectively commute the death sentences of six inmates, but also of Ross, to life in prison. Amann feared that the pro–capital punishment Republicans, who held barely one-third of the seats, would flail Democrats with being soft on crime. He imagined an attack campaign, especially in eastern Connecticut, with the message: Did your legislator vote to spare Michael Ross?

The Judiciary Committee by a twenty-four to fifteen margin approved and sent to the House a bill for abolition. Co-chairman Michael Lawlor, a Democrat from East Haven, castigated capital punishment as a "fraud on public policy."[88] There was vocal opposition to the death penalty, including from Vivian Dobson, who revealed herself as the only surviving victim of a Ross assault.[89] The general wisdom, however, was that the bill would not pass. A Quinnipiac University poll indicated that 48 percent of Democrats, 71 percent of Republicans, and 62 percent of unaffiliated voters endorsed the death penalty.[90] Governor Rell promised a veto. "Who are we," William Hamzy, a Republican from Plymouth, queried legislators, "to second guess those juries and judges?"[91] After a five-hour debate, the House on March 30 turned down the repeal bill eighty-nine to sixty.

The partisan divide was clear: Republicans voted forty-eight to four against repeal of capital punishment, and Democrats split fifty-six to forty-one for abolition. Although more than 90 percent of Republicans stood together, Democrats were significantly divided. Of the four dissident Republicans, only one represented a district (Stonington) east of the Connecticut River. Representative Dyson, the senior Democrat from New Haven who had held a one-man vigil against the death penalty that January, declared, "We have killed some innocent people." In contrast, Representative Steven Mikutel, who represented Griswold, the home of some of Ross's victims, demanded, "These people [on death row] deserve to die."[92] Representative Mike Alberts asked his constituents in a northeastern district, "Do you support the death penalty for certain crimes?" He reported that 73 percent said yes, 23 percent indicated no, and 4 percent were undecided.[93] In the cultural wars, Republicans in Connecticut were overwhelmingly for capital punishment, whereas what pundits called a wedge issue fractured the Democrats.

Continuous Intravenous Lethal Injection

The way was cleared for execution. On Monday, May 9, the Connecticut Supreme Court rejected a petition from special counsel Groark challenging Judge Clifford's finding of April 22 that Ross was competent. Chief Justice William J. Sullivan ruled, "Accordingly, we conclude that the trial court's determination that the preponderance of the evidence established that the defendant's mental disorder did not substantially affect his capacity to make and act on a rational decision so as to render him incompetent was supported by the evidence and was not clearly erroneous."[94] Justice Norcott reiterated his opposition to the death penalty, but agreed "with the majority's well reasoned resolution of the jurisdictional and competency issues that this case presents us with, despite the ineluctable fact that this court's decision in the present case clears one of the last remaining obstacles to Connecticut's first execution in nearly forty-five years."[95] The next day, Groark desisted from further appeals. "We feel we have advocated as well as we can for the position of incompetence," he stated. "The court has come to a decision, and we do not think there would be any interest by the United States Supreme Court in reviewing the decision."[96]

All other appeals were stillborn. The Connecticut Supreme Court at the end of April refused to hear a petition from the Missionary Society of Connecticut that Hartford Superior Court Judge Beach dismissed. The society sought to compel the Board of Pardons and Paroles to establish specific guidelines for commutation hearings before the impending execution.[97] Attorney Antonio Ponvert III on behalf of Dan Ross complained to Dr. J. Robert Galvin, the state's commissioner of public health, that physician involvement with lethal injection violated medical ethics, but Dr. Galvin on May 6 said that he would not act on the matter.[98] With no more legal barriers, Blumenthal, the attorney general, announced at 11 p.m. on Thursday, May 12, "We are prepared to go forward."[99] With only a few hours left before the scheduled execution at 2:01 a.m. on Friday, May 13, Ross could exercise his legal rights and stop the execution. He appeared firmly resolved to proceed.

At 8:10 a.m. on Thursday, prison officials at the Osborn prison moved Ross to the execution holding cell. The barred cell was encased in Plexiglas with holes midway in front so that communication, but not physical contact, could occur. The exception was priests, who were admitted to give him communion at 9 a.m. and later last rites. Ross had returned enthusiastically to the faith he had been baptized in while in prison. As an oblate, a lay affiliate of the Roman Catholic Order of Saint Benedict, he had adopted the name Brother Dismas. According to church tradition, Saint Dismas was one of two thieves the Romans had crucified next to Jesus. He was a penitent who asked for Jesus's blessing, a spiritual vision that appealed to Ross. "If it is God's will," he said, "I will achieve that reconciliation that I so desire, and hopefully complete my transformation into one who is worthy of redemption and forgiveness."[100] His religious advisors assured him that in accepting a lawfully imposed death sentence he was not committing suicide. A devout Catholic, he understood his decision as a moral one: expiation for heinous sins. During his last moments, the prisoner, strapped prone to the gurney with arms outstretched for the administration of the deadly drugs, bore a surreal resemblance to the crucifixion.

There was, ironically, controversy over the use of lethal injection from both those who supported and those who opposed capital punishment. The transition from electrocution to lethal injection began in Oklahoma in 1977 largely as a means to avoid the expense of repairing the electric chair or building a gas chamber. In response to an inquiry from the legislature, Dr. Stanley Deutsch, head of the Department of Anesthesiology at the University of Oklahoma Health Sciences Center, recommended a chemical cocktail given intravenously that cost less than $100 and would cause rapid, certain death without the grotesqueries of the electric chair or gas chamber. Texas adopted lethal injection the same year and after hundreds of executions became expert in the application. During November 2004, personnel from Connecticut's Department of Correction traveled to the Texas State Prison at Huntsville to learn the procedure, which had never been used in New England.[101]

Despite claims that it was more humane, Deborah W. Denno, a professor at Fordham University Law School, indicated that only nine of thirty-seven states made public their protocols and drug dosages. Connecticut and Texas were two of the nine. In addition to secrecy, she questioned whether the procedures were adequate, whether they were consistently carried out, and whether personnel were competently trained.[102] Three faculty members of the Yale University School of Medicine pointed out on May 8 that research published in the *Lancet*, Britain's leading medical journal, showed that anesthesia levels administrated during lethal injection in the United States were too low according to best practices. Without adequate anesthesia, the condemned person would experience extreme pain before death. They added that the code of ethics of the American Medical Association prohibited physicians from participating directly or training executioners. They concluded, "Connecticut's execution protocol is both medically flawed and ethically and morally repugnant."[103]

Advocates of retribution thought that lethal injection was too benign. Some family members and police officers believed that Ross was getting off too lightly by not experiencing the pain and suffering of his young victims. Robert Blecker, a New York Law School professor, complained, "There is something fundamentally inappropriate when someone who is, himself, a sadistic torturer goes out in an opiate haze." His perspective was echoed by U.S. Supreme Court Justice Antonin Scalia, who remarked in 1994 about a man sentenced to death for the rape and murder of an eleven-year-old girl, "How enviable a quiet death by lethal injection compared to that."[104] Agreeing with his Yale colleagues on medical ethics, Dr. Stanley Rosenbaum countered that the dosage of 2,500 milligrams of sodium thiopental, a quick-acting barbiturate called for in Connecticut, would render one unconscious, even to the point of death, before the two other drugs were administered.[105] State and federal courts upheld the procedure.[106]

Up until the moment of lethal injection, Ross had the right to stop the execution and declare that he wanted to appeal. Until then, a specially trained team of six correctional staff and six alternates, whose identities were kept confidential, was overseen by the warden of Osborn Correctional Institution, who carried out a prescribed death ritual.[107] Guards had the prisoner under continuous watch during the preceding four days, and as the final evening approached, heightened security was maintained throughout the prison and its perimeter. Officials allowed demonstrators to convene a mile from the prison. Around midnight, several hundred opponents of the death penalty held a candlelight vigil with signs that said, "Don't Kill for Me." Some had marched from "the state house to the death house." At 12:45 a.m. on Friday, May 13, they walked toward the Osborn prison, where they held a moment of silence shortly before the execution. Only a dozen pro–death penalty people congregated in a separate parking lot.[108]

On Thursday, Ross had received family and friends, including his attorney Paulding, and had his last meal at 3 p.m. As of Friday morning at 1:30 a.m., visitors were barred. Guards took Ross from the adjoining "death cell" to the "execution enclosure" where he was strapped to the "execution surface." At that time, a heart monitor was connected and intravenous access was established, one a primary line and the other a backup. According to guidelines, this procedure was not done by a physician, which violated medical ethics, but by "a person or persons, properly trained to the satisfaction of a Connecticut licensed and practicing physician."[109] Thirty minutes prior to execution, the warden accompanied the executioner, an unidentified person also certified by a physician, to the "execution ante room" that was obscured by one-way glass to maintain confidentiality. Here the apparatus for lethal injection was kept.

Ten minutes later, the warden escorted witnesses to the observation room, whose window that looked out on the condemned man was blocked by curtains. The witnesses included victims' families, five representatives from the media, and no more than three adults and a clergyman designated by the inmate. All had earlier passed through a metal detector and had been frisked. No photographic or recording devices were permitted; only notepads and pencils or pens were allowed. The commissioner of the Department of Correction and a physician were also in attendance. Two guards were stationed in the observation room, and various witnesses were separated from each other.

After a seven-minute delay, the curtain was opened at 2:08 a.m. Having checked on a designated telephone line that no stays had been received, Christine Whidden, warden of the prison and the first woman in the history of Connecticut in such a role, gave the order to proceed with the execution at 2:13 a.m. There were three injections: 2,500 milligrams of thiopental sodium, a lethal dose; 100 milligrams of pancuronium bromide; and a 120 milliequivalent of potassium chloride. After the first injection, Ross, who had his eyes shut and lay quietly except for one audible gasp, ceased to move.

When the infusion was completed, personnel closed the curtains at 2:23 a.m., and the warden summoned the medical examiner to certify death. The warden pronounced Ross dead at 2:25 a.m. Guards escorted the witnesses out of the observation room, and the corpse was removed. Outside, the anti–death penalty vigil dispersed.

Afterward, there was a gamut of reactions to the execution. According to one account, Shelly Sindland, a television reporter and media witness, said, "It looked like he was sleeping"; media witnesses heard one of the victim's family say, "It's too peaceful"; and another was said to comment, "He didn't have the balls to say anything . . . he didn't even look over here."[110] Kathy Jaeger, one of Ross's spiritual advisors and a witness, countered that Ross had contemplated making a final statement but feared he would break down and garble his message. She indicated that he wanted to say, "It's over. I'm sorry it took so long. At least there's no more court, and I hope you find peace."[111] Attorney Paulding concurred that Ross "sought to do what he thought was right."[112] Edwin Shelley, whose daughter Ross killed in 1984, lamented that his family "waited 21 years for justice." Jennifer Taylor, whose sister was a victim, reflected, "The anger caused by Ross' crimes can now soon fade to a safe place." Retired detective Michael Malchik, who had arrested Ross in 1984, warned that there are "other Michael Rosses out there." Blumenthal, Connecticut's attorney general observed, "It shows that the criminal justice system works and that we can impose a lawful punishment after a lawful sentence." How well, though, had the criminal justice system actually worked?

EPILOGUE
An Unworkable Death Penalty

> But, for reasons of philosophy, policy and law, we can't have it both ways.
> We can't pretend that we will fulfill the wishes of the people and kill off the
> occasional murderer but then actually never do it.
>
> Laurence D. Cohen, public policy consultant, May 15, 2005

THE ARREST, adjudication, and execution of Michael Ross took place over two decades. The duration far surpassed that of the 157 other people put to death in Connecticut in civilian courts over nearly four centuries. Rather than a vindication of the criminal justice system, the interminable process points to contradictions and complexities in Connecticut's commitment to capital punishment. Simply put, the death penalty for almost a half century has been unworkable, unless the prisoner—Joseph Taborsky in 1960 and Michael Ross in 2005—waived appeals and volunteered for execution. Even then, in the latter example, there were extraordinary efforts to block the outcome. In concurring with a Connecticut Supreme Court decision that cleared the way for Ross's execution, Justice Flemming L. Norcott Jr., an opponent of the death penalty, also dissented. He asked on May 9, 2005:

> And yet, at the end of the day, the question remains: After the execution, what will the state of Connecticut have gained from all of this? The answer seems to be that, minimally, the state has secured the proverbial pound of flesh for the crimes of this one outrageously cruel man. But now, what is to be? Has our thirst for this ultimate penalty now been slaked, or do we, the people of Connecticut, continue down this increasingly lonesome road?[1]

Surveys of public opinion provide an answer. A Quinnipiac University poll in January 2005 indicated that 59 percent of Connecticut residents favored the death penalty, 31 percent opposed, and 10 percent did not know. The results were comparable to national sentiment. If the question were rephrased to ask which punishment was preferred for a murder conviction, 37 percent favored the death penalty, 49 percent selected a life sentence without parole, and 14 percent did not know. A plurality, almost a majority, of those canvassed chose the alternative to capital punishment, which was somewhat above the national outcome. It seemed that citizens might support the abolition of the death penalty. Once the fate of Michael Ross was interjected into the question, however, the results were highly skewed. Seventy percent endorsed his execution, 23 percent opposed it, and 8 percent offered no opinion. One-fourth of those who had previously indicated that they opposed the death penalty wanted Ross executed. An additional question revealed further polarization. Eighty-five percent thought that Ross should be allowed to die without further appeals.[2] Most citizens in Connecticut approved the death penalty when it applied to horrific murders.[3]

There has been greater discrimination in defining capital crime, to whom it can be applied, and how the execution is carried out. The seventeenth century saw the last executions for witchcraft, bestiality, and incest. The statute of 1750 dropped biblical language from the capital code, and around the same time the last young woman went to the gallows for infanticide. During the Enlightenment and early days of the republic, the concept of proportionality of punishment led to the substitution of imprisonment at Newgate and Wethersfield prisons in place of mutilation, other corporal punishment, and execution for the third offense of robbery. Since 1786, when a twelve-year-old girl of mixed race was hanged, an unofficial gender convention has so far limited the condemned to males. The mentally incompetent and eventually minors under eighteen years of age were excluded. The last convicted rapist was hanged in 1817, and this African American was the last person executed for a crime other than murder. A pivotal statute in 1842 more specifically defined murder as a homicide carried out with malice aforethought and premeditation.

The last public execution occurred in 1833. Hangings were sequestered to the confines of county jails, but sheriffs admitted scores of spectators. In 1893, executions occurred in the state prison with only a few witnesses permitted. The electric chair replaced the automatic gallows in 1937, and the General Assembly adopted lethal injection in 1995.

In the era before the Civil War, a few governors opposed the death penalty. The Taborsky rampage of the mid-1950s caused Governor Abraham Ribicoff and the *Hartford Courant* to moderate their call for an end to capital punishment. After a Democratic sweep of legislative seats in November 2008, the General Assembly, embracing a national trend, voted for abolition the next year. The outcome was all the more remarkable because of state attention on the horrific slayings of three members of the Petit family during a home invasion in Cheshire in July 2007. The surviving member of the family, a physician, applauded Republican Governor M. Jodi Rell's veto.[4] The rationale was that notorious murderers ought to be executed.

Joseph Taborsky and Michael Ross were cases in point. Their executions made Connecticut the only state in New England to carry out executions since the 1950s. They were admitted serial murderers, and their heinous acts produced widespread outrage. The recent revelations made in dozens of cases through DNA evidence that innocent men had been convicted—and some undoubtedly executed—did not apply. They were white men; racial bias was not a factor in any way. Their sensational, highly publicized, repetitive violence—six execution-style murders and eight sexual killings—stood apart in Connecticut's long annals of crimes. In that sense, their death sentences were not arbitrary or capricious compared with others serving life in prison. Neither was prosecuted in the judicial district of Waterbury, from which a majority of death row inmates hailed by 2005. They both waived appeals and volunteered for death. Ross was the greater anomaly. Most of the scores of people executed over the centuries have been on the margins of society, not unlike Taborsky. Ross was Ivy League and solidly middle class. Juries rejected his initial contention that he was not legally culpable because he suffered from the psychiatric disorder of sexual sadism. There was no glaring disparity in the application of the capital code.

The controversy was largely ethical. Was the death penalty right or wrong? According to the 2005 Quinnipiac University poll, 57 percent of those who supported capital punishment offered retribution as their reason.[5] As Lera Shelley, the mother of one of Ross's victims, said after watching his execution, "My daughter and the other victims finally have the justice they deserve."[6] The ancient law of the talion, measure for measure, was at the core of support for the death penalty. Three hundred and fifty years earlier, a colonial statute had repeated the divine mandate of Genesis 9:6, "Whoever shed the blood of man, by man his blood shall be shed." Only 10 percent of death penalty advocates indicated that deterrence was their primary rationale.[7] The debate did not hinge on the unpersuasive argument that the death penalty made society safer. It had not deterred Taborsky or Ross. The majority of people in Connecticut thought that those men got what they deserved.

For opponents of capital punishment, the fundamental objection was that killing—whether done by the state or not—was abhorrent. They pointed to the hidden, secretive nature of the act, done in early morning darkness. Physicians objected that lethal injection perverted medical techniques to take life so as to make execution more efficient and less objectionable. Many based their rationale on religious injunctions and human rights ideals. Life in prison without parole was an alternative for the worst of the worst. Joshua Rubenstein, northeast regional director of Amnesty International, explained, "The state can protect people from Michael Ross by locking him up, not killing him."[8] Abolitionists also pointed out the long, agonizing ordeal the current law presented to victims' families. Due to the duration of appeals, capital cases were also very expensive. In addition, opponents found capital punishment to be arbitrary, racially biased, and unfair. In recent years, Connecticut Supreme Court Justices Robert Berdon, Joette Katz, and Flemming L. Norcott Jr. have held that executions violated the Eighth Amendment's prohibition against cruel and unusual punishment. As Justice Norcott put it in January 2005, "My long-standing belief [is] that the death penalty has no place whatsoever in a civilized and rational criminal justice system."[9] These judicial opinions, however, have remained in the minority.

Today, the paradox of capital punishment in Connecticut remains ensconced, although under mounting challenge. Public opinion supports the death penalty for killers such as Taborsky and Ross. So far, every General Assembly (except in 2009), almost all governors, and the courts (state and federal) have concurred. Ever since the antebellum period, abolitionists have been a vocal minority, unable to enact their principles. They find the death penalty ethically abhorrent and facially unconstitutional; they argue the application of the capital code is biased and iniquitous. The Kafkaesque outcome is a death penalty law in which no condemned are executed unless they want to be. This bizarre situation has existed for the last half century. With ten men on death row in 2010, Connecticut remains committed to a contradictory public policy.[10]

NOTES

Introduction

1. See *Trial of Amos Adams for a Rape, Committed on the Body of Lelea Thorp* (New Haven: T. G. Woodward, 1817); William Andrews, *A **Sermon** Delivered at Danbury, Nov. 13th, 1817; Being the Day Appointed for the Execution of **Amos Adams** for the Crime of **Rape*** (New Haven: T. G. Woodward, 1817); *Connecticut Courant,* Nov. 25, 1817, 2; and James Montgomery Bailey, *History of Danbury, Connecticut* (New York: Burr, 1896), 117–18.

2. http://www.boston.com/news/local/connecticut/articles/2010/06/04/connecticut_death_row_inmates/. New Hampshire, the only other state in the region with a death row, had one man there. See Epilogue, note 10.

3. The phrase "the solemn sentence of death" was routinely used when judges sentenced defendants to be executed. See *Connecticut Journal,* Aug. 18, 1790, 3, in regard to the death sentence for Joseph Mountain.

4. David Garland, *Punishment and Modern Society: A Study in Social Theory* (Chicago: University of Chicago Press, 1990), 175.

5. On November 13, 1967, George Mackie, a research assistant to Governor John Dempsey, wrote to Douglas Lyons, chairman of Citizens Against Legalized Murder, "I know of no history of the death penalty, which has been involved in Connecticut since early colonial times, which could be summarized." Record Group (RG) 5, Office of the Governor, John Dempsey, 1961–1970, box A-233, Connecticut State Library, Hartford (CSL). This study is an effort to fill this void.

Two important historical works have recently been published: Alan Rogers, *Murder and the Death Penalty in Massachusetts* (Amherst: University of Massachusetts Press, 2008); and Stuart Banner, *The Death Penalty: An American History* (Cambridge, Mass.: Harvard University Press, 2002), which is an overview of the subject on the national level.

The identification of people judicially executed by state includes William J. Bowers, *Legal Homicide: Death as Punishment in America, 1864–1982* (Boston: Northeastern University Press, 1984); M. Watt Espy and John Ortiz Smykla, "Executions in the U.S. 1608–1987: The Espy File Executions by State (chronologically)," www.deathpenaltyinfo.org/ESPYstate.pdy; and most comprehensively Daniel Allen Hearn, *Legal Executions in New England, 1623–1960* (Jefferson, N.C.: McFarland, 1999). For Connecticut alone, see "Connecticut State Prisons—Executions" [1894–1960], Connecticut—Executions, Subject File, History and Genealogy, CSL; and M. S. Richmond [warden, Connecticut State Prison, Wethersfield] to Robert J. Beckwith [Special Assistant—Governor's Office], RG 5, Office of the Governor, Abraham Ribicoff, 1955–1961, box 647, folder "Capital Punishment," Archives, CSL.

6. A number of studies of capital punishment focus on recent events and ethics. They include Helen Prejean, *Dead Man Walking* (New York: Random House, 1993); James Marquant, Sheldon Ekland-Olson, and Jonathan R. Sorensen, *The Rope, the Needle, and the Chair: Capital Punishment in Texas* (Austin: University of Texas Press, 1994); Hugo Adam Bedau, ed., *The Death Penalty in America: Current Controversies* (New York: Oxford University Press, 1997); Kathleen O'Shea, *Women and the Death Penalty in the United States, 1900–1998* (Westport, Conn.: Praeger, 1999); Jesse L. Jackson Sr., Jesse L. Jackson Jr., and Bruce Shapiro, *Legal Lynching: The Death Penalty and America's Future* (New York: New Press, 2001); Austin Sarat, *When the State Kills: Capital Punishment and the American Condition* (Princeton, N.J.: Princeton University Press, 2001); Barry Scheck, Peter Neufeld, and Jim Dwyer, *Actual Innocence: When Justice Goes Wrong and How to Make It Right* (New York: Signet, 2001); David R. Dow and Mark Dow, eds., *Machinery of Death: The Reality of America's Death Penalty Regime* (New York: Routledge, 2002); Robert Jay Lifton and Greg Mitchell, *Who Owns Death? Capital Punishment, the American Conscience, and the End of Executions* (New York: Perennial, 2002); Victor L. Streib, *Death Penalty in a Nutshell* (St. Paul, Minn.: West Group, 2003); Mary Welek Atwell, *Evolving Standards of Decency: Popular Culture and Capital Punishment* (New York: Peter Lang, 2004); Craig Haney, *Death by Design: Capital Punishment as a Social Psychological System* (New York: Oxford University Press, 2005); and Andrew Welsh-Huggins, *No Witnesses Here Tonight: Race, Politics, and Geography in One of the Busiest Death Penalty States* (Athens: Ohio University Press, 2009).

7. Governor M. Jodi Rell to the Honorable Susan Bysiewicz, Secretary of State, June 5, 2009, www.ct.gov; and Christopher Keating, "Rell Vetoes Bill That Would Have Abolished Death Penalty," www.courant.com/news/politics/hc-death-penalty-rell-0605,0,78884211.

8. See www.deathpenaltyinfo.org.

9. "Anger and Restraint," *New York Times*, June 26, 2008.

10. Recorded in a photograph taken by Anna Goodheart on Route 97 in Hampton, Connecticut, during January 2005.

1. Biblical Retribution, 1636–1699

1. In a discussion before the United States Supreme Court of the constitutionality of a monument of the Ten Commandments in a park surrounding the Texas Capitol, Justice Antonin Scalia commented that the Decalogue is "a symbol of the fact that government derives its authority from God." The Puritans would have concurred. Linda Greenhouse, "The Justices Consider Religious Displays," *New York Times*, Mar. 3, 2005, A18.

2. "Fundamental Orders of Connecticut." The full document is at www.bartleby .com/43/7.htlm.

3. Albert E. Van Dusen, *Connecticut* (New York: Random House, 1961), 49.

4. Isabel M. Calder, "John Cotton and the New Haven Colony," *New England Quarterly* 3 (1930), 93.

5. Perry Miller, *The New England Mind: The Seventeenth Century* (New York: Macmillan, 1939), 489.

6. Norman Pettit, "Hooker's Doctrine of Assurance: A Critical Phase in New England Spiritual Thought," *New England Quarterly* 47 (1974), 518–34.

7. Miller, *The New England Mind*, 22. Increase Mather similarly commented, "Altho'it is true, (as has been shewed) that sinners cannot convert themselves, their *Cannot* is a willful *Cannot*." "Predestination and Human Exertions," in *Sinners in the*

Hands of an Angry God and Other Puritan Sermons, ed. David Dutkanicz (Mineola, N.Y.: Dover, 2005), 99.

8. Thomas Hooker, "A True Sight of Sin, Meditation, Wandering Thoughts, Repentant Sinner and Their Ministers," in *Sinners in the Hands of an Angry God and Other Puritan Sermons,* ed. David Dutkanicz (Mineola, N.Y.: Dover, 2005), 32, 45.

9. Puritan thought represented a transition between the organicism of medieval society and the individualism of Lockean liberalism. See Max Weber, *The Protestant Ethic and the Spirit of Capitalism,* trans. Talcott Parsons (London: G. Allen and Unwin, 1930); and Michael Walzer, *Revolution of the Saints: A Study in the Origins of Radical Politics* (Cambridge, Mass.: Harvard University Press, 1965).

10. Quoted in M. Louise Greene, *The Development of Religious Liberty in Connecticut* (Freeport, N.Y: Books for Libraries Press, 1970; originally 1905), 92 note b. See Christopher Grasso, *A Speaking Aristocracy: Transforming Public Discourse in Eighteenth-Century Connecticut* (Chapel Hill: Published for the Omohundro Institute of Early American History and Culture by the University of North Carolina Press, 1999).

11. John Cotton, "Limitation of Government," in *Sinners in the Hands of an Angry God and Other Puritan Sermons,* ed. David Dutkanicz (Mineola, N.Y.: Dover, 2005), 3–4.

12. John D. Cushing, ed., *The Earliest Laws of the New Haven and Connecticut Colonies, 1639–1673* (Wilmington, Del.: Michael Glazier, 1977), 132.

13. See Dave Thomas Konig, *Law and Society in Puritan Massachusetts: Essex County, 1629–1692* (Chapel Hill: University of North Carolina Press, 1979); and Edgar J. McManus, *Law and Liberty in New England* (Amherst: University of Massachusetts Press, 1993). For a modern example of stoning, see "Islamists in Somalia Say They Plan to Execute 5 Rapists by Stoning," *New York Times,* June 27, 2006, A9.

14. Edmund S. Morgan, *The Puritan Dilemma: The Story of John Winthrop* (Boston: Little, Brown, 1958), 31.

15. Quoted in Van Dusen, *Connecticut,* 66.

16. *The Code of 1650, Being a Compilation of the Earliest Laws and Orders of the General Court of Connecticut* (Hartford: S. Andrus and Son, 1821), 26.

17. Cushing, *The Earliest Laws,* 509.

18. Cushing, *The Earliest Laws,* 17.

19. Cushing, *The Earliest Laws,* viii.

20. Cushing, *The Earliest Laws,* 2–3, 77.

21. Cushing, *The Earliest Laws,* 9.

22. Cushing, *The Earliest Laws,* 73.

23. See Gail Sussman Marcus, "'Due Execution of the Generall Rules of Righteousness': Criminal Procedure in New Haven Town and Colony, 1638–1658," in *Saints and Revolutionaries: Essays in Early America,* ed. David D. Hall, John M. Murrin, and Thad W. Tate (New York: W. W. Norton, 1984), 99–137.

24. Cushing, *The Earliest Laws,* 14, 69, 143. The two-eyewitness rule applied in both New Haven and Connecticut colonies.

25. Mary J. A. Jones, *Congregational Commonwealth: Connecticut, 1636–1662* (Middletown: Wesleyan University Press, 1968), 99–137; John M. Murrin, "Magistrates, Sinners, and a Precarious Liberty: Trial by Jury in Seventeenth-Century New England," in *Saints and Revolutionaries,* ed. Hall, Murrin, and Tate, 152–206; and McManus, *Law and Liberty,* 90–93.

26. McManus, *Law and Liberty,* 207–8; and M. P. Baumgartner, "Law and Social Status in Colonial New Haven, 1639–1665," *Research in Law and Sociology* 1 (1978), 155–72.

27. The statutes prescribing punishment examples can be found in the law codes of 1642, 1650, 1656, and 1673 in Cushing, *The Earliest Laws*. Specific cases are in Norbert B. Lacy, ed., "Records of the Court of Assistants of Connecticut, 1665–1701," 2 vols. (master's thesis, Yale University, 1937); *Records of the Particular Court of Connecticut, 1639–1663* (Hartford: Connecticut Historical Society, 1928); Franklin Bowditch Dexter, ed., *Ancient Town Records*, 3 vols. (New Haven: New Haven Colony Historical Society, 1917); Charles J. Hoadly, ed., *Records of the Colony and Plantation of New Haven, from 1638–1649* (Hartford: Case, Tiffany, 1857), hereafter cited as *Records of . . . New Haven;* and Charles J. Hoadly, ed., *Records of the Colony or Jurisdiction of New Haven from May, 1653, to the Union* (Hartford: Case, Lockwood, 1858).

In 1673, a man who cursed and violently resisted one of his majesty's officers was banished, at his own cost, to Barbados. Lacy, "Records," 1:51–52. More commonly, banishment was just from the colony itself, as with Will Harding being banished from New Haven in 1642 for repeated sexual infractions, and the Quaker Humphrey Norton from the same place in 1657/58. Hoadly, *Records of . . . New Haven*, 81; and Dexter, *Ancient Town Records*, 1:339–43. On the Hartford house of correction, see Jones, *Congregational Commonwealth*, 124.

28. Hoadly, *Records of . . . New Haven*, 260.

29. Lacy, "Records," 1:3.

30. Dexter, *Ancient Town Records*, 1:238–40.

31. Lacy, "Records," 1:174; and Peter C. Hoffer and N. E. H. Hull, *Murdering Mothers: Infanticide in England and New England, 1558–1803* (New York: New York University Press, 1981), 45. In psychiatric terms, Mercy Brown may have suffered severe postpartum psychosis. In a notable contemporary case, Andrea Yates was convicted in Houston, Texas, in 2002 of drowning her five children despite an insanity plea. Her conviction was overturned on appeal, and a retrial is scheduled. Fred Moss, an associate professor of law at Southern Methodist University, commented, "This part of the country in particular is very retributive in their notions of justice and think somebody has to pay for a death." The contrast between Connecticut in the seventeenth century and Texas today is important in the assessment of the insanity defense in cases of mothers murdering their children. "Retrial to Begin for Mother of 5 in Drownings," *New York Times*, June 26, 2006, A16.

32. Lacy, "Records," 1:279.

33. Daniel Allen Hearn, *Legal Executions in New England, 1623–1960* (Jefferson, N.C.: McFarland, 1999), 50–52. Hearn includes in his comprehensive list two Native Americans, Canonchet, sachem of the Narragansetts, and Choos, who were executed in 1676. The best evidence indicates that their executions were directly linked to King Philip's War. I have therefore excluded them from this study because they do not fit into the category of civilian judicial proceedings. Neither case, for example, is cited in the public records of Connecticut and New Haven, nor do any court records apparently exist. In addition, Hearn cites a firing squad, a form of military execution, as the cause of Canonchet's death. For Connecticut's role in the Pequot War and King Philip's War, see Van Dusen, *Connecticut*, 33–40, 75–82; and more broadly, John J. Navin, "Cross-Cultural 'Murther' and Retribution in Colonial New England," in *Murder on Trial*, ed. Robert Asher, Lawrence B. Goodheart, and Alan Rogers (Albany: State University of New York Press, 2005), 33–59.

34. Katherine Hermes, "Justice Will Be Done Us," in *The Many Legalities of Early America*, ed. Christopher L. Tomlins and Bruce H. Mann (Chapel Hill: University of North Carolina Press, 2001), 144–45. See Jenny Hale Pulsipher, *King: Indians, English,*

and the Contest for Authority in Colonial New England (Philadelphia: University of Pennsylvania Press, 2005).

35. See John Mason, *A Brief History of the Pequot War: Especially of the Memorable Taking of Their Fort at Mistick in Connecticut in 1637* (Boston: S. Kneeland and T. Green, 1736); and Ben Kiernan, *Blood and Soil: A World History of Genocide and Extermination* (New Haven: Yale University Press, 2007), 225–36.

36. Hoadly, *Records of . . . New Haven*, 22–24.

37. Hoadly, *Records of . . . New Haven*, 135, 149; and John Winthrop, *The Journal of John Winthrop, 1630–1649*, ed. Richard S. Dunn, James Savage, and Laetitia Yeandle (Cambridge, Mass.: Belknap Press, 1996), 534.

38. Lacy, "Records," 1:112.

39. Lacy, "Records," 1:147–48.

40. See Van Dusen, *Connecticut*, 83–84.

41. Lacy, "Records," 1:58–59; and William K. Holdsworth, *Law and Society in Colonial Connecticut, 1636–1672* (Ann Arbor, Mich.: University Microfilms International, 1974), 384.

42. Lacy, "Records," 1:68–69; and *Crimes and Misdemeanors*, series 1 (1663–1706), 1:28, 81–82, CSL.

43. Lacy, "Records," 1:77–78; *Crimes and Misdemeanors*, series 1 (1663–1706), 1:26–28, 107–14; and Nancy Steenburg, *Children and the Criminal Law in Connecticut, 1635–1855* (New York: Routledge, 2005), 64–68. In a modern ruling, *Thompson v. Oklahoma*, the U.S. Supreme Court in a five-to-three decision barred executions of juveniles younger than sixteen years old as a violation of the "cruel and unusual punishment" provision of the Eighth Amendment. Stuart Taylor, "Justices Put Age Limit on Executions," *New York Times*, Newspaper Clipping Files, CSL.

44. Lacy, "Records," 1:7–8; and Holdsworth, *Law and Society*, 384.

45. *Crimes and Misdemeanors*, series 1 (1663–1706), 1:182.

46. *Crimes and Misdemeanors*, series 1 (1663–1706), 1:174.

47. *Crimes and Misdemeanors*, series 1 (1663–1706), 1:26, 219–23; and Hoffer and Hull, *Murdering Mothers*, 61–62.

48. Charles J. Hoadly, ed., *The Public Records of the Colony of Connecticut*, vol. 4, *From August, 1689, to May, 1706* (Hartford: Case, Lockwood, and Brainard, 1868), 248; Hoffer and Hull, *Murdering Mothers*, x, xiii, 37; and McManus, *Law and Liberty*, 54, 118.

49. There is no positive record of Amy Mun's execution. Because she was found guilty as charged in the indictment, I find it more likely than not that she was hanged. See *Crimes and Misdemeanors*, series 1 (1663–1706), 1:26, 219–23.

50. Hoadly, *Records of . . . New Haven*, 577.

51. See Edmund Morgan, "The Puritans and Sex," *New England Quarterly* 15 (1942), 591–607; and John Demos, *A Little Commonwealth: Family Life in Plymouth Colony* (New York: Oxford University Press, 1970).

52. Hoadly, *Records of . . . New Haven*, 577.

53. William K. Holdsworth, "Adultery or Witchcraft: A New Note on an Old Case in Connecticut," *New England Quarterly* 48 (1975), 405n34. I differ from Holdsworth in dating Newberry's execution as late 1647, not 1648. The court convicted Newberry on December 2. Because executions usually occurred within three weeks of sentencing, I assume that he was hanged before January 1, 1648.

54. *Records of the Particular Court of Connecticut, 1639–1663*, 3; and Richard Goldbeer, *The Sexual Revolution in Early America* (Baltimore: Johns Hopkins University Press, 2002), 115. Lawrence M. Friedman, speaking generally of colonial justice, writes,

"Most of the thousands punished for petty crimes, and for fornication, idleness, and other forms of misconduct, were people at the bottom of the ladder. Ministers of the gospel and substantial merchants were rarely whipped, put in stocks, or branded. . . . The lash of the law, in all of the colonies fell overwhelmingly on servants, apprentices, slaves, smallholders, and laborers." *Crime and Punishment in American History* (New York: Basic Books, 1993), 51. Holdsworth adds, "When Connecticut convicted a gentleman of forgery, sedition, and a host of other serious crimes in 1664, the Particular Court fined him, imprisoned him, and stripped him of office and political privileges, though the magistrates thought he merited 'very sore corporal punishments, in various manners." *Law and Society, 666.*

55. *Records of the Particular Court of Connecticut, 1639–1663,* 13. Officials whipped the irrepressible Stark again in 1843 and put him in the service of Captain John Mason.

56. Spencer was the third New Englander put to death for bestiality in 1641–1642. William Hatchet of Salem and Thomas Granger of Plymouth were the other two. New Haven officials sought advice from Massachusetts in the Spencer case. Winthrop, *Journal,* 385n46.

57. Hoadly, *Records of . . . New Haven,* 62–63. The fetal monstrosity may not have been a teratoma. Nonetheless, consider Elizabeth Svoboda's description: "A tumor's encroachment is always terrifying, but teratomas, literally 'monster tumors,' exert a macabre hold on the imagination because they contain human elements remixed with Frankensteinian logic. It is not unusual for a teratoma to contain patches of hair, errant wedges of cartilage and even fully formed teeth." *New York Times,* June 6, 2006, D5.

58. Hoadly, *Records of . . . New Haven,* 64–68.

59. Hoadly, *Records of . . . New Haven,* 68.

60. Hoadly, *Records of . . . New Haven,* 69–73.

61. Hoadly, *Records of . . . New Haven,* 293–96.

62. Hoadly, *Records of . . . New Haven,* 295–96.

63. *Records of the Particular Court of Connecticut, 1639–1663,* 48–49.

64. Holdsworth, *Law and Society,* 411.

65. Winthrop, *Journal,* 771.

66. Hoadly, *Records of . . . New Haven,* 440–43; see also Dexter, *Ancient Town Records,* 3:1–2.

67. Cotton Mather, *Pillars of Salt* (Boston: B. Green and J. Allen, 1699), 63–66.

68. Hoadly, *Records of . . . New Haven,* 1656, 577; Leviticus 20:13; and Louis Compton, "Homosexuals and the Death Penalty in Colonial America," *Journal of Homosexuality* 1 (1976), 277–93. Connecticut maintained the wording of Leviticus 20:13 in its capital code until 1822.

69. Holdsworth, "Adultery," 405n34.

70. Winthrop, *Journal,* 629.

71. Dexter, *Ancient Town Records,* 2:30–32; and Hoadly, *Records of . . . New Haven,* 577.

72. Holdsworth, *Law and Society,* 417.

73. *Crimes and Misdemeanors,* series 1 (1663–1706), 1:39–40, 87–102.

74. Lacy, "Records," 1:67–68; and Cornelia Hughes Dayton, *Women before the Bar: Gender, Law and Society in Connecticut, 1639–1789* (Chapel Hill: University of North Carolina Press, 1995), 164n11. See Richard Godbeer, "'The Cry of Sodom': Discourse, Intercourse and Desire in Colonial New England," *William and Mary Quarterly* 52 (1995), 267–75. Godbeer emphasizes that the community tolerated Sen-

sion's homoeroticism over a long time. He neglects to mention that Sension suffered a severe punishment, one just short of execution, which undermines his argument. Class and social status are paramount factors in explaining why Plaine and Knight, but not Sension, were executed.

75. Holdsworth, "Adultery," 406; and Hoadly, *Records of . . . New Haven*, 577n.

76. Holdsworth, "Adultery," 407–8; and McManus, *Law and Liberty*, 174.

77. Crimes and Misdemeanors, series 1 (1663–1706), 1:32–33; Holdsworth, *Law and Society*, 384; Hoffer and Hull, *Murdering Mothers*, 45; and Dayton, *Women before the Bar*, 166.

78. Leviticus 20:11–12, 14, 17, 19–21.

79. Lacy, "Records," 1:35–37; J. Hammond Trumbull, ed., *The Public Records of the Colony of Connecticut*, vol. 2, *From 1665 to 1678* (Hartford: F. A. Brown, 1852), 184; Holdsworth, *Law and Society*, 542; Robert C. Black, *The Younger John Winthrop* (New York: Columbia University Press, 1966), 325; and Dayton, *Women before the Bar*, 276–77.

80. Lacy, "Records," 1:46.

81. Trumbull, *Public Records of the Colony of Connecticut*, 2:184n. Although the Puritans would not have embraced the divine right theory of Robert Filmer's *Patriarcha* (1680), the assumption of male rule as God's will was part of their worldview.

82. See Deuteronomy 22:22–28.

83. Cushing, ed., *The Earliest Laws*, 19, 83; and McManus, *Law and Liberty*, 31–32.

84. Dayton, *Women before the Bar*, 10.

85. Holdsworth, *Law and Society*, 423.

86. Dayton, *Women before the Bar*, 237–38.

87. *Crimes and Misdemeanors*, series 1 (1663–1706), 1:34, 197–201.

88. Hoadly, *Public Records of the Colony of Connecticut*, 4:32–33, 195 (John Rogers Jr. and William Wright, an Indian, aided Matthews's escape from the Hartford jail); and Lacy, "Records," 1:200–201.

89. Briggs's execution for adultery and infanticide occurred in New Haven in 1668. The date is shortly after the merger of the New Haven and Connecticut colonies.

90. See Leviticus 20:27 and Deuteronomy 18:10, 11.

91. Quoted in McManus, *Law and Liberty*, 142.

92. Quoted in Perry Miller, *The New England Mind: Colony to Providence* (Cambridge, Mass.: Harvard University Press, 1953), 184. William Perkins, *A Discourse of the Damned Art of Witchcraft* (London: Printer to the University of Cambridge, 1608), was a representative text that New England divines consulted on the subject.

93. Quoted in John M. Taylor, *The Witchcraft Delusion in Colonial Connecticut, 1647–1697* (Stratford: J. Edmund Edwards, 1969; originally 1908), 42.

94. See Carol F. Karlsen, *The Devil in the Shape of a Woman: Witchcraft in Colonial New England* (New York: W. W. Norton, 1986); Elizabeth Reis, "The Devil, the Body, and the Feminine Soul in Puritan New England," *Journal of American History* 82 (1995), 15–36; and Elizabeth Reis, *Damned Women: Sinners and Witches in Puritan New England* (Ithaca, N.Y.: Cornell University Press, 1997).

95. Data on witchcraft are in Taylor, *The Witchcraft Delusion;* R. G. Tomlinson, *Witchcraft Trials of Connecticut* (Hartford, Conn.: Bond Press, 1978); John Putnam Demos, *Entertaining Satan: Witchcraft and the Culture of Early New England* (New York: Oxford University Press, 1982); McManus, *Law and Liberty;* Richard Godbeer, *The Devil's Dominion: Magic and Religion in Early New England* (New York: Cambridge University Press, 1992); and Richard Godbeer, *Escaping Salem: The Other Witch Hunt of 1692* (New York: Oxford University Press, 2005). See also Paul S. Boyer and Stephen

Nissenbaum, *Salem Possessed: the Social Origins of Witchcraft* (Cambridge, Mass.: Harvard University Press, 1974); Mary Beth Norton, *In the Devil's Snare: The Salem Witchcraft Crisis of 1692* (New York: Knopf, 2002); and Richard Latner, "'Here Are No Newters': Witchcraft and Religious Discord in Salem Village and Andover," *New England Quarterly* 79 (2006), 92–122. On European witchcraft, see Norman Cohn, *Pursuit of the Millennium* (London: Secker and Warburg, 1957); Norman Cohn, *Warrant for Genocide* (New York: Harper and Row, 1967); H. R. Trevor-Roper, *The European Witch-Craze of the Sixteenth and Seventeenth Centuries, and Other Essays* (New York: Harper and Row, 1967); Keith Thomas, *Religion and the Decline of Magic* (London: Weidenfeld and Nicholson, 1971); H. C. Erik Midelfort, *Witch-Hunting in Southwestern Germany, 1582–1684* (Stanford, Calif.: Stanford University Press, 1972); Norman Cohn, *Inner Demons: An Enquiry Inspired by the Great Witch-Hunt* (New York: Basic Books, 1975); Christina Larner, *Enemies of God: The Witch-Hunt in Scotland* (Baltimore: Johns Hopkins University Press, 1981); Carlo Ginzburg, *The Night Battles: Witchcraft and Agrarian Cults in the Sixteenth and Seventeenth Centuries* (Baltimore: Johns Hopkins University Press, 1983); Brian Levack, *The Witch-Hunt in Early Modern Europe* (New York: Longman, 1995); Robin Briggs, *Witches and Neighbors: The Social and Cultural Context of European Witchcraft* (New York: Viking, 1996); James Sharpe, *Instruments of Darkness: Witchcraft in England, 1550–1750* (London: Hamish Hamilton, 1996); Stuart Clark, *Thinking with Demons: The Idea of Witchcraft in Early Modern Europe* (New York: Oxford University Press, 1997); and Lyndal Roper, *Witch Craze: Terror and Fantasy in Baroque Germany* (New Haven: Yale University Press, 2006).

96. Walter W. Woodward, "Prospero's America: John Winthrop, Jr., Alchemy, and the Creation of New England Culture" (Ph.D. diss., University of Connecticut, 2001), 307; and John Noble Wilford, "Transforming the Alchemists," *New York Times,* Aug. 1, 2006, D1, D4.

97. Quoted in Tomlinson, *Witchcraft Trials,* 60–62. A slander by one James Redfin in 1696 that Mercy Disborough bore an illegitimate child while a servant of Buckeley was strongly refuted. Buckeley confided to his nephew, "I can not but wonder at ye bloody malice of some men who, having by Good Providence missed theire marke, by taking away her life by one project would now do it, if possible, by another, for I can make no other construction out of it." The historical point is that once a woman was maligned as a witch, she was vulnerable to various accusations of wrongdoing. Gershom Buckeley to Joseph Buckeley, Jan. 3, 1696, manuscript 64768, Connecticut Historical Society, Hartford.

98. Increase Mather, "Cases of Conscience Concerning Evil Spirits, Personating Men, Witchcrafts, infalliable Proofs of Guilt in such as are accused with the crime" (Boston: Bemnjamin [sic] Harris, 1693), 66. Mather added, "I had rather judge a Witch to be an honest woman than judge an honest woman as a witch" (10). In contrast to his father's condemnation of spectral evidence, Cotton Mather published an apology for the Salem executions in October 1692 in which he validated its use. See *The Wonders of the Invisible World* (Bostun [sic]: John Dunton, 1693).

99. Quoted in David D. Hall, *Witch-hunting in Seventeenth-Century New England, 1638–1693* (Boston: Northeastern University Press, 1999), 349–50.

100. Quoted in Hall, *Witch-hunting,* 351.

101. Stephen Taylor Squires recounts his experience in recovering the past of Mercy Disbrow [a variant spelling] in *Are There Witches? Being a True Tale of Discovering a Fairfield Ancestor Accused of Witchcraft* (Mansfield, Conn.: n.p., 1995), 17-page pamphlet.

102. Jones recorded seven prerequisites, each of which might warrant examination, but not conviction or condemnation, of an alleged witch: (1) widespread accusations; (2) identification by a known witch; (3) death or mishap that followed a curse; (4) misdeeds that occurred after a quarrel or threat; (5) close association with a known witch; (6) witch marks, especially "teats" on the private parts of the body; and (7) contradictory responses to interrogation. These grounds for examining a witch were preliminary to establishing guilt or innocence. In medieval Aristotelian fashion, Jones noted, "For conviccion it must be grounded on just and sufficient proofes. The proofes for conviccion of 2 sorts, 1, Some be less sufficient, some more sufficient." He concurred with an unidentified author that extreme physical tests by red-hot iron and scalding water were "utterly condemned." So too he wrote the practice that a bound suspect who floated because she rejected the pure baptismal water was "supstitious and unwarrantable." Taylor, *The Witchcraft Delusion*, 40–41.

103. In Connecticut, several other accusations are worth noting. In 1692, Winifred Benham of Wallingford and Hugh Croasia of Stratford were accused in separate incidents of witchcraft, but grand juries dismissed the charges. Then, in 1697, the same accusers charged Benham and her thirteen-year-old daughter of witchcraft, a pairing of parent and offspring seen only before in Connecticut in the case of the Harveys in 1692. The case was heard by a special court in New Haven, which found no grounds for indictment and released the defendants. The family nonetheless found it prudent to move to New York and escape what was a bitter local quarrel. Winifred Benham's husband, Joseph Benham, at one point threatened to shoot antagonists of his wife and daughter. The Benham trial was the last of its kind in Connecticut. See Lacy, "Records," 1:263; and Taylor, *The Witchcraft Delusion*, 64–65, on the Benhams. See also *Crimes and Misdemeanors*, series 1 (1663–1706), 1:43–44, 186–87; Lacy, "Records," 1:193; Taylor, *The Witchcraft Delusion*, 117–19; and Tomlinson, *Witchcraft Trials*, 64.

2. The Emergence of Yankee Justice, 1700–1772

1. The era of the American Revolution would accelerate changes already in progress. See Gordon S. Wood, *The Radicalism of the American Revolution* (New York: Vintage, 1993).

2. On the shift from moral to property crimes, see Richard Gaskins, "Changes in the Criminal Law in Eighteenth-Century Connecticut," *American Journal of Legal History* 25 (1981), 309–42.

3. On the double standard for women, see Cornelia Hughes Dayton, *Women before the Bar: Gender, Law and Society in Connecticut, 1639–1789* (Chapel Hill: University of North Carolina Press, 1995).

4. See Max Weber, *The Protestant Ethic and the Spirit of Capitalism*, trans. Talcott Parsons (New York: Scribner, 1958); and Richard L. Bushman, *From Puritan to Yankee: Character and the Social Order in Connecticut, 1690–1765* (New York: W. W. Norton, 1967).

5. See Bernard Bailyn, "The Apologia of Robert Keayne," *William and Mary Quarterly* 7 (1950), 568–87. Keayne's guilt over his sharp business practices in seventeenth-century Boston is a foreshadowing from an individual example to the anxiety of the many a century later during a period of economic expansion.

6. In separate incidents in 1713 at Colchester, Joseph Chapman was convicted of bestiality with a cow, and John Brown with a mare. They were not hanged for the "horrible crime of buggery" even though sexual penetration had occurred. Instead,

they sat for one hour on the gallows with a rope around the neck and were whipped thirty-nine times. *Crimes and Misdemeanors,* series 1 (1707–1724), 2:4–5, 74–76, 83, 88, CSL. In 1770, a divided jury acquitted Thomas Alderman of the "fowl [*sic*] and unnatural crime" of bestiality. *Connecticut Courant,* Sept. 17, 1770, 2.

7. In 1724 at Colchester, Elizabeth Ackley charged Sarah Spencer, a poor, aged widow, with bewitching her. The local minister spoke up for Spencer, who turned the tables on her accuser by convicting her of slander. *Crimes and Misdemeanors,* series 1 (1702–1724), 2:36, 398–401, CSL.

8. Shortly after the decapitalization of incest, Thomas Hall and his daughter-in-law Hannah Rude in 1703 at Norwich were punished by a symbolic hanging, whipping, and wearing the letter *I.* Norbert B. Lacy, "The Records of the Court of Assistants of Connecticut, 1665–1701" (M.A. thesis, Yale University, 1937), 2:412–13; and *Crimes and Misdemeanors,* series 1 (1663–1706), 1:19–20, 322–30, CSL. The General Assembly in 1725 released Sarah Perkins from the above penalty for a conviction of incest with her father, because of her ignorance and repentance. *Crimes and Misdemeanors,* series 1 (1707–1721), 3:29, 42–43, CSL; and *Public Records,* 6:526.

9. For example, in 1701 William Hoadley of Branford impregnated Elizabeth Randall, whose husband had deserted her. Hoadley was fined and was made financially responsible for the child, but Elizabeth was "Severely whipt upon her naked body" for adultery. A clear sexual differentiation in punishment occurred: the man suffered a pecuniary penalty; the woman a corporal punishment. Lacy, *Records,* 1:358–59.

10. *Acts and Laws Passed by the General Court or Assembly of His Majesties Colony of Connecticut . . . 1717* (New London: T. Green, 1702–1776), 225. Adultery was defined as "any Man be found in Bed with another Mans wife." It was contingent on discovering the miscreants *in flagrante delictu,* and there was a sexual double standard. A married man who committed sexual intercourse with an unmarried woman was guilty of fornication, not adultery. The same standard did not apply to a married woman with an unmarried man. The patriarchal bias was to protect the purity of the husband's bloodline. On conviction, both were whipped no more than thirty stripes.

11. M. Louise Greene, *The Development of Religious Liberty in Connecticut* (Freeport, N.Y.: Books for Libraries Press, 1970; originally 1905); Albert E. Van Dusen, *Connecticut* (New York: Random House, 1961), 105–6; and Robert V. Wells, *The Population of the British Colonies in America before 1776: A Survey of Census Data* (Princeton, N.J.: Princeton University Press, 1975), 79. The population in 1670 was less than 10,000 but on the eve of the Revolution was 200,000. Jackson Turner Main, *Society and Economy in Colonial Connecticut* (Princeton, N.J.: Princeton University Press, 1983), 13.

12. See Anne Farrow, Joel Lang, and Jenifer Frank, *Complicity: How the North Promoted, Prolonged, and Profited from Slavery* (New York: Ballantine, 2005).

13. See Bruce Daniels, *The Connecticut Town: Growth and Development, 1635–1790* (Middletown: Wesleyan University Press, 1979).

14. Van Dusen, *Connecticut,* 114–16.

15. See Charles Grant, *Democracy in the Frontier Town of Kent* (New York: Columbia University Press, 1961).

16. See Philip Greven, *Four Generations: Population, Land and Family in Colonial Andover, Massachusetts* (Ithaca, N.Y.: Cornell University Press, 1970); Kenneth Lockridge, *A New England Town: The First Hundred Years: Dedham, Massachusetts, 1636–1736* (New York: W. W. Norton, 1970); James A. Henretta, *The Evolution of American Society, 1700–1815: An Interdisciplinary Analysis* (Lexington, Mass.: D. C. Heath, 1973), 38;

and Lawrence B. Goodheart, *Abolitionist, Actuary, Atheist: Elizur Wright and the Reform Impulse* (Kent, Ohio: Kent State University Press, 1990), chap. 1.

17. Leonard Woods Labaree and Catherine Fennelly, eds., *The Public Records of the State of Connecticut, From May 1793 through October 1796* (Hartford: published by the state, 1951), 8:87n3.

18. Charles J. Hoadly, ed., *The Public Records of the Colony of Connecticut*, vol. 5, *From October, 1706, to October, 1717* (Hartford: Case, Lockwood and Brainard, 1870), 5.

19. *Crimes and Misdemeanors*, series 1 (1756–1773), 5:30, 408–11, CSL; and *Connecticut Courant*, Oct. 27, 1772, 3.

20. Charles J. Hoadly, ed., *The Public Records of the Colony of Connecticut*, vol. 7, *From May, 1726, to May, 1735, Inclusive* (Hartford: Case, Lockwood and Brainard, 1873), 127–29.

21. Zara Jones Powers, ed., *Ancient Town Records*, vol. 3 (New Haven: New Haven Colony Historical Society, 1962), 794.

22. Lorenzo Johnston Green, *The Negro in Colonial New England, 1620–1776* (New York: Columbia University Press, 1942); Edgar J. McManus, *Black Bondage in the North* (Syracuse, N.Y.: Syracuse University Press, 1973); Ira Berlin, "Time, Space, and the Evolution of Afro-American Society on British Mainland North America," *American Historical Review* 85 (1980), 44–78; and Jackson Turner Main, *Society and Economy in Colonial Connecticut* (Princeton, N.J.: Princeton University Press, 1983).

23. Lacy, "Records," 1:534.

24. Hoadly, *Public Records of the Colony of Connecticut,* 5:52.

25. Charles J. Hoadly, ed., *The Public Records of the Colony of Connecticut*, vol. 6, *From May, 1717, to October, 1725* (Hartford: Case, Lockwood and Brainard, 1872), 340.

26. Hoadly, *Public Records of the Colony of Connecticut,* 7:290, 575n; and Albert E. Van Dusen, *Puritans against the Wilderness: Connecticut History to 1763* (Chester: Pequot Press, 1975), 98–99.

27. Van Dusen, *Connecticut,* 116; Greene, *The Development,* 101–7; and Bushman, *From Puritan to Yankee,* 147–48.

28. Bushman, *From Puritan to Yankee,* 149; and Greene, *The Development,* 129–30.

29. Greene, *The Development,* 138–46; Van Dusen, *Connecticut,* 166–67; and Bushman, *From Puritan to Yankee,* 150–51.

30. Greene, *The Development,* 158–59, 165.

31. Greene, *The Development,* 155–56.

32. Denise Schenk Grosskopf, "The Limits of Dissent in Seventeenth-Century Connecticut: The Rogerene Heresy" (Ph.D. diss., University of Connecticut, 1999).

33. Greene, *The Development,* 214–15; and Bushman, *From Puritan to Yankee,* 166–68.

34. On the Great Awakening in Connecticut, see Greene, *The Development,* 220–32, 270–72; Robert Sklar, "The Great Awakening and Colonial Politics: Connecticut's Revolution in the Minds of Men," *Connecticut Historical Society Bulletin* 28 (1963), 81–95; and Bushman, *From Puritan to Yankee,* 183–95. On broader issues, see Harry S. Stout, "Religion, Communication and the Ideological Origins of the American Revolution," *William and Mary Quarterly* 34 (1977), 519–41; and Jon Butler, "Enthusiasm Described and Decried: The Great Awakening as Interpretative Fiction," *Journal of American History* 69 (1982): 305–25.

35. Main, *Society and Economy,* 115.

36. See David Dutkanicz, ed., *Sinners in the Hands of an Angry God and Other Puritan Sermons* (Mineola, N.Y.: Dover, 2005), 178.

37. See Joshua Hempstead, *Diary of Joshua Hempstead of New London, Connecticut, Covering a Period of Forty-seven Years from September, 1711, to November, 1758* (New London: New London County Historical Society, 1901), 380, 406–7.

38. Greene, *The Development,* 242–51, 270–72; and Bushman, *From Puritan to Yankee,* 191.

39. Greene, *The Development,* 269; and Sklar, "The Great Awakening," 89–95.

40. See Everett C. Goodwin, *The Magistracy Rediscovered: Connecticut, 1636–1818* (Ann Arbor, Mich.: UMI Research Press, 1979), chap. 3; Bruce H. Mann, *Neighbors and Strangers: Law and Community in Early Connecticut* (Chapel Hill: University of North Carolina Press, 1987), 10, 168–69; Cornelia Hughes Dayton, "Turning Points and the Relevance of Colonial Legal History," *William and Mary Quarterly* 50 (1993), 12–13; and Joette Katz, "350 Years of the Death Penalty in Connecticut," *Connecticut Law Tribune* 25:17 (Apr. 25, 1994), 14.

41. Charles J. Hoadly, ed., *The Public Records of the Colony of Connecticut,* vol. 4, *From August, 1689, to May, 1706* (Hartford: Case, Lockwood and Brainard, 1868), 468.

42. Hoadly, *Public Records of the Colony of Connecticut,* 5:238.

43. *Acts and Laws of His Majesties Colony of Connecticut . . . [1702]* (Boston: Bartholomew Green and John Allen, 1702), 13.

44. *Acts and Laws [1702],* 13–14; and David H. Wrinn, "Manslaughter and Mosaicism in Early Connecticut Law," *Valparaiso University Law Review* (1986–1987), 284n43, 285n43, 293.

45. Hoadly, *Public Records of the Colony of Connecticut,* 5:351*.

46. J. Hammond Trumbull, ed., *The Public Records of the Colony of Connecticut,* vol. 2, *From 1665 to 1678* (Hartford: F. A. Brown, 1852), 184.

47. Hoadly, *Public Records of the Colony of Connecticut,* 5:351.

48. Hoadly, *Public Records of the Colony of Connecticut,* 6:144.

49. Quoted in Wrinn, 317; see also 307–11, 318.

50. Quoted in Charles M. Andrews, ed., *Reports on the Laws of Connecticut* (n.p.: Acorn Club, 1915), 5.

51. Quoted in Arthur M. Schlesinger, "Colonial Appeals to the Privy Council. II," *Political Science Quarterly* 28 (1913), 441–42.

52. Quoted in Andrews, *Reports,* 22.

53. *Acts and Laws, of His Majesties Colony of Connecticut in New-England* (New London: Timothy Green, 1715), 12–14.

54. Quoted in Andrews, *Reports,* 65.

55. Quoted in Andrews, *Reports,* 65–66.

56. Quoted in Andrews, *Reports,* 59.

57. See Adam Liptak, "Louisiana Court Backs Death in Child Rape," *New York Times,* May 23, 2007, A16.

58. *Crimes and Misdemeanors,* series 1 (1737–1755), 4:164–66, CSL; and Charles J. Hoadly, ed., *The Public Records of the Colony of Connecticut,* vol. 10, *From May, 1751, to February, 1757, Inclusive* (Hartford: Case, Lockwood and Brainard, 1877), 134–35. Hartford County Superior Court in 1768 imposed the penalty of the pillory, not the statutory death penalty, on Thomas Baldwin, a convicted blasphemer. *Connecticut Courant,* Feb. 8, 1768, 3. No one was ever executed for the crime in what is now Connecticut.

59. See Richard Gaskins, "Changes in the Criminal Law in Eighteenth-Century Connecticut," *American Journal of Legal History* 25 (1981), 309–12. In contrast, William E. Nelson places decisive changes in the criminal law of Massachusetts after, not before, the American Revolution—"Emerging Notions of Modern Criminal Law in the Revolutionary Era: An Historical Perspective," *New York Law Review* 42 (1967),

450–82. For New York, see Douglas Greenburg, *Crime and Law Enforcement in the Colony of New York, 1691–1776* (Ithaca, N.Y.: Cornell University Press, 1976), chap. 8.

60. *Connecticut Courant,* May 2, 1768, 3.

61. Gaskins, "Changes," 338–39.

62. Timothy Dwight, *A Statistical Account of the City of New Haven* (New Haven: Connecticut Academy of Arts and Sciences, 1811), 35–36; Christopher P. Bickford, ed., *Voices of the New Republic: Connecticut Towns, 1800–1832* (New Haven: Connecticut Academy of Arts and Sciences, 2003), 1:318.

63. Lacy, "Records," 2:435, 2:506–7.

64. Hoadly, *Public Records of the Colony of Connecticut,* 6:551, 7:23n.

65. *Crimes and Misdemeanors,* series 1 (1663–1706), 1:24, 384–87, CSL; and Lacy, "Records," 2:472.

66. Lacy, "Records," 2:796–801; Hoadly, *Public Records of the Colony of Connecticut,* 5:259; and *Crimes and Misdemeanors,* series 1 (1707–1724), 2:20, 66, CSL.

67. Hoadly, *Public Records of the Colony of Connecticut,* 5:28, which involves a 1707 murder in Fairfield; and Hoadly, *Public Records of the Colony of Connecticut,* 6:362, a Pequot man at New London in 1707 who was suspected of killing a "squaw."

68. Lacy, "Records," 2:435.

69. *Connecticut Courant,* Dec. 26, 1768, 3.

70. Timothy Pitkin, *A Sermon, Delivered at Litchfield, on the 2d Day of November, A.D. 1768 . . .* (Hartford: Green, and Watson, 1768), 4.

71. Pitkin, *Sermon,* 12.

72. Pitkin, *Sermon,* 13.

73. Pitkin, *Sermon,* title page.

74. *Crimes and Misdemeanors,* series 1 (1756–1773), 5:29–30, 362–64, CSL; and Samson Occom, *A Sermon Preached at the Execution of Moses Paul, an Indian . . .* (New Haven: T. Green, 1772), reprinted in *The Collected Writings of Samson Occom, Mohegan: Leadership and Literature in Eighteenth-Century Native America,* ed. Joanna Brooks (New York: Oxford University Press, 2006), 194–95. For a full account, see Ava Chamberlain, "The Execution of Moses Paul: A Story of Crime and Contact in Eighteenth-Century Connecticut," *New England Quarterly* 77 (2004), 414–50.

75. *Connecticut Courant,* Dec. 31, 1771.

76. *Crimes and Misdemeanors,* series 1 (1756–1773), 5:362–64, CSL; and *Connecticut Courant,* Dec. 17, 1771, 3.

77. *Crimes and Misdemeanors,* series 1 (1756–1773), 5:362–64, CSL; and *Connecticut Courant,* June 9, 1772, 3.

78. Occom, *Sermon,* 177; and *Connecticut Courant,* Sept. 8, 1772, 3.

79. Occom, *Sermon,* 188, 190.

80. Occom, *Sermon,* 192.

81. Occom, *Collected Writings,* 87, 176–95.

82. This and following from Occom, *Sermon,* 193.

83. Joseph Johnson, *Letter from J-h J-n, one of the Mohegan Tribe of Indians, to his Countryman, Moses Paul, under Sentence of death, in New Haven Gaol* (New London [?]: Timothy Green [?], 1772).

84. See John Wood Sweet, *Bodies Politic: Negotiating Race in the American North, 1730–1830* (Baltimore: Johns Hopkins University Press, 1973), 127–28; and www.mohegan.nsn.us, accessed May 25, 2007.

85. *Crimes and Misdemeanors,* series 1 (1756–1773), 5:28, 81–84, CSL. For two other homicides involving whites, juries ruled for manslaughter, not murder; see William Samuel Johnson, *The Superior Court Diary of William Samuel Johnson, 1772–1773,* ed.

John T. Farrell (Washington, D.C.: American Historical Association, 1942), xlv; and Lacy, "Records," 2:318.

86. Fairfield County Superior Court Files, 1720–1729, RG 3, box 2, CSL.

87. New Haven County Superior Court Files, 1728-1740, box 308, folder 15, CSL.

88. Lacy, "Records," 2:605.

89. New London County Court Files, African Americans, RG 3, box 2, folder 19, CSL.

90. New London County Court Files, African Americans, RG 3, box 2, folder 20, CSL. See Orlando Patterson, *Slavery and Social Death: A Comparative Study* (Cambridge, Mass.: Harvard University Press, 1982).

91. Lacy, "Records," 2:493.

92. Lacy, "Records," 2:490.

93. Hoadly, *Public Records of the Colony of Connecticut*, 5:62.

94. See Lacy, "Records," 2:485–93; Hoadly, *Public Records of the Colony of Connecticut*, 5:12, 28, 62; and *Crimes and Misdemeanors*, series 1 (1707–1724), 2:20, documents 4–6, CSL.

95. Charles J. Hoadly, ed., *Public Records of the Colony of Connecticut*, vol. 11, *From May, 1757, to March, 1762, Inclusive* (Hartford: Case, Lockwood and Brainard, 1880), 313, 590–91; and Richard Alfred Hunter, *Three Hundred Years of Psychiatry, 1535–1860* (New York: Oxford University Press, 1963), 436–37.

96. See Henretta, *Evolution*, 132–33.

97. Dayton, *Women*, chap. 1.

98. *Acts . . . 1702*, 13. Compare David Owens, "Woman Who Killed Her Baby Seeks Release," *Hartford Courant*, May 25, 2005. Dawn March was indicted for killing her baby by throwing her into the Housatonic River. March was the first person in Connecticut acquitted of infanticide based on a defense of postpartum psychosis. She claimed that voices told her to kill the six-month-old infant. Since the birth, she has had a tubal ligation.

99. Peter C. Hoffer and N. E. H. Hull, *Murdering Mothers: Infanticide in England and New England, 1558–1803* (New York: New York University Press, 1981), x, 38–39, 45, 80.

100. *Crimes and Misdemeanors*, series 1 (1663–1706), 1:25–26, 273–83, CSL; and Lacy, "Records," 2:381–82.

101. Nancy Hathaway Steenburg, *Children and the Criminal Law in Connecticut, 1635–1855: Changing Perceptions of Childhood* (New York: Routledge, 2005), 152.

102. For Abigail Wilson, see Steenburg, *Children*, 153. For Lucretia Smith, see *Crimes and Misdemeanors*, series 1 (1756–1773), 5:30, 240–242, CSL; and Charles J. Hoadly, ed., The *Public Records of the Colony of Connecticut*, vol. 12, *From May, 1762, to October, 1767, Inclusive* (Hartford: Case, Lockwood and Brainard, 1881), 390–91.

103. *Crimes and Misdemeanors*, series 1 (1737–1755), 4:34, 213–16, CSL.

104. *Crimes and Misdemeanors*, series 1 (1756–1773), 5:27, 198–99, CSL.

105. New London County Superior Court Files, Sept.–1736–Mar. 1738, folder "Katherine Garrett Execution 1737," CSL; *Crimes and Misdemeanors*, series 1 (1737–1755), 4:3, 33, CSL; and Frances Manwaring Caulkins, *History of New London, Connecticut* (New London: published by the author, 1852), 410.

106. Charles J. Hoadly, ed., The *Public Records of the Colony of Connecticut*, vol. 8, *From October, 1735, to October, 1743, Inclusive* (Hartford: Case, Lockwood, and Brainard, 1874), 122.

107. Eliphalet Adams, *A Sermon Preached on the Occasion of the Execution of Katherine Garrett (who Was Condemned for the Murder of her Spurious Child), On May 3, 1738* (New London: T. Green, 1738), 29–30.

108. Adams, *Sermon*, 37.

109. Adams, *Sermon*, 40.

110. Hempstead, *Diary*, 384.

111. Adams, *Sermon*, 43.

112. Adams, *Sermon*, 42.

113. Hartford County Superior Court Files, RG 3, box 86, CSL; Connecticut Superior Court Files, RG 3, vol. 11, 201, CSL. Kate pleaded not guilty.

114. Daniel Wadsworth, *Diary of Reverend Daniel Wadsworth* (Hartford: Case, Lockwood and Brainard, 1894), 100.

115. Wadsworth, *Diary*, 106.

116. Wadsworth, *Diary*, 106.

117. I am indebted to Robert Burgoyne of the Hampton Historical Society who provided me with copies of Angela Fichter's transcripts of the original judicial proceedings involving Elizabeth Shaw. Attorney Fichter spoke about Elizabeth Shaw on March 6, 2003, at the Hampton Historical Society.

118. Ellen D. Larned, *History of Windham County, Connecticut*, 2 vols. (Worcester, Mass.: published by the author, 1874, 1880), 288–89.

119. For an abortion in Pomfret that killed Sarah Grosvenor in 1742 and for which the two men involved escaped conviction, see Cornelia Hughes Dayton, "Taking the Trade: Abortion and Gender Relations in an Eighteenth-Century New England Village," *William and Mary Quarterly*, 3rd series, 48 (1991), 19–49.

120. "A brief Relation of a MURDER committed by ELIZABETH SHAW . . ." (New London: Timothy Green, 1772).

121. New London County Superior Court Files, box 12, Mar. 1753, case 13, and Box 7, Sept. 1753, case 35; Hempstead, *Diary*, 619; and Caulkins, *History of New London*, 468.

122. *Connecticut Courant*, June 18, 1770, 3, Sept. 17, 1770, 2.

123. See Winthrop D. Jordan, *White over Black: American Attitudes toward the Negro, 1550–1812* (Baltimore: Penguin, 1968); and compare Eldridge Cleaver, *Soul on Ice* (New York: Laurel/Dell, 1991).

124. *Acts and Laws* [1702], 12. Chief Justice Zephaniah Swift made clear in 1796 what had been earlier practice: "To constitute this crime, there must be actual penetration." *System of the Laws of the State of Connecticut: In Six Books* (Windham: Imprint, 1795–1796), 2:308.

125. New London County Court Files, African Americans, RG 3, box 2, folder 25, CSL.

126. *Crimes and Misdemeanors*, series 1 (1756–1773), 5:31, 47–53, CSL; and Dayton, *Women*, 256–58.

127. Hartford County Superior Court Files, 1742–1744, RG 3, box 11, folder 1743, *Rex v. Negro Man named Jack* (Sept. 1743), CSL; and Dayton, *Women*, 265–66.

128. *Pennsylvania Gazette*, July 7, 1743, 2, that was copied from a Boston notice of June 27.

129. *Crimes and Misdemeanors*, series 1 (1737–1755), 4:34, 71–73, CSL.

130. Wadsworth, *Diary*, 106.

131. Hartford County Superior Court Files, 1711–1899, RG 3, box 11 (1742–1744), CSL.

132. Hoadly, *Public Records of the Colony of Connecticut*, 8:579; and *Crimes and Misdemeanors*, series 1 (1737–1755), 4:67, CSL.

133. Connecticut Superior Court Files, RG 3, vol. 11 (Sept. 1741–Aug. 1745), 237, CSL; Hartford County Superior Court Files, RG 3, dockets, 1713–1806, box 101, CSL; and Hoadly, *Public Records of the Colony of Connecticut*, 8:579*.

134. On fears, unfounded in actuality, that black prisoners would castrate white guards held hostage at Attica Prison in 1971, see Tom Wicker, *Time to Die* (New York: Ballantine, 1975).

135. Connecticut Superior Court Files, RG 3, vol. 11 (Sept. 1741–Aug. 1745), 237, CSL; Hartford County Superior Court Files, RG 3, dockets, 1713–1806, box 101, CSL; and Hoadly, *Public Records of the Colony of Connecticut*, 8:579*. See Samuel Peters, *A General History of Connecticut* (Upper Saddle River, N.J.: Literature House/Gregg Press, 1970; originally 1781), 85. Daniel Allen Hearn, *Legal Executions in New England, 1623–1960* (Jefferson, N.C.: McFarland, 1999), 135–36, speculates that the punishment killed Barney, which is possible, but was not the literal intent of the court's sentence. The court directed that he be "discharged" from jail after the castration.

136. New Haven County Superior Court Files, Judicial Department, RG 3, 1712–1798, box 310, *Rex v. Cuff*, CSL; New Haven County Superior Court Files, drawer 327, CSL; and Dayton, *Women*, 265–68.

137. *Crimes and Misdemeanors*, series 1 (1737–1755), 4:34, 118–19, CSL.

138. *Crimes and Misdemeanors*, series 1 (1756–1773), 5:31–32, 144–46, CSL; Fairfield County Superior Court Files, RG 3, vol. 7 (Feb. 1760–March 1763), 44, *Rex v. Vanskelly Mully*, CSL; and Dayton, *Women*, 254–56.

139. *Crimes and Misdemeanors*, series 1 (1756–1773), 5:31–32, 144–46, CSL.

140. "An Act in Addition to the Law Entitled An Act against Theft and Burglary," in Hoadly, *Public Records of the Colony of Connecticut*, 7:561.

141. See, for example, Lacy, *Records*, 2:460; and *Connecticut Courant*, Sept. 17, 1770, 17, Dec. 30, 1767, 3, Sept. 12, 1768, 3, Dec. 19, 1768, 3.

142. *Connecticut Journal*, Apr. 8, 1768, 2.

143. *Connecticut Journal*, Aug. 26, 1768, 2; see also Apr. 29, 1768, 4, July 29, 1768, 2 Sept. 9, 1768, 4; and *Connecticut Courant*, May 2, 1768, 3, Sept. 12, 1768, 3 (quotation).

144. *A Brief Account of the Life and Abominable Thefts, of the Notorious Isaac Frasier, who was Executed at Fairfield, Sept. 7th, 1768, penned from his own Mouth, and signed by him a few Days before his Execution* (New Haven: T. & S. Green [1768]), cover.

145. See Karen Halttunen, *Murder Most Foul: The Killer and the American Gothic Imagination* (Cambridge, Mass.: Harvard University Press, 1998).

146. *A Brief Account*, 3.

147. *A Brief Account*, 6.

148. *Crimes and Misdemeanors*, series 1 (1756–1773), 5:5, 16, 246–48, 261, 302, CSL.

149. Noah Hobart, *Excessive Wickedness, the Way to an Untimely Death, a Sermon Preached at Fairfield, in Connecticut, September 7th, 1768, at the Execution of Isaac Frasier* (New Haven: Thomas and Samuel Green, 1768), 12.

150. Hobart, *Excessive Wickedness*, 21.

151. Hobart, *Excessive Wickedness*, 23–24.

152. *Connecticut Courant*, Aug. 22, 1764, 4.

153. Quoted in Lynn Hunt, *Inventing Human Rights: A History* (New York: W. W. Norton, 2007), 103.

154. *Connecticut Courant*, Aug. 22, 1764, 4.

155. Quoted at www.constitution.org/cb/crim_pun22.htm, accessed Apr. 17, 2007.

156. *Connecticut Courant*, Aug. 2, 1767, 4.

3. The Era of Newgate Prison, 1773–1827

1. Lynn Hunt, *Inventing Human Rights: A History* (New York: W. W. Norton, 2007). See also Arthur Koestler, *Reflections on Hanging* (New York: Macmillan, 1957).

2. *New Haven Gazette,* Apr. 6, 1786, 60–61. The serialized publication of Beccaria's book can be found in the newspaper from Jan. 12, 1786, through Aug. 3, 1786. The first English translation of *On Crimes and Punishment* appeared in 1768 in London.

3. *New Haven Gazette,* Jan. 12, 1786, 4.

4. See Louis P. Masur, "The Revision of the Criminal Law in Post Revolutionary America," *Criminal Justice History* 8 (1987), 21–36.

5. See Peter Linebaugh, *The London Hanged: Crime and Civil Society in the Eighteenth Century* (Cambridge: Cambridge University Press, 1992); V. A. C. Gatrell, *The Hanging Tree: Execution and the English People* (New York: Oxford University Press, 1994); Richard J. Evans, *Rituals of Retribution: Capital Punishment in Germany, 1600–1987* (New York: Oxford University Press, 1996); and Erick H. Monkkonen, *Murder in New York City* (Berkeley: University of California Press, 2001), 168.

6. Quoted in Eric Foner, ed., "Common Sense," *Thomas Paine: Collected Writings* (New York: Library of America, 1995), 5. See also Gordon Wood, *The Creation of the American Republic, 1776–1787* (Chapel Hill: University of North Carolina Press, 1969); and *The Radicalism of the American Revolution* (New York: A. A. Knopf, 1992).

7. Merrill D. Peterson, ed., *Writings / Thomas Jefferson* (New York: Literary Classics of the U.S., 1984), 349.

8. See Charles Roy Keller, *The Second Great Awakening in Connecticut* (New York: Anchor, 1942), chapters 1 and 2.

9. See Norbert Elias, *The Civilizing Process: the History of Manners,* trans. Edmund Jephcott (New York: Urizen, 1978); Thomas Bender, ed., *Antislavery Debate: Capitalism and Abolitionism as a Problem in Historical Interpretation* (Berkeley: University of California Press, 1992); and Hunt, *Inventing Human Rights,* for different perspectives on the foundations of humanitarianism.

10. *Crimes and Misdemeanors,* series 1 (1756–1773), 5:402, CSL.

11. *The Public Records of the State of Connecticut* (Hartford: Case, Lockwood and Brainard, 1894–), 2:271, hereafter cited as *State Public Records.*

12. See Stuart Banner, *The Death Penalty: An American History* (Cambridge, Mass.: Harvard University Press, 2002), chapter 2, for an overview of the United States.

13. Joel Barlow, *A Letter to the National Convention of France on the Defects in the Constitution of 1791 and the Extent of the Amendments which Ought to Be Applied* (London: J. Johnson, 1792), 58, 54, 55, 54.

14. Zephaniah Swift, *A System of Laws of the State of Connecticut: In Six Books* (Windham, Conn.: John Byrne, 1795–1796), 5:295.

15. Swift, *System,* 5:295.

16. Swift, *System,* 5:303–4.

17. Quoted in Keller, *Second Great Awakening,* 226.

18. *President Dwight's Decisions of Questions Discussed by the Senior Class in Yale College, in 1813 and 1814* (New York: Jonathan Leavitt; Boston: Crocker and Brewster, 1833), 8.

19. *President Dwight's Decisions,* 10, 11–12, 13.

20. Charles J. Hoadly, ed., *The Public Records of the Colony of Connecticut,* vol. 14, *From October, 1772, to April, 1775, Inclusive* (Hartford: Case, Lockwood and Brainard, 1887), 92–93, 205–8; and Noah Amherst Phelps, *A History of the Copper Mine and Newgate Prison, at Granby, Connecticut* (Hartford: Case, Tiffany and Burnham, 1845), 12–13.

21. *Crimes and Misdemeanors,* series 1 (1774–1778), 6:20, 350, CSL; and Hoadly, *Public Records of the Colony of Connecticut,* 14:206–8, 260.

22. Hoadly, *Public Records of the Colony of Connecticut,* 14:205–6.

23. Phelps, *History,* 12–16; *State Public Records,* 1:34, 261, 2:184; 7:118n.

24. Samuel Peters, *General History of Connecticut* (Upper Saddle River, N.J.: Literature House/Gregg Press, 1970; originally 1781), 143.

25. See "An Act containing an Abstract and Declaration of the Rights and Privileges of the People of this State, and securing the same," in *Acts and Laws of the State of Connecticut in America* (1784), 18, hereafter cited as *Acts* (year).

26. *State Public Records,* 1:4–5, 227, 365, 416; and Richard Gaskins, "Changes in the Criminal Law in Eighteenth-Century Connecticut," *American Journal of Legal History,* 25 (1981), 340.

27. *State Public Records,* 5:204; and *Crimes and Misdemeanors,* series 1 (1774–1788), 6:20, 234.

28. *State Public Records,* 5:323–24.

29. *Acts* (1784), 84; and Phelps, *History,* 17–18.

30. *State Public Records,* 7:118–20, 494.

31. *Acts* (1792), 458–59; and *State Public Records,* 5:494–95. For example, the following men were sentenced to imprisonment at Newgate for attempted rape: Thomas Evans for life in 1803; John Ely for life in 1804; Johann Jost Salim [?] for life in 1806; Samuel Rude for ten years in 1807; Deming Latimer for seven years in 1808; and Ezekiel Ball for life in 1813. See also, respectively, *Crimes and Misdemeanors,* series 2 (1671–1820), 4:119, CSL; *Crimes and Misdemeanors,* series 2 (1671–1820), 4:114–18, CSL; *Crimes and Misdemeanors,* series 2 (1671–1820), 4:135–36, CSL; *Crimes and Misdemeanors,* series 2 (1671–1820), 4:132–34, CSL; *Crimes and Misdemeanors,* series 2 (1671–1820), 4:121–23, CSL; and Petition of Ezekiel Ball, May 7, 1824, Rejected Bills, RG 2, box 7, folder 3, document 145, CSL.

32. *Acts* (1793), 494.

33. Juries were reluctant to convict under the 1699 statute. Such was the case for infanticide in general. See, for example, the case in 1791 of Prudence Foster, Saul Foster, and Hannah Bishop—New Haven County Superior Court Files, Judicial Department, 1712–1798, RG 3, box 322, CSL.

34. New London County Superior Court Files, Judicial Department, 1808–1809, RG 3, box 37, no. 123.

35. *Connecticut Courant,* Feb. 7, 1808, 1; and *State Public Records,* 14:xvii.

36. *Acts* (1808), 808.

37. *Crimes and Misdemeanors,* series 2 (1671–1820), 4:11, 92a–92b.

38. The phrases "a woman of colour" and "a black woman" are the racial designations, identifying her apart from white society, in the trial record. See New London County Superior Court Files, Judicial Department, 1808–1809, RG 3, box 37, no. 123, CSL.

39. New London County Superior Court Files, Judicial Department, 1808–1809, RG 3, box 37, no. 123, CSL.

40. *Crimes and Misdemeanors,* series 2 (1671–1820), 4: 11, 92c–92d, 93a, 96a–96b, CSL.

41. *Courier* (Norwich), June 1, 1808, 3; *State Public Records,* 14:55–56; and Nancy Hathaway Steenburg, *Children and the Criminal Law in Connecticut, 1635–1855: Changing Perceptions of Childhood* (New York: Routledge, 2005), 154.

42. *Acts* (1808), 808–9; *State Public Records,* 14:36–37, 55n32; and *Crimes and Misdemeanors,* series 2 (1671–1820), 4:8, 68–69, CSL.

43. Douglas Arnold, ed., *Public Records of Connecticut,* vols. 18 and 19 (Hartford: Connecticut State Library, 2007), 31.

44. *Crimes and Misdemeanors,* series 2 (1671–1820), 2:5, 57–58, CSL; *State Public Records,* 17:291–91; and *State Public Records,* 18:31, 31n17. Gaskin, "Changes," 337n118, is incorrect. The General Assembly overturned the verdict before Polly Rogers was branded.

45. *Crimes and Misdemeanors,* series 2 (1671–1820), 2:5, 57–58, CSL. Zephaniah Swift was the lead editor of the 1821 statutes, and I presume that the unattributed statement is his; see also *Stat. Conn. 1821,* 107, 107n1.

46. *Stat. Conn. 1821,* 103, 237, 310.

47. Christopher Reinhart, "Legislature's Power to Commute Death Sentences and Effect on Pending Cases," http://www.cga.ct.gov/2004/rpt/2004-R-0930. htm; and Richard Buel Jr. and George Willauer, eds., *Original Discontents: Commentaries on the Creation of Connecticut's Constitution of 1818* (Hartford: Acorn Club, 2007), 188, 191.

48. *Stat. Conn. 1821,* 97–108.

49. *Stat. Conn. 1821,* 121, 121n5.

50. *Connecticut Courant,* Mar. 27, 1781, 1.

51. See David Hackett Fischer, *Washington's Crossing* (New York: Oxford University Press, 2004).

52. Quoted in Albert E. Van Dusen, *Connecticut* (N.Y.: Random House, 1961), 144–45. See also *Connecticut Courant,* Jan. 27, Feb. 3, 1777; *Pennsylvania Evening Gazette,* Feb. 11, 1777, 72; and *Norwich Packet,* Mar. 17–24, 1777, 3.

53. Nathan Strong, *The Reasons and Design of Public Punishments: A Sermon Delivered before the People who Were Collected to the Execution of Moses Dunbar, who Was Condemned for High Treason Against the State of Connecticut, and Executed March 19, 1777* (Hartford: Ebenezer Watson, 1777), 17.

54. Henry Channing, *God Admonishing His people of Their Duty as Parents and Ministers* (New London: T. Green, 1786), second page of the unpaginated Appendix, which are probably not the words of the Reverend Channing.

55. Swift, *System of the Laws,* 2:368; Koestler, *Reflections,* 13–15; Steenburg, *Children,* 69–71; and Victor L. Streib, *Death Penalty for Juveniles* (Bloomington: Indiana University Press, 1987).

56. *Connecticut Journal* (New Haven), Oct. 25, 1786, 1. See also Oct. 11, 1786, 3; and *Connecticut Courant,* Oct. 9, 1786, 3.

57. *Crimes and Misdemeanors,* series 1 (1774–1788), 6:306a–306b, CSL.

58. Channing, *God Admonishing,* 6.

59. Channing, *God Admonishing,* 8.

60. *Connecticut Journal* (New Haven), Dec. 27, 1786, 3.

61. Channing, *God Admonishing,* 26–27.

62. Channing, *God Admonishing,* "Appendix"; *Connecticut Journal,* Dec. 27, 1786, 3; and, Frances Manwaring Caulkins, *History of New London, Connecticut* (New London: published by author, 1852), 576.

63. For a related study, see Victor L. Streib, *The Fairer Death: Executing Women in Ohio* (Athens: Ohio University Press, 2006). Only four women have been executed in Ohio since statehood in 1804. Streib finds a reluctance to execute women. "Masculine traits" displayed by a woman defendant accused of homicide, however, facilitated a capital conviction.

64. *Connecticut Courant,* Dec. 7, 1795, 3; and *Boston Courier,* Nov. 28, 1795, 175. See also Ellen D. Larned, *History of Windham County, Connecticut,* 2 vols. (Worcester, Mass.: published by the author, 1874, 1880), 2:290.

65. *American Mercury,* Aug. 9, 1816, 3.

66. *Connecticut Courant*, Sept. 6, 1815, 2; and Middlesex County Superior Court, Judgments, and Defaults, 1815–1816, RG 3, box 7, Dec. 19, 1815, CSL.

67. David D. Field, *Warning Against Drunkenness* (Middletown: Seth Richards, 1816), 25; Middlesex County Superior Court, Judgments, and Defaults, 1815–1816, RG 3, box 7, Sept. 6, 1815, CSL; and *State Public Records*, 17:480, 480n27, 513–14.

68. *Styles v. Tyler*, 64 Conn. 448 (1894). See I. Ridgeway Davis, David Mars, and Fred Kort, *Administration of Justice in Connecticut* (Storrs: Institute of Public Service, 1963), 24.

69. *Connecticut Courant*, Jan. 2, 1816, 3.

70. *Hamden Federalist* (Springfield, Mass.), Jan. 4, 1816, 3.

71. *Connecticut Courant*, Feb. 6, 1816, 3.

72. Zephaniah Swift, *A Vindication of the Calling of the Special Superior Court, at Middletown, on the 4th Tuesday of August, 1815* (Windham: J. Byrne, 1816), 4.

73. Swift, *Vindication*, 5.

74. Swift, *Vindication*, 11.

75. Swift, *Vindication*, 48.

76. *Connecticut Courant*, Mar. 19, 1816, 2; and *Middlesex Gazette* (Middletown), Apr. 11, 1816, 4.

77. Peter Lung, *Brief Account of the Life of Peter Lung* (Hartford: William S. Marsh, 1816). Marsh copyrighted the pamphlet on behalf of Lung and himself (as "proprietor") on March 11, 1816. Marsh sold the pamphlet at his Hartford bookstore.

78. Lung, *Brief Account*, 4.

79. Field, *Warning*, includes an afterword, "Sketch of the Life and Hopeful Repentance of Peter Lung."

80. Field, *Warning*, 19.

81. Field, *Warning*, 21.

82. *Connecticut Courant*, July 2, 1816, 3. The account is taken from the *Middlesex Gazette* (Middletown).

83. Field, *Warning*, 28.

84. On public opinion, see Gordon S. Wood, *Revolutionary Characters* (New York: Penguin, 2006), 245–75; and Christopher Grasso, *A Speaking Aristocracy: Transforming Public Discourse in Eighteenth-Century Connecticut* (Chapel Hill: University of North Carolina Press, 1999). On the Toleration Party, see Richard J. Purcell, *Connecticut in Transition, 1775–1818* (Middletown: Wesleyan University Press, 1963: originally 1918), chapter 8.

85. Field, *Warning*, 28.

86. *Connecticut Courant*, July 2, 1816, 3.

87. *Connecticut Courant*, July 2, 1816, 3.

88. *Connecticut Courant*, July 2, 1816, 3.

89. Field, *Warning*, 28.

90. Purcell, *Connecticut in Transition*, chapter 8.

91. *Connecticut Courant*, May 9, 1780, 3. Much of the story of Davenport is taken from Lawrence B. Goodheart, "Home Invasion—1780," *Hartford Courant*, Aug. 5, 2007, C3.

92. Barnett Davenport, *A Brief Narrative of the Life and Confession of Barnett Davenport* (n.p.: n.p., [1780?]), 8. The only known copy at the American Antiquarian Society is imperfect.

93. *Connecticut Gazette* (New London), May 19, 1780, 2.

94. Davenport, *Narrative*, 14.

95. *Connecticut Gazette* (New London), May 19, 1780, 2.

96. *Crimes and Misdemeanors,* series 1 (1774–1788), 6:119 (see also 118a–c, 120–21, 171–72), CSL.

97. *Norwich Courier,* June 12, 1816, 3. See also New London County Superior Court, Papers by subject: Inquest, c. 1711–1875, RG 3, A-M, box 134, Main Vault, CSL; New London County Record of Trials, 1798–1874, 14 vols., vol. 3 (Apr. 1810—Oct. 1817), RG 3, case 50, Jan. 1816, CSL; *Connecticut Courant,* July 5, 1815, Oct. 18, 181, Feb. 3, 1816, June 18, 1816, 3; and Steenburg, *Children,* 71–72.

98. *Connecticut Courant,* Nov. 20, 1805, 2; and Moses C. Welch, *Execution Sermon of Samuel Freeman . . .* (Windham: John Byrne, 1805), especially the "Appendix."

99. *Connecticut Courant,* May 4, 8, June 8, 1824, 3; *Connecticut Gazette,* May 12, 1824, 1; and Petition of Elijah Johnson, General Assembly Papers, RG 2, box 8, folder 20, document 114, archives, CSL. The General Assembly reimbursed Johnson, sheriff of Tolland County, $40 for the refreshment of a company of cavalry and light infantry.

100. Nathan Strong, *A Sermon Preached in Hartford, June 10, 1797, at the Execution of Richard Doane* (Hartford: Elisha Babcock, 1797), 11. See also *State Public Records,* 8:454, 454n15; and *Connecticut Courant,* June 12, 1797, 3.

101. "To Which is Added, A Short Account of his Life, As given by Himself," in Strong, *Sermon,* 20.

102. *Litchfield Monitor,* Nov. 15, 1785, 3; and *Connecticut Courant,* Aug. 29, 1785, 2.

103. *Connecticut Courant,* Aug. 29, 1785, 2.

104. *Connecticut Courant,* Mar. 1, 1785, 3.

105. *The Last Words and Dying Speech of Thomas Goss, in Private Conference, Previous to His Execution* [Connecticut?: n.p. 1778]; Crimes and Misdemeanors, ser. 1 (1774–1788), 6:26, 285–90; CSL; *State Public Records,* 6:131; *Connecticut Courant,* Aug. 22, 1785, 2, Nov. 28, 1785, 3; and *Litchfield Monitor,* Nov. 15, 1785, 3.

106. *Courier* (Norwich), Sept. 19, 1803, 3; *Connecticut Courant,* Sept. 28, 1803, 2; *Windham Herald,* Sept. 15, 1803, 3; and Elijah Waterman, *A Sermon Preached at Windham, November 29th, 1803, Being the Day of Execution of Caleb Adams, for the Murder of Oliver Woodworth* (Springfield, Mass.: Henry Brewer, [1803]), "Appendix," 21–23.

107. *Courier* (Norwich), Sept. 19, 1803, 3. See also Larned, *History of Windham County,* 2:291–92.

108. Waterman, *Sermon,* "Appendix," 27–29.

109. Waterman, *Sermon,* 8.

110. "Mr. Welch's Address at the Place of Execution," in Waterman, *Sermon,* 20.

111. Waterman, *Sermon,* "Appendix," 32.

112. *Connecticut Courant,* Dec. 14, 1803, 3. See also *Windham Herald,* Dec. 1, 1803, 3; and *Norwich Courier,* Dec. 7, 1803, 2.

113. *Connecticut Journal* (New Haven), Nov. 25, 1778, 3; and *Connecticut Courant,* Dec. 1, 1778, 2.

114. *Connecticut Courant,* Oct. 26, 1779, 3; and Christopher P. Bickford, *Voices of the New Republic: Connecticut Towns, 1800–1832,* 2 vols. (New Haven: Connecticut Academy of Arts and Sciences, 2003), 1:216, 450n58.

115. *Connecticut Courant,* May 1, 1781, 3; and *State Public Records,* 4:212.

116. *State Public Records,* 16:245–46.

117. *State Public Records,* 8:116–17.

118. *Connecticut Courant,* July 2, 1793, 3; *Vermont Journal,* Sept. 30, 1793, 2; and *State Public Records,* 8:117n27.

119. *State Public Records,* 8:87, 9:90n13; *Crimes and Misdemeanors,* series 2 (1671–1820), 4: 9, 74, CSL; *Conn. Statutes 1821,* 228; *Conn. Statutes 1824,* 314; and Edward W.

Capen, *The Historical Development of the Poor Law of Connecticut* (New York: Columbia University Press, 1905), 155.

120. See Lawrence B. Goodheart, *Mad Yankees: The Hartford Retreat for the Insane and Nineteenth-Century Psychiatry* (Amherst: University of Massachusetts Press, 2003), chap. 1.

121. Levi Hart, *Liberty Described and Recommended . . .* (Hartford: Eben. Watson, 1775), 14, 16, 18.

122. *State Public Records,* 14:329.

123. Theodore Dwight, *An Oration . . .* (Hartford: Hudson and Goodwin, 1794), 6. See also James Dana, *The African Slave Trade* (New Haven: Thomas and Samuel Green, 1791); Zephaniah Swift, *An Oration on Domestic Slavery* (Hartford: Hudson and Goodwin, 1791); and Noah Webster, *Effects of Slavery on Morals and Industry* (Hartford: Hudson and Goodwin, 1793). See also Dwight L. Dumond, *Antislavery: The Crusade for Freedom in America* (New York: W. W. Norton, 1966), 47.

124. *State Public Records,* 17:xviii, xviii n. 36, 49, 546. See also Buel and Willauer, *Original Discontents.*

125. See Anne Farrow, Joel Lang, and Jenifer Frank, *Complicity: How the North Promoted, Prolonged and Profited from Slavery* (New York: Ballantine, 2005).

126. New Haven County Superior Court Files, 1789–1790, RG 3, box 31, *Connecticut v. Joseph Mountain,* CSL; *Connecticut Journal,* June 2, 1790, 3, Aug. 11, 1790, 3, Aug. 18, 3; and *Connecticut Courant,* June 7, 1790, 3, Aug. 16, 1790, 3.

127. *Crimes and Misdemeanors,* series 2 (1671–1820), 4:16, 131.

128. James Dana, *The Intent of Capital Punishment* (New Haven: T. and S. Green, 1790), 6.

129. Dana, *Intent,* 7n.

130. Dana, *Intent,* 9.

131. Dana, *Intent,* 13.

132. *Connecticut Journal,* Oct. 20, 1790, 3, Oct. 27, 1790, 3. See also Daniel A. Cohen, "In Defense of the Gallows: Justification of Capital Punishment in New England Execution Sermons, 1674–1825," *American Quarterly* 40 (1988), 147–64.

133. *Connecticut Journal,* Oct. 27, 1790, 3.

134. [David Daggett], *Sketches of the Life of Joseph Mountain, A Negro . . .* (New Haven: T. & S. Green, 1790).

135. [Stephen Mix Mitchell], *A Narrative of the Life of William Beadle, Of Wethersfield . . .* (Hartford: Bavil Webster, 1783). Other editions appeared in 1794, 1795, 1796, and 1805, including a German language edition in Pennsylvania.

136. See Charles Brockden Brown, *Three Gothic Novels* (New York: Library of America, 1998); and Karen Halttunen, *Murder Most Foul: The Killer and the American Gothic Imagination* (Cambridge, Mass.: Harvard University Press, 1998).

137. *Connecticut Journal* (New Haven), Mar. 15, 1798, 3.

138. *Crimes and Misdemeanors,* series 2 (1671–1820), 4:109a, CSL.

139. Timothy Langdon, *A Sermon, Preached at Danbury, November 8th, A.D. 1798* (Danbury: Douglas and Nichols, 1798), 19.

140. Langdon, *Sermon,* 16.

141. Langdon, *Sermon,* 22.

142. *Connecticut Journal,* Dec. 15, 1798, 3; and James Montgomery Bailey, *History of Danbury, Conn., 1684–1896* (New York: Burr, 1896), 116–17.

143. *Connecticut Courant,* Sept. 9, 1817, 3.

144. Quoted in Peter Hinks, "How White or Black Must the Voter Be: The Parameters of Suffrage and the Constitution of 1818," in my possession.

145. William Andrews, *A Sermon, Delivered at Danbury, Nov. 13, 1817 . . .* (New Haven: T. G. Woodward, 1817), 13.

146. Andrews, *Sermon,* 15.

147. Andrews, *Sermon,* 16.

148. Andrews, *Sermon,* 17.

149. Andrews, *Sermon,* 18.

150. Andrews, *Sermon,* 18.

151. *Connecticut Courant,* Nov. 25, 1817, 2; and Bailey, *History,* 117–18.

152. Hartford County Superior Court Files, 1763–1849, RG 3, folder Mar. to Sept. 1783, CSL; *Connecticut Courant,* Mar. 18, June 10, 1783, 3; and *Connecticut Journal,* March 18, 1783, 3.

153. *Connecticut Courant,* June 10, 1783, 3. In 1786, the *New Haven Gazette* published verbatim Beccaria's tract calling for reforms in capital punishment.

154. *Crimes and Misdemeanors,* series 2 (1671–1820), 4:120a.

155. *Crimes and Misdemeanors,* series 2 (1671–1820), 4:124b. See also Fairfield County Superior Court Files, 1798–1808, RG 3, CSL; *State Public Records,* 12:244; *Litchfield Monitor,* Feb. 13, 1805, 3; *Republican Farmer* (Bridgeport), June 5, 1805, 3; and *Windham Herald,* June 13, 1805, 3.

156. Petition of Eli Lyon, May 20, 1818, RG 2, Rejected Bills, box 4, folder 19, document 123; and *Crimes and Misdemeanors,* series 2 (1671–1820), 4:126a.

157. *Connecticut Mirror* (Hartford), Dec. 3, 1821, 3; *The Times and Hartford Advertiser,* Jan. 15, 1822, 3; *Connecticut Courant,* Jan. 15, 1822, 3; *Middlesex Gazette,* Jan. 17, 1822, 3; *Rhode-Island American* (Providence), Jan. 22, 1822, 1; and *New Hampshire Gazette* (Portsmouth), Jan. 29, 1822, 3.

158. *The Times and Weekly Advertiser,* Dec. 4, 1821, 3.

159. Petition of Henry Wilson, African Americans, 1821–1869, RG 2, 1822, box 1, folder 2, documents 19–21, 38A-38C, CSL; Petition of Henry Wilson, African Americans, Rejected Bills, RG 2, 1810–1869, box 2, folder 4 (1825), documents 89–91, folder 5 (1828), documents 63–65, 73–74, 88–89, CSL; and Petition of Henry Wilson, African Americans, 1835, RG 2, 1821–1869, box 1, folder 12, 1835–1836, CSL.

160. *The Times and Hartford Advertiser,* June 4, 1822, 2; and *Middlesex Gazette,* June 6, 1822, 2.

161. Petition of Henry Wilson, African Americans, 1810–1869, Rejected Bills, RG 2, May 1826, box 7, folder 19, document 89, CSL.

162. *Litchfield Monitor,* Oct. 2, 1799, 1.

163. *Crimes and Misdemeanors,* series 2 (1671–1820), 2:87–89; and *State Public Records,* 9:437, 438n26.

164. *Litchfield Monitor,* Nov. 16, 1799, 3, Jan. 15, 1800, 3; and *Connecticut Courant,* Jan. 20, 1800, 3.

165. See Bickford, *Voices,* 1:133.

166. *Connecticut Courant,* June 9, 1772, 3.

167. *A poem, Wrote upon the Execution of a Man, who [was] Whipt, Cropt, and Branded at Fairfield, for burglary, the first Day of March, in the Year 1769* (New Haven: n.p., 1769). It is not clear if the verse is directed at John Brown. Nonetheless, the punishment described was the same.

168. Litchfield County Superior Court Files, 1770–1779, A–Z, RG 2, CSL; and *Crimes and Misdemeanors,* series 1 (1756–1773), 5:381–83, 390–95. The *Connecticut Courant* documents the criminal saga of Brown after 1770 in well over a dozen separate citations.

169. *Crimes and Misdemeanors,* series 2 (1671–1820), 2:70.

170. *Columbian Centinel* (Boston), Aug. 6, 1794, 3.

171. Denis R. Caron, *A Century in Captivity: the Life and Trials of Prince Mortimer, a Connecticut Slave* (Durham: University of New Hampshire Press, 2006).

172. Petition of [Theresa] Mansfield, General Assembly Papers, RG 2, Apr. 15, 1825, box 5, folder 13, document 20, CSL.

173. Report of the Committee on Newgate Prison [1825], General Assembly Papers, RG 2, box 6, folder 14, CSL.

174. Edward Kendall, *Travels through the Northern Parts of the United States in the Years 1807 and 1808,* 3 vols. (New York I. Riley, 1809), 1:215.

175. Kendall, *Travels,* 1:216.

176. *State Public Records,* 15:xiv–xv.

177. *Connecticut Courant,* May 3, 1815, 3.

178. *Crimes and Misdemeanors,* series 2 (1671–1820), 5:152; and *State Public Records,* 17:478, 478n25, 479n25.

179. *Report. Committee on Governor's Message regarding Penitentiaries and Newgate. May 1821,* General Assembly Papers, RG 2, box 1, folder 12, document 70, CSL; *Report of the Committee on Newgate* [1825], General Assembly Papers, RG 2, box 6, folder 14, document 8, CSL; and Gregg Mangan, "Newgate Prison in 1825: A Nursery of Crime," *Connecticut History* 47 (2008), 1–37.

180. Louis Dwight to Martin Wells, Hawley Olmsted, and Joseph Paton, May 20, 1826, document 5, Papers Related to Newgate Prison . . . 1822–1827, CSL.

4. The Debate over Capital Punishment, 1828–1879

1. *Public Statute Laws of the State of Connecticut, 1835* (Hartford: John B. Eldridge, 1835), section 146, 155. The law was passed in 1830, but a capital case lingering in the judicial system resulted in the last public execution in 1831.

2. For a detailed discussion of the development of the insanity defense in capital cases, see Lawrence B. Goodheart, "Murder and Madness: The Ambiguity of Moral Insanity in Nineteenth-Century Connecticut," in *Murder on Trial, 1620–2002,* ed. Robert Asher, Lawrence B. Goodheart, and Alan Rogers (Albany: State University of New York Press, 2005), 135–54.

3. See V. A. C. Gatrell, *The Hanging Tree: Execution and the English People* (New York: Oxford University Press, 1994), 610.

4. For example, where nativity is known, in 1831 there were three Irish born and thirty-five African Americans in the state prison; in 1855, thirty Irish born and thirty-three African Americans; in 1865, thirty-one Irish and eighteen African Americans; and in 1880, thirty-five Irish born and twenty-five African Americans. See the annual *Report of the Directors of the Connecticut State Prison* at the CSL.

5. *Report of the Directors and Warden of the Connecticut State Prison . . . 1829* (Hartford: C. Babcock, 1829), 10.

6. Basil Hall, *Travels in North America in the Years 1827 and 1828,* 3 vols. (Edinburgh: Cadell, 1829), 2:188.

7. Gustave de Beaumont and Alexis de Tocqueville, *On the Penitentiary System in the United States and Its Application in France* (Carbondale, Ill.: Southern Illinois Press, 1964), 28, 38.

8. Beaumont and Tocqueville, *On the Penitentiary System,* 121, 134, 129.

9. Mathew Carey, *Thoughts on Penitentiaries and Prison Discipline* (Philadelphia: Clark and Raser, 1831), 3.

10. *Report of the Directors and Warden of the Connecticut State Prison . . . 1828* (New Haven: Hezekiah Howe, 1828), 5.

11. *Report of the Directors and Warden of the Connecticut State Prison . . . 1830* (New Haven: H. Howe, 1828–1831), 7, 10.

12. *Report of the Directors of the Connecticut State Prison . . . 1834* (Hartford: John Russell, 1834), 33.

13. *Report of the Directors of the Connecticut State Prison . . . 1835* (Hartford: John Russell, 1835), 17–19.

14. Dorothea L. Dix, *Remarks on Prisons and Prison Discipline in the United States* (Philadelphia: Joseph Kite, 1845), 25.

15. Nathan Mayer, *Report on the State Prison and County Jails in Connecticut* (Hartford: Case, Lockwood and Brainard, 1873), 7, 5, 6.

16. *The General Statutes of the State of Connecticut: Revision of 1875,* 498.

17. *Norwich Courier,* May 12, 1830, 2.

18. *The General Statutes of Connecticut* (1866) (New Haven: John H. Benham, 1866), 292.

19. *Norwich Courier,* Aug. 10, 1831, 3.

20. *General Statutes . . . 1875,* 497.

21. Quoted in *Connecticut v. Dowd,* 19 Conn. 390, 391 (1849).

22. *General Statutes . . . 1866,* 247, reprints the 1846 law.

23. *General Statutes . . . 1875,* 498.

24. *Truth Stranger than Fiction. Lydia Sherman. Confession of the Arch Murderess of Connecticut . . .* (Philadelphia: T. R. Calender, 1873); *The Poison Fiend! Life, Crimes and Conviction of Lydia Sherman* (Philadelphia: Barclay, 1872); and *Hartford Daily Courant,* July 3, 8, 1871, 2, July 10, 12, 1871, 1, July 13, 1871, 4, and Jan. 8, 1873, 3.

25. *State v. Potter,* 18 Conn. 166, 175–76 (1846).

26. *Connecticut v. Watkins,* 9 Conn. 47, 54 (1831).

27. *Connecticut v. Dowd,* 19 Conn. 390, 392, 393 (1849).

28. *State v. John R. Johnson,* 40 Conn. 136, 144, 143–44 (1873)

29. *State v. John R. Johnson,* 41 Conn. 584, 585, 588 (1874).

30. *John Andersen v. The State,* 43 Conn. 514, 517, 526 (1876).

31. *John Andersen v. The State,* New Haven County Superior Court, Criminal Files, RG 3, no. 119, Archives, CSL.

32. Rejected Bills, RG 2, 1852, box 32, folder 7, document 31, CSL. See David Brion Davis, "The Movement to Abolish Capital Punishment in America," *American Historical Review* 63 (1957), 23–46.

33. Leonard Bacon, "Shall Punishment Be Abolished?," *New Englander* 4 (1846), 564.

34. Joseph Thompson, *Right and Necessity of Inflicting the Punishment of Death for Murder* (New Haven: J. M. Patten, 1842), 16–17, 50, 23, 50–51, 54.

35. Editorial, "Capital Punishment," *New Englander* 1 (1843), 33.

36. Jonathan Cogswell, *A Treatise on the Necessity of Capital Punishment* (Hartford: Elihu Geer, 1843), 27, 29, 57. See also W. T. Dwight, *Discourse on the Rightfulness and Expediency of Capital Punishments* (Portland, Maine: printed at the Temperance Office, 1843).

37. *Hartford Daily Courant,* May 12, 1841, 2, June 24, 1843, 2, and July 24, 1846, 2.

38. *Hartford Daily Courant,* May 12, 1842, 2.

39. *Colored American* (New York), July 18, 1840, 3. See also *Hartford Daily Courant,* June 21, 1840, 2, for further opposition to the death penalty.

40. See, for example, the May 1847 petition from Hampton—RG 2, Rejected Bills, folder 2, document 49a, CSL.

41. See RG 2, Rejected Bills, box 21, 1843–1844, folder 2, documents 27–29; box 23, 1846, folder 10, documents 35–36, 45–51; box 26, 1847, documents 40–53; box 32, 1852,

folder 7, document 100; box 35, 1853–1854, folder 1, documents 52–64; and General Assembly Papers, RG 2, box 58, 1850–1851. This tally is not definitive; there may well be more petitions in other collections, and some may not have made it to the archives.

42. *Hartford Daily Courant,* June 10, 1842, 2.

43. *Journal of the Senate of the State of Connecticut* (Hartford: Elihu Geer, 1842), 118–19; *Journal of the House of Representatives of the State of Connecticut* (New Haven: Osborn and Baldwin, 1842), 124–25; and *Report of the Joint Select Committee on that Part of the Governor's Message Relating to Capital Punishment,* General Assembly Papers, RG 2, 1842, box 35, folder 3, document 28, p. 10, CSL. Chauncey told the legislators, "I recommend that the punishment for death for crime be abolished and solitary imprisonment for life be substituted in its place." *Hartford Daily Courant,* May 9, 1842, 2.

44. *Journal of the Senate of the State of Connecticut* (New Haven: Osborn and Baldwin, 1843), 129–30; *Journal of the House of Representatives of the State of Connecticut* (Hartford: W. S. Williams, 1843), 132–33; [Chauncey Cleveland—Governor's Message], General Assembly Papers, RG 2, 1843, box 38, folder 3, document 1, p. 3; *Report of the Joint Select Committee on Capital Punishment* and *Report of the Minority Committee . . .* , Rejected Bills, RG 2, box 21, 1843–1844, folder 2, documents 26, 30.

45. *Message of His Excellency, Thomas H. Seymour . . .* (New Haven: Osborn and Baldwin, 1850), 11–12; and *Report of the Joint Select Committee on So Much of the Governor's Message as Relates to Capital Punishment . . .* (New Haven: Osborn and Baldwin, 1850), 35.

46. *Report of the Minority of the Joint Select Committee . . .* (New Haven: Osborne and Baldwin, 1850), 1. A minority of the committee, but the majority of the General Assembly, supported the current laws. See *Journal of the Senate of the State of Connecticut* (New Haven: Osborn and Baldwin, 1850), 188.

47. *Message of His Excellency, Thomas H. Seymour . . .* (Hartford: Boswell and Faxon, 1851), 10.

48. *Journal of the Senate of the State of Connecticut* (New Haven: Osborn and Baldwin, 1852), 197, 162; and *Journal of the Senate of the State of Connecticut* (Hartford: Alfred E. Burr, 1853), 269–70.

49. *Report of the Joint Select Committee on So Much of the Governor's Message as Relates to Capital Punishment* (New Haven: Osborn and Baldwin, 1852), 4, 9, 17.

50. *Report of the Minority of the Committee on Capital Punishment* (Hartford: Connecticut General Assembly, 1853), 8.

51. *Hartford Daily Courant,* June 29, 1854, 2; and *Report of the Joint Select Committee on Capital Punishment, June 27, 1854,* Rejected Bills, RG 2, 1853–1854, box 35, folder 12, document 81, CSL.

52. Bruce Clouette, "Irish-Americans in Hartford City Politics, 1850–1890," *Connecticut History* 34 (1993), 36; and Bruce Clouette, "Getting Their Share: Irish and Italian Immigrants in Hartford, Connecticut, 1850–1940" (Ph.D. diss., University of Connecticut, 1992).

53. See Mark Voss-Hubbard, *Beyond Party: Cultures of Anti-Partisanship in Northern Politics before the Civil War* (Baltimore: Johns Hopkins University Press, 2002).

54. *Windham County Advertiser,* May 26, 1830, reported in *Norwich Courier,* June 2, 1830, 2. See *Connecticut Courant,* May 18, 1830, 2; and *Norwich Courier,* May 26, June 2, 1830, 2.

55. *Connecticut Courant,* Oct. 19, 26, 1830, 2. See *Norwich Courier,* Oct. 20, 1830, 2, and Feb. 16, 1831, 3.

56. *State v. Watkins,* 9 Conn. 47, 51 (1831).

57. *Connecticut Courant,* Aug. 2, 1831, 3.

58. *Account of the Execution of Oliver Watkins (Convicted of the Murder of His Wife)* (broadside, 1831); see also *Brooklyn Advertiser,* Aug. 3, 1831, 3.

59. Henry Leander Foote, *A Sketch of the Life and Adventures of Henry Leander Foote . . .* (New Haven: T. J. Stafford, 1850).

60. Foote, *Sketch,* 53, 14.

61. Foote, *Sketch,* 43, 48, 43.

62. Isaac Minor, *A Poem on the Murder of Miss Emily Cooper, and Mrs. Olive Foote, in North Branford, Sept. 14, 1849* (New Haven: published by the author, 1850), 16.

63. William Goodwin, *Death Cell Scenes, or, Notes, Sketches and Memorandums of the Last Sixteen Days and Last Night of Henry Leander Foote; Together With an Account of His Execution for the Murder of Emily H. Cooper . . .* (New Haven: J. H. Benham, 1850), 2, 3, 22.

64. *New Haven Morning Journal and Chronicle,* Oct. 3, 1850, 2.

65. Goodwin, *Death Cell Scenes,* 30.

66. *Trial at Middletown, Conn., of Hall, Roberts, and Bell, for the Murder of Mrs. Lavinia Bacon* (Middletown: Charles H. Pelton, 1844), 39, 40.

67. *Trial at Middletown,* 37, 9.

68. *Hartford Daily Courant,* June 22, 1844, 2.

69. *Hartford Daily Courant,* July 26, 1853, 2; and *Constitution* [Middletown], July 27, 1853, 2.

70. *Hartford Daily Courant,* Feb. 9, 1854, 2; and *Trenton State Gazette,* Feb. 112, 1854, 2.

71. Rejected Bills, RG 2, 1853–1854, box 35, folder 12, documents 72–80, CSL.

72. Rejected Bills, RG 2, 1853–1854, box 35, folder 12, documents 66–68, CSL.

73. Rejected Bills, RG 2, 1853–1854, box 35, folder 12, document 69, CSL. See *Hartford Daily Courant,* Feb. 9, May 12, 22, 23, 24, 31, and June 1, 17, 24, 29, 1854—all on p. 2.

74. *Hartford Daily Courant,* July 12, 1854, 2; *Trenton State Gazette,* July 12, 1854, 2; and *Weekly Herald* [New York], July 15, 1854, 217.

75. See *Trial and Confession of Andrew P. Potter, for the Murder of Lucius P. Osborn* (New Haven: William Goodwin, 1845).

76. Joseph P. Thompson, *Lewdness and Murder* (New Haven: J. H. Benham, 1845), 4–5, 7, 11, 9.

77. Bacon, "Shall Punishment Be Abolished?," 568.

78. Thompson, *Lewdness and Murder,* 16, 18.

79. *Hartford Daily Courant,* Oct. 22, 1845, 2.

80. "Sundry Petitions for the Commutation of Andrew P. Potter; together with the Minority Report of the Committee thereon," RG 2, Rejected Bills, box 24, folder 6, documents 169–180, CSL.

81. *State v. Potter,* 18 Conn. 165–180 (1846).

82. *Confessions of Two Malefactors, Teller & Reynolds . . .* (Hartford: Hanmer and Comstock, 1833), 69–70, 50, 58.

83. *The Times and Hartford Advertiser,* Sept. 10, 1822, 2.

84. *Confessions,* 73.

85. See *Confessions,* 2–42.

86. See *Confessions,* 43–47, 71–73; and *Connecticut Courant,* May 7, 1833, 3, May 14, 1833, 2, May 27, 1833, 2.

87. *Confessions,* 77–78.

88. *Confessions,* 78; RG 3, Conn. Superior Court, Hartford County Records, 1798–1952, Vol. 5–9, 1830–1842, box 15–69B, 214–17, CSL; and *Connecticut Courant,* May 20, 1833, 3.

89. RG 2, Rejected Bills, African Americans, 1810–1869, box 2, folder 7, 1833, CSL.

90. RG 2, Rejected Bills, African Americans, 1810–1869, box 2, folder 6, folder 27, 1833, CSL.

91. RG 2, Rejected Bills, African Americans, 1810–1869, box 2, folder 6, folders 29–30, 1833, CSL.

92. *Norwich Courier,* May 29, 1833, 2, 3.

93. *Connecticut Courant,* June 17, 1833, 3.

94. *Confessions,* 82; RG 2, General Assembly papers, African Americans, 1821–1869, box 1, folder 9, 1833, CSL; and *Connecticut Courant,* June 6, 1833, 2.

95. *Confessions,* 83–84; and *Connecticut Courant,* June 19, 26, 1833, 3.

96. *Confessions,* 81–82; and *Connecticut Courant,* July 1, 1833, 3.

97. *Connecticut Courant,* Sept. 9, 1833, 3; and *Norwich Courier,* Sept. 11, 1833, 2.

98. RG 3, Superior Court, Hartford County Files, 1764–1864, Feb.–Sept. 1833, *State v. William Teller,* alias *John Scott,* Warrant of Execution, May 18, 1833, CSL.

99. *Confessions,* 43.

100. RG 3, Superior Court, Hartford County Files, 1764–1864, Feb.–Sept. 1833, *State v. William Teller,* alias *John Scott,* Warrant of Execution, May 18, 1833, CSL.

101. *Connecticut Courant,* Sept. 9, 1833, 1.

102. *Hartford Daily Courant,* Mar. 28, 29, 1962, 2; *Middletown Constitution,* May 2, 1862, 2; and *Report of the Directors of the Connecticut State Prison, 1862,* 5, 18.

103. Gerald Toole, *An Autobiography of Gerald Toole* (Hartford: Case, Lockwood, 1862), 3, 27.

104. *Hartford Daily Courant,* June 20, 25, 1862, 2.

105. *Hartford Daily Courant,* June 22, 1862, 2.

106. Toole, *Autobiography,* 26.

107. *Hartford Daily Courant,* Sept. 20, 1862, 2.

108. *Hartford Daily Courant,* Aug. 15, 16, 1870, 2.

109. *Hartford Daily Courant,* August 15, 2, Nov. 2, 1870, 2; and Records of the Department of Correction, 1827–1960, RG 017, Series 1, Wethersfield Prison Records, Warrants for Commitment, 1800–1903, CSL.

110. [Amherst, N.H.], *Farmer's Cabinet,* Oct. 18, 1870, 2; *Trenton State Gazette,* August, 16, 1870, 2; *Pittsfield Sun,* Sept. 1, 1870, 2; and *Hartford Daily Courant,* Feb. 16, 1870, 2, Oct. 14, Nov. 2, 1870, 2.

111. *Hartford Daily Courant,* Oct. 14, 1871, 2.

112. *Middletown Constitution,* Oct. 12, 1870, 2; *Amherst [N.H.] Farmer's Cabinet,* Oct. 13, 1870; *Hartford Daily Courant,* Sept. 29, Oct. 5, 1870, 2; and *State v. Wilson,* 38 Conn. 126 (1871).

113. *Amherst [N.H.] Farmer's Cabinet,* Oct. 13, 1870, 2.

114. *Wilson,* 38 Conn. 126; and *Hartford Daily Courant,* Mar. 3, 11, 1871, 2.

115. *Hartford Daily Courant,* Mar. 22, 1871, 2; and *Philadelphia Inquirer,* Mar. 28, 1871, 4.

116. *Hartford Daily Courant,* June 24, 1871, 2.

117. *Hartford Daily Courant,* Oct. 13, 1871, 2.

118. *Hartford Daily Courant,* Oct. 14, 1871, 2.

119. *Hartford Daily Courant,* May 8, 1844, 2.

120. Nancy Hathaway Steenburg, *Children and the Criminal Law in Connecticut, 1635-1855; Changing Perceptions of Childhood* (New York: Routledge, 2005), 73–74; and *Connecticut Courant,* May 7, 1833, 2; RG2, Rejected Bills, 1846, box 24, folder 17, document 86, CSL; and RG2, Rejected Bills, 1851, box 31, folder 17, document 51, CSL. I thank Kevin Johnson for these last two citations.

121. New Haven County, Superior Court, Criminal Files, 1797–1899, RG 2, box 532, 1841–1846, A–Z, case 256, CSL; *Resolutions and Private Acts, 1842,* 8; and *Hartford Daily Courant,* June, 4, 1842, 2.

122. *Hartford Daily Courant,* June 17, 1842, 2.

123. *State v. John R. Johnson,* 40 Conn. 136, 142 (1873).

124. C. Gardiner, ed. *Speeches and Public Correspondence of Ratcliffe Hicks* (N.p.: University Press Cambridge, 1896), 266.

125. *State v. John R. Johnson,* 40 Conn. at 143–44.

126. *State v. John R. Johnson,* 41 Conn. 584, 588 (1874).

127. *Speeches . . . Ratcliffe Hicks,* 269.

128. *Hartford Daily Courant,* Oct. 24, 1842, 2; and New Haven County, Superior Court, Criminal Files, 1797–1899, RG 3, box 552, 1841–1846, A–Z, case 257, CSL.

129. General Assembly Papers, African Americans, 1821–1869, RG 2, 1843, box 1, folder 17, CSL.

130. General Assembly Papers, African Americans, 1821–1869, RG 2, 1843, box 1, folder 17, CS; see also and *Hartford Daily Courant,* June 20, 26, 1843, 2.

131. Rejected Bills, 1841–1842, RG 2, box 20, folder 6, documents 78–81, CSL; and *Hartford Daily Courant,* June 11, 1842, 2.

132. *Hartford Daily Courant,* June 6, 12, 1848, 2.

133. African Americans, 1821–1869, RG 2, box 1, 1849, folder 19, folders 21–27, CSL.

5. The Menace of the Criminal Class, 1880–1929

1. David R. Meyer, *From Farm to Factory to Urban Pastoralism: Urban Change in Central Connecticut* (Cambridge, Mass.: Ballinger, 1976); Jeremy Brecher, Jerry Lombardi, and Jan Stackhouse, *Brass Valley: The Story of Working People's Lives and Struggles in an American Industrial Region* (Philadelphia: Temple University Press, 1982); Cecilia Bucki, *Bridgeport's Socialist New Deal, 1915–1936* (Urbana: University of Illinois Press, 2001); and David K. Leff, "Nicknames Recall Town's Gilded Heyday," *Hartford Courant,* Feb. 17, 2008, C4.

2. *Historical Census Statistics on the Foreign Born Population of the United States, 1850–1990* (Washington, D.C.: U.S. Bureau of the Census, 1999); Sando Bologna and Richard M. Marano, *Growing Up Italian and American in Waterbury* (Portland, Conn.: Waverly, 1997); and Bruce M. Stave and John F. Sutherland with Aldo Salerno, *An Oral History of the European Migration to America* (New York: Twayne, 1993).

3. *General Statutes of Connecticut, Revision of 1902,* 349; see also Paul Avrich, *The Haymarket Tragedy* (Princeton, N.J.: Princeton University Press, 1984).

4. See Robert J. Embardo, "'Summer Lightning,' 1907: The Wobblies in Bridgeport," *Labor History* 30 (1989), 518–35.

5. *General Statutes of Connecticut: Revision of 1918,* 1712. This revision occurred in 1903.

6. *General Statutes of Connecticut, Revision of 1902,* 348.

7. Robert Wiebe, *The Search for Order, 1877–1920* (New York: Hill and Wang, 1967).

8. *Hartford Daily Courant,* Apr. 7, 1883, 1.

9. *Public Acts . . . 1883,* 753–55; *General Statutes . . . 1902,* 753; and *Palka v. Walker,* 124 Conn. 121 (1938).

10. *Hartford Daily Courant,* Dec. 4, 1883, 3.

11. *Hartford Daily Courant,* May 4, 1883, 2.

12. Edward Wilson, *Sociobiology: The New Synthesis* (Cambridge, Mass.: Harvard University Press, 1975).

13. "About Hanging Women," *Hartford Courant*, July 7, 1917, 8.

14. "How James Plew Killed Wakefield" and "Plew Meets Fate Without a Quiver," *Hartford Courant*, Mar. 4, 1914, 10, 1.

15. "Bessie Wakefield Guilty of Murder," *Hartford Courant*, Nov. 1, 1913, 1.

16. "Movement to Save Bessie Wakefield," *Hartford Courant*, Nov. 11, 1913, 1. See also "State Suffragists Protest Hanging," *Hartford Courant*, Nov. 22, 1913, 5.

17. "Should a Woman Hang for Murder?" *Hartford Courant*, Dec. 12, 1913, 7.

18. "Mrs. Wilson Asked to Use Her Influence," *Hartford Courant*, Mar. 8, 1914, 5.

19. "Orphan Girl Writer: 'Don't Kill the Lady,'" *Hartford Courant*, Nov. 26, 1913, 1.

20. "Child Executed in This State," *Hartford Courant*, Nov. 5, 1913, 11.

21. *Connecticut v. Bessie J. Wakefield*, 88 Conn. 174 (1914); and "Supreme Court Grants New Trial to Bessie Wakefield," *Hartford Courant*, Apr. 17, 1914, 1.

22. "Escapes Gallows to Live in Prison," *Hartford Courant*, July 13, 1914, 2; and "Bessie Wakefield Begins Life Term," *Hartford Courant*, Aug. 7, 1914, 2.

23. "About Murder," *Hartford Courant*, Apr. 18, 1914, 8.

24. "Board Frees Woman, Held for 19 Years," *Hartford Courant*, Nov. 7, 1933, 1.

25. In the indictment, Cross stated, "I raped her until I satisfied my passion." Justice Alberto T. Roraback of Fairfield County Superior Court instructed the jury in more qualified description of the sexual assault, "The defendant was perpetrating or attempting to perpetrate the crime of rape, and thereby caused her death." The State of *Connecticut v. Charles B. Cross*, 72 Conn. 722, 723, 726 (1900).

26. "Misplaced Sympathy," *Hartford Courant*, July, 19, 1900, 10.

27. "Negro Murderer of Henry Osborn Didn't Leave House," *Hartford Courant*, Aug. 6, 1904, 1.

28. "Plea for Watson by Counsel," *Hartford Courant*, Sept. 30, 1904, 11.

29. "Watson to Die November 17," *Hartford Courant*, Oct. 1, 1904, 11.

30. "Did Marx Kill Two Other Men?" *Hartford Courant*, Aug. 31, 1904, 13.

31. "'Innocent' Was Marx's Last Word," *Hartford Courant*, May 18, 1905, 1.

32. See *Historical Census Statistics on the Foreign Born Population of the United States, 1850–1900*.

33. "Imposino Hanged," *Hartford Courant*, Dec. 17, 1897, 1.

34. "Judge Case Alone to Decide Fate of Simonelli Slayer," *Hartford Courant*, Oct. 10, 1917, 4; and "Wild Scene in Court As Murderers Are Sentenced," *Hartford Courant*, Oct. 5, 1917, 4.

35. "Two Pay Penalty for Italian Feud," *Hartford Courant*, Nov. 16, 1917, 1.

36. "Confess Killing Man for Sake of Watch," *Hartford Courant*, Nov. 29, 1916, 20; and "Three Gunmen Pay Penalty of Death," *Hartford Courant*, June 17, 1918, 1.

37. "Goes to Delaware on Zebris Case," *Hartford Courant*, Mar. 16, 1915, 1.

38. "Lithuanian Affairs," Hartford Courant, July 26, 1915, 8; see also "'Not Guilty,' Cries Montvid, Just As Trap Is Sprung," *Hartford Courant*, Aug. 16, 1915, 1; and "Father Zebris Baptized Montvid," *Hartford Courant*, June 18, 1915, 1.

39. See Charles S. Johnson, *The Negro Population of Hartford* (New York: National Urban League, 1921).

40. "Why He Killed Osborn," *Hartford Courant*, Sept. 29, 1904, 11.

41. "Negro Murderer of Henry Osborn Didn't Leave House," *Hartford Courant*, Aug. 6, 1904, 1.

42. "Watson to Be Tried on September 27," *Hartford Courant*, Sept. 2, 1904, 3.

43. "Watson on Trial for His Life," *Hartford Courant*, Sept. 28, 1904, 1.

44. "Negro Murderer of Henry Osborn Didn't Leave House," *Hartford Courant*, Aug. 6, 1904, 1.

45. "Why He Killed Osborn," *Hartford Courant*, Sept. 29, 1904, 11.

46. "Negro Murderer of Henry Osborn Didn't Leave House," *Hartford Courant*, Aug. 6, 1904, 1.

47. I found no evidence of any lynching or extrajudicial vigilantism that Susan D. Pennybacker cites in "The Life and Death of Joseph Watson: Anniversary of an Execution," *Northeast*, Nov. 17, 1996, 15. She wrote, "The state's most recent lynching had occurred less than 20 years before when a white man accused of murder was hanged by his neighbors in Litchfield County without benefit of trial or jury." No reference is provided for this putative event or any others in Connecticut. I did find accounts of two attempted lynchings in the Litchfield area roughly at the time period mentioned, but they involved sexual assaults, not homicide. See "The Rascal Caught; Miss Cook's Assailant in Jail in Litchfield—He Escaped Lynching," *Hartford Courant*, Apr. 22, 1889, 6; and "The New Milford Outrage: An Attempt at Lynching Prevented—the Man in Litchfield Jail," *Hartford Courant*, May 21, 1889, 6. Moreover, I have found no record of an actual lynching—an extrajudicial execution of an alleged criminal—taking place at any time in what is now Connecticut.

48. "Negro Murderer of Henry Osborn Didn't Leave House," *Hartford Courant*, Aug. 6, 1904, 1.

49. "Plea for Watson by Counsel," *Hartford Courant*, Sept. 30, 1904, 11.

50. "City News in Brief," *Hartford Courant*, Nov. 18, 1904, 8; and "Watson's Message from the Gallows," *Hartford Courant*, Nov. 21, 1904, 6.

51. A document in my possession from the research of David Ransom in preparing Spring Grove Cemetery for nomination in the National Register of Historic Places, June 12, 2008.

52. "Chinese Hanged for Murder of Laundry Worker," *Hartford Courant*, Nov. 8, 1927, 1.

53. "Tong Buries Executed Men with Honors," *Hartford Courant*, Nov. 11, 1927, 1.

54. "Hangman's Noose," *Hartford Daily Courant*, Sept. 2, 1882, 2; and "'Chip' Smith's Last Home," *Hartford Daily Courant*, Sept. 1, 1882, 2.

55. "A Murderer's Funeral," *Hartford Daily Courant*, Sept. 4, 1882, 3.

56. Newspapers had variant spellings of Pallidona, which reflected a lack of fluency with Italian by English speakers. "Palladona Dying," *Hartford Daily Courant*, Apr. 24, 1888, 4; "Philip Palladoni," *Hartford Daily Courant*, Oct. 5, 1888, 2; "Philip Palladini," *Hartford Daily Courant*, Oct. 6, 1888, 1; "Pallidoni's Grave," *Hartford Daily Courant*, Oct. 8, 1888, 1.

57. "'Innocent' Was Marx's Last Word," *Hartford Courant*, May 18, 1905, 1.

58. "Did Marx Kill Two Other Men?" *Hartford Courant*, Aug. 31, 1904, 13; and "'Innocent' Was Marx's Last Word," *Hartford Courant*, May 18, 1905, 1.

59. "Hebrews Want New Trial for Saxon," *Hartford Courant*, Jan. 24, 1913, 17.

60. "Saxon's Only Hope in Federal Action," *Hartford Courant*, June 26, 1913, 11.

61. "Louis Saxon Loses Hope of Retrial," *Hartford Courant*, Apr. 19, 1913, 6; and "Saxon Hanged; Appeared Sane," *Hartford Courant*, June 27, 1913, 1.

62. "Wise Is Cool and Unshaken on Stand in Murder Trial," *Hartford Courant*, Oct. 30, 1917, 2.

63. "Wise Refuses to Change His Story of Cutting Affray," *Hartford Courant*, Sept. 21, 1917, 4; and "W.J. Wise Executed at State Prison," *Hartford Courant*, Dec. 14, 1917, 1.

64. "A Disgrace All Around," *Hartford Courant*, Sept. 26, 1903, 10.

65. See *Connecticut v. Joseph Buonomo*, 88 Conn. 177 (1914).

66. "Mrs. Schutte Urges Husband to Leave with Clean Heart," *Hartford Courant*, Oct. 24, 1922, 1.

67. "Mrs. Schutte Urges Husband to Leave with Clean Heart," *Hartford Courant*, Oct. 24, 1922, 1; see also "Expert Asserts Bones Found in Haddam Are Those of Human Being," *Hartford Courant*, May 27, 1921, 1; and "Aged Prisoner Admitted Burning Body of LaDuc," *Hartford Courant*, July 7, 1921, 1.

68. "Schutte Kisses His Children Farewell," *Hartford Courant*, Oct. 23, 1922, 1; and "Schutte Under Spell of Terror Hanged As He Clutches Flowers," *Hartford Courant*, Oct. 24, 1922, 1.

69. "Negro Murderer of Henry Osborn Didn't Leave House," *Hartford Courant*, Aug. 6, 1904, 1.

70. "Grela Must Pay the Death Penalty," *Hartford Courant*, July 1, 1915, 3.

71. "The Nichols Murder," *Hartford Courant*, Dec. 9, 1897, 11; "To Save Her Brother," *Hartford Courant*, Dec. 10, 1897, 11; and "Said He Died Happy," *Hartford Courant*, Apr. 15, 1898, 8.

72. "Benjamin Willis's Crime," *Hartford Courant*, Dec. 28, 1898, 5; see also "Confession a Surprise," *Hartford Courant*, May 5, 1898, 2; "Benjamin Willis Hanged," *Hartford Courant*, Dec. 30, 1898, 1; and "Brockhaus Hanged," *Hartford Courant*, Sept. 6, 1899, 1.

73. "Led to Murder by Infatuation," *Hartford Courant*, Mar. 1, 1912, 1.

74. "Redding Keeps His Nerve to The Last," *Hartford Courant*, Nov. 1, 1912, 1.

75. "A Disgrace All Around," *Hartford Courant*, Sept. 26, 1903, 10.

76. "The State Prison Murderers," *Hartford Daily Courant*, Apr. 25, 1879, 1.

77. "'Chip' Smith's Last Hours," *Hartford Daily Courant*, Sept. 1, 1882, 2.

78. "Murderer Scheele," *Hartford Courant*, May 2, 1889, 6.

79. "The Chapman Problem," *Hartford Courant*, Oct. 16, 1924, 16; and "Chapman Executed," *Hartford Courant*, Apr. 6, 1926, 16.

80. "Pleads Rum As Excuse," *Hartford Courant*, Feb. 8, 1889, 5; "The Case of Young Swift," *Hartford Courant*, Feb. 14, 1889, 4; "Saves His Neck," *Hartford Courant*, Mar. 29, 1889, 2; "Murderer Swift," *Hartford Courant*, Apr. 6, 1889, 3; "About Swift," *Hartford Courant*, Apr. 11, 1889, 8; "Voting by Request," *Hartford Courant*, Apr. 13, 1889, 4; and "The General Assembly," *Hartford Courant*, Apr. 13, 1889, 4.

81. "Premeditated Murder," *Hartford Daily Courant*, July 8, 1887, 2.

82. "The Case of Swift," *Hartford Courant*, Apr. 9, 1889, 4.

83. Editorial, "For Women to Think Of," *Hartford Courant*, Mar. 29, 1889, 4; and "Law Appeased," *Hartford Courant*, Apr. 19, 1889, 1.

84. "Kippie Found Guilty," *Hartford Courant*, Feb. 5, 1897, 8; and "Kippie's Last Hours," *Hartford Courant*, July 13, 1897, 3.

85. "Imposino Hanged," *Hartford Courant*, Dec. 17, 1897, 1.

86. "Negro Murderer of Henry Osborn Didn't Leave House," *Hartford Courant*, Aug. 6, 1904, 1.

87. "Grela Dies Tonight on Prison Gallows," *Hartford Courant*, June 12, 1915, 7; and "Woman May Have Done Slashing," *Hartford Courant*, Sept. 20, 1917, 2.

88. "Chapman Executed," *Hartford Courant*, Apr. 6, 1926, 16.

89. "Chapman Arrested After Long Search," *Hartford Courant*, Jan. 19, 1925, 1.

90. See RG 5, John H. Trumbull, 1925–1931, box 324A, flat file box, Letters, telegrams, etc. pertaining to Gerald Chapman, CSL. Petitions are on pp. 44–76, a death threat is on p. 32, and Kerr's comments are on p. 184.

91. Editorial, "The Chapman Problem," *Hartford Courant*, Oct. 16, 1924, 16.

92. "Hang Chapman, Dead at 12:13," "Crowd of 300 Follows Body of Chapman," and "Reprisals Feared As Chapman Dies," *Hartford Courant*, Apr. 6, 1926, 1.

93. "Chapman Executed," *Hartford Courant*, Apr. 6, 1926, 1.

94. "Life for Life," *Hartford Daily Courant*, May 13, 1880, 1.

95. "Life for Life," *Hartford Daily Courant*, May 13, 1880, 1.

96. "Life for Life," *Hartford Daily Courant*, May 13, 1880, 1.

97. "Hangman's Noose," *Hartford Courant*, Sept. 2, 1892, 2.

98. "Litchfield's Murderer," *Hartford Courant*, Jan. 11, 1892, 1; "The Litchfield Hanging," *Hartford Courant*, Jan. 13, 1892, 1; and "Sheriff Tomlinsen's Views," *Hartford Courant*, July 18, 1894, 4.

99. "Petrillo to Hang," *Hartford Courant*, Oct. 21, 1892, 6; and "Petrillo Executed," *Hartford Courant*, Nov. 15, 1892, 3.

100. "Sheriff Tomlinsen's Views," *Hartford Courant*, July 18, 1894, 4; see also "Petrillo Executed," Harford Courant, Nov. 15, 1892, 3.

101. *General Statutes . . . 1902*, 416–17.

102. Editorial, "A Capital Punishment," *Hartford Daily Courant*, Feb. 14, 1876, 2.

103. "Old Hanging Machine Will Come Down," *Hartford Courant*, Apr. 9, 1936, 2.

104. "How Cronin Will Hang," *Hartford Courant*, Aug. 1, 1894, 1; and "Forced to Execute Himself," *New York Times*, Dec. 18, 1894, 3.

105. "The Gallows Approved," *Hartford Courant*, July 10, 1894, 5.

106. "The Gallows Approved," *Hartford Courant*, July 10, 1894, 5.

107. RG 5, John H. Trumbull, 1925–1931, box 324A, flat file box, Letters, telegrams, etc. pertaining to Gerald Chapman, p. 136, Apr. 1926, CSL.

108. "Model Gallows Tested," *Hartford Courant*, May 14, 1894, 4; "How Cronin Will Hang," *Hartford Courant*, Aug. 1, 1894, 5; "Cronin Must Hang," *Hartford Courant*, Dec. 4, 1894, 3; and "John Cronin Talks," *Hartford Courant*, Dec. 17, 1894, 3.

109. "Cronin Hanged," *Hartford Courant*, Dec. 18, 1894, 1.

110. "Forced to Execute Himself," *New York Times*, Dec. 18, 1894, 3.

111. "Zuppa Execution Quickest on Record," *Hartford Courant*, Mar. 10, 1916, 17.

112. "Trap Sprung Twice for One Murder," *Hartford Courant*, Feb. 2, 1909, 1.

113. "Williams and Roe Hanged; Denying Guilt to the Last," *Hartford Courant*, Mar. 3, 1916, 1.

114. "Deaf Mutes Pay Penalty Calmly," *Hartford Courant*, Oct. 5, 1917, 1.

115. "Two Pay Penalty for Italian Feud," *Hartford Courant*, Nov. 16, 1917, 1.

116. "Three Gunmen Pay Penalty for Death," *Hartford Courant*, June 17, 1918, 1.

117. "Perrettas, Near Collapse, Pay Murder Penalty," *Hartford Courant*, June 27, 1919, 1.

118. "Cerone [Cerrone] Moans As Trap Is Sprung," *Hartford Courant*, Mar. 5, 1920, 1.

119. "No Confession; Sherrie Hanged," *Hartford Courant*, Jan. 1, 1906, 1.

120. "Partial Confession Made by Murderer before Execution," *Hartford Courant*, Dec. 3, 1919, 1.

121. "Hang Chapman, Dead At 12:13," *Hartford Courant*, Apr. 6, 1926, 1.

122. "Chinese Hanged for Murder of Laundry Worker," *Hartford Courant*, Nov. 8, 1927, 1.

123. John Kelly, "John Feltovic Is Hanged for Store Murder," *Hartford Courant*, Dec. 10, 1929, 1.

124. "The Death Penalty," *Hartford Courant*, Dec. 14, 1929, 14.

125. *General Statutes . . . 1902*, 382.

126. *Public Acts Passed by the General Assembly . . . 1909*, 1135–36; see also Harry Hamilton Laughlin, *Eugenical Sterilization in the United States* (Chicago: Psychopathic Laboratory of the Municipal Court of Chicago, 1922), 19; and J. H. Landman, *Human Sterilization: The History of the Sexual Sterilization Movement* (New York: Macmillan, 1932), 289, 291.

127. Simeon E. Baldwin, "Whipping and Castration As Punishments for Crime," *Yale Law Journal* 8 (1899), 371–86. Baldwin recalled that whipping was an effective punishment for African American criminals.

128. *The Menace of the Feeble-Minded in Connecticut* (Lakeville: Connecticut School for Imbeciles, between 1912 and 1915).

129. Stephen Jay Gould, *The Mismeasurement of Man* (New York: W. W. Norton, 1981).

130. "The Pallidoni [*sic*] Murder Trial," *Hartford Courant*, Sept. 21, 1887, 6; and "Philip Palladini [*sic*]," *Hartford Courant*, Oct. 6, 1888, 1.

131. "Guiseppe Fuda Hanged," *Hartford Courant*, Dec. 3, 1897, 1.

132. "Story of the Murder," *Hartford Courant*, Dec. 18, 1894, 1.

133. "Kippie Found Guilty," *Hartford Courant*, Feb. 5, 1897, 8.

134. "A Disgrace All Around," *Hartford Courant*, Sept. 26, 1903, 10.

135. "Charles B. Cross Hanged," *Hartford Courant*, July 20, 1900, 7.

136. "Negro Murderer of Henry Osborn Didn't Leave House," *Hartford Courant*, Aug. 8, 1904, 1.

137. "Bailey Must Die, Hanging April 16," *Hartford Courant*, Apr. 9, 1907, 3.

138. "James Plew Born of Long Lineage Cradled in Crime," *Hartford Courant*, Jan. 12, 1914, 3.

139. Francis Wayland, *Opening Address Before the American Social Science Association, at its Annual Meeting, Saratoga Springs, Sept. 3d, 1833, on Capital Punishment* (New Haven: Hoggron and Robinson, 1883), 18.

140. C. Gardiner, ed. *Speeches and Public Correspondence of Ratcliffe Hicks* (N.p: University Press Cambridge, 1896), 17, 20.

141. *Hartford Courant*, Feb. 18, 1893, 4, and Mar. 22, 1893, 8.

6. The Waning of Executions, 1930–1960

1. Electrocution, Section 1727C, *Cumulative Supplement to the General Statutes. Revision of 1930. January Sessions, 1931, 1933, 1935* (Hartford: printed by the state, 1935), 751.

2. "Kemmler's Execution," *Hartford Courant*, Oct. 10, 1890, 1; "Killed by Electricity," *Hartford Courant*, July 8, 1891, 1; and Mark R. Essig, *Edison and the Electric Chair* (New York: Walker, 2003).

3. Gilbert King, "Cruel and Unusual History," *New York Times*, Mar. 23, 2008, A25.

4. "Electrocution Proposed at State Prison," *Hartford Courant*, May 3, 1935, 16; "Electric Chair in Place of Hanging at Prison Sought from Legislature," *Hartford Courant*, May 18, 1935; "Prison Will Put Electric Chair in Soon," *Hartford Courant*, June 20, 1935, 16; and "Old Hanging Machine Will Come Down," *Hartford Courant*, Apr. 9, 1936, 2.

5. George Ross Wells, "Connecticut Goes Modern," *Hartford Courant*, Oct. 11, 1935, 11.

6. "State Won't Hire Own Executioner, Cummings Says," *Hartford Courant*, Aug. 7, 1953, Capital Punishment, Clipping File, 1939–1992, CSL.

7. M. S. Richmond to Robert J. Beckwith, RG 5, Office of the Governor, Abraham Ribicoff, 1855–1961, box 647, folder Capital Punishment, CSL; and Gerald J. Demeusy, *Ten Weeks of Terror: A Chronicle of the Making of a Killer* (N.p.: n.p., 2002), 5.

8. "Plea Is Lost by McElroy, Waits Chair," *Hartford Courant*, Feb. 2, 1937, 12.

9. *New York Review of Books*, Apr. 10, 2003, 52.

10. "McElroy Is Executed at State Prison," *Hartford Courant*, Feb. 11, 1937, 1; and "M'Elroy Is Executed," *New York Times*, Feb. 11, 1937, 5.

11. *New Haven Journal Courier,* Mar. 25, 1959, in Office of the Governor, Abraham Ribicoff, 1955–1961, RG 5, box 648, folder 3, CSL.

12. Demeusy, *Ten Weeks,* 1.

13. Demeusy, *Ten Weeks,* 145.

14. Demeusy, *Ten Weeks,* 8–11. See Gerald J. Demeusy, "Witness for the Execution," *Hartford Courant (Northeast),* Jan. 10, 1988, Capital Punishment, Clipping File, 1939–1992, CSL; and Edwin M. Kent, "One Waved Farewell," *Hartford Times Sunday Magazine,* Feb. 9, 1969, Capital Punishment, Clipping File, 1939–1992, CSL.

15. "Study of Murders Key to Death Penalty Debate," *Hartford Times,* Mar. 25, 1961.

16. "Murder of Samuel Kamaroff," *Hartford Courant,* Feb. 21, 1930, 1.

17. "DiBattista's Verdict Just, Court Asserts," *Hartford Courant,* Jan. 25, 1930, 1.

18. "The DiBattista Case," *Hartford Courant,* Feb. 20, 1930, 14.

19. "Plea for Lorenz Fails: Youth Will Be Hanged for Anderson Slaying," *Hartford Courant,* June 24, 1930, 1.

20. "Usefulness of Gallows," *Hartford Courant,* Apr. 8, 1930, 10.

21. "Lorenz and Death Penalty," *Hartford Courant,* Apr. 14, 1930, 10.

22. "John Simborski Put to Death Early Today," *Hartford Courant,* Apr. 7, 1936, 1.

23. "John Simborski Put to Death Early Today," *Hartford Courant,* Apr. 7, 1936, 1.

24. "Plea Is Lost by McElroy, Waits Chair," *Hartford Courant,* Feb. 2, 1937, 1.

25. *Palka v. Walker,* 124 Conn. 121 (1938); and I. Ridgway Davis, David Mars, and Fred Kort, *The Administration of Justice in Connecticut* (Storrs: Institute of Public Service, University of Connecticut, 1963), 104–7.

26. "Frank Palka Executed in Wethersfield," *Hartford Courant,* Apr. 13, 1938, 1.

27. "The Case of Frank Palka," *Hartford Courant,* Oct. 17, 1936, 10.

28. "Bound Over," Harford Courant, July 16, 1931, 2.

29. "Justice Tempered with Mercy," *Hartford Courant,* Nov. 5, 1931, 14; see also "Father Makes Klim Confess," July 16, 1931, 1; and "Windsor Slayers Saved from Death by Pardons Board," *Hartford Courant,* Nov. 3, 1931, 1.

30. "3 Indicted for Murder in Fairfield County," *Hartford Courant,* Jan. 12, 1935, 7; "Must Die June 4 for Norwalk Murder," *Hartford Courant,* Mar. 6, 1935, 22; and "Santella, Doomed to Die, Gets 15 Years in Retrial," *Hartford Courant,* Feb. 8, 1936, 5.

31. "John Palm Held Insane, Life Saved," *Hartford Courant,* Feb. 25, 1938, 1; and "Palm's Sentence Is Commuted to Life by Board," *Hartford Courant,* Mar. 19, 1938, 1.

32. "Jury Finds Trio Guilty of Murder," *Hartford Courant,* July 4, 1945, 1.

33. "Three Guard Slayers Are Electrocuted," *Hartford Courant,* Oct. 2, 1946, 2.

34. "Jury Finds Trio Guilty of Murder," *Hartford Courant,* July 4, 1945, 1.

35. Demeusy, *Ten Weeks,* 182–84.

36. "Funderburk Put to Death for Murder," *Hartford Courant,* Apr. 21, 1943, 1.

37. "Two Confess Killing of Mrs. Wegner," *Hartford Courant,* Sept. 27, 1943, 1; "Stolen Auto Brings Back Two Negroes," *Hartford Courant,* Sept. 28, 1943, 1; "Robert Rossi Wins Change of Sentence," *Hartford Courant,* June 12, 1945, 12; and "Elder Rossi Pays Penalty for Slaying," *Hartford Courant,* June 19, 1945, 1.

38. "State Board Final Resort for Bradley," *Hartford Courant,* Feb. 2, 1948, 2; "Robert Bradley Pays Penalty for Murder of Three Men," *Hartford Courant,* Apr. 13, 1948, 1; and Demeusy, *Ten Weeks,* 112–13.

39. "Two Slayers Scheduled to Die Tonight," *Hartford Courant,* Apr. 30, 1940, 1; and "Cotts, Weaver Pay Penalty for Slaying," *Hartford Courant,* May 1, 1940, 1.

40. "Thomaston Woman Slain by Attacker," *Hartford Courant,* July 2, 1942, 22; "Hunch Leads to Arrest in Terryville Murder," *Hartford Courant,* July 3, 1942, 16;

"Peter Gurski Convicted in Murder Case," *Hartford Courant,* Oct. 17, 1942, 1; and "Gurski Is Electrocuted at Prison for Slaying of Woman in Plymouth," *Hartford Courant,* Feb. 24, 1943, 1.

41. "Nine Jurors Selected for DeCaro Trial," *Hartford Courant,* Dec. 2, 1943, 3; "Youth Guilty, Must Die in Chair in May," *Hartford Courant,* Dec. 16, 1943, 1; and "Slayer Dies in Chair at State Prison," *Hartford Courant,* Apr. 4, 1944, 6.

42. "Youth Guilty, Must Die in Chair in May," *Hartford Courant,* Dec. 16, 1943, 1.

43. "Robert Bradley Pays Penalty for Murder of Three Men," *Hartford Courant,* Apr. 13, 1948, 1.

44. Affectator, "It Does Not Permit Murder," *Hartford Courant,* July 10, 1945, 8.

45. "Bridgeport Slayer Gets Life Term," *Hartford Courant,* Apr. 4, 1943, 2; and Gerald J. Demeusy, "Pardons Board Cuts Murderer's Sentence," *Hartford Courant,* Apr. 8, 1958, Crime, Clipping File, CSL. In 1958, the board granted Richards clemency, and he was released from prison.

46. "Board of Pardons Will Hear Murder Pleas February 15," *Hartford Courant,* Jan. 20, 1943, 7.

47. "Two Youths, 16, Are Given Life Terms," *Hartford Courant,* June 17, 1944, 1.

48. "Robert Rossi Convicted of Murder," *Hartford Courant,* Apr. 28, 1945, 2; and "Robert Rossi Wins Change of Sentence," *Hartford Courant,* June 12, 1945, 12.

49. "Peterson's Sentence Commuted," *Hartford Courant,* Aug. 14, 1945, 1.

50. Albert Camus, "Reflections on the Guillotine," in *Resistance, Rebellion and Death* (New York: Vintage, 1974), 175–234; and Arthur Koestler, *Reflections on Hanging* (New York: Macmillan, 1957).

51. Camus, *Reflections on the Guillotine,* 194.

52. Gunnar Myrdal, *The American Dilemma* (New York: Harper, 1944).

53. "Judge Henchel—A Profile," *New Haven Journal,* Mar. 26, 1959, Capital Punishment, Clipping File, 1939–1992, CSL; and "Dead!" *New York Daily News,* Jan. 12, 1928, 1.

54. "Henchel Asks Abolition of Capital Punishment," Hartford Courant, Feb. 27, 1947, 18.

55. "Robert Bradley Pays Penalty for Murder of Three Men," *Hartford Courant,* Apr. 13, 1941, 1.

56. Roger Dove, "Seven Men in Death Row—Shall They Die?" *Hartford Courant,* Feb. 27, 1955, 1.

57. William J. Bowers, *Legal Homicide: Death as Punishment in America, 1864–1962* (Boston: Northeastern University Press, 1984), 40.

58. On Ehrmann, see Alan Rogers, *Murder and the Death Penalty in Massachusetts* (Amherst: University of Massachusetts Press, 2008), 332–34, 336, 344, 353, 354, 365, 374, 377.

59. "Hickey Would Retain Murder Death Penalty," *Hartford Courant,* May 23, 1951, Capital Punishment, Clipping File, 1939–1992, CSL.

60. "On Capital Punishment," *Hartford Courant,* Jan. 7, 1951, A2.

61. Gerald J. Demeusy, "Bill to End Death Penalty Brings Plea for Reprieves," *Hartford Courant,* Jan. 12, 1955, 1 discusses the 1951 legislation.

62. Title LXIV, chap. 417, S. 8351, p. 1018 (Hartford: published by the state, 1953). See also William T. Souney, "Law Signed after Three Convicted," *Hartford Courant,* July 4, 1951; "GOP for Easing Death Penalty," *Hartford Times,* May 23, 1951; and "Death Penalty," *Hartford Times,* May 25, 1951—all Clipping File, CSL; and William R. Ginsberg, "Punishment of Capital Offenders: A Critical Examination of the Connecticut Statute," *Connecticut Bar Journal* 27 (1953), 273–81.

63. Bowers, *Legal Homicide,* 166–67.

64. Ginsberg, "Punishment of Capital Offenders," 273–81.

65. *Connecticut v. Wallace M. Walters,* 145 Conn. 60 (1958); and Gerald J. Demeusy, "Court Upholds Jury Power in Death Cases," *Hartford Courant,* Feb. 4, 1958, 1.

66. "Our Prisons Are Social Dinosaurs," *Hartford Courant,* May 5, 1954, 16.

67. Charles Henchel to Governor Ribicoff, Jan. 10, 1955, RG 5, Office of the Governor, Abraham Ribicoff, 1955–1961, box 647, folder capital punishment, CSL.

68. Meredith S. Kohlberg to Governor Ribicoff, Jan. 19, 1955, RG 5, Office of the Governor, Abraham Ribicoff, 1955–1961, box 647, folder capital punishment, CSL. See also Clarence A. Pickett to Governor Ribicoff, Feb. 8, 1955, RG 5, Office of the Governor, Abraham Ribicoff, 1955–1961, box 647, folder capital punishment, CSL.

69. Roger Dove, "Seven Men in Death Row—Shall They Die?" *Hartford Courant,* Feb. 27, 1955, 1.

70. Editorial, "Should the State Kill?" *Hartford Courant,* Feb. 27, 1955, A2.

71. Roger Dove, "Seven Men in Death Row—Shall They Die?" *Hartford Courant,* Feb. 27, 1955, 1.

72. Roger Dove, "Police Argue That More Murders Would Follow Abolition of 'Chair,'" *Hartford Courant,* Feb. 28, 1955, 1A.

73. Roger Dove, "Police Argue That More Murders Would Follow Abolition of 'Chair,'" *Hartford Courant,* Feb. 28, 1955, 1A.

74. Roger Dove, "Prosecutors Back Death Penalty as a Deterrent to Violent Crime," *Hartford Courant,* Mar. 1, 1955, 1.

75. Roger Dove, "Prosecutors Back Death Penalty as a Deterrent to Violent Crime," *Hartford Courant,* Mar. 1, 1955, 1.

76. Roger Dove, "Clergy of Three Faiths Criticize Defenders of Capital Punishment," *Hartford Courant,* Mar. 2, 1955, 1.

77. Roger Dove, "Is 'Chair' for Friendless Only? Few Killers Pay Extreme Penalty," *Hartford Courant,* Mar. 3, 1955, 1.

78. Roger Dove, "Legislature Must Rule on Pleas to Abolish State's Electric Chair," *Hartford Courant,* Mar. 6, 1955, 1.

79. Roger Dove, "Atrocities Prompted Seven States to Restore Capital Punishment," Mar. 5, 1955, 1.

80. Roger Dove, "Murderers Sentenced for 'Life' Have Good Records on Parole," *Hartford Courant,* Mar. 4, 1955, 2, 1.

81. "Compromise on Capital Punishment," *Hartford Courant,* Mar. 6, 1955, A2.

82. "The Death Penalty Is Still Wrong," *Hartford Courant,* Mar. 13, 1955, A2; and "End the Death Penalty," *Hartford Times,* Apr. 25, 1955, Capital Punishment, Clipping File, 1939–1992, CSL.

83. On capital punishment, see RG 5, Office of the Governor, Abraham Ribicoff, 1955–1961, box 647, folder 1, and box 648, folders 2 and 3, CSL; "Governor Would End Executions," *Hartford Times,* Apr. 21, 1955, Capital Punishment, Clipping File, 1939–1992, CSL; and Keith Schonrock, "Governor for Abolition of Capital Punishment," *Hartford Courant,* May 22, 1955, 1.

84. Keith Schonrock, "Keep Death Penalty Police Chiefs Demand," *Hartford Courant,* Mar. 11, 1955, 1.

85. "State Senate Refuses to End Death Penalty," *Hartford Courant,* June 4, 1955, 3; see also "Connecticut Senate Blocks End of Capital Punishment," *Hartford Times,* June 4, 1955, Capital Punishment, Clipping File, 1939–1992, CSL.

86. William T. Souney, "Buteau Saved from Chair by Pardon Vote," *Hartford Courant,* May 9, 1950, 3.

87. "Death Penalty of Tomassi Commuted to Life Sentence," *Hartford Courant*, Dec. 19, 1950, 1.

88. Gerald J. Demeusy, "Smith's Sentence Commuted to Life Term," *Hartford Courant*, June 8, 1954, 1; see also Gerald J. Demeusy, "Smith Leaves 'Death Row'; Starts New Life in Prison," *Hartford Courant*, June 9, 1954, 19.

89. "Frank Smith," *Hartford Courant*, June 9, 1954, Crime, Prisons, Police, Clipping File, 1939–1992, CSL; see also "A Life Is Spared," *Hartford Times*, June 9, 1954, Crime, Prisons, Police, Clipping File, 1939–1992, CSL.

90. "William T. Souney, "Board of Pardons Saves Krooner from Death in Chair, Decrees Life Term," *Hartford Courant*, Nov. 14, 1950, 1; see also "Murder Held Deliberate in Ames Case," *Hartford Courant*, July 20, 1948, 1.

91. Gerald J. Demeusy, "Chair Claims 13th Victim as W. J. Lorain Is Executed," *Hartford Courant*, July 12, 1955, 1.

92. Gerald J. Demeusy, "Dortch's Execution Stayed by Lodge at Last Minute," *Hartford Courant*, Feb. 17, 1953, 1; and Demeusy, *Ten Weeks*, 110–12.

93. "Eight Jurors Are Selected for Lorainne [sic] Trial," *Hartford Courant*, Nov. 15, 1952, 1; William T. Souney, "Lorain to Die May 4 for Slaying Zgierski," *Hartford Courant*, Dec. 5, 1952, 1; Gerald J. Demeusy, "Chair Claims 13th Victim as W. J. Lorain Is Executed," *Hartford Courant*, July 12, 1955, 1; Demeusy, *Ten Weeks*, 156–64; and *State v. Lorain*, 141 Conn. 694 (1954).

94. Gerald J. Demeusy, "Chair Claims 13th Victim as W. J. Lorain Is Executed," *Hartford Courant*, July 12, 1955, 1.

95. "Connecticut Resumes Capital Punishment," *Hartford Courant*, July 13, 1955, 12.

96. Gerald J. Demeusy, "Donahue, Malm Die in State's Electric Chair," *Hartford Courant*, July 19, 1955, 1.

97. "Donahue Given Death Sentence," *Hartford Courant*, June 13, 1953, 1.

98. Gerald J. Demeusy, "Chair Claims 13th Victim as W. J. Lorain Is Executed," *Hartford Courant*, July 12, 1955, 1; see also Demeusy, *Ten Weeks*, 8–9.

99. Demeusy, *Ten Weeks*, 8.

100. Gerald J. Demeusy, "Malm Convicted, Sentenced to Electric Chair July 12," *Hartford Courant*, Feb. 12, 1954, 1.

101. Gerald J. Demeusy, "Donahue, Malm Die in State's Electric Chair," *Hartford Courant*, July 19, 1955, 1.

102. "Institution Sought for Care of 'Abnormal' Criminals," *Hartford Courant*, Mar. 20, 1955, 22.

103. "Tighter Control of Known Perverts," *Hartford Courant*, Dec. 18, 1953, 18; see also "The Need to Know the Roots of Perversion," *Hartford Courant*, Dec. 17, 1953, 18.

104. Gerald J. Demeusy, "Malm Convicted, Sentenced to Electric Chair July 12," *Hartford Courant*, Feb. 12, 1954, 1.

105. Demeusy, *Ten Weeks*, 9.

106. *Connecticut v. Robert N. Malm*, 142 Conn. 113, 118 (1955).

107. "State Police Oppose Bill to End Death Penalty," *Hartford Courant*, Mar. 27, 1957, 3.

108. Demeusy, *Ten Weeks*, chapters 3, 5.

109. Gerald J. Demeusy, "Taborsky Set Free after Long Ordeal," *Hartford Courant*, Oct. 7, 1955, 1.

110. "Two Are Arrested on Policeman's Tip in Connection with Two of Holdups," *Hartford Courant*, Jan 14, 1951, 1; "Confession Solves Wolfson Murder in West Hartford," *Hartford Courant*, Jan. 18, 1951; and Demeusy, *Ten Weeks*, chapter 7.

111. *Joseph L. Taborsky v. State of Connecticut,* 142 *Conn. 619, 633* (1955).

112. Gerald J. Demeusy, "Also Admits Killing of Wolfson in 1950," *Hartford Courant,* Mar. 2, 1957, 1.

113. Taborsky to Gerald J. Demeusy, "My Years in a Death Cell," *Hartford Courant,* Oct. 30, 1955, SM3.

114. "Taborsky Tells of Death Row Ordeal in Magazine Story on Sale Thursday," *Hartford Courant,* Dec. 14, 1955, 6.

115. Gerald J. Demeusy, "Nolle or Dismissal to Free Taborsky," *Hartford Courant,* Oct. 5, 1955, 1.

116. "Taborsky, "Pal Seized in Probe of Slayings," *Hartford Courant,* Feb. 26, 1957, 1; and Demeusy, *Ten Weeks,* chapters 13, 15, 17.

117. Gerald J. Demeusy, "Also Admits Killing of Wolfson in 1950," *Hartford Courant,* Mar. 2, 1957, 1; "Taborsky's Large Feet Gave Police 'Big Break' in Hunt for Two Slayers," *Hartford Courant,* Mar. 3, 1957, 1; Gerald J. Demeusy, "The Man who Cracked the 'Mad Dog' Cases," *Courant Magazine,* June 9, 1957, 4–5; and Demeusy, *Ten Weeks* 19.

118. Governor [Abraham Ribicoff] to Jon Colvin, Mar. 18, 1958, RG 5, Office of the Governor, Abraham Ribicoff, 1955–1961, Box 647, folder capital punishment, CSL.

119. "The Death Penalty," *Hartford Courant,* Feb. 19, 1957, 14.

120. "To the Police: Well Done," *Hartford Courant,* Mar. 1, 1957, 18; see also "Capital Punishment as a Prophylaxis," *Hartford Courant,* Mar. 28, 1957, 14.

121. Mrs. Louis L. Wolfson, "Capital Punishment and the Taborsky Case," *Hartford Courant,* Mar. 6, 1957, 14.

122. N. K. Borland, "Legislators Study Death Law Changes," *Hartford Times,* Feb. 28, 1957, 1; and "State Police Oppose Bill to End Death Penalty," *Hartford Courant,* Mar. 27, 1957, 3.

123. "State Police Oppose Bill to End Death Penalty," *Hartford Courant,* Mar. 27, 1957, 3.

124. Keith Schonrock, "House Rejects Abolishing Death Penalty in State," *Hartford Courant,* May 3, 1957, 1.

125. Robert Satter, "Murder and the Due Process of Law," *Hartford Courant,* Apr. 14, 1957, SM12.

126. N. K. Borland, "Legislators Study Death Law Changes," *Hartford Times,* Feb. 28, 1957, 1.

127. "Delaware Outlaws Capital Punishment," *Hartford Courant,* Apr. 5, 1958, Crime and Punishment, Clipping File, 1939–1992, CSL.

128. Gerald J. Demeusy, "Taborsky, Culombe Guilty, to Die in Chair," *Hartford Courant,* June 28, 1957, 1; see also "12th Juror Is Selected for Taborsky, Culombe," *Hartford Courant,* Apr. 25, 1957, 2.

129. "Guilty As Charged," *Hartford Courant,* June 29, 1957, 8.

130. Joseph L. Taborsky to Governor Abraham Ribicoff, Dec. 7, 1958, RG 5, Office of the Governor, Abraham Ribicoff, 1955–1961, box 647, folder capital punishment, CSL.

131. *State of Connecticut v. Joseph L. Taborsky; State of Connecticut v. Arthur Culombe,* 147 Conn. 194, 213 (1960).

132. Gerald J. Demeusy, "Taborsky Refuses to Lift Finger to Save Himself from Electric Chair," *Hartford Courant,* May 15, 1960, B1; Gerald J. Demeusy, "State Puts Taborsky to Death," May 18, 1960, 1; and Demeusy, *Ten Weeks,* chapters 29, 30, 32.

133. Demeusy, *Ten Weeks,* epilogue, i–iv.

134. "Suspect in Killing at Wolcott Admits Slaying of Second Girl," *Hartford Courant,* May 23, 1957, 1; "Davies Guilty, Sentenced to Die in Chair Feb. 17," *Hartford*

Courant, Nov. 8, 1957, 1A; Gerald J. Demeusy, "Davies Is Executed for Slaying of Girl," *Hartford Courant,* Oct. 21, 1959, 1; and Demeusy, *Ten Weeks,* 115. Davies wrote Governor Ribicoff on Dec. 3, 1958 from prison, "I say it is better to die in the chair then [*sic*] to spend your life in prison with no chance to get out." RG 5, Office of the Governor, Abraham Ribicoff, 1955–1961, box 647, folder capital punishment, CSL.

135. William T. Souney, "Many Prisons Have known Wojculewicz Who Has Been in Trouble Since Age of 10," *Hartford Courant,* Nov. 7, 1951, 1; and William T. Souney, "Wojculewicz Convicted Given Death Sentence," *Hartford Courant,* Mar. 19, 1952, 1.

136. Harlan L. Reycroft, "He's Had His Share of Justice," *Hartford Courant,* Feb. 5, 1956, A2; and Grace Lee Kenyon, "This Ridiculous Farce of 'Justice and Mercy,'" *Hartford Courant,* Apr. 24, 1959, 18; see also Grace Lee Kenyon, "Legal Loopholes Protect Criminals," *Hartford Courant,* July 31, 1958, 10.

137. *Frank Wojculewicz v. George A. Cummings,* 145 Conn. 11, 23 (1958).

138. "Shall Mercy Alter Sentence?," *Hartford Times,* Jan. 23, 1958, Crime and Punishment, Clipping File, 1939–1992, CSL.

139. Gerald J. Demeusy, "Paralyzed Police Killer Dies in Electric Chair," *Hartford Courant,* Oct. 27, 1959, 1.

140. Demeusy, *Ten Weeks,* 77–80.

141. "An Act Concerning the Board of Pardons," Public Acts 410 and 643, *Connecticut Public Acts* (1959), 752–53, 1298.

142. "Capital Punishment Is Still with Us," *Hartford Courant,* June 4, 1959, Crime and Punishment, Clipping File, 1939–1992, CSL.

7. An Unofficial Moratorium, 1961–2004

1. There is an exception on the state level. Connecticut in 1969 repealed treason as a capital crime. See *Connecticut Public Acts* (1969), 828, "An Act Concerning Revision and Codification of the Substantive Criminal Law," Section 214, which repealed Connecticut General Statute Section 53-1 Treason. I thank Hilary Frye at the CSL for her help.

2. Charles Kochakian, "Death Law Severity Questioned," *Hartford Times,* Oct. 30, 1974, Capital Punishment, Clipping File, 1939–1992, CSL.

3. *State of Connecticut v. Joseph L. Taborsky; State of Connecticut v. Arthur Culombe,* 147 Conn. 194, 247 (1960).

4. *Arthur Culombe v. State of Connecticut,* 367 U.S. 568 (1961), 635; and "Killers Appeal Backed by Assn. for Retarded," *Hartford Courant,* Nov. 13, 1960, 18A.

5. *Culombe* 367 U.S. at 640 (1961).

6. Gerald J. Demeusy, "Conviction of Culombe Upset by Supreme Court," *Hartford Courant,* June 20, 1961, 1.

7. *Culombe,* 367 U.S. at 635. A well-publicized example of abusive interrogation by the state police led to the conviction of eighteen-year-old Peter Reilly for slashing his mother's throat and running over her with a car. Judge John A. Speziale set events in motion that led to Reilly's exoneration in 1977 and an investigation that faulted the tactics of the state police. Speziale subsequently served as chief justice of the state supreme court from 1981 to 1984. Edmund H. Mahony, "Ex-Chief Justice Speziale Dies," *Hartford Courant,* Jan. 4, 2005, A1.

8. "Don't Let Him Loose," *Hartford Courant,* June 21, 1961, 14.

9. Editorial, "Culombe Pleads Guilty," *Hartford Courant,* June 30, 1961, 16.

10. Gerald J. Demeusy, "Culombe to Stay Behind Bars," *Hartford Courant,* June 29, 1961, 1; Gerald J. Demeusy, "Culombe Due to Begin Sentence of Life Today," *Hartford*

Courant, June 30, 1961, 1; and "Culombe Dies in Cell at Age 46," *Hartford Courant,* Dec. 25, 1970, 26.

11. *State of Connecticut v. Harold D. Rogers,* 143 Conn. 167 (1956).

12. *Rogers v. Richmond, Warden,* 365 U.S. 534, 540–41 (1961).

13. "Slayer Wins Fight against Electric Chair," *Hartford Courant,* May 27, 1961, 18A.

14. "State Moves to Conform to Recent Court Rulings," *Hartford Courant,* July 18, 1961, 3.

15. Gerald J. Demeusy, "Prison Records Show: Death Penalty Fell on 67 Whites—4 Negroes," *Hartford Courant,* June 23, 1963, part B, Capital Punishment, Clipping File, 1939–1992, CSL.

16. Gerald J. Demeusy, "6 Await Death at Prison," *Hartford Courant,* Aug. 10, 1958, 1B.

17. William Styron, "The Death-in-Life of Benjamin Reid," *Esquire* 57 (1962), 145; see also Joseph A. LaPlante, "Connecticut Criminal Law: Deficiencies Disclosed in the Reid Case," *Connecticut Bar Journal* 37 (1963), 19.

18. Gerald J. Demeusy, "Legal Resources Fail, Reid Resentenced to Die," *Hartford Courant,* Feb. 9, 1962, 9.

19. Styron, "Death," 114, 141.

20. Styron, "Death," 145.

21. Gerald J. Demeusy, "5 Years in 'Death Row' End for Reid June 25," *Hartford Courant,* June 3, 1962, Capital Punishment, Clipping File, 1939–1992, CSL.

22. "Who Would Still Vote Death Had Benjamin Reid's Story Been Told," *Hartford Times,* Apr. 18, 1962, Capital Punishment, Clipping File, 1939–1992, CSL; William Styron, "The Aftermath of Benjamin Reid," *Esquire* 58 (1962), 81–82.

23. "Judge Wright Intercedes in Killer Reid's Behalf, Citing Case of Culombe," *New Britain Herald,* June 25, 1962, 1; and Styron, "Aftermath," 158, 160.

24. Gerald J. Demeusy, "Jaycees in Drive to Stop Execution," *Hartford Courant,* June 17, 1962, Capital Punishment, Clipping File, 1939–1992, CSL; and Petition for the Life of Benjamin Reid of the Greater Hartford Jaycees and Theodore Paullin [Society of Friends] to Isadore L. Kotler [Board of Pardons], May 5, 1962, in RG-5, John Dempsey Papers (1961–1971), box A-289, CSL. There are a number of letters against capital punishment in this source.

25. "Who Is without Guilt?" *Hartford Times,* Apr. 18, 1962, 22.

26. "Sentence Commuted," *Hartford Courant,* June 26, 1962, Capital Punishment, Clipping File, 1939–1992, CSL.

27. Various letters during May 1960 in RG 5, John Dempsey Papers (1961–1971), box A-289, CSL.

28. Styron, "Aftermath," 164.

29. LaPlante, "Connecticut Criminal Law," 49–50.

30. Ivan Robinson, "Justice King Says He's against Capital Punishment," *Hartford Times,* Dec. 2, 1964, 4.

31. John Dempsey to Virginia Slomske, Apr. 5, 1962, RG 5, John Dempsey Papers (1961–1971), box A-289, CSL.

32. "Capital Punishment Is to Be Retained," *Hartford Courant,* June 1, 1963, Capital Punishment, Clipping File, 1939–1992, CSL. In the same year, the House in Massachusetts voted 124 to 108 to retain the death penalty. "Bay State Fails to End Execution," *Hartford Courant,* May 7, 1963, Capital Punishment, Clipping File, 1939–1992, CSL.

33. "Priest Urges Death Law Be Kept in State," *New Haven Register,* Mar. 22, 1963, Capital Punishment, Clipping File, 1939–1992, CSL.

34. "House Vote Retains the Death Penalty," *Hartford Courant,* May 19, 1965, A1.

35. "Study of Murders Key to Death Penalty Debates," *Hartford Times,* Mar. 25, 1961, 7.

36. "House Vote Retains the Death Penalty," *Hartford Courant,* May 19, 1965, A1.

37. "The Executioner is Obsolete," *Hartford Times,* Jan. 18, 1963, 14. The *Hartford Courant* typically argued at the time, "Indeed, the only absolute and unmistakable method now of preventing repetitious murders is through capital punishment." "Note on Capital Punishment," *Hartford Courant,* Feb. 27, 1967, Capital Punishment, Clipping File, 1939–1992, CSL.

38. Mrs. J. Robert Reynolds [Unitarian] to John Dempsey, July 26, 1966, Adelaide N. Baker to Senator John Pritchard, Mar. 3, 1967, Stephen A. Richardson [Quaker] to Dempsey, Mar. 23, 1967, Harold W. Richardson [United Church of Christ] to Dempsey, Mar. 31, 1967, Connecticut State Committee to Abolish Capital Punishment, Apr. 4, 1967, all in RG 5, John Dempsey Papers (1961–1971), box A-289, CSL. John A. Russell [Methodist] to John Dempsey, Mar. 1, 1961, RG 5, John Dempsey Papers (1961–1971), box A-233.

39. George Mackie to Edward Morrison, Oct. 21, 1970, RG 5, John Dempsey Papers (1961–1971), box A-289, CSL. Mackie, an aide to Dempsey, wrote, "The Governor has never made any public statement regarding his views on capital punishment." "Dempsey Disclaims Measure to Outlaw Capital Punishment," *New Haven Register,* Jan. 11, 1967, and "A Rejected Compromise on the Death Penalty," *Hartford Courant,* May 28, 1971, Capital Punishment, Clipping File, 1939–1992, CSL.

40. Charles F. J. Morse, "Meskill Backs Death Penalty," *Hartford Courant,* Feb. 23, 1972, Capital Punishment, Clipping File, 1939–1992, CSL.

41. "Death Penalty Issue Faces Connecticut," *New Haven Register,* May 5, 1971, Capital Punishment, Clipping File, 1939–1992, CSL.

42. *Witherspoon v. Illinois,* 319 U.S. 510, 519 (1968).

43. "Won't Benefit Two on Death Row," *Hartford Courant,* June 4, 1968, 36A; and Victor Sasson, "3 in State Face Death Despite Court Ruling," *Hartford Courant,* June 29, 1971, 23.

44. "The Vanishing Death Penalty," *Hartford Courant,* Jan. 12, 1967, 14, and "Changing Attitudes toward Execution," *Hartford Courant,* Jan. 5, 1969, 2B.

45. *Delgado v. Connecticut,* 408 U.S. 940 (1972).

46. *Furman v. Georgia,* 408 U.S. 238, 242 (1972).

47. See *Brown v. Board of Education,* 347 U.S. 483 (1954); *Mapp v. Ohio,* 367 U.S. 643 (1961); *Abington School District v. Schempp,* 374 U.S. 203 (1963); *Gideon v. Wainwright,* 372 U.S. 335 (1963); *Escobedo v. Illinois,* 378 U.S. 478 (1964); *Griswold v. Connecticut,* 381 U.S. 479 (1965); and *Miranda v. Arizona,* 384 U.S. 436 (1966).

48. "Public Expected to Support Nixon on Death Penalty," *Hartford Courant,* Mar. 14, 1973, 41.

49. James J. Kilpatrick, "Judicial Activism vs. Death Penalty," *Hartford Courant,* July 5, 1972, 18.

50. *Furman,* 408 U.S. at 400.

51. Charles F. J. Morse, "State Panel Adopts Death Penalty Bill," *Hartford Courant,* Mar. 28, 1973, 1A; "Death Penalty Voted," *Hartford Courant,* Apr. 12, 1973, 9; and Ann Hall, "Senate Votes Death Penalty," *Hartford Courant,* Apr. 20, 1973, 1A.

52. "An Act Concerning the Death Penalty," *Public Acts* 38 (1973), 224–28.

53. "Return of the Death Penalty Leads Crime Fighting Package," *Hartford Courant,* June 3, 1973, 35.

54. Charles Kochakian, "Death Law Severity Questioned," *Hartford Times,* Oct. 30, 1974, Capital Punishment, Clipping File, 1939–1992, CSL.

55. Tom Barnes, "Massacre Largest Since 1966," *Hartford Courant,* Oct. 20, 1974, 2A.

56. "Death Penalty 'Unlikely' Here, Prosecutor States," *Hartford Times,* July 3, 1976, Capital Punishment, Clipping File, 1939–1992, CSL.

57. Gerald J. Demeusy, "Delgado Sentenced to Electric Chair," *Hartford Courant,* A1.

58. Luis Lugo to Gov. Dempsey, Dec. 14, 1967, RG 5, John Dempsey Papers (1961–1971), box A-289, CSL.

59. C. J. Trankle Jr., "New Haven Gunman Slays Five: Suspect Nabbed in New Jersey," *Hartford Courant,* Aug. 27, 1966, 1; and "Execution Date Passes: Appeal Review Awaited," *Hartford Courant,* Jan. 19, 1967, 46.

60. "Cofone Scheduled to Die in Chair Oct. 7 at Somers," *Hartford Courant,* June 6, 1970, 5; and "Convicted Killer Gets Life Term," *Hartford Courant,* Jan. 20, 1973, 19A.

61. "New Terms Sought for Two Killers," *Hartford Courant,* Oct. 4, 1972, 72; "Man, 32, Given 6 Life Terms," *Hartford Courant,* Nov. 18, 1972, 6; "Slayer Gets Death Term Cut to Life," *Hartford Courant,* Dec. 20, 1972, 34; and "Court Sets Review of Death Penalty," *Hartford Courant,* Jan. 23, 1976, 8.

62. William J. Bowers, *Legal Homicide: Death as Punishment in America, 1864–1962* (Boston: Northeastern University Press, 1984), 107–8.

63. William Cockerham, "3 Somers Inmates Spared by Ruling," *Hartford Courant,* June 30, 1972, 1.

64. *Gregg v. Georgia,* 428 U.S. 153 (1976); "Supreme Court Upholds Death Penalty," *Hartford Courant,* July 3, 1976, 1; and "High Court Rulings Sweeping in Nature," *Hartford Courant,* July 4, 1976, 8A.

65. "George Gallup, "Support for Death Penalty Highest in 25 Years," *Hartford Courant,* Apr. 29, 1976, 84.

66. "The Penalty of Death," *Hartford Courant,* July 7, 1976, 18.

67. "State Laws Similar to Those Upheld," *Hartford Courant,* July 3, 1976, 6.

68. *Lockett v. Ohio,* 438 U.S. 586 (1978); and Richard L. Madden, "Judge in Connecticut Rules the Death Penalty Is Illegal," *New York Times,* Dec. 13, 1979, B1.

69. Antoinette Martin, "Deal Averts Battle over Death Penalty Bill," *Hartford Courant,* Apr. 18, 1980, 50.

70. "Most Governors Back Capital Punishment," *Hartford Courant,* June 5, 1975, Capital Punishment, Clipping File, 1939–1992, CSL; "Capital Punishment Needed," *Hartford Times,* July 21, 1976, Capital Punishment, Clipping File, 1939–1992, CSL; "Grasso Vetoes Sunday Racing, Jai Alai Bill," *Hartford Courant,* May 29, 1980, 1C; and "Act Revising Sentencing Procedures for Imposition of Death Penalty," Public Act No. 80-332, *Connecticut Public Acts* (1980), 494–96.

71. *District Attorney for the Suffolk District v. James Watson and others,* 381 Mass. 648 (1980); "Massachusetts Court Rejects Death Penalty," *Hartford Courant,* Oct. 29, 1980, B2; and "Cruel and Unusual," *Hartford Courant,* Nov. 5, 1980, A26.

72. "High Court Gets Appeal on Death Penalty Ruling, *Hartford Courant,* Apr. 10, 1980, 7; Gerald J. Demeusy, "Castonguay Sentenced to 50 Years in Slaying," *Hartford Courant,* Nov. 13, 1980, A5; and "Slain Man's Peers Favor Death Penalty," *Hartford Courant,* Nov. 13, 1980, C1A.

73. Lynne Garnett, "Wood Sentenced to 120 Years for Murders," *Hartford Courant,* Nov. 17, 1984, A1B.

74. John Hyland, "Student, 18, Held in Rape-Slaying," *Hartford Courant,* Oct. 23, 1982, B1E.

75. *State v. Kevin Usry,* 205 Conn. 298 (1987).

76. Lynne Garnett, "Is the State Death Penalty Moribund?" *Hartford Courant,* June 30, 1985, Capital Punishment, Clipping File, 1939–1992, CSL.

77. Yolanda Barnes, "Man Arrested in Slaying of Mother, Tot," *Hartford Courant,* June 18, 1984, D1E.

78. Barbara Roessner, "Ultimate Penalty Is Injustice," *Hartford Courant,* Apr. 4, 1986, Capital Punishment, Clipping File, 1939–1992, CSL.

79. *Connecticut v. Daniels,* 209 Conn. 225, 231 (1988).

80. *Glass v. Louisiana,* 471 U.S. 1080 (1985). In dissent, Justice Brennan joined by Justices Marshall and Harry Blackmun found the death penalty absolutely unconstitutional. Justice Brennan commented, "The death penalty is in all circumstances cruel and unusual punishment prohibited by the Eighth and Fourteenth Amendments." *Glass,* 471 U.S. at 1084.

81. Michele Jacklin, "Polls Show Residents Back Harsh Penalty for Murder," *Hartford Courant,* Feb. 11, 1987, Capital Punishment, Clipping File, 1939–1992, CSL.

82. *State v. Ross,* 230 Conn. 183, 187n16 (1994).

83. "Death Penalty Issue Debated," *Hartford Times,* Apr. 14, 1975, Capital Punishment, Clipping File, 1939–1992, CSL.

84. "CCLU to Seek Death Penalty Repeal," *Hartford Courant,* July 16, 1976, 5.

85. Andrew Welch, "Archbishop Re-Enters Capital Punishment Debate," *Hartford Courant,* July 7, 1984. Earlier, Whealon had stated that the criminal killer "has in a sense abdicated his own right to live." *Hartford Courant,* Aug. 11, 1974. Compare a later statement: "Precisely when persons appear worthless and expendable and when people are tempted to destroy, the church must speak out in defense of their lives." On this premise, the church opposed capital punishment and abortion, particularly *Roe v. Wade* (1973). David Fink, "Capital Punishment Debate Mixes Tears with Anger," *Hartford Courant,* Apr. 7, 1987. All references from Capital Punishment, Clipping File, 1939–1992, CSL.

86. "Don't Revive Death Penalty," *Hartford Courant,* Dec. 17, 1979, Capital Punishment, Clipping File, 1939–1992, CSL. See also "Electric Chair Justice," *Hartford Courant,* May 27, 1979, Capital Punishment, Clipping File, 1939–1992, CSL; "One Murder Follows Another," *Hartford Courant,* Aug. 12, 1982, A22; and "Let's Fix the Death Penalty," *Hartford Courant,* Apr. 20, 1986, Capital Punishment, Clipping File, 1939–1992, CSL.

87. William A. O'Neill to Susan Killian, Mar. 25, 1985, RG 5, Governor William A. O'Neill, 1979–1991, box 47, folder 69, CSL; O'Neill to Nathan Adams, June 19, 1986, RG 5, Governor William A. O'Neill, 1979–1991, box 47, folder 70, CSL; and O'Neill to Katie Brearton, June 22, 1989, RG 5, Governor William A. O'Neill, 1979–1991, box 47, folder 73, CSL. Steve Grant, "Senator Seeking Override of Death-Penalty Veto, *Hartford Courant,* June 18, 1986; and "Let the Death Bill Die . . . ," *Hartford Courant,* June 28, 1986, Capital Punishment, Clipping File, 1939–1992, CSL.

88. *Thompson v. Oklahoma,* 487 U.S. 815 (1988); see also Stuart Taylor Jr., "Justices Put Age Limit on Executions," *New York Times,* June 30, 1988, Capital Punishment, Clipping File, 1939–1992, CSL.

89. Lynne Tuohy and Mark Pazniokas, "Weicker Vetoes Death Penalty Bill," *Hartford Courant,* June 29, 1991—Capital Punishment, Clipping File, 1939–1992, CSL; see also "Not a Matter of Balancing," *Hartford Courant,* Apr. 24, 1986; David Rink, "State Senate Blocks Death Penalty Bill for Current Session," *Hartford Courant,* May 7, 1987; Jacqueline Cutler, "House Votes Not to Ban Death Penalty," *Hartford Courant,* Apr. 30, 1987; and Michael Reniez and David Fink, "Senate Re-

jects Death Penalty," *Hartford Courant,* June 2, 1989, Capital Punishment, Clipping File, 1939–1992, CSL.

90. "An Act Concerning the Death Penalty," Public Act No. 95-19, *Connecticut Public Acts* (1995), 34; and "A Court Asks That a New Jury Reconsider a Death Penalty," *New York Times,* Aug. 22, 1995, B5.

91. *Connecticut General Statutes,* sec. 53a-46(b)(3), adopted in 1980.

92. *Pulley v. Harris,* 465 U.S. 37 (1984).

93. "An Act Concerning Lethal Injection, Proportionality Review of Death Sentences and Murder of a Child," Public Act No. 95-16, Connecticut Public Acts, 1995, 29–31; and Christopher Keating, "Broader Death Penalty in Place[,] Many New Laws in Effect Today," *Hartford Courant,* Oct. 1, 1995, C1.

94. *Collins v. Collins,* 510 U.S. 1141, 1145 (1994).

95. *Collins,* 510 U.S. at 1143.

96. I have relied heavily in this paragraph and the preceding one on Attorney Christopher Reinhart, "Death Penalty Laws and Statistics," *Office of Legislative Research Report,* Apr. 27, 2000, 2000-R-0504.

97. *State v. Ross,* 230 Conn. at 249–250.

98. *State v. Webb,* 238 Conn. 389, 405 (1996).

99. *State v. Cobb,* 251 Conn. 285 (1999).

100. *State v. Johnson,* 253 Conn. 1, 75 (2000).

101. *Johnson,* 253 Conn. 1.

102. Lynne Tuohy, "Trooper's Murderer Won't Be Executed," *Hartford Courant,* May 3, 2000, A1.

103. Lynne Tuohy, "Bagshaw Ruling Challenged," *Hartford Courant,* May 23, 2000, A3.

104. Georgia in 1986 was the first state to bar such executions, and a number of other states followed. In *Atkins v. Virginia,* 536 U.S. 304 (2002), the high court legitimated nationally what it saw as the emerging standard on the state level. In similar reasoning, the Court had previously found that the death penalty was inappropriate for the crime of rape in *Coker v. Georgia,* 433 U.S. 584 (1977), or for those convicted of felony murder who neither themselves killed, attempted to kill, or intended to kill in *Enmund v. Florida,* 458 U.S. 782 (1982).

105. *State of Connecticut Commission on the Death Penalty* (submitted to the Connecticut General Assembly, Jan, 8, 2003), 1 and appendix A.

106. "A Useless Death Penalty," *Hartford Courant,* Jan. 10, 2002, A10.

107. *Commission,* 3, 5.

108. *Commission,* 6.

109. *Commission,* 8.

110. *McCleskey v. Kemp,* 481 U.S. 279 (1987); and *Commission,* 18.

111. *State v. Cobb,* 234 Conn. 735, 748 (1995); see also *Commission,* 19.

112. *Commission,* 21–25.

113. *Commission,* 25–27.

114. *Commission,* 28–35.

115. *Commission,* 15.

116. Quoted in *Commission,* 32.

117. *State v. Reynolds,* 264 Conn. 1, 265–66 (2003).

118. Lynne Tuohy, "Dissenting Justice Accuses Prosecutor of 'Deliberate Misconduct,'" *Hartford Courant,* May 30, 2003, A1.

119. *Reynolds,* 264 Conn. 1; and Lynne Tuohy, "Dissenting Justice Accuses Prosecutor of 'Deliberate Misconduct,'" *Hartford Courant,* May 30, 2003, A1.

120. *Reynolds,* 264 Conn. at 138.

121. Lynne Tuohy, "Cop Killer to Remain in Death Row," *Hartford Courant,* May 20, 2003, A1.

122. *Connecticut v. Rizzo,* 266 Conn. 171, 242 (2003).

123. *Rizzo,* 266 Conn. at 269.

124. *Connecticut Public Acts,* PA 04-234, 982–84; and Christopher Reinhart, "Legislature's Power to Commute Death Sentences and Effect on Pending Cases," *Office of Legislature's Research Report,* Dec. 6, 2004, 4.

125. *Roper v. Simmons,* 543 U.S. 551 (2005). This decision revised *Sanford v. Kentucky,* 492 U.S. 361 (1989), which permitted the execution of juveniles from the age of sixteen. Adam Liptak, "Another Step in Reshaping the Capital Justice System," *New York Times,* Mar. 2, 2005, A1; and Christopher Reinhart, "Connecticut Death Penalty Laws," *Office of Legislative Research Report,* Jan. 28, 2005, 4.

126. "Chipping Away at the Death Penalty," *Hartford Courant,* Mar. 3, 2005, A10.

127. Helen Prejean, *Dead Man Walking: An Eyewitness Account of the Death Penalty in the United States* (New York: Random House, 1993); *Dead Man Walking,* directed by Tim Robbins (New York: PolyGram Video, 1996); Helen Prejean, *The Death of Innocents: An Eyewitness Account of Wrongful Executions* (New York: Random House, 2005); and Helen Prejean, "Above All Else, Life," *New York Times,* Apr. 4, 2005, A27.

128. "DNA's Weight as Evidence," *New York Times,* Jan. 18, 2006, A22. For Connecticut examples, see William Yardley, "Inmate Freed After 18 Years on Basis of DNA Evidence," *New York Times,* June 7, 2006, A23; William Yardley, "DNA Samples Link 4 Murders in Connecticut," *New York Times,* June 8, 2006, A23; and David Altimari and David Owens, "DNA Reprieve for Convicted Killer?" *Hartford Courant,* Dec. 17, 2008, www.courant.com.

129. *Commission,* 15.

130. *New Haven Advocate,* Jan. 15, 2004, Capital Punishment, Clipping File, 1939–1992, CSL.

131. For a more detailed discussion of the numbers, see Christopher Reinhart, "Capital Felony Case Statistics," *Office of Legislative Research Report,* Feb. 24, 2005. For data from 1973 to 2003, see *Commission,* appendixes D, E, and F.

132. Christopher Reinhart, "Prisoners Sentenced for Capital Felonies," *Office of Legislative Research Report,* Mar. 14, 2005, 1–3; and "On Death Row," *Hartford Courant,* May 14, 2005, A9. Reinhart noted that the length of Eric Amado's non-death sentence is unclear. I have assumed that it is life without release because he was sentenced in 1993.

133. Katie Zezima, "Jury Issues First Death Sentence in New Hampshire Since the 1950s," *New York Times,* Dec. 19, 2008, A19. On December 18, 2008, a New Hampshire jury issued the state's first death sentence since 1959. Michael Addison, a twenty-eight-year-old African American, was convicted of shooting Michael Briggs, a white police officer, at close range in the head. In the only other capital murder trial in 2008, John J. Brooks, a wealthy white businessman, was sentenced to life in prison for hiring three men to kill a handyman, who Brooks accused of stealing from him. These two cases raise the question of race and class in death sentences. In 2008, New Hampshire joined Connecticut as the only New England state with inmates on death row.

134. Lynne Tuohy, "On Death Row, Webb's Life Goes On," *Hartford Courant,* July 25, 1996, A1; and "Life on Death Row," *Hartford Courant,* Mar. 8, 2005, A11.

135. On "death row phenomenon," see Diane Struzzi and Roselyn Tantraphol, "Death Row: Extreme Nothingness," *Hartford Courant,* Mar. 8, 2005, A1.

136. Matt Bugard, "Murder-for-Hire Case Brings Death Sentence," *Hartford Courant*, Feb. 1, 2005, B1.

137. Rosemary Keogh, "Insurance Agent Held in Girl's Death," *Hartford Courant*, June 29, 1984, A1C; Miriam Silver, "Murder Case Leaves Brooklyn in Shock," *Hartford Courant*, June 30, 1984, A1A; Theodore A. Driscoll, "Ross to Get Public Aid for Defense," *Hartford Courant*, July 3, 1984, B1; and Theodore A. Driscoll, "Accused Slayer Pleads Not Guilty, Asks Jury Trial," *Hartford Courant*, Nov. 3, 1984, C1.

138. Lynne Tuohy and Alaine Griffin, "8 Lives Cut Short," *Hartford Courant*, Jan. 23, 2005, A1; and "Chronology of a Killer," *Hartford Courant*, Jan. 29, 2005, A8.

139. Lynne Tuohy and Alaine Griffin, "8 Lives Cut Short," *Hartford Courant*, Jan. 23, 2005, A1; William Yardley and Julia Preston, "Parents Knew of Confession in '81 Murder, Records Show," *New York Times*, Jan. 26, 2005, A19; and "Chronology of a Killer," *Hartford Courant*, Jan. 29, 2005, A8.

140. "I Really Didn't Feel Anything," *Hartford Courant*, May 11, 2005, A5.

141. Richard l. Madden, "Ross's Trial Puts Capital Punishment Back in Spotlight," *New York Times*, Capital Punishment, Clipping File, 1939–1992, CSL; David Fink, "Survey Finds Support for Death by Injection," *Hartford Courant*, Capital Punishment, Clipping File, 1939–1992, CSL; and *Connecticut v. Ross*, 225 Conn. 559 (1993).

142. *Ross*, 230 Conn. at 286.

143. *Ross*, 230 Conn. at 286–287.

144. *Ross v. Connecticut*, 513 U.S. 1165 (1995).

145. Deborah Peterson, "State's Death Penalty Ruled Unconstitutional," *Hartford Courant*, Mar. 11, 1989, Capital Punishment, Clipping File, 1939–1992, CSL; *Connecticut v. Robert J. Breton, Sr.*, 212 Conn. 258 (1989); and *Connecticut v. Robert J. Breton, Sr.*, 235 Conn. 206 (1995).

146. *Breton*, 212 Conn at 263.

147. *Breton*, 212 Conn at 271.

148. *Breton*, 212 Conn at 271.

149. *Trop v. Dulles*, 356 U.S. 86 (1958).

150. *Breton*, 235 Conn. at 211–212.

151. "A Court Asks That a New Jury Reconsider a Death Penalty," *New York Times*, Aug. 22, 1995, B5.

152. "Judicial Panel Reinstates Death Sentence for Killer," *New York Times*, Apr. 21, 1997, B6; and *Connecticut v. Robert J. Breton, Sr.*, 264 Conn. 327 (2003).

153. *Breton*, 264 Conn. at 327; and *Connecticut v. Robert J. Breton, Sr.*, 540 U.S. 1055 (2003).

154. *Webb*, 238 Conn. at 259.

155. *Connecticut v. Webb*, 252 Conn. 128, 147 (2000).

156. *Webb*, 252 Conn. at 147–148.

157. Lynne Tuohy, "Court Backs Use of Lethal Injection," *Hartford Courant*, Feb. 4, 2000, A3.

158. *Cobb v. Connecticut*, 251 Conn. 285 (1999).

159. *Cobb*, 251 Conn. at 523.

160. Lynne Tuohy, "Death Penalty Upheld in '89 Waterbury Case," *Hartford Courant*, Nov. 30, 1999, A1.

161. Michael Remiz, "Supreme Court Rejects Death Row Inmates' Appeals," *Hartford Courant*, Oct. 10, 2000, A4.

162. Kenton Robinson, "Death Penalty's Constitutionality Questioned," *Willimantic Chronicle*, Feb. 17, 2005, 9. More recently, see Thomas Kaplan and Alison Leigh Cowan, "Arguing the Death Penalty, in a Gym Near Death Row," *New York*

Times, Dec. 14, 2007, C15; and Katie Melone, "Death Penalty May Be Tested," *Hartford Courant,* Feb. 28, 2008, B1.

In 1987, the U.S. Supreme Court ruled that evidence specific to an individual, not a pattern of statewide discrimination, was necessary to establish a claim of racial bias. Unlike most states, in Connecticut, Superior Court Judge Stanley T. Fuger Jr. allowed the claim because the state's constitution afforded greater protection than the U.S. Constitution. The inmates' attorneys had commissioned two studies.

The first study covered ninety-six cases from 1973 to 1998. It was completed in 2003, but was withheld from the public and prosecutors for four years. Chief Public Defender Susan Storey explained that the 2003 study was not released until December 2007 because the sample was too small, not because it contradicted the second study. The 2003 report concluded that there was geographic disparity in convictions, but it did not conclude that a defendant's race was a factor in a death sentence. The murder victim's race, however, was found to be a factor.

The second study, of November 30, 2007, was "Capital Punishment in Connecticut, 1973–2007: A Comprehensive Evaluation from 4600 Murders to One Execution" conducted by Professor John J. Donohue III of Yale University Law School. This extensive study cost $256,000 and took four and one-half years to complete. It was in line with the innovative, statistical work of Professor David Baldus of the University of Iowa College of Law, who studied bias in the death penalty in four states and the city of Philadelphia. Among other findings, Donohue concluded that blacks were more likely than whites to get the death penalty, a conclusion different from that of the 2003 study. In addition, he reported that the adjudication of capital punishment was capricious and arbitrary; that nonwhite defendants were treated more harshly than whites, especially when the victim was white; and that the egregious nature of the crime did not correlate with who was sentenced to death, either within or across judicial districts.

As of 2008, seven death row inmates—four black, two white, and one Latino— are part of this consolidated habeas corpus challenge. The other two death row inmates—one white and one Latino—are not a part of the appeal. The litigation on this pivotal challenge continues today.

8. The Execution of Michael Ross, 2005

1. Trip Jennings, "More Twists in Ross Case," *Willimantic Chronicle,* Jan. 27, 2005, A1.

2. Michael Ross's homepage at http://www.ccadp.org/michaelross-timeforme. htm, accessed on Mar. 22, 2005. The essay by Ross, "It's Time for Me to Die: An Inside Look at Death Row," appeared in various outlets in the winter of 1998. The quotations are on pages 4 and 7.

3. Ross, "It's Time," 7.

4. Lynne Tuohy, "Ross Appeal Begins Major Challenge to Death Penalty," *Hartford Courant,* May 16, 1992, Capital Punishment, Clipping File, 1939–1992, CSL.

5. *Connecticut v. Ross,* 230 Conn. 183 (1994).

6. Brigitte Greenberg, "In Reversal, Serial Killer Decides to Fight Death Penalty," *Hartford Courant,* Aug. 6, 1998, A6.

7. Edmund H. Mahony, "Ross Fails in Suicide Try, Serial Killer in Hospital after Being Found in Cell," *Hartford Courant,* Nov. 3, 1998, A3.

8. "Death Recommended for Man Convicted in 1980's Murders," *New York Times,* Apr. 7, 2000, B5.

9. Janice D'Arcy, "A Killer Cries in Court 'I'm Sorry I Didn't Take My Own Life,'" May 13, 2000, A1.

10. "Killer to Be Extradited to New York," *New York Times,* July 9, 2001, B5; Amy Pagnozzi, "Her Friends Recall Their 'Little Lamb,'" *Hartford Courant,* July 20, 2001, A3; and William Yardley and Julia Preston, "Parents Knew of Confession in '81 Murder, Records Show," *New York Times,* Jan. 26, 2005, A19.

11. *Connecticut v. Ross,* 269 Conn. 213, 282 (2004). See "Court Upholds Death Sentence," *New York Times,* June 25, 2004, B6; and Lynne Tuohy, "Ross' Death Sentence Stands," *Hartford Courant,* May 25, 2004, B1.

12. *Ross,* 269 Conn. at 284.

13. Lynne Tuohy, "Ross Signals End to Appeals," *Hartford Courant,* Oct. 2, 2004, A1.

14. "Execution Date Set for Killer," *New York Times,* Oct. 7, 2004, B8; and Lynne Tuohy, "Ross Gets a Date to Die," *Hartford Courant,* Oct. 7, 2004, A1.

15. Lynne Tuohy, "Ross a Crusade for Group," *Hartford Courant,* Nov. 9, 2004, B1.

16. Lynne Tuohy, "Campaign Launched to Stop Ross Execution," *Hartford Courant,* Oct. 23, 2004, B1.

17. William Yardley, "Governor Denies Reprieve in Rare Northeast Execution," *New York Times,* Dec. 7, 2004, A25.

18. Terese Karmel, "Sister of Ross Victim Seeks Closure," *Willimantic Chronicle,* Jan. 20, 2005, A1.

19. Editorial, "Ross Has Earned His Punishment," *Willimantic Chronicle,* Dec. 15, 2004, 7.

20. Michael Ross, "Letter from Death Row," *Hartford Courant,* Dec. 12, 2004, 2 (Northeast).

21. Lynne Tuohy, "Ruling Bars Public Defenders in Ross Case," *Hartford Courant,* Dec. 16, 2005, A1.

22. "A Killer Weighs His Fate," *Hartford Courant,* Dec. 29, 2004, A4.

23. Lynne Tuohy, "Ross Ruled Competent to Choose Execution," *Hartford Courant,* Dec. 29, 2004, A1.

24. "European Union Asks State to Halt Ross Execution," Associated Press, ctnow.com, accessed Dec. 17, 2004.

25. Michael A. Fitzpatrick, "Capital Punishment Tests State's Values," *Hartford Courant,* Dec. 26, 2004, C3; see also Lynne Tuohy, "Some Heinous Killers Given Life Sentences," *Hartford Courant,* Jan. 16, 2005, A1.

26. Lynne Tuohy, "Implore Governor to Spare Ross," *Hartford Courant,* Jan. 14, 2005, B1.

27. Frances Grandy Taylor, "Death Penalty Fight Escalates," *Hartford Courant,* Jan. 6, 2005, A1; and Matthew Kauffman and Frances Grandy Taylor, "Catholics Debate Death Penalty," *Hartford Courant,* Jan. 9, 2005, B1.

28. Frances Grandy Taylor, "A Stand Against 'Inhumanity,'" *Hartford Courant,* Jan. 13, 2005, A6.

29. Robert C. Goodwin, "Too Ill for Execution," *Hartford Courant,* Jan. 16, 2005, C1.

30. Christopher Keating, "Legislator Takes Stand Against Death Penalty," *Hartford Courant,* Jan. 25, 2005, A7.

31. Trip Jennings, "More Twists in Ross Case," *Willimantic Chronicle,* Jan. 27, 2005, A1.

32. Lynne Tuohy, "Attempts to Save Ross Stall Again," *Hartford Courant,* Jan. 4, 2005, A1.

33. Lynne Tuohy, "ACLU Argues for a Stay," *Hartford Courant,* Jan. 8, 2005, A1.

34. *Connecticut v. Ross,* 272 Conn. 577, 614 (2005).

35. Lynne Tuohy, "Ross Court Battles Intensify," *Hartford Courant,* Jan. 21, 2005, B1.

36. Lynne Tuohy, "Legal Wrangling over Ross Continues," *Hartford Courant,* Jan. 19, 2005, B1; see also Lynne Tuohy, "Society's Ross Appeal Denied," *Hartford Courant,* Jan. 20, 2005, B1.

37. John A. Connolly, "Death Penalty Reserved for the Worst of the Worst," *Hartford Courant,* Jan. 23, 2005, C3.

38. Michele Jacklin, "The Big Lie about Capital Punishment," *Hartford Courant,* Jan. 23, 2005, C3.

39. Matthew Kaufman, "On to High Court," *Hartford Courant,* Jan. 26, 2005, A1.

40. Lynne Tuohy and Alaine Griffin, "Judge's Stay Might Last Only a Day," *Hartford Courant,* Jan. 25, 2005, A1.

41. Kenton Robinson, "Supreme Court Rejects Father's Bid," *Willimantic Chronicle,* Jan. 26, 2003, 3.

42. Matthew Kaufman, "On to High Court," *Hartford Courant,* Jan. 26, 2005, A1; Lynne Tuohy, "Justices' Review to Make Countdown More Tense," *Hartford Courant,* Jan. 26, 2005, A1; and Patricia Hurtado, "Court Upholds Stay of Execution," *Willimantic Chronicle,* Jan. 26, 2005, 1.

43. Editorial, "A Reasonable Execution Delay," *Hartford Courant,* Jan. 25, 2005, A8.

44. This and following quotations from Lynne Tuohy and Alaine Griffin, "One Obstacle to Execution Left," *Hartford Courant,* Jan. 28, 2005, A1.

45. Lynne Tuohy and Alaine Griffin, "One Obstacle to Execution Left," *Hartford Courant,* Jan. 28, 2005, A1.

46. Lynne Tuohy, "As Clock Ticks, Ross' Fate Unclear," *Hartford Courant,* Jan. 27, 2005, A1.

47. See "Inmate in Ross Case Claims Retaliation," *Hartford Courant,* Feb. 17, 2005, B5. Lopez claimed that he and Ross communicated through air ducts because the prisoners were isolated.

48. See the comments by John H. Blume and Stephen Bright in Lynne Tuohy, "Ross' Lawyer Likely to Stay," *Hartford Courant,* Feb. 10, 2005, A1.

49. Telephone conference before Hon. Robert N. Chatigny, Chief U.S.D.J., Hartford, Conn., Jan. 28, 2005, 17. Chatigny made the printed transcript public. It was available at ctnow.com on Jan. 20, 2005. See Matthew Kauffman, "Federal Judge Berates, Pleads with Ross Lawyer," *Hartford Courant,* Jan. 29, 2005, A12.

50. For a discussion of forensic ambiguities, see Harold I. Schwartz, M.D., "Misusing Psychiatry to Abolish the Death Penalty," *Hartford Courant,* Feb. 6, 2005, C1.

51. Telephone conference, Jan, 28, 2005, transcript 13–14.

52. Telephone conference, Jan, 28, 2005, transcript, 21, 22, 25, 26.

53. Lynne Tuohy, "T.R. Paulding," *Hartford Courant,* Jan. 29, 2005, A11.

54. Lynne Tuohy, "Focus on Ross Turns to His Lawyers," *Hartford Courant,* Jan. 30, 2005, A6.

55. Lynne Tuohy, "Ross to Delay Execution," *Hartford Courant,* Jan. 1, 2005, A1.

56. "A Different Conclusion," *New York Times,* Feb. 1, 2005, A1.

57. Rinker Buck, "FOI Officer Seeks Ross Execution File," *Hartford Courant,* Feb. 16, 2005, B7.

58. William Yardley and Stacey Stowe, "Connecticut Delays Death of Serial Killer Indefinitely," *New York Times,* Feb. 1, 2005, A20.

59. Lynne Tuohy, "Indefinite Reprieve for Ross," *Hartford Courant,* Feb. 1, 2005, A1.

60. William Yardley and Stacey Stowe, "Connecticut Delays Death of Serial Killer Indefinitely," *New York Times,* Feb. 1, 2005, A20.

61. In July 2006, a federal panel of judges cleared Judge Chatigny of any misconduct in his unusual involvement in the case. Paulding did not file a complaint. Judge Chatigny said that some of his remarks were too vehement, and he indicated that he apologized to Paulding the next day.

62. Edmund H. Mahony, "Three Views on Chatigny's Challenge," *Hartford Courant*, Jan. 30, 2005, A7.

63. Editorial, "Long Path to Death Chamber," *Hartford Courant*, Jan. 30, 2005, C2.

64. "Casting Stones at Judge Chatigny," *Hartford Courant*, Feb. 13, 2005, C2.

65. Lynne Tuohy, "Ross to Delay Execution," *Hartford Courant*, Jan. 31, 2005, A1–A2. See Edmund H. Mahony, "Judge's Teleconference Has Experts Talking," *Hartford Courant*, Feb. 2, 2005, A1; and William Yardley, "Reprieve for Serial Killer Places Spotlight on Judge," *New York Times*, Feb. 2, 2005, C18.

66. Lynne Tuohy, "Ross to Delay Execution," *Hartford Courant*, Jan. 1, 2005, A2.

67. Robert Blecker, " 'God Love Him'? May Ross End in Hell," *Hartford Courant*, Feb. 6, 2005, C3.

68. Lynne Tuohy, "Indefinite Reprieve for Ross," *Hartford Courant*, Feb. 1, 2005, A1.

69. Gary Libow, "Death Penalty Foes to Rally Forces," *Hartford Courant*, Jan. 31, 2005, A2.

70. Bill Leukhardt and Christopher Keating, "Death Penalty Revisited," *Hartford Courant*, Feb. 1, 2005, A1, A4.

71. Editorial, "Death Penalty Doesn't Work," *Hartford Courant*, Feb. 1, 2005, A6.

72. Edward J. Crowder, "Inmates Hunger for Better Conditions on Death Row," *Willimantic Chronicle*, Feb. 4, 2005, 2.

73. Roselyn Tantraphol, "Death Row Inmates on Hunger Strike," *Hartford Courant*, Feb. 4, 2005, B1.

74. Lynne Tuohy, "Ross' Attorney Given a Week to Ponder Role," *Hartford Courant*, Feb. 4, 2005, A1.

75. Kyn Tolson, "Judge Chews Out Defenders over Missing Ross Evidence," *Willimantic Chronicle*, Feb. 4, 2005, 2.

76. Lynne Tuohy, "Ross' Attorney Given a Week to Ponder Role," *Hartford Courant*, Feb. 4, 2005, A1.

77. Lynne Tuohy, "Ross Case: Advocacy Roles Shifting," *Hartford Courant*, Feb. 16, 2005, B1; see also Mark Pazniokas, "A Different Challenge," *Hartford Courant*, Feb. 11, 2005, A5; and "New Ross Defender to Have His Say," *Willimantic Chronicle*, Feb. 14, 2005, 2.

78. Lynne Tuohy, "Execution Set for May 11," *Hartford Courant*, Feb. 11, 2005, A1.

79. Lynne Tuohy, "Psychiatrists in Ross Case Have Varied Experiences," *Hartford Courant*, Apr. 7, 2005, A14; Lynne Tuohy, "Focus Again on Ross' Mind," *Hartford Courant*, Apr. 7, 2005, A1; and Lynne Tuohy, "In a Postscript, Ross to Doctor: 'Checkmate,' " *Hartford Courant*, June 14, 2005, A1.

80. *Connecticut v. Ross*, Superior Court, Judicial District of New London at New London, Apr. 22, 2005, "Memorandum of Decision Re: Competency and Voluntariness," Judge Patrick J. Clifford, 5. Accessed Apr. 22, 2005, at www.courant.com via links.

81. Lynne Tuohy, "Witness: Ross Able to Make Decision," *Hartford Courant*, Apr. 8, 2005, A1.

82. Lynne Tuohy, "Another Psychiatrist Backs Ross," *Hartford Courant*, Apr. 13, 2005, A1.

83. Lynne Tuohy, "Ross Painted as a Fraud," *Hartford Courant*, Apr. 12, 2005, A1.

84. Lynne Tuohy, "Witness: Ross Can't Back Down," *Hartford Courant,* Apr. 14, 2005, B1; see also Izaskun E. Larraneta, "Doctor No. 4: Ross Not Competent," *Willimantic Chronicle,* Apr. 14, 2005, 2.

85. Lynne Tuohy, "Judge Set to Rule on Ross Again," *Hartford Courant,* Apr. 15, 2005, A1.

86. "Memorandum of Decision," 8, 7, 15, 16, 22.

87. Mark Pazniokas, "GOP Plots Values War," *Hartford Courant,* Apr. 10, 2005, A1.

88. "Alternative to Death Penalty," *Hartford Courant,* Mar. 13, 2005, C2.

89. Helen Ubinas, "Breaking the Hold of Michael Ross," *Hartford Courant,* Mar. 30, 2005, A1; and Helen Ubinas, "Big Issue Gets Little Attention," *Hartford Courant,* Mar. 31, 2005, B1.

90. Mark Pazniokas, "GOP Plots Values War," *Hartford Courant,* Apr. 10, 2005, A5.

91. Mark Pazniokas, "Panel Takes Long Shot Against Death Penalty," *Hartford Courant,* Mar. 10, 2005, B1.

92. Mark Pazniokas, "Death Penalty Survives," *Hartford Courant,* Mar. 31, 2005, A1.

93. Mike Alberts, 2005 Legislative Survey Results, copy in the author's possession.

94. *State of Connecticut v. Michael Ross,* 273 Conn. 684, 713 (2005).

95. *State v. Ross,* 273 Conn. at 721.

96. Lynne Tuohy, "Groark to End His Ross Effort," *Hartford Courant,* May 11, 2005, B7.

97. "High Court Refuses to Hear Missionary Society's Appeal," *Willimantic Chronicle,* Apr. 27, 2005, 7.

98. Lynne Tuohy, "Ross Ruling Again Upheld," *Hartford Courant,* May 10, 2005, A1.

99. Lynne Tuohy, "Confronting Death," *Hartford Courant,* May 13, A7.

100. Alaine Griffin, "Killer Said to Be Clinging to a Spiritual Vision," *Hartford Courant,* May 12, 2005, A7.

101. See Lynne Tuohy, "A Lethal Routine, A Grim Debate," *Hartford Courant,* Jan. 9, 2005, A7.

102. http://moritzlaw.osu.edu/lawjournal/issues/volume63/number1/denno .pdf, accessed Jan. 24, 2009.

103. August H. Fortin VI, Andre Sofair, and Asghar Rastegar, "Lethal Objection," *Hartford Courant,* May 8, 2005, C3.

104. Lynne Tuohy, "A Lethal Routine, A Grim Debate," *Hartford Courant,* Jan. 9, 2005, A7.

105. William Hathaway, "Report Suggests a Review of Lethal Injections," *Hartford Courant,* Apr. 15, 2005, B1.

106. Linda Greenhouse, "Justices Uphold Lethal Injection in Kentucky Case," *New York Times,* Apr. 7, 2008, A1. The seven-to-two majority in *Baze v. Rees* approved the method of administration procedure in Kentucky, one used widely. Chief Justice John G. Roberts ruled that some pain incurred in the process did not violate the prohibition against cruel and unusual punishment. The constitutionality of lethal injection was not in question. Denise Grady, "Doctors See Way to Cut Risks of Suffering in Lethal Injection," *New York Times,* June 23, 2006, A1; and Adam Liptak, "Court Rules for Kentucky on Executions," *New York Times,* Nov. 23, 2006, A20. The *New York Times,* an opponent of capital punishment, entitled an editorial "Lethal Cruelty" in arguing that, if administered improperly, lethal injection "can in fact be particularly barbaric." See *New York Times,* Apr. 26, 2006, A22.

107. See "Administration of Capital Punishment," State of Connecticut Department of Correction, Administrative Directive, July 23, 1997, on file at the Law Library, CSL.

108. Sean O'Leary, "Activists on Both Sides Make Trek to Osborn," *Willimantic Chronicle*, May 13, 2005, 1.

109. Administration of Capital Punishment," 7.

110. Sean O'Leary, " 'Justice Has Been Given,' " *Willimantic Chronicle*, May 13, 2005, 1.

111. Lynne Tuohy, "Ross Goes Quietly, No Final Statement, No Emotion," *Hartford Courant*, May 14, 2005, A9.

112. This and following quotations from Sean O'Leary, " 'Justice Has Been Given,' " *Willimantic Chronicle*, May 13, 2005, 1.

Epilogue

1. *State v. Ross*, 273 Conn. 684, 723 (2005).

2. Mark Pazniokas, "Poll Finds Support for Execution," *Hartford Courant*, Jan. 13, 2005, A1.

3. Dave Collins, "63 Percent of State Residents Support Death Penalty, Poll Says," *Norwich Bulletin*, Apr. 8, 2007, B5.

4. William A. Petit Jr., "Death Penalty Is Justice for Murderers," *Hartford Courant*, May 31, 2009, C1.

5. Mark Pazniokas, "Poll Finds Support for Execution," *Hartford Courant*, Jan. 13, 2005, A1.

6. Lynne Tuohy, "Ross Goes Quietly: No Final Statement, No Emotion," *Hartford Courant*, May 14, 2005, A9.

7. Mark Pazniokas, "Poll Finds Support for Execution," *Hartford Courant*, Jan. 13, 2005, A1.

8. Sean O'Leary, "Activists on Both Sides Make Trek to Osborn," *Willimantic Chronicle*, May 13, 2005, 1.

9. *State v. Ross*, 272 Conn. 577, 613 (2005).

10. On June 4, 2010, the Connecticut Supreme Court overturned Robert Courchesne's capital felony conviction. Nine other inmates remain on death row. There is a striking racial/ethnic disparity among them, because six are black, two are white, and one is Hispanic. *State of Connecticut v. Robert Courchesne*, 2010 Conn. LEXIS 227; and Stephen Busemeyer and Jenna Carlesso, "Was Fetus Alive? Retrial Ordered," *Hartford Courant*, June 5, 2010, A1. On December 2, 2010, Judge Jon C. Blue of the New Haven County Superior Court sentenced Steven J. Hayes to death according to the mandate of the jury on November 8. The jury found the defendant guilty of six capital crimes for his part in the brutal invasion of the family home of Dr. William A. Petit Jr., which resulted in the rape/murders of his wife, Jennifer Hawke-Petit, and their two daughters, Hayley and Michaela. Alaine Griffen, "No End to Pain," *Hartford Courant*, Dec. 3, 2010, Al, and William Glaberson, "At Sentencing, Connecticut Killer Says He Is Tormented and Welcomes Death," *New York Times*, Dec. 3, 2020, A23.

INDEX